DR. JANG'S
SAT* 800

MATH WORKBOOK

FOR THE DIGITAL EXAM
2024

Simon Jang and Tiffany T. Jang

*SAT is a registered trademark of the College Board, which was not involved in the production of, and does not endorse, this book.

Published in the United States by Amazon KDP Publishing, Seattle, WA.

Jang, Simon.
    Dr. Jang's SAT 800 Math Workbook For The Digital Exam 2024 / Simon Jang and Tiffany T. Jang
    376 p. 28 cm.
1. SAT (Educational test)—Study guides. 2. Mathematics—Examinations—Study guides. 3. Mathematics / Study & Teaching. 4. Study Aids / SAT. 5. Redesigned SAT
378.1664 – dc23

ISBN-13: 9798396873537

www.DrJang800.com

*SAT is a registered trademark of the College Board, which was not involved in the production of, and does not endorse, this book.

Table of Contents

How To Use This Book

Starting Spring 2024, the digital SAT will completely replace the paper-and-pencil SAT. This book is our SAT math workbook for the digital SAT. For over 20 years, we have taught math to students in both high schools and private settings. One observation we have made during our years of teaching is the lack of comprehensive learning material for students of all levels preparing for the math section of the SAT exam. To address this issue, we have created this book, which contains all the necessary material to achieve a high score. Based on our extensive teaching experience, we firmly believe that anyone can attain an excellent math score on the SAT with focused preparation on the test's content and skills required to tackle questions quickly and effectively.

Since the digital SAT applies multistage adaptive testing, where subsequent module of questions dynamically adjusts based on a student's performance in their previous module, students will need to adapt their test preparation strategies to effectively handle an exam in which the difficulty of questions progressively increases. It is important to note that as students encounter more challenging questions on the digital SAT, their likelihood of achieving higher scores also increases. Therefore, this book helps students practice Math SAT questions of varying difficulty levels, ranging from easy to high.

Required Content Knowledge
In this book, we have divided the required content knowledge into four chapters in corresponding to the guideline provided by the College Board for the digital SAT tests in 2024:
- Chapter One: Algebra
- Chapter Two: Problem-Solving and Data Analysis
- Chapter Three: Advanced Math
- Chapter Four: Geometry and Trigonometry

Within each chapter, we delve deeply into all necessary sub–concepts and provide a multitude of practice questions that closely resemble those found in the actual SAT.

The problems and techniques presented in this book help to prepare and acquaint students for the digital SAT tests. The breakdown of topics in this book aligns with the emphasis of the digital SAT.

Problem Solving Skills
Within each concept section, the math questions are grouped into three levels of difficulty:
- Easy
- Medium
- Hard

The critical thinking advice, answers, and detailed explanations are conveniently located to the right of the problems. Students can easily refer to the answers, but they also have the option to cover the page if they prefer to attempt the problem on their own. By engaging with the problem-solving skills sections, students can develop a strong intuition for problem-solving and make educated guesses.

1500+ Practice Problems and 10 Mock Tests

In addition to a thorough overview of materials, this book provides over 1500 practice problems for you to reinforce your understanding of the material and pinpoint the weak areas you need to improve on. The digital SAT tests allow students to use a calculator throughout the test. Students have the option to use their own approved calculator or utilize the system-provided graphical calculator.

Multistage Adaptive Testing Strategy

In Chapter 5 of our book, "Ten Mock Tests," we provide a series of tests designed to assess your knowledge. Each test consists of three module tests: Module 1, Module 2 Easy, and Module 2 Hard. Module 1 encompasses a diverse range of questions, including easy, medium, and hard ones. Module 2 Easy is intentionally easier than Module 1, while Module 2 Hard is intentionally more challenging.

After completing the Module 1 test, it is important to review your answers. If you have answered more than 8 questions incorrectly in Module 1, it is recommended to proceed with the Module 2 Easy test. On the other hand, if you have answered 8 or fewer questions incorrectly in Module 1, you should move on to the Module 2 Hard test. Each module consists of 22 questions.

More SAT Practices Like the Real Test

We have published this edition to better align with the content and format of the actual digital SAT test. We express our gratitude to our readers for providing us with valuable feedback, which has allowed us to enhance our mock tests and create a more realistic simulation of the actual exam. We are committed to continuous imporovement in order to help students be as prepared as possicle for the digital SAT Math exam.

Based on feedback from students and teachers, we have also reorganized the questions in the problem-solving skills section to better align with their respective difficulty levels. Additionally, we have revised the concept overview sections to provide more comprehensive coverage of the content that will be tested in the digital SAT Math exam.

About the Authors

Dr. Simon Jang and Mrs. Tiffany Jang have been teaching in public high schools and in their own private tutoring studio for more than 20 years. They have developed a unique and proven SAT Math learning system that suits the students' needs and helps them efficiently prepare for the Math section of the SAT. Over the years, their innovative methods and effective teaching materials have benefitted not only their students' scores, but also their students' endeavors in college and beyond.

Dr. Jang received a Ph.D in Chemical Engineering from New York Polytechnic University. He worked as a software developer before he became a high school teacher. He has been teaching math, physics, and chemistry in New Jersey public high schools for many years. He has dedicated his spare time to developing innovative and effective methods of teaching high school math, chemistry, and physics in his established tutoring studio.

Tiffany Jang earned a Master's degree in Library and Information Sciences from the University of Wisconsin-Madison and a Master's degree in Computer Science from the New Jersey Institute of Technology. After several years of teaching high school math, now she is working as a school librarian in the New Jersey public school system.

Through years of experience, they have developed innovative teaching methods and effective learning materials. These methods are designed to introduce new students to the subject while also addressing any weaknesses and helping them efficiently prepare for the SAT Math exam.

Acknowledgements

We would like to acknowledge the help and support from our daughters, Jennifer and Justine, as well as the countless students over the years who have provided feedback on our system. Without the help of everyone around us, this enormous project would never even have been conceptualized.

About the Digital SAT Math Test

What Content Knowledge Is Included
According to the College Board, the digital SAT Math assesses knowledge and skills that are largely similar to those tested in their paper and pencil SAT exams.

On each module of the test, questions from four content areas of math applear, arranged in order of increasing difficulty from easiest to hardest:
- Algebra (35%)
- Advanced Math (35%)
- Problem-Solving and Data Analysis (15%)
- Geometry and Trigonometry (15%)

What Application and Device Are Used for the Digital Test
The digital SAT tests are administered through College Board's customized digital testing application called the Bluebook. Students should download the most updated Bluebook App on their approved device in advance of the test day. The approved devices can be the labtops with Windows or MacOS, tablet, ipads, or school-managed Chromebooks.

How the Test Is Organized
The digital SAT Math exam lasts a total of 70 minutes with two separate equal-length modules. There are 22 questions in each module. After students finish their first module, the second module will be generated individually basen on their performance in the previous module. Within each module, questions are arranged from easy to hard, with the easier problems at the beginning and the more difficult ones at the end. There are totally 44 questions, 75% of which are four-option multiple-choice questions and 25% are student-produced response (SPR) questions. Here is the breakdown of the digital SAT Math content specifications:

Digital SAT Math Testing Time (70 minutes)	Module 1: 22 questions	35 minutes
	Module 2: 22 questions	35 minutes
Types of Questions (44 questions)	33 4-option multiple-choice questions	75%
	11 student-produced response questions	25%
Content Areas	Algebra • Linear equations in one variable • Linear equations in two variables • Linear functions • Systems of linear equations • Linear inequalities	13-15 questions 35%

Content Areas	**Advanced Math** • Equivalent algebraic expressions • Nonlinear equations in one variable • System of equations in two variables • Nonlinear functions	13-15 questions 35%
	Problem-Solving and Data Analysis • Ratios, rates, proportions, and units • Percentages • One-variable data: distributions and measures of center and spread • Two-variable data: models and scatterplots • Probability • Inference from sample statistics and margin of error • Evaluating statistical claims: observational studies and experiments	5-7 questions 15%
	Geometry and Trigonometry • Area and volume • Lines, angles, and triangles • Right triangles and trigonometry • Circles	5-7 questions 15%

How the SAT Is Scored

On the digital SAT assessment, test-takers receive three scores: a total score (400-1600) and two section scores (200-800 each), one for Reading-and-Writing and the other for Math. Test-takers can receive scores in a few days. The more difficult questions students can take, the higher score they can possibly get.

What to Do before the Test
- Download the most current Bluebook from the College Board's website
- Become accustomed to the digital testing environment by taking the digital SAT practice tests through Bluebook.
- Get a good night's sleep.

- Have your photo ID, admission ticket, watch, and a scientific or graphing calculator ready the night before.
- Have a nutritious but not too filling breakfast.
- Be there 15 minutes before the test is expected to start.

What to Be Aware of during the Test

- Read the questions completely and carefully.
- Solve the easy questions with caution; careless mistakes tend to occur when solving easy questions too confidently.
- Don't struggle on one question for too long. flag the question and work on it at the end.

About The Digital SAT Math Problem Solving Strategies

Strategies and Some Shortcuts to Solving SAT Math Questions

When taking a math test, you have to think mathematically. To think mathematically, you must become familiar with some keywords and their definitions or mathematical equivalents:

- Even Integer: $2n$
- Odd Integer: $2n + 1$
- Order of Operation: Follow the PEMDAS Rules
- Union, Intersection, and Venn diagram
- GCF (Greatest Common Factor) and LCM (Least Common Multiple)
- Prime Numbers
- Common Denominator
- Multiplying and Dividing Exponents
- Percent and Percent Change
- Ratio and Proportion: Direct Proportion and Inverse Proportion
- Average, Sum, Median, and Mode
- Rate
- Probability of an Event
- Parallel Lines and Their Transversals
- Triangles and Special Triangles
- Interior and Exterior Angles of a Triangle
- Polygons
- Area of Geometric Figures

Read questions carefully and pay attention to the most important key points, such as "average," "sum," "maximum," etc. so that you can catch the scope of the question quickly. One of the most important aspects that you must get used to in SAT Math test is the reading comprehension feature. You will need excellent reading comprehension skills to translate word problems into math problems.

Pay attention to hints in the questions that you can use to decide whether or not to use shortcuts to solve the problem. Do not use shortcuts without understanding the question first. Certain types of example questions can be easily solved by shortcuts. Some examples are shown below.

Shortcuts

1. Plugging in Easy Numbers: If a question is along the lines of "which of the following must be true or must NOT be true," and the answer choices contain variables, you can try to assign an easy number to the variable to find the answer.

Example 1: If X, Y and Z represent consecutive positive odd integers, which of the following is NOT true?

    a) $X + Y + Z$ is an odd integer

    b) $X + Y$ is an even integer

    c) $\frac{Z - X}{2}$ is an even integer

    d) $\frac{X + Y}{2}$ is an odd integer

This question looks complicated, but if we plug in, X = 1, Y = 3, and Z = 5, you will find out that only answer (d) is not true. Of course, make sure that the numbers you plug in satisfy the requirements. 1, 3, and 5 are obviously consecutive positive odd integers.

Example 2: If $|x| < 1$, which of the following is the greatest?

    a) 2

    b) $1 - x$

    c) $1 + x$

    d) $2x$

Instead of solving this inequality, you can easily find the right answer (a) by plugging in a value of x that satisfies the inequality. If we plug in $x = \frac{1}{2}$, we see that the answer (a) is the greatest.

Example 3: The figure below shows a square and a right triangle. What is the area of shaded region?

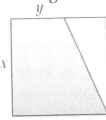

    a) $\frac{x(x + y)}{2}$

    b) $\frac{(x^2 + y^2)}{2}$

    c) xy

    d) $2xy$

To find the answer fast, we can plug in $x = 5$ and $y = 3$. If we do this, the shaded region has area $5^2 - \frac{1}{2}(2)(5) = 20$. Only (a) gives an equivalent answer.

2. In geometry, when you are given a set of parallel lines and possibly a transversal, many times the degree of two angles end up being congruent or supplementary. Many times you can tell which one is which just by looking at the graph (but this is not always the case and sometimes graphs are not drawn to scale).

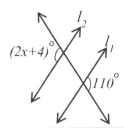

Example 4: In the figure above, if $l_1 \parallel l_2$, what is the value of x?
   a) 45
   b) 53
   c) 57
   d) 60

Since we have two parallel lines and a transversal, there are only two different types of angles here: angles with degree equal to 110° and angles supplementary to 110°. By just looking at that graph, we can tell, $2x + 4 = 110$, so $x = 53$. Answer is (b).

3. Sometimes if you can't solve the problem mathematically, you can still use logic to eliminate the answer choices. The more answer choices you can eliminate, the higher the probability of you answering a question right.

Example 5: John can complete a job in 20 minutes. Bob can complete the same job in 40 minutes. If they work together, approximately how many minutes will it take them to complete the job?
   a) 60 minutes
   b) 40 minutes
   c) 30 minutes
   d) 15 minutes

If they work together, the job should be completed faster than 2 Bobs and slower than 2 Johns. The only reasonable answer should be between 10 to 20 minutes. Answer is (d).

Example 6: Sam drove to work at an average speed of 50 miles per hour from her house and then returned along the same route at an average speed of 40 miles per hour. If the entire trip took her 2.25 hours, what is the entire distance, in miles, for the round trip?

   a) 90
   b) 100
   c) 120
   d) 125

In this problem, since distance = time × speed, the entire distance is between 40 × 2.25 and 50 × 2.25 miles. The reasonable answer is 100 miles, answer (b).

4. Take advantage of your calculator during the test. Learn to use a calculator efficiently by practicing. As you approach a problem, focus on how to solve that problem and then decide whether the calculator will be helpful. Using a calculator may help to prevent you from careless mistakes and save you some time performing calculations. However, a calculator will not solve a problem for you. You must understand the problem first. Keep in mind that every SAT Math question can be solved without a calculator and some questions can be solved faster mentally than with a calculator.

Example 7: What is the average (arithmetic mean) of 192, 194, and 196? We can get the answer, 194, without using a calculator since the median of three consecutive odd integers is also the average.

5. When applicable, use the plug–and–chug technique to solve a question backwards. This method works best when you see simple numbers as answer choices. Plug the numbers from the answer choices into the question until you find the right one. Plug–and–chug is sometimes faster than setting up an equation.

Example 8: Together, Ken, Justin, and Tiff have read a total of 65 books. Justin read 3 times as many books as Ken and Tiff read 3 times as many books as Justin. How many books did Ken read?

   a) 12
   b) 9
   c) 7
   d) 5

Plugging and chugging this question is faster than setting up an equation. You can start with plugging in the number from choice (c) and notice that the number 7 is too big, so you pick a smaller number, (d), to plug in. Thus you arrive at the right answer, (d).

6. Working backwards can sometimes help you organize your thoughts in order to solve a word problem. First, identify what the question is asking. Then, ask yourself what data you might need. Finally, look for the data you need from the question, and use it to solve the problem.

Example 9: On an Algebra exam, class A has 10 students taking the test and an average score of 90. Class B has 20 students taking the test and an average score of 85. What is the average score of all the students in both class A and B?
- By reading the last sentence, we know the question is asking for the average of all the students.
- In order to answer this question, we will use the formula to find averages:

$$Average = \frac{Total\ Score}{Number\ of\ Students}$$

- The total number of students is 10 + 20 and the total score is $10 \times 90 + 20 \times 85$.
- Finally, set up an equation to solve this problem.
$$\frac{10 \times 90 + 20 \times 85}{10 + 20} = 86.666$$

7. Most of the word problems can be translated from English into mathematical expressions by following a few guidelines:

a. Keywords in the problem can help translating the words into algebraic expressions. For instance, the words "greater than," "more," and "increase" indicate addition and "less than," "fewer," and "decrease" indicate subtraction. "2 times" refers to multiplying a number or a variable by 2, and "is" indicates equality in an equation. If the question mentions finding "a number" without specifying the value of the number, assign a variable for that number and then solve for the value of the variable.

b. When dealing with percent problems, the following keywords usually translate to the following actions:
   ▪ Percent in decimal form → divide by 100
   ▪ Decimal in percent form → multiply by 100
   ▪ 'is' → =

- 'of' → ×
- 'what' or 'a number' (the value you are solving for) → x

Examples:	*Solutions:*

i. What is 15% of 60?

ii. 20% of what number is 16?

iii. What percent of 20 is 5?

i. $x = \frac{15}{100} \times 60 = 9$

ii. $\frac{20}{100} \times x = 16$

  $x = 80$

iii. $\frac{x}{100} \times 20 = 5$

  $x = \frac{5 \times 100}{20}$

  $x = 25\%$

c. If a geometry question is given in words, make a sketch and label points according to the question. It becomes easier to find the answer once you have drawn your own sketch.

8. It's okay to trust their geometric figures unless when it is stated that the figure is not drawn to scale. You may estimate the answer based on the figure itself if you cannot solve the problem or you run out of time. If it is stated that the figure is not drawn to scale, you may redraw the figure based on the data presented.

About the Diagnostic Test In This Book

This diagnostic test contains 58 questions on topics that are most frequently found on the SAT Math test. The purpose of the diagnostic test is to allow you to measure your level of proficiency and identify your weakest areas.

It is important that you take this diagnostic test to find out your weakest areas and then study those areas accordingly. All the questions in the diagnostic test are on a medium to hard level on the actual SAT. So if you quite comfortable with some of these questions, you should be able to do well on SAT Math test in those areas. If you have no idea how to solve a question, you should leave a mark on the question and spend more time studying that area in the future.

After taking the diagnostic test and checking the solutions, group each question based on your confidence level when you were solving it:
1. <u>Low</u>: Questions that you skipped or had absolutely no idea how to solve.
2. <u>Medium</u>: Questions that you may be able to solve but are not completely familiar with and/or made careless mistakes on.
3. <u>High</u>: Questions that you are very confident and you know how to solve.

For the topic areas you have confidence low, you need to read through the concept overviews on each section, try to understand them, and do questions from easy to hard on the problems solving skills sections. Remember, only after recognizing your problem areas, you can tackle them by lots of practices.

For those areas that you have medium confidence in, you may quickly glance at the concept overviews to see if there are some concepts or tricks that you don't know and then jump straight to the medium and hard level practice problems.

If you still have time after dealing with low and medium confidence questions, you can focus on the hard-level questions of the topics you have high confidence in. By doing so, you will improve your skills across the board and become a master of the SAT Math test. Practice makes perfect!

SAT Math Diagnostic Test

Evaluating Algebraic Expressions

1. If $z = \frac{12x^4}{y}$, what happens to the value of z when both x and y are doubled?
    - a) z is multiplied by 32.
    - b) z is multiplied by 16.
    - c) z is multiplied by 8.
    - d) z is doubled.

Evaluating Variables in Terms of Another

2. A right circular cylinder with radius 3 and height 7 has a volume v. In terms of v, what is the volume of the right circular cylinder with radius 3 and height 14?
    - a) $v + 7$
    - b) $7v$
    - c) $5v$
    - d) $2v$

Solving Equations

3. A litter of milk can fill up 3 large cups or 5 small cups. If there are 12 large cups and 10 small cups, about how many litters of milk will be needed to fill up all the cups?
    - a) 6
    - b) 4
    - c) 3
    - d) 2

Solving Linear Equations

4. If a linear function passes through the points $(1, s)$, $(3, t)$ and $(5, 10)$, what is the value of $2t - s$?
    - a) 2
    - b) 4
    - c) 8
    - d) 10

Solving Quadratic Equations

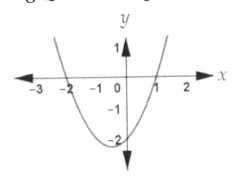

5. Which of the following equations best describes the curve in the figure above?
    - a) $y = x^2 - 2$
    - b) $y = x^2 + x - 2$
    - c) $y = x^2 + x + 2$
    - d) $y = x^2 + x$

Solving Systems of Equations

6. There is $180 of cash in John's pocket. John only has 10 and 20 dollar bills. If John has a total of 13 bills, how many 20 dollar bills are in his pocket?

Solving Inequalities

7. If $x < 5 < \frac{1}{x-1}$, then x could be which of the following?
    - a) 5
    - b) 1
    - c) $\frac{7}{6}$
    - d) $\frac{10}{3}$

Word Problems

8. Six erasers cost as much as 3 pencils. If Matt bought one eraser and one pencil for $1.50, how much does one pencil cost in dollars?
    - a) 0.25
    - b) 0.50
    - c) 0.75
    - d) 1.00

Rate Word Problems

9. Sam drove from home at an average speed of 50 miles per hour to her working place and then returned along the same route at an average speed of 40 miles per hour. If the entire trip took her 2.25 hours, what is the entire distance, in miles, for the round trip?
    a) 90
    b) 100
    c) 120
    d) 125

Percentage Word Problems

10. A store sells a certain brand of TVs for $550 each. This price is 25 percent more than the cost at which the store buys one of these TVs. The store employees can purchase any of these TVs at 20 percent off the store's cost. How much would it cost an employee to purchase a TV of this brand?
    a) $352
    b) $330
    c) $413
    d) $440

Ratio and Proportion Word Problems

11. A recipe of a cake for 8 people requires 1.2 pounds of flour. Assuming the amount of flour needed is directly proportional to the number of people eating the cake, how many pounds of flour are required to make a big cake for 240 people?
    a) 20
    b) 26
    c) 30
    d) 36

Ratios, Proportions, and Rates

12. If y is inversely proportional to x and y is equal to 12 when x is equal to 8, what is the value of y when $x = 24$?
    a) $\frac{1}{6}$
    b) 4
    c) 1
    d) $\frac{1}{4}$

13. If y is directly proportional to x and y is equal to 40 when x is equal to 6, what is the value of y when $x = 9$?
    a) 40
    b) 45
    c) 50
    d) 60

14. Freddy's family owns two different types of cars, a sedan and an SUV. The sedan has gas mileage of 25 miles per gallon, and the SUV has gas mileage of 20 miles per gallon. If both cars use the same amount of gasoline and the sedan travels 100 miles, how many miles does the SUV travel?

Percentages

15. Two rectangles X and Y are shown above. If the width of rectangle Y in the figure below is 25 percent less than the width of rectangle X and the length of rectangle Y is 25 percent greater than the length of rectangle X. What is the area of rectangle Y compared to the area of rectangle X?
    a) The area of rectangle Y is 25 percent less than the area of rectangle X.

b) The area of rectangle Y is 6 percent less than the area of rectangle X.
c) Both rectangles have the same area.
d) The area of rectangle Y is 6 percent greater than the area of rectangle X.

Averages

16. Which of the following could be the sum of 8 numbers if the average of these 8 numbers is greater than 9 and less than 10?
    a) 85
    b) 83
    c) 82
    d) 79

Data Analysis

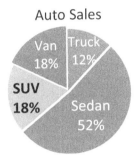

Auto Sales

17. The pie graph above represents the automobiles that were sold by a dealer in 2010, according to their records. If the dealer sold 40 more Sedans than all others combined, how many automobiles did it sell altogether?

Probability

18. A bag contains red, blue, and green marbles. The probability of pulling out a red marble randomly is $\frac{1}{4}$ and the probability of pulling out a blue marble randomly is $\frac{1}{5}$. Which of the following could be the total number of marbles in the bag?
    a) 10
    b) 12
    c) 18
    d) 20

Factors and Multiples

19. What is the greatest three-digit integer that has the factors 10 and 9?
    a) 100
    b) 900
    c) 955
    d) 990

20. Which of the following must be a factor of x if x is a multiple of both 9 and 12?
    a) 8
    b) 24
    c) 27
    d) 36

Fraction Operations

21. If $x = -\frac{1}{2}$, what is the value of $\frac{1}{x} - \frac{1}{x+1}$?
    a) −4
    b) −2
    c) 4
    d) 2

Algebraic Factoring

22. If $x^2 - y^2 = 15$, and $x - y = 3$, what is the value of $x + y$?
    a) 1
    b) 3
    c) 5
    d) 10

Functions

23. The quadratic function f is given by $f(x) = ax^2 + bx + c$, where a and c are positive real numbers. Which of the following is the possible graph of $f(x)$?

    a)

    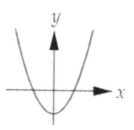

    b)

    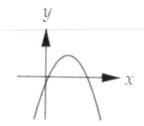

    c)

    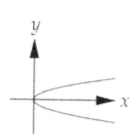

    d)

    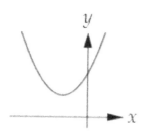

Complex Numbers

24. Which of the following is the expression $\frac{3-2i}{4+3i}$ equivalent to?

    a) $\frac{12-4i}{7}$

    b) $\frac{6+17i}{25}$

    c) $\frac{6-10i}{7}$

    d) $\frac{6-17i}{25}$

25. If $3 - 2i$ is a root of $2x^2 + ax + b = 0$, then $b = ?$

    a) 7.5

    b) –7.5

    c) 26

    d) It cannot be determined.

Quadratic Functions and Equations

26. Which of the following could be a graph of the equation $y = ax^2 + bx + c$, where $b^2 - 4ac = 0$?

    a)

    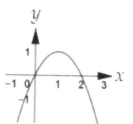

    b)

    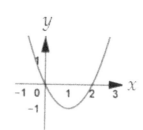

c)

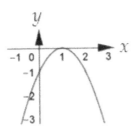

d)

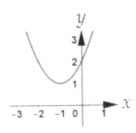

27. A baseball is hit and flies into a field at a trajectory defined by the equation $d = -1.2t^2 + 100$, where t is the number of seconds after the impact and d is the horizontal distance from the home plate to the outfield fence. How many seconds have passed if the ball is 50 meters away from the outfield fence ?

   a) 3.78
   b) 4.33
   c) 5.12
   d) 6.45

Exponent Operations

28. If $8 = a^y$, then $8a^2 =$?

   a) a^{y^2}
   b) a^{y+2}
   c) $8a^y$
   d) a^{8y}

Roots and Radical Operations

29. If $x^{\frac{3}{2}} = \frac{1}{27}$, then what does x equal?

   a) -9
   b) -3
   c) $\frac{1}{9}$
   d) $-\frac{1}{9}$

30. $\dfrac{2}{(x+y)^{-\frac{2}{3}}} = (x+y)^{-\frac{1}{3}}$, which of the following must be true?

   a) $x = 0$
   b) $\sqrt{x+y} = 2$
   c) $\sqrt{x+y} = \frac{1}{2}$
   d) $x + y = \frac{1}{2}$

Lines and Angles

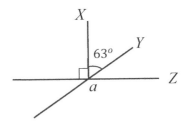

31. What is the value of a in the figure above?

Parallel Lines and Their Transversal

32. In the figure below, $\overline{AB} \parallel \overline{CD}$ and $\overline{CD} \perp \overline{BC}$. What is the value of $x + y$?

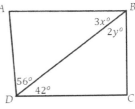

   a) 21
   b) 34
   c) 36
   d) 38

Triangle Interior and Exterior Angles

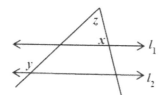

33. In the figure above, if $l_1 \parallel l_2$, what does z equal in terms of x and y?
    a) $x-y$
    b) $y-x$
    c) $180° - y + x$
    d) $180° - x - y$

Special Triangles

34. In the figure below, AB = 2. What is the length of AD?

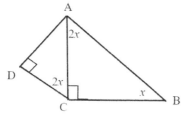

    a) $\sqrt{3}$
    b) 1
    c) $\frac{1}{2}$
    d) $\frac{\sqrt{3}}{2}$

Areas of Triangles

35. In the figure below, the area of the shaded region is 26 square units. What is the height of the smaller triangle?

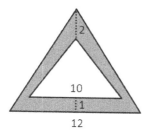

Segments of a Circle

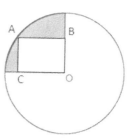

36. In the figure above, rectangle ABOC is drawn in circle O. If OB = 3 and OC = 4, what is the area of the shaded region?
    a) $6\pi - 3$
    b) $\frac{25\pi}{4} - 12$
    c) $25\pi - 12$
    d) $\frac{25\pi}{4} - 3$

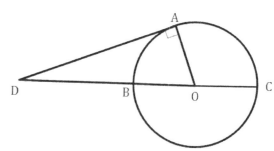

37. Point O is the center of the circle in the figure above. If DA = 12 and DB = 8, what is the area of the circle?

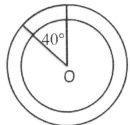

38. In the figure above, O is the center of the two circles. If the bigger circle has a radius of 5 and the smaller circle has a radius of 4, what is the area of shaded region?
    a) 3π
    b) 2π
    c) π
    d) $\frac{2}{3}\pi$

Cubes

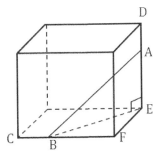

39. The cube shown above has edges of length 3. If $\overline{CB} = \overline{AD} = 1$, what is the length of $\overline{AB}$?

Volumes and Surface Areas

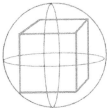

40. A cube is inscribed in a sphere as shown in the figure above. Each vertex of the cube touches the sphere. If the diameter of this sphere is $3\sqrt{3}$, what is the volume of the cube?
    a) 8
    b) 27
    c) 36
    d) 48

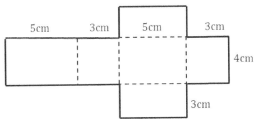

41. If the figure above is folded along the dashed lines, a rectangular box will be formed. What is the volume of the box in cubic centimeters?
    a) 15
    b) 20
    c) 40
    d) 60

Coordinate Geometry

42. Which of the following is the equation of a parabola whose vertex is at (–3, –4)?
    a) $y = (x + 3)^2 - 4$
    b) $y = (x - 3)^2 + 4$
    c) $y = (x - 4)^2 - 3$
    d) $y = x^2 - 4$

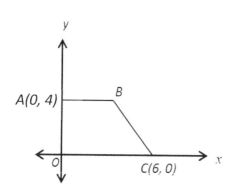

Trigonometric Functions

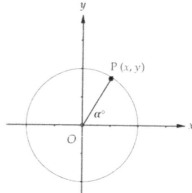

43. In the xy-coordinate plane, AB is parallel to the x-axis. If AO = AB, what is the area of quadrilateral ABCO?
    a) 12
    b) 16
    c) 18
    d) 20

44. If the center of the circle defined by $x^2 + y^2 - 4x + 2y = 20$ is (h, k) and the radius is r, then $h + k + r = ?$

45. On the unit circle above, if the values of sine and cosine of the angle $\alpha°$ are equal, what is the sum $x + y$?
    a) $2\sqrt{2}$
    b) $\sqrt{2}$
    c) $\frac{\sqrt{2}}{2}$
    d) $\frac{\sqrt{2}}{3}$

46. The graph of $y = 3cos\,(2x) + 3$ intersects the y–axis at what value of y?
    a) 3
    b) 6
    c) 9
    d) 0

Diagnostic Test Answer Keys

1.	C	2.	D	3.	A	4.	D	5.	B	6.	5	7.	C	8.	D	9.	B	10.	A
11.	D	12.	B	13.	D	14.	80	15.	B	16.	D	17.	1000	18.	D	19.	D	20.	D
21.	A	22.	C	23.	D	24.	D	25.	C	26.	C	27.	D	28.	B	29.	C	30.	D
31.	153	32.	D	33.	B	34.	D	35.	8	36.	B	37.	78.5	38.	C	39.	4.12	40.	B
41.	D	42.	A	43.	D	44.	6	45.	B	46.	B								

Diagnostic Test Answer Explanations

1. Answer: (C)
$$\frac{12(2x)^4}{(2y)} = 2^3 \left(\frac{12x^4}{y}\right)$$

2. Answer: (D)
$$v = \pi (3)^2 \times 7$$
$$v_2 = \pi (3)^2 \times 14$$
$$\frac{v}{v_2} = \frac{\pi(3)^2 \times 7}{\pi(3)^2 \times 14} = \frac{1}{2}$$
$$v_2 = 2v$$

3. Answer: (A)
12 large cups need 4 litters and 10 small cups need 2 litters.
The amount of milk needed:
$4 + 2 = 6$ litters

4. Answer: (D)
The line segment connecting the first two points must have the same slope as the line segment connecting the last two points.
$$\frac{10-s}{5-1} = \frac{10-t}{5-3}$$
$$\frac{10-s}{4} = \frac{10-t}{2}$$
$$40 - 4t = 20 - 2s$$
$$4t - 2s = 20$$
$$2t - s = 10$$

5. Answer: (B)
From the graph, there are two roots, −2 and 1.
$$y = (x + 2)(x - 1) = x^2 + x - 2$$

6. Answer: 5
Let x be the number of $20 bills and y be the number of $10 bills.
$$x + y = 13, y = 13 - x$$
$$20x + 10y = 180$$
$$20x + 10(13 - x) = 180$$
$$130 + 10x = 180$$
$$10x = 50$$
$$x = 5$$

7. Answer: (C)
$$5 < \frac{1}{x-1}, \frac{1}{5} > x - 1$$
$$1 < x < \frac{6}{5}$$

8. Answer: (D)
Let the price of one eraser be x and the price of one pencil be y. The price of 6 erasers = the price of 3 pencils.
$$6x = 3y, x = \frac{1}{2}y$$
The Price of One Eraser = $\frac{1}{2}$ the Price of One Pencil.
$$x + y = 1.50 ; \frac{1}{2}y + y = 1.50$$
Solve for y to get the price of one pencil $1.00.

9. Answer: (B)
Let one trip have x miles.
$$Time = 2.25 = t_1 + t_2 = \frac{x}{50} + \frac{x}{40}$$
$$2.25 = x\left(\frac{1}{50} + \frac{1}{40}\right) ; x = 50$$
Total Distance = $2 \times 50 = 100$

10. Answer: (A)
$$Store's\ Cost \times (1 + 25\%) = 550$$
$$Store's\ Cost = \frac{550}{1.25} = 440$$
20 percent off the store's cost:
$$440 \times (1 - 0.2) = 352$$

11. Answer: (D)
$$\frac{8\ People}{1.2\ Pounds} = \frac{240\ People}{x\ Pounds}$$
$$8x = 1.2 \times 240$$
$$x = 36\ pounds\ of\ flour$$

12. Answer: (B)
$$8 \times 12 = y \times 24$$
$$y = 4$$

13. Answer: (D)
$$\frac{40}{6} = \frac{y}{9}$$
$$y = 60$$

14. *Answer: 80*

Small car uses $\frac{100}{25} = 4$ gallons

SUV Miles = $4 \times 20 = 80$ miles

15. *Answer: (B)*

Let X's width be w and length be l. Then Y's width is $0.75w$ and length is $1.25l$.

Area of Y = $0.75w \times 1.25l = 0.9375wl = 93.75\%$ of area of X.

$100\% - 93.75\% = 6.25\%$ (less)

16. *Answer: (D)*

Sum = Number of Elements × Average

$9 \times 8 < Sum < 10 \times 8$

$72 < Sum < 80$

17. *Answer: 1000*

Solve this problem using proportions.

There were 4% (52% − 48%) more Sedans sold than all other cars combined.

$4\% : 40 = 100\% : x$

$x = 1,000$ cars

18. *Answer: (D)*

The total number of marbles should be a common multiple of 4 and 5.

The LCM of 4 and 5 is 20, so the total number of marbles has to be a multiple of 20.

19. *Answer: (D)*

Find the greatest number that ends in 0 and where the sum of the digits is divisible by 9.

20. *Answer: (D)*

The LCM of 12 and 9 is 36.

21. *Answer: (A)*

$$\frac{1}{-\frac{1}{2}} - \frac{1}{-\frac{1}{2}+1} = -2 - 2 = -4$$

22. *Answer: (C)*

$x^2 - y^2 = (x - y)(x + y)$

$3(x + y) = 15, x + y = 5$

23. *Answer: (D)*

A positive value of a will make the quadratic function's graph open upward and a positive value of c will show that the function has a positive y-intercept.

24. *Answer: (D)*

Rationalize the denominator.

$$\frac{3-2i}{4+3i} \times \frac{4-3i}{4-3i} = \frac{(3-2i)(4-3i)}{16+9} = \frac{6-17i}{25}$$

25. *Answer: (C)*

If $(3 - 2i)$ is a root of the quadratic equation, then its conjugate $(3 + 2i)$ is also the root of the equation.

The product of the roots is $\frac{b}{2}$; the sum of the roots is $-\frac{b}{a}$.

$(3 - 2i)(3 + 2i) = 13 = \frac{b}{2}$

$9 - (-4) = 13 = \frac{b}{2} \rightarrow b = 26$

26. *Answer: (C)*

The discriminant, $b^2 - 4ac$, of a quadratic equation reveals the type of its roots.

When $b^2 - 4ac = 0$, the quadratic equation two equal, real roots.

- When $b^2 - 4ac > 0$, the quadratic equation has two unequal, real roots.
- When $b^2 - 4ac < 0$, the quadratic equation has no real roots.

27. *Answer: (D)*

$50 = -1.2t^2 + 100$

$t = 6.45$

28. *Answer: (B)*

$8a^2 = a^y \times a^2 = a^{y+2}$

29. *Answer: (C)*

$x^{\frac{3}{2}} = \frac{1}{27}$

$x = (\frac{1}{27})^{\frac{2}{3}}$

$\frac{1}{27} = 3^{-3}$

$x = (3^{-3})^{\frac{2}{3}} = 3^{-2} = \frac{1}{9}$

30. *Answer: (D)*

$\frac{2}{(x+y)^{-\frac{2}{3}}} = (x + y)^{-\frac{1}{3}}$,

$2 = (x + y)^{-\frac{2}{3}}(x + y)^{-\frac{1}{3}} = (x + y)^{-1}$

$x + y = \frac{1}{2}$

31. *Answer: 153*

$a + (90 - 63)° = 180°$

$a = 153°$

32. Answer: (D)
$3x = 42$
$x = 14$
$2y + 42 = 90$
$y = 24$
$x + y = 14 + 24 = 38$

33. Answer: (B)
$y = x + z$ (exterior angle theorem and corresponding angles)
$z = y - x$

34. Answer: (D)
$2x + x = 90º$
$x = 30º$
Two special 30–60–90 right triangles: AB = 2
$AC = \frac{1}{2} \times 2 = 1; AD = \frac{\sqrt{3}}{2} \times AC = \frac{\sqrt{3}}{2}$

35. Answer: 8
If h is the height of smaller triangle, then the height of the big triangle is h + 3.
Area of Big Δ – Area of Small Δ = 26
$\frac{1}{2}(h + 3) \times 12 - \frac{1}{2}h \times 10 = 26$
$6h + 18 - 5h = 26; h = 8$

36. Answer: (B)
OA is the radius of the circle and the shaded area is the area of the quarter circle minus the area of the rectangle.
Radius $= \sqrt{OB^2 + OC^2} = \sqrt{3^2 + 4^2} = 5$
Shaded Area = Area of $\frac{1}{4}$ Circle – Area of Rectangle =
$\frac{1}{4}(\pi \times 5^2) - 4 \times 3 = \frac{1}{4} \times 25\pi - 12 = \frac{25\pi}{4} - 12$

37. Answer: 78.5
$DA^2 + OA^2 = OD^2$
$12^2 + r^2 = (8 + r)^2 = 64 + 16r + r^2 ; r = 5$
Area $= \pi \times 5^2 = 78.54$

38. Answer: (C)
Area $= \frac{40}{360}(\pi \times 5^2 - \pi \times 4^2) = \pi$

39. Answer: 4.12
BF = 2; EF = 3; EA = 2
$AB = \sqrt{EA^2 + EB^2} = \sqrt{EA^2 + BF^2 + EF^2}$
$AB = \sqrt{2^2 + 2^2 + 3^2} = \sqrt{17} = 4.123$

40. Answer: (B)
Let x be the length of one side of the cube.
Diameter of Sphere = Diagonal of Cube
Diagonal of Cube $= \sqrt{x^2 + x^2 + x^2} = x\sqrt{3}$
$\sqrt{x^2 + x^2 + x^2} = 3\sqrt{3}$
$x\sqrt{3} = 3\sqrt{3}$
$x = 3$
Volume of Cube $= 3^3 = 27$

41. Answer: (D)
After folding, the height of the box will be 3 cm, the length will be 5 cm, and the width will be 4cm.
Volume = 3 cm × 4 cm × 5 cm = 60 cm³

42. Answer: (A)
The equation of a parabola with vertex (h, k) is
$y = (x - h)^2 + k$.
$(h, k) = (-3, -4)$
$y = (x + 3)^2 - 4$

43. Answer: (D)
This is a trapezoid of whose area is equal to $\frac{1}{2}$ (AB + OC) × OA.
Area $= \frac{1}{2}(4 + 6) \times 4 = 20$

44. Answer: 6
Rewrite the equation in standard form:
$(x - h)^2 + (y - k)^2 = r^2$
$x^2 + y^2 - 4x + 2y = 20$
$(x^2 - 4x + 2^2) + (y^2 + 2y + 1^2) = 20 + 2^2 + 1^2 = 25$
$(x - 2)^2 + (y + 1)^2 = 5^2$
The center of circle is $(2, -1)$ and the radius is 5.
$h + k + r = 2 - 1 + 5 = 6$

45. Answer: (B)
In the first Quadrant, only when $\alpha = 45$, $cos(\alpha°) = sin(\alpha°) = \frac{\sqrt{2}}{2}$
For a unit circle:
$x = y = \frac{\sqrt{2}}{2}$
$x + y = \sqrt{2}$

46. Answer: (B)
The graph of y = 3cos (2x) + 3 intersects the y–axis at x = 0.
$y = 3\cos(2 \times 0) + 3 = 3\cos(0) + 3$
$= 3 \times 1 + 3 = 6$

Chapter 1 Algebra

I.   ALGEBRAIC EXPRESSIONS

Like Terms

Terms that share a base and the same power are called like terms. For instance, the terms x, $3x$, and $8x$ are like terms because these terms all have the same base, x, and the same exponent (the exponent is one because it is not explicitly stated). The terms $3x$ and $3x^2$ are **unlike terms**, because the variables have different exponents.

Addition and Subtraction of Algebraic Expressions Consist of Combining Like Terms

To add like terms, combine them by adding their coefficients, for example, $3x + 4x = 7x$. To subtract like terms, subtract their coefficients, for example, $9a^2 - 6a^2 = 3a^2$.

Multiply and Divide Terms with Same Base

To **multiply** terms with same base, multiply the coefficients of the terms and add the exponents: $(3b^4)(2b^3) = 6b^7$. To divide terms with same base, divide the coefficients of the terms and subtract the exponents: $\frac{15x^5}{5x^2} = 3x^3$.

- The **reciprocal** of a number x is equivalent to $\frac{1}{x}$ where x is not 0.
- To divide by a fraction term is the same as multiplying by its reciprocal. For instance: $\frac{x^5}{\frac{1}{x^2}} = x^5 \times x^2 = x^7$

Distributive Law

Use the **distributive law** when multiplying algebraic expressions with more than one term. The distributive law states that in order to get rid of the parentheses, each element within the parentheses should be multiplied by the term outside.
Examples:

$$A (B + C) = AB + AC$$
$$A (B - C) = AB - AC$$

- If the sign before the parentheses is −, change the sign of every term inside and take away the parentheses. This can be thought of as distributing −1. For instance, $x^2 - (-2x^2 + 3x - 1) = x^2 + 2x^2 - 3x + 1 = 3x^2 - 3x + 1$

- Use **FOIL** to multiply a binomial by another binomial

$$\text{(a + b)(c + d)} = ac + ad + bc + bd$$

F   O   I   L

Example: $(x + 3)(x - 1) = x^2 - x + 3x - 3 = x^2 + 2x - 3$

Evaluate an Expression

To evaluate an expression by substitution is **to replace a variable by its value** and then perform the calculations by using the **PEMDAS** as the order of the operations.

Example: Evaluate $x^2 + 3x + 5$ when $x = -1$
Solution: Substitute x with -1, so $(-1)^2 + 3(-1) + 5 = 1 - 3 + 5 = 3$.

Evaluate One Variable in Terms of Another

An equation that contains two variables can be written so that the value of one variable is given in terms of the other. For instance, $y = 3x + 3$ is an equation with two variables, x and y, in which the value of variable y is written in terms of the other variable x. The value of y is $3x + 3$.

Steps to Evaluate One Variable in Terms of Another
1) Combine **like terms.**
2) Isolate the **variable** you wish to solve for by using **opposite operations** to move all other terms to the other side of the equation.

Example: If $4a + 8b = 16$, what is the value of a in terms of b?
Solution: $4a = 16 - 8b$, Isolate $4a$ on one side of the equation, move $8b$ to the other side of the equation and change the sign of $8b$ to negative.
$a = 4 - 2b$, after dividing all terms by 4, the value of a in terms of b is $4 - 2b$.

Problem Solving Skills

Easy

1. If $x = 4y$ and $y = 2$, what is the value of $5x$?
   a) 4
   b) 10
   c) 20
   d) 40

   Answer: (D)
   Plug $y = 2$ into the first equation.

   $x = 4(2) = 8$
   $5x = 5(8) = 40$

2. If $x + 2y = 5$, what is the value of $x + 2y - 5$?

   Answer: 0
   $x + 2y = 5$
   $(x + 2y) - 5 \rightarrow 5 - 5 = 0$

3. If $x + y = 8$, $y = z - 3$, and $z = 1$, then what is the value of x?
   a) 10
   b) 3
   c) -8
   d) -6

   Answer: (A)
   If $z = 1$, then $y = 1 - 3 = -2$.

   $x + (-2) = 8$
   $x = 10$

4. If $f(x) = \frac{2-x^2}{x}$ for all nonzero x, then $f(1)=?$
   a) 1
   b) 2
   c) 3
   d) 4

   Answer: (A)
   Plug $x = 1$ into the function.
   $f(1) = \frac{2-(1)^2}{1} = \frac{1}{1} = 1$

5. Which of the following is not equal to $6x^2$?
   a) $2x^2 + 4x^2$
   b) $2x + 4x$
   c) $(2x)(3x)$
   d) $(6x)(x)$

   Answer: (B)
   $2x + 4x = 6x \neq 6x^2$

6. If $ab + 3b = a - 2c$, what is the value of b when $a = -2$ and $c = -1$?

   Answer: 0
   Plug $a = -2$ and $c = -1$ into equation.
   $(-2)b + 3b = -2 - 2 \times (-1)$
   $-2b + 3b = 0 \rightarrow b = 0$

7. If $x = y(y - 2)$, then $x + 3 = ?$
   a) $y^2 - y$
   b) $y^2 - 3y$
   c) $y^2 - 2y + 2$
   d) $y^2 - 2y + 3$

   Answer: (D)
   Use Distribution Law.
   FOIL: $x = y(y - 2) = y^2 - 2y$
   $x + 3 = y^2 - 2y + 3$

8. If $5x = 4y$ and $2y = 5z$, what is the value of x in terms of z?

    a) z
    b) $2z$
    c) $3z$
    d) $4z$

Answer: (B)
Substitute 2y with 5z in the first equation.
$5x = 2(2y) = 2(5z) = 10z$
$x = 2z$

9. If x is $\frac{3}{4}$ of y, y is $\frac{2}{3}$ of z, and $z > 0$, and then what is x in terms of z?

    a) $\frac{3}{4}z$
    b) $\frac{1}{2}z$
    c) $\frac{1}{4}z$
    d) $2z$

Answer: (B)
$x = \frac{3}{4}y = \frac{3}{4}\left(\frac{2}{3}z\right)$
$x = \frac{1}{2}z$

10. If $xy^3 = z$, $z = ky^2$, and $ky \neq 0$, which of the following is equal to k?

    a) xy
    b) $\frac{x}{y}$
    c) $x - 1$
    d) $x + y$

Answer: (A)
$xy^3 = z = ky^2$

$k = \frac{xy^3}{y^2} = xy$

Medium

11. If $2x + y = x + 5$, what is y in terms of x?
    a) $5 - x$
    b) $x + 5$
    c) $1 - 5x$
    d) $1 - 2x$

Answer: (A)
Isolate the terms that contain the variable you wish to solve for and then move all other terms to the other side of the equation.
$2x + y = x + 5$
$y = x + 5 - 2x$
$y = -x + 5$

12. If $\frac{x}{2} = 0$, what is the value of $1 + x + 2x^2 + 3x^3 =$?
    a) 2
    b) 1
    c) 0
    d) 3

Answer: (B)
$\frac{1}{2}x = 0$
$x = 0$
$1 + 0 + 2(0)^2 + 3(0)^3 = 1$

13. If $x = 3$, $y = 5$, what is the value of $2 \times \left(\frac{x}{y}\right)^2 \times y^2$?

    a) 5
    b) 10
    c) 15
    d) 18

Answer: (D)
$2 \times \left(\frac{3}{5}\right)^2 \times 5^2 = 18$

14. $f(x) = \frac{x^3 - 5}{x^2 - 2x + 8}$, then what is $f(3)$?
    a) 0
    b) 2
    c) 4
    d) 6

Answer: (B)

$f(3) = \frac{3^3 - 5}{3^2 - 2(3) + 8} = \frac{22}{11} = 2$

15. If $z = \frac{12x^4}{y}$, what happens to the value of z when both x and y are doubled?
    a) z is multiplied by 32.
    b) z is multiplied by 16.
    c) z is multiplied by 8.
    d) z is doubled.

Answer: (C)

$\frac{12(2x)^4}{(2y)} = 2^3 \times \frac{12x^4}{y}$

16. If one soft drink costs \$0.40 and one burger cost \$2, which of the following represents the cost, in dollars, of S soft drinks and B burgers?
    a) S × B
    b) 0.8(S × B)
    c) 2.4(B + S)
    d) 2B + 0.4S

Answer: (D)
Total = 2 × B + 0.4 × S

17. If $x = -5$ and $y = 3$, what is the value of $x^2(2y + x)$?
    a) –275
    b) –75
    c) –25
    d) 25

Answer: (D)
$(-5)^2 \times (2 \times 3 + (-5)) = 25$

18. If $x^{-1}y = 5$, what does y equal in term of x?
    a) –5x
    b) x
    c) –x
    d) 5x

Answer: (D)
$x^{-1} = \frac{1}{x}$
$x^{-1}y = 5$
$\frac{y}{x} = 5 \rightarrow y = 5x$

19. If $x = y^2$ for any positive integer x, and if $z = x^3 + x^4$, what is z in terms of y?
    a) $y^2 + y^3$
    b) y^3
    c) $y^6 + y^3$
    d) $y^6 + y^8$

Answer: (D)
Replace x with y^2.

$z = (y^2)^3 + (y^2)^4 = y^6 + y^8$

20. The price of green tea leaves is D dollars for 5 ounces and each ounce makes x bottles of green tea drink. In terms of D and x, which of the following expressions shows the cost of making 1 bottle of green tea drink?

    a) $5Dx$
    b) $\frac{5D}{x}$
    c) $\frac{5x}{D}$
    d) $\frac{D}{5x}$

Answer: (D)

$D = 5\ ounces \times \frac{x\ Bottles}{Ounce} \times$
$Price\ of\ One\ Bottle$

$Price\ of\ One\ Bottle = \frac{D}{5x}$

Hard

21. If $\frac{x+y}{z} = 9$, $\frac{x}{y} = 8$,and $\sqrt{x} = 4$,what is the value of z?

    a) 1
    b) 2
    c) 3
    d) 4

Answer: (B)
If $\sqrt{x} = 4$, then $x = 4^2 = 16$.
$\frac{x}{y} = \frac{16}{y} = 8 \rightarrow y = 2$
$\frac{16 + 2}{z} = 9 \rightarrow z = 2$

22. The table below gives values of the quadratic function $f(x)$ at selected values of x. Which of the following defines $f(x)$?

x	0	1	2	3
$f(x)$	5	7	13	23

    a) $f(x) = x^2 + 5$
    b) $f(x) = x^2 + 1$
    c) $f(x) = 2x^2 - 5$
    d) $f(x) = 2x^2 + 5$

Answer: (D)
Plug in $x = 0$ and $x = 1$ to try out until the answer found.

(d) $2(0)^2 + 5 = 5$
$2(1)^2 + 5 = 7$

II. SOLVING ONE VARIABLE EQUATIONS

Definition of Equation

An **equation** is a statement that two expressions are equal. The both sides of the equation are equal. The key of solving for a variable in the equation is to isolate the variable on one side and everything else on the other side of the equal sign.

Opposite Operations

To **isolate an variable**, use operations that are opposite to the existing operations in the equation in order to move variables or numbers between both sides of an equation and keep the two sides equal. Some pairs of opposite operations include **+ verses −** , **× verses ÷**, and **square verses square root**.

Solving an equation involves isolating the variable you want to solve for by using opposite operations and reversing the order of PEMDAS to move all other terms to the opposite side of the equation.

For example, let's consider the equation $3x^2 - 1 = 11$. In this equation, there is multiplication by 3, an exponent of 2, and subtraction of 1. According to the reverse order of PEMDAS and opposite operations, you need to add 1, divide by 3, and take the square root on both sides of the equal sign.

$$3x^2 - 1 = 11$$
$$3x^2 = 12$$
$$x^2 = 4$$
$$x = \pm 2$$

Problem Solving Skills

Easy

1. If $-3x + 8 = -2x - 7$, what is the value of x?
   a) 15
   b) 3
   c) -3
   d) -15

   Answer: (A)
   Isolate x on one side of equation and use opposite operations.
   $-3x + 8 = -2x - 7$
   $-3x + 8 - 8 + 2x$
   $= -2x - 7 - 8 + 2x$
   $-x = -15 \rightarrow x = 15$

2. If $x^3 + 6 = x^3 + y$, then $y = ?$
   a) -6
   b) -3
   c) 6
   d) 3

   Answer: (C)
   Definition of equation. Both sides of the equation are equal.

   $x^3 + 6 = x^3 + y$
   $y = 6$

3. If $3x + 2 = 5$, what is the value of $3x - 6$?
   a) -1
   b) -2
   c) -3
   d) 1

   Answer: (C)
   Subtract 8 on both sides.

   $3x + 2 - 8 = 5 - 8 = -3$
   $3x - 6 = -3$

4. If $a^2 - 1 = b^3$, and $2a = 6$, which of the following could be the value of b?
   a) -1
   b) 0
   c) 1
   d) 2

   Answer: (D)
   $2a = 6$
   $a = 3$
   $3^2 - 1 = b^3$
   $8 = b^3 = 2^3$
   $b = 2$

5. If $m^2 + 8 = 39$, then $m^2 - 7 = ?$
   a) 31
   b) 29
   c) 26
   d) 24

   Answer: (D)
   $m^2 + 8 = 39$
   $m^2 = 31$
   $m^2 - 7 = 31 - 7 = 24$

6. If $3(x + 5) = 18$, then what is the value of x?
   a) 1
   b) 3
   c) 6
   d) 9

   Answer: (A)
   Divide both sides by 3.
   $3(x + 5) = 18$
   $x + 5 = 6$
   $x = 1$

7. If $(0.0010) \times y = 10$, then $y = ?$
   a) 0.01
   b) 0.001
   c) 100
   d) 10000

Answer: (D)
Divide both sides by 0.001.
$(0.0010) \times y = 10$
$y = \frac{10}{0.001} = 10000$

Medium

8. If $\frac{x}{3} = \frac{3x}{z}$ and $z \neq 0$, what is the value of z?
   a) 9
   b) 6
   c) 4
   d) 3

Answer: (A)
Apply cross multiplication.
$\frac{x}{3} = \frac{3x}{z}$
$\frac{1}{3} = \frac{3}{z}$
$z = 3 \times 3 = 9$

9. If $2a + 3b = 2b$, which of the following must equal $6a + 3b$?
   a) 0
   b) 1
   c) b
   d) $3b$

Answer: (A)
$2a + 3b = 2b$
$2a + b = 0$
$6a + 3b = 3(2a + b) = 0$

Hard

10. If $3(x + y)(x - y) = 30$ and $x - y = 5$, what is the value of $x + y$?
    a) 1
    b) 2
    c) 3
    d) −1

Answer: (B)
$3 \times 5 \times (x + y) = 30$
$x + y = 2$

11. If $xy = 4$, $z - y = 3$, and $2z = 10$, what is the value of $x + y + z$?

Answer: 9
Solve for z first. Then solve for y, and finally solve for x.
$2z = 10 \rightarrow z = 5$
$5 - y = 3 \rightarrow y = 2$
$x(2) = 4 \rightarrow x = 2$
$x + y + z = 9$

III. SOLVING A LINEAR EQUATION

Slope of Two Points $= \dfrac{Rise}{Run} = \dfrac{y_2 - y_1}{x_2 - x_1}$

The slope of a line represents the rate of change of that line, specifically indicating the change in y for each unit increase in x.

Slope-intercept Form: $y = mx + b$ where m is the slope and b is the y-intercept. A linear equation written as slope-intercept form has the properties illustrated by the following graph:

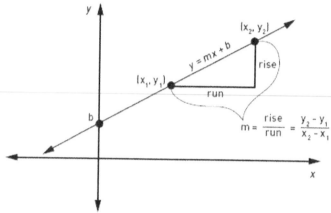

The y-intercept, the point where the line intersects the y-axis, of a line represents the initial value of y when x is zero.

Standard Form: The standard form of a line is written as $ax + by = c$, where the slope of the line is $-\dfrac{a}{b}$.

Example: Find the slope of the line from the equation $4x - 2y + 2 = 0$.
Answer: Change the equation to any of the forms listed above.

Convert to slope-intercept form: $2y = 4x + 2$ → $y = 2x + 1$
$m = 2$ So, the slope is 2. (The graph slopes upward from left to right.)

Convert to the standard form: $4x - 2y = -2$
The slope of a linear equation $ax + by + c = 0$ will be $-\dfrac{a}{b}$.
$$m = -\frac{a}{b} = -\frac{4}{-2} = 2$$

Two lines are perpendicular if their slopes are **opposite reciprocals**, i.e., the product of their slopes is –1.

Two different lines are parallel if their **slopes are equal** but they are not the same line.

Problem Solving Skills

Easy

1. What is the y-intercept of the linear equation
   $7y - x = -14$?
   - a) −4
   - b) −2
   - c) 0
   - d) 2

   Answer: (B)
   The y-intercept occurs when x = 0.
   $7y - 0 = -14$
   $y = -2$

2. What is the slope of a line that passes through the points
   $(1, -1)$ and $(-1, 5)$?
   - a) −3
   - b) −2
   - c) 0
   - d) 2

   Answer: (A)
   $Slope = \frac{Rise}{Run} = \frac{5 - (-1)}{-1 - 1} = -3$

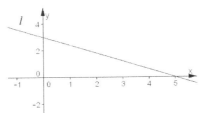

3. In the figure above, what is the slope of line l?
    - a) $\frac{1}{4}$
    - b) $\frac{1}{2}$
    - c) $\frac{2}{5}$
    - d) $-\frac{3}{5}$

   Answer: (D)
   $Slope = \frac{Rise}{Run} = \frac{0-3}{5-0} = -\frac{3}{5}$

[Figure: coordinate axes with line l passing through $A(-3, 2)$ and $B(5, y)$]

4. In the figure above, the slope of line l is $-\frac{1}{2}$. What is the
    value of y?
    - a) $\frac{1}{2}$
    - b) 1
    - c) $-\frac{1}{2}$
    - d) −2

   Answer: (D)
   $Slope = \frac{y-2}{5 - (-3)} = -\frac{1}{2}$
   $y - 2 = -4$
   $y = -2$

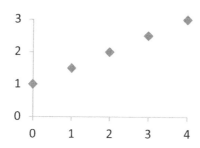

5. Which of the lines described by the following equations best fits those points above?
   a) $y = 0.5x - 1$
   b) $y = 0.5x + 1$
   c) $y = -0.5x - 1$
   d) $y = -0.5x + 1$

Answer: (B)
$Slope = \dfrac{Rise}{Run} = \dfrac{2-1}{2-0} = 0.5$
y-intercept = 1
$y = 0.5x + 1$

x	1	2	3	4
y	1	4	7	10

6. The table above represents a relationship between x and y. Which of the following linear equations describes the relationship?
   a) $y = 4x - 1$
   b) $y = 3x + 1$
   c) $y = 3x - 2$
   d) $y = -3x + 4$

Answer: (C)
The slope of the linear equation is
$\dfrac{4-1}{2-1} = 3.$
Point-slope-form: $y - 1 = 3(x - 1)$
$y = 3x - 2$

7. Which two lines are perpendicular to each other?
   a) $y = x - 1; x = 1$
   b) $y = x + 1; x = 1$
   c) $y = -1; x = 1$
   d) $x = -1; x = 1$

Answer: (C)
The value of the y coordinate is constant for a horizontal line.

8. In the xy-coordinate system above, which of the following lines has a slope closest to 1?
   a) A
   b) B
   c) C
   d) D

Answer: (A)
Line A has the slope closest to 1.

9. Which of the following is the graph of a linear function with a negative slope and a negative y-intercept?

a)

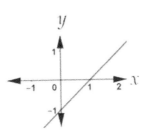

b)

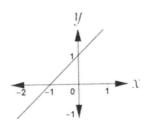

c)

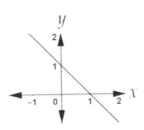

d)

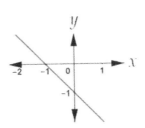

10. What is the y-intercept of the line that passes through the points $(1, 1)$ and $(5, 13)$?
   a) −2
   b) −1
   c) 1
   d) 2

11. In the xy-plane, the line $x - 2y = k$ passes through point (4, −1). What is the value of k?
    a) 6
    b) 4
    c) 2
    d) −2

Answer: (A)
Plug in the values for x and y into the equation.
4 − 2(−1) = k = 6

Medium

12. The equation of line l is $x - 2y = 3$. Which of the following is an equation of the line that is perpendicular to line l?
    a) $y = x + 2$
    b) $y = -x + 2$
    c) $y = 2x - 1$
    d) $y = -2x + 1$

Answer: (D)
x − 2y = 3
$y = \frac{1}{2}x - 1.5$
Line l has a slope of $\frac{1}{2}$.
A line that is perpendicular to line l would have a slope of −2.

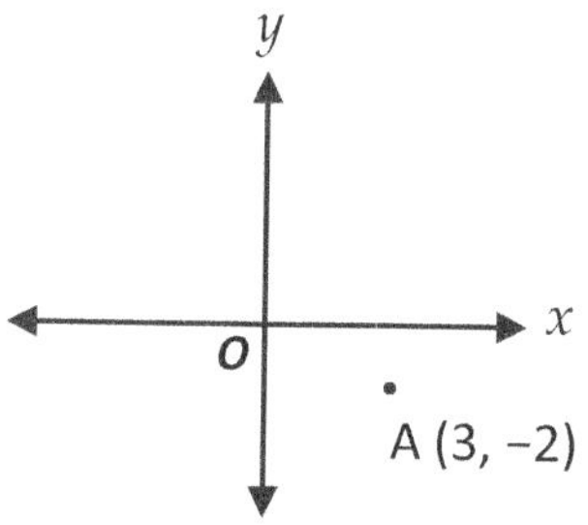

13. In the figure above, a line is to be drawn through point A so that it has a slope of 1. Through which of the following points must the line pass?
    a) (−5, 1)
    b) (−4, 1)
    c) (1, 4)
    d) (1, −4)

Answer: (D)
Slope $= 1 = \frac{y-(-2)}{x-3}$
x − 3 = y + 2
y = x − 5
Out of 5 answer choices, only (1, −4) satisfies the equation y = x − 5.

14. Which of the following could be the coordinates of point R in a coordinate plane, if points P(1, 1), Q(−1, 5), and R(x, y) lie on the same line?
    a) (0, 2)
    b) (2, −1)
    c) (0, −2)
    d) (2, 2)

Answer: (B)
Slope $= \frac{Rise}{Run} = \frac{5-1}{-1-1} = -2$
Point-slope-form: y − 1 = −2(x −1)
The point (2, −1) satisfies the above equation.

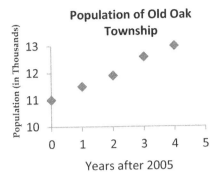

15. The graph above shows the population of Old Oak Township since 2005. If y represents the population, in thousands, and x represents the number of years after 2005, which of the following equations best describes the data shown?
    a) $y = x + 11$
    b) $y = 2x + 11$
    c) $y = 2x - 11$
    d) $y = \frac{1}{2}x + 11$

Answer: (D)
Find the slope and y-intercept from the graph.
Slope = $\frac{1}{2}$
y-intercept = 11
$y = \frac{1}{2}x + 11$

16. What is the product of the slopes of all four sides of a rectangle if all four sides' slopes are not equal to zero?
    a) −2
    b) −1
    c) 0
    d) 1

Answer: (D)
The product of the slopes of two perpendicular lines is −1.
The product of the slopes of all four sides of rectangle is
$−1 \times (−1) = 1$.

Hard

17. If a linear function passes through the points $(1, s)$, $(3, t)$ and $(5, 10)$, what is the value of $2t - s$?
    a) 2
    b) 8
    c) 10
    d) 12

Answer: (C)
The line segment connecting the first two points must have the same slope as the line segment connecting the last two points.
$\frac{10-s}{5-1} = \frac{10-t}{5-3} \rightarrow \frac{10-s}{4} = \frac{10-t}{2}$
$40 - 4t = 20 - 2s \rightarrow 2t - s = 10$

18. Joe goes on a business trip that includes 3 different types of transportation: bike, bus, and airplane, in that order. If all three transportations take roughly the same amount of time, which of the following could be the graph of the distance traveled by the three transportations?

Answer: (B)
The higher the speed of the vehicle, the steeper (greater) the slope of the graph. Since bikes are slower than buses which are slower than planes, the graph must have three segments of increasing slope.

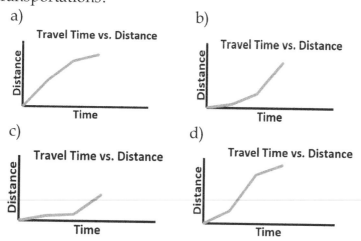

a)

Travel Time vs. Distance

Distance

Time

b)

Travel Time vs. Distance

Distance

Time

c)

Travel Time vs. Distance

Distance

Time

d)

Travel Time vs. Distance

Distance

Time

IV. SOLVING A SYSTEM OF EQUATIONS

There must be at least one equation given in order to solve for one variable. In the same vein, at least two equations must be given to solve two variables, at least three equations for three variables, and so on. **In order to solve a system of equations, there must be at least the same number of equations given as the variables being solved for.** In the real world, tools such as matrices or computer algorithms are necessary to solve complicated system of equations. On the SAT, however, it is sufficient to use the following two methods:

- **Substitution**

    Example: Solve the following system of equations by substitution:
    $$x - y = 1 \qquad (1)$$
    $$2x + 3y = 7 \qquad (2)$$
    Solution: $x = y + 1$, from the first equation
    $2(y+1) + 3y = 7$, because they are equivalent, substitute x with $y + 1$ into the second equation
    $$2y + 2 + 3y = 7$$
    $$5y = 5$$
    $$y = 1$$
    $$x = y + 1$$
    $$= 1 + 1$$
    $$= 2$$
    $$x = 2 \text{ and } y = 1$$

- **Elimination**

    Example: Solve the following system of equations by elimination:
    $$3x - y = 3 \quad ---(1)$$
    $$x + 2y = 15 \quad ---(2)$$
    Solution: In order to eliminate y, multiply equation (1) by 2.
    $2(3x - y) = 3 \times 2 ---(3)$, add equations (2) and (3).
    $$2(3x - y) + (x + 2y) = 3 \times 2 + 15$$
    $6x - 2y + x + 2y = 21$, cancel out $-2y$ and $2y$.
    $$7x = 21$$
    $x = 3$, plug in the value for x into equation (1).
    $$3 \times 3 - y = 3$$
    $$y = 6$$
    $$x = 3 \text{ and } y = 6$$

Problem Solving Skills

Easy

1. $y = x + 1$ and $x + 2y = 8$, what is the value of x?
   a) 1
   b) 2
   c) 3
   d) −2

   Answer: (B)
   Use the substitution method.
   $y = x + 1$
   $x + 2(x + 1) = 8$
   $3x + 2 = 8$
   $x = 2$

2. What is the value of x if $x + 2y = 6$ and $x + y = 5$?
   a) 2
   b) 3
   c) 4
   d) 5

   Answer: (C)
   Substitute y with 5 − x.
   $x + 2(5 − x) = 6$
   $x = 4$

3. If $3a − b = 3$ and $a + 2b = 15$, then $a + b$?
   a) −2
   b) −4
   c) 9
   d) 5

   Answer: (C)
   It is easier to use the method of elimination for this question.
   $3a − b = 3$ (1)
   $6a − 2b = 6$ (1a)
   $a + 2b = 15$ (2)
   Add (1a) and (2) to eliminate b.
   $(1) + (2) → 7a = 21 → a = 3$
   $3 × 3 − b = 3 → b = 6$
   $a + b = 9$

4. There are 25 high school seniors who are taking the total of 112 AP classes this year. Some of them take 4 APs and the others take 5. How many seniors are taking 5 APs?
   a) 11
   b) 12
   c) 13
   d) 14

   Answer: (B)
   Let x be the number of students taking 5 APs and y be the number of students taking 4 APs.
   $x + y = 25$
   $y = 25 − x$
   $5x + 4y = 112$ *(substitution rule)*
   $5x + 4(25 − x) = 112$
   $x + 100 = 112$
   $x = 12$

Medium

5. Six erasers cost as much as 3 pencils. If Matt bought one eraser and one pencil for $1.50, how much does one pencil cost in dollars?
   a) 0.25
   b) 0.50
   c) 0.75
   d) 1.00

   Answer: (D)
   Let the price of one eraser be x and the price of one pencil be y.
   Price of 6 Erasers = Price of 3 Pencils
   $6x = 3y → x = \frac{1}{2}y$
   Price of 1Eraser = $\frac{1}{2}$ Price of 1 Pencil
   $x + y = 1.50$
   $\frac{1}{2}y + y = 1.50 → y = 1.0$
   The price of one pencil is $1.00.

6. There is $180 of cash in John's pocket. John only has 10 and 20 dollar bills. If John has a total of 13 bills, how many 20 dollar bills are in his pocket?

Answer: 5
Let x be the number of $20 bills and y be the number of $10 bills.
$x + y = 13 \rightarrow y = 13 - x$
$20x + 10y = 180$
$20x + 10(13 - x) = 180$
$130 + 10x = 180 \rightarrow x = 5$

Hard

7. At the school cafeteria, there are 30 tables and each table can seat either 2 or 4 students. If there are a total 80 students in one of the lunch sections, how many tables must seat exactly 4 students in this lunch section?
    a) 9
    b) 10
    c) 11
    d) 12

Answer: (B)
Let x be the number of tables that seat 4 students and y be the number of tables that seat 2 students.
$x + y = 30$
$y = 30 - x$
$4x + 2y = 80$ *(substitution rule)*
$4x + 2(30 - x) = 80$
$2x + 60 = 80 \rightarrow x = 10$

$$3x - 4y = 8$$
$$5x + 3y = 23$$

8. Based on the above system of 2-equations, which of the following values will $(x + y)$ equal?
    a) 10
    b) 8
    c) 7
    d) 5

Answer: (D)
Use the method of elimination.
$(3x - 4y = 8) \times 5 \rightarrow$
$15x - 20y = 40 \qquad (1)$
$(5x + 3y = 23) \times (-3) \rightarrow$
$-15x - 9y = -69 \qquad (2)$
Add the equations (1) and (2)
$-29y = -29 \rightarrow y = 1$
$3x - 4 \times 1 = 8 \rightarrow x = 4$
$x + y = 5$

V. SOLVING AN INEQUALITY

Definition of an Inequality: When comparing two real numbers, one number is greater than, less than, or equal to the other number.

To solve inequalities, follow rules that are similar to those applicable to equations. Isolate the variable that needs to be solved for on one side, move all other numbers or constants to the other side, and combine the like terms.

All the rules and techniques used in solving an equation apply to solving an inequality EXCEPT for multiplication and division by a **negative. When you multiply or divide both sides by a negative number, reverse the direction of the inequality**.

> *Example:* 4 > 3, but if you multiply –1 on both sides, the inequality becomes
> –4 < –3.

The inequality is not preserved when both sides are multiplied by zero.

Absolute Value Inequality

The absolute value of a number is the distance from that number to the zero-mark on the number line. The absolute value of any number is always nonnegative.

- If $|x - a| \leq b$, all values of x are between $a - b$ and $a + b$, inclusive, on the number line:
  $a - b \leq x \leq a + b$

  Example: $|x - 1| \leq 3$
  $-3 \leq x - 1 \leq 3$
  $1 - 3 \leq x \leq 1 + 3$
  $-2 \leq x \leq 4$

- If $|x - a| \geq b$, all values of x are either less than or equal to $a - b$ or larger than or equal to $a + b$ on the number line: $x \geq a + b$ or $x \leq a - b$.

  Example: $|x - 1| \geq 3$
  $3 \leq x - 1$ or $x - 1 \leq -3$
  $1 + 3 \leq x$ or $x \leq 1 - 3$
  $x \geq 4$ or $x \leq -2$

To graph the solution of an inequality with two variables, first graph the linear equation as the boundary line using the appropriate line style (dashed for strict, solid for inclusive), and then select a test point outside the boundary to determine the solution side.

Example: Graph $x + 2y < 4$

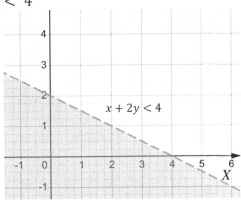

Problem Solving Skills

Easy

1. What is the smallest positive integer value of x for which $2x - 7 > 0$?

   Answer: 4
   If $2x - 7 > 0$, then $2x > 7$.
   $x > 3.5$
   So the smallest positive integer is 4.

2. Given that $4x + 3 < 12$, which of the following cannot be the value of x?
   a) 3
   b) 2
   c) 1
   d) 0

   Answer: (A)
   $4x + 3 < 12$
   $4x < 12 - 3$
   $4x < 9 \rightarrow x < 2.25$

3. What is the least value of integer x such that the value of $2x - 1$ is greater than 9?
   a) 7
   b) 6
   c) 5
   d) 4

   Answer: (B)
   $2x - 1 > 9$
   $2x > 10$
   $x > 5$
   The least value of integer is 6.

4. Alex has less money than Bob and Bob has less money than Chris. If a, b, and c represent the amounts of money that Alex, Bob, and Chris have, respectively, which of the following is true?
   a) $a < b < c$
   b) $c < b < a$
   c) $b < a < c$
   d) $a < c < b$

   Answer: (A)
   "Alex has less money than Bob"
   $\rightarrow a < b$
   "Bob has less money than Chris"
   $\rightarrow b < c$
   $a < b < c$

5. There are 15 boxes of apples in the storage room. Each box has at least 21 apples, and at most 28 apples. Which of the following could be the total number of apples in the storage room?
   a) 200
   b) 250
   c) 300
   d) 350

   Answer: (D)
   Set up the inequality for the number of apples and then multiply the inequality by 15.
   $(21 < x < 28) \times 15$
   $315 < 15x < 420$

6. If 3 less than x is a negative number and if 1 less than x is a positive number, which of the following could be the value of x?
   a) 3

   Answer: (B)
   "3 less than x is a negative" $\rightarrow$
   $x - 3 < 0$
   $x < 3$
   "1 less than x is a positive" $\rightarrow$
   $x - 1 > 0$

b) 2
c) 1
d) 0

7. Which of the following conditions would make $2x - y < 0$?
a) $2x = y$
b) $x > 0$
c) $y > 0$
d) $2x < y$

Answer: (D)
If $2x - y < 0$, then $2x < y$.

8. If $x - 1 > 2$ and $x + 2 < 7$, which of the following could be a value for x?
a) 1
b) 2
c) 3
d) 4

Answer: (D)
Solve the inequalities.
$x - 1 > 2 \rightarrow x > 3$
$x + 2 < 7 \rightarrow x < 5$
Combine them together.
$3 < x < 5$

Medium

9. If $a + 3b < a$, which of the following must be true?
a) $a > 0$
b) $a = 0$
c) $a < 0$
d) $b < 0$

Answer: (D)
Subtract a from both sides.
$a + 3b < a$
$a + 3b - a < a - a$
$3b < 0 \rightarrow b < 0$

10. If $5 \leq x \leq 7$ and $-3 \leq y \leq 1$, which of the following gives the set of all possible values of xy?
a) $-15 \leq xy \leq 7$
b) $0 \leq xy \leq 7$
c) $-21 \leq xy \leq 5$
d) $-21 \leq xy \leq 7$

Answer: (D)
Try out different combinations of x and y.
$-21 \leq xy \leq 7$

11. If $0 > x > y$, which of the following is less than $\frac{x}{y}$?
a) 1
b) 2
c) xy
d) $\frac{x}{2y}$

Answer: (D)
If $0 > x > y$, then $1 > \frac{x}{y} > 0$.
$\frac{x}{y} > \frac{x}{2y}$

Hard

12. If $|5 - 2x| < 3$, which of the following is a possible value of x?
    a) 3
    b) 4
    c) 5
    d) 6

Answer: (A)
If $|5 - 2x| < 3$, then $-3 < 5-2x < 3$.
$-3 -5 < -2x < 3 -5$
$-8 < -2x < -2$
$8 > 2x > 2$ → $4 > x > 1$

13. If $0 < xy$ and $y < 0$, which of the following statements must be true?
    I. $x < 0$
    II. $x < y$
    III. $x > 0$
    a) I only
    b) III only
    c) I and II
    d) II and III

Answer: (A)
$xy > 0$ → both x and y must have the same sign. (Both are positive or both are negative.)
$y < 0$ and $x < 0$

VI. WORD PROBLEMS

Translating from English to Algebraic Expressions
Keywords in the problem can help translating the words into algebraic expressions. For instance, the word "increase" indicates addition and "less" indicates subtraction. "2 times" refers to multiplying a number or variable by two, and "is" indicates equality in an equation.

If the question mentions finding "a number" without specifying the value of the number, assign a variable for that number and then solve for the value of the variable.

The following table lists the most common phrases and their translations.

Operations	Keywords	Sample Phrases	Algebraic Expressions
Addition	plus sum added to more than increased by	three plus a number the sum of a number and 3 three added to a number three more than a number a number increased by 3	$x + 3$
Subtraction	difference minus subtracted from less than decreased by reduced by deducted from	the difference of a number and three a number minus 3 three subtracted from a number three less than a number a number decreased by three a number reduced by three three deducted from a number	$x - 3$
Multiplication	of multiply times twice product of multiplied by	30% of 50 is 15. multiplying 3 by a number four times a number twice a number the product of a number and three a number multiplied by five	$0.3 \times 50 = 15$ $3x$ $4x$ $2x$ $3x$ $5x$
Division	divided by quotient of	a number divided by 3 the quotient of a number and 3	$\frac{x}{3}$
Equal	equal is is equal to	Three multiplied by a number equals 4. Half of 20 is 10. The sum of 5 and 4 is equal to 9.	$3x = 4$ $\frac{1}{2} \times 20 = 10$ $5 + 4 = 9$

Examples: Translate each of the following into an algebraic expression.
1. Three more than four times a number: $4x + 3$
2. Five times the sum of a number and two: $5(x + 2)$
3. Eleven subtracted from the product of two and a number: $2x - 11$

4. The quotient of two less than a number and twice the number: $\frac{(x-2)}{2x}$

5. The sum of a number and its reciprocal is equal to three: $x + \frac{1}{x} = 3$

6. Six times the difference of a number and two is equal to twice the number: $6(x - 2) = 2x$

7. The product of a number and five is increased by the number: $5x + x$

8. Eight less than five times a number divided by twice the number: $\frac{(5x-8)}{2x}$

9. The product of two numbers, if one number is three less than twice the other number: $x(2x - 3)$

10. If nine times a number is reduced by five, the result is three less than the number: $9x - 5 = x - 3$

11. The sum of three consecutive odd integers is 51: $x + (x + 2) + (x + 4) = 51$

12. The sum of three consecutive even integers is 36: $x + (x + 2) + (x + 4) = 36$

13. The product of the sum and difference of two numbers is equal to 15: $(x + y)(x - y) = 15$

Problem Solving Skills

Easy

1. During a lunch in the school cafeteria, if Kristin paid $3.50 for her lunch from her pocket and borrowed $1.50 from a friend, how much did she spend for this lunch?

   Answer: 5
   If she spent x money, then
   $3.5 - x = -1.5.$
   $3.5 - x = -1.5 \rightarrow x = 5$

2. The value of $5n - 7$ is how much greater than the value of $5n - 8$?
   a) 15
   b) 1
   c) $10n + 1$
   d) $5n - 1$

   Answer: (B)
   Find the difference between the two expressions.
   $(5n - 7) - (5n - 8) = 1$

3. A smartphone costs $30 less than four times the cost of a basic cell phone. If the smartphone and the basic phone together cost $570, how much more does the smartphone cost than the basic phone?
   a) $216
   b) $330
   c) $415
   d) $450

   Answer: (B)
   Let the price of a basic phone be x, then the price of a smartphone is $4x – 30$. Solve the equation x + (4x – 30) = 570, and get x = 120. Therefore, a basic phone costs $120 while a smartphone costs $4 × 120 – 30 = $450.
   450 – 120 = 330

4. Triangles A, B, and C are different in size. Triangle A's area is twice the area of triangle B, and triangle C's area is four times the area of triangle A. What is the area of triangle C, in square inches, if the area of triangle B is 10 square inches?
   a) 20
   b) 40
   c) 60 .
   d) 80

   Answer: (D)
   A = 2B,
   C = 4A
   If B = 10, then
   A = 20, and C = 4 × 20 = 80.

5. The local route from Maya's house to her college is 4 miles longer than the expressway. When she drives by the local route and returns by the expressway, the round trip is 30 miles. How many miles does Maya have to drive if she goes to school through the expressway?
   a) 13
   b) 15
   c) 17
   d) 19

   Answer: (A)
   Let the express way be x miles between Maya's house and her college. The local route would be x + 4 miles, which means that the round trip would be x + (x + 4) = 30.
   x = 13

Subtract 5 from y
Divide this difference by 5
Multiply this quotient by 5

6. After completing the operations described above, which of the following is showing the result?

   a) $\frac{y-5}{5}$

   b) $\frac{y}{5}$

   c) $\frac{y+5}{5}$

   d) $y - 5$

Answer: (D)
Since division and multiplication are the inverse functions to each other, the last two operations will cancel each other. Hence, it will only need to perform the first operation: subtract 5 from y.

7. Which of the following is an equation you would use to find x if it is given that 10 more than the product of x and 5 is 30?

   a) $5(x - 10) = 30$

   b) $5x - 10 = 30$

   c) $5(x + 10) = 30$

   d) $5x + 10 = 30$

Answer: (D)
10 more than the product of x and 5 → 10 + 5x
5x + 10 = 30

8. If 10 percent of 40 percent of a positive number is equal to 20 percent of y percent of the same positive number, find the value of y.

   a) 10

   b) 15

   c) 20

   d) 35

Answer: (C)
$\frac{10}{100} \times \frac{40}{100} \times A = \frac{20}{100} \times \frac{y}{100} \times A$
$\frac{10 \times 40}{100 \times 100} = \frac{20y}{100 \times 100}$
Therefore, $10 \times 40 = 20y$
$y = 20.$

9. After 20 customers entered a deli store and 4 customers left, there were 3 times as many customers as there were at the beginning. How many customers were in that deli store at the very beginning?

   a) 6

   b) 7

   c) 8

   d) 12

Answer: (C)
Let x be the original number of customers, then x + 20 − 4 = 3x.
x = 8

10. The sum of $5x$ and 3 is equal to the difference of $2x$ and 3. Which of the following represents the above statement?

   a) $5x + 3 = 2x - 3$

   b) $5(x + 3) = 2(x - 3)$

   c) $5x - 3 = 2x + 3$

   d) $5x - 3 = 2x - 3$

Answer: (A)
Convert words into algebraic expressions.
5x + 3 = 2x − 3

Medium

11. How old was William 5 years ago if a years ago he was b years old (given that $a > 5$ and $b > 5$)?
    a) $a + b$
    b) $a + b + 5$
    c) $b - a - 5$
    d) $a + b - 5$

Answer: (D)
Let x be the current age.
$x - a = b \rightarrow x = a + b$
Current Age $= a + b$
William's Age 5 Years Ago $=$
$a + b - 5$

12. If 14% of x is equal to 7% of y, which of the following is equivalent to y?
    a) 200% of x
    b) 20% of x
    c) 2% of x
    d) 98% of x

Answer: (A)
$\frac{14}{100}x = \frac{7}{100}y$
$y = \frac{14}{100} \times \frac{100}{7} x$
$y = 2x = 200\%x$

13. Which of the following represents the statement "When the square of the sum of x and y is added to the sum of the squares of x and $2y$, the result is 5 less than z"?
    a) $x^2 + y^2 + (x + 2y)^2 = z - 5$
    b) $(x + y)^2 + x^2 + 2y^2 = z - 5$
    c) $(x + y)^2 + (x + 2y)^2 = z - 5$
    d) $(x + y)^2 + x^2 + (2y)^2 = z - 5$

Answer: (D)
The square of the sum of x and y
$\rightarrow (x + y)^2$
The sum of the squares of x and
$2y \rightarrow x^2 + (2y)^2$
$(x + y)^2 + x^2 + (2y)^2 = z - 5$

14. The rate for a long distance call is \$1.00 for the first minute and \$.75 for each additional minute. Which of the following represents the cost, in dollars, of a phone call made for n minutes?
    a) $1.75n$
    b) $1.00 + n$
    c) $1.00 + 0.75(n - 1)$
    d) $1.00 + 1.75(n - 1)$

Answer: (C)
Each additional minute costs
\$0.75.
For the n-minute phone call, the
total cost would be the first minute
(\$1.00) plus additional $(n - 1)$
minutes (\$0.75$(n - 1)$), so the
total cost of n minute call is
$1.00 + 0.75(n - 1)$ dollars.

Hard

15. Bob needs two 60" pieces of duct tape to protect each window in his house during hurricane season. There are 12 windows in the house. Bob had an m-foot roll of duct tape when he started. If no tape was wasted, which of the following represents the number of feet of duct tape left after he finished taping all of his windows?

    a) $m - 240$
    b) $m - 120$
    c) $m - 60$
    d) $m - 20$

Answer: (B)
Every window needs 2 pieces of tape and each piece of tape is 60 inches long, so $60 \times 2 = 120$ inches needed for each window. Twelve windows, in total, would need 12×120 inches of tape. 12×120 inches = 120 feet $(m - 120)$ feet left after the use.

Chapter 2 Advanced Math

I.   FACTORS AND MULTIPLES

Prime Number: An integer number greater than 1 that has only two positive divisors: 1 and itself.
- Prime numbers up to 50: 2, 3, 5, 7, 11, 13, 17, 19, 23, 29, 31, 37, 41, 43, 47

Prime Factorization: The prime factorization of an integer x is to find all the prime numbers that multiply together equal to x.

Example: 36 is equal to 2 × 2 × 3 × 3.

GCF (Greatest Common Factor) of Two Integers: the largest integer that divides exactly into both integers.

Example: GCF of 24 and 30 is 6.

Two numbers are relatively prime if their GCF is 1.

Example: 6 and 35 are relative prime with GCF 1.
         25 and 35 are not relative prime with their GCF equal to 5.

LCM (Least Common Multiple) of Two Integers: the smallest integer that is divisible by both integers. For example, LCM of 24 and 30 is 120.

We can use ladder method to figure out GCF and LCM of two integers.

GCF of 24 and 30 is 2 × 3 = 6 (numbers on the side)
LCM of 24 and 30 is 2 × 3 × 4 × 5 = 120 (all the numbers on the side and bottom)

GCF among multiple terms with exponents of x is the term with the lowest degree of power, while LCM is the term with the highest degree of power. For instance, when considering the terms x, x^2, x^3, and x^4, the GCF is x, and the LCM is x^4.

Example: what is the GCF of $6x^2, 18x^3$ and $9x^5$?
Solution: the GCF of 6, 18, and 9 is 3 and GCF of x^2, x^3, and x^5 is x^2, therefore the GCF of $6x^2, 18x^3$ and $9x^5$ is $3x^2$.

Problem Solving Skills

Easy

1. What is the least common multiple of 12, 16, and 28?
   a) 4
   b) 84
   c) 168
   d) 336

   Answer: (D)
   The least common multiple is the smallest multiple of all three numbers.
   Find the multiples of 28, then find the smallest one that is divisible by 12 and 16.

2. What is the greatest common factor of 75, 125, 225?
   a) 5
   b) 9
   c) 25
   d) 35

   Answer: (C)
   The easiest strategy is to divide each of the numbers by each answer choice. 5, 9, and 25 are factors of all the numbers. 25 is the highest common factor of 75, 125, and 225.

3. Which of the following must be a factor of x if x is a multiple of both 9 and 12?
   a) 8
   b) 24
   c) 27
   d) 36

   Answer: (D)
   The LCM of 12 and 9 is 36.

4. If each cubical block has edges of length 6 inches, what is the number of such blocks needed to fill a rectangular box with inside dimensions of 30 inches by 36 inches by 42 inches?

   Answer: 210
   Calculate how many for each side and multiply them together.
   $\frac{30}{6} \times \frac{36}{6} \times \frac{42}{6} = 5 \times 6 \times 7 = 210$

5. If x is the greatest prime factor of 34 and y is the greatest prime factor of 49, what is the value of $x - y$?
   a) 8
   b) 9
   c) 10
   d) 15

   Answer: (C)
   The greatest prime factor of 34 is 17 and the greatest prime factor of 49 is 7.
   $x - y = 17 - 7 = 10$

6. Two numbers are relatively prime if their GCF is 1. Which of the following pairs of numbers are relatively prime?
   a) 22, 33
   b) 17, 34
   c) 35, 49
   d) 21, 64

   Answer: (D)
   a)   GCF = 11
   b)   GCF = 17
   c)   GCF = 7
   d)   GCF = 1

Medium

7. A supermarket has brand A juice smoothie on sale every 7 days and has brand B juice smoothie on sale every 4 days. Within a year (365 days), how many times does this supermarket have both brands of juice smoothie on sale on the same day?
   a) 9
   b) 12
   c) 13
   d) 24

Answer: (C)
The LCM of 7 and 4 is 28.
Every 28 days, A and B will be on sale on the same day.
$\frac{365}{28} = 13.035$

8. In a toy factory production line, every 10th toy has their electronic parts checked and every 5th toy will have their safety features checked. In the first 150 toys, what is the probability that a toy will have both its electronic parts and safety features checked?

Answer: $\frac{1}{10}$
The LCM of 10 and 5 is 10.
The every 10th toy will have both of their electronic parts and safety features checked.
There are 15 such toys (150 divided by 10) $\frac{15}{150} = \frac{1}{10}$

9. If x, y, and z are all integers greater than 1 and $xy = 14$ and $yz = 21$, which of the following must be true?
   a) $z > x > y$
   b) $y > z > x$
   c) $y > x > z$
   d) $x > z > y$

Answer: (B)
The only common factor of 14 and 21 other than 1 is 7, so y = 7.
y = 7
$x = \frac{14}{7} = 2$
$z = \frac{21}{7} = 3$

Hard

10. If the area of a rectangle is 77 and its length and width are integers, which of the following could be the perimeter of the rectangle?
    a) 36
    b) 37
    c) 38
    d) 39

Answer: (A)
The length and width of the rectangle must be factors of 77. There are only two ways to factor 77 into 7 × 11 and 1 × 77.
77 = 7 × 11
Perimeter = 2 (7 + 11) = 36 (a); 77 = 1 × 77
Perimeter = 2(1 + 77) = 156 (not among the options)

11. If x, y and z are three different prime numbers greater than 2 and $m = x \times y \times z$, how many positive factors, including 1 and m itself, does m have?
    a) 9
    b) 8
    c) 6
    d) 4

Answer: (B)
$m = x \times y \times z = x^1 \times y^1 \times z^1$
The total number of factors including 1 and m is (1 + 1) × (1 + 1) × (1 + 1) = 8.

II. OPERATIONS ON FRACTIONS

A **Fraction** is a number of the form $\frac{a}{b}$ where a and b are integers and b is not a zero. A fraction can be expressed as a terminating or repeating decimal.

-   To add two fractions with different denominators, you must first convert both fractions to a **common denominator**, a common multiple of the two denominators. Then convert both fractions to equivalent fractions with the common denominator. Finally, add the numerators and keep the common denominator.

    Example: $\frac{2}{3} + \frac{2}{5} = \left(\frac{2}{3}\right)\left(\frac{5}{5}\right) + \left(\frac{2}{5}\right)\left(\frac{3}{3}\right) = \frac{10+6}{15} = \frac{16}{15}$

    $\frac{1}{x} + \frac{1}{y} = \frac{y}{xy} + \frac{x}{xy} = \frac{y+x}{xy}$

    $\frac{1}{x+1} - \frac{1}{x+2} = \frac{x+2}{(x+1)(x+2)} - \frac{x+1}{(x+1)(x+2)} = \frac{1}{(x+1)(x+2)}$

-   To multiply two fractions, the resulting numerator is the product of the two numerators and the resulting denominator is the product of the two denominators.

    Example: $\frac{2}{5}\left(\frac{-3}{7}\right) = \frac{2 \times (-3)}{5 \times 7} = \frac{-6}{35} - \frac{6}{35}$

-   To divide one fraction by another, first **invert** the second fraction (find it's **reciprocal**), then multiply the first fraction by the inverted fraction.

    Example: $\frac{3}{5} \div \frac{6}{7} = \frac{3}{5} \times \frac{7}{6} = \frac{3 \times 7}{5 \times 6} = \frac{21}{30} = \frac{7}{10}$

-   **Cross multiplying** is a way to solve an equation that involves a variable as part of two equal fractions.

    Example: If $\frac{9}{x} = \frac{3}{5}$, what is the value of x?
    Solution: Applying cross multiplying: $x \times 3 = 9 \times 5$
    $$x = \frac{45}{3} = 15$$

Problem Solving Skills

Easy

1. An hour-long workshop included 10 minutes of self-studies. What fraction of the hour-long workshop were self-studies?

   Answer: $\frac{1}{6}$
   $\frac{10}{60} = \frac{1}{6}$

2. If a movie is 120 minutes long, what fraction of the movie has been completed 20 minutes after it begins?
   a) $\frac{1}{5}$
   b) $\frac{1}{6}$
   c) $\frac{1}{4}$
   d) $\frac{1}{3}$

   Answer: (B)
   $\frac{20}{120} = \frac{1}{6}$

3. Which of the following numbers is between 1 and 2?
   a) $\frac{8}{9}$
   b) $\frac{7}{3}$
   c) $\frac{10}{4}$
   d) $\frac{11}{9}$

   Answer: (D)
   $1 < \frac{11}{9} < 2$

4. In a poll, 25 people supported the current city mayor, 14 people were against him, and 6 people had no opinion. What fraction of those polled supported the city mayor?

   Answer: $\frac{5}{9}$
   $\frac{Part}{Whole} = \frac{25}{25 + 14 + 6} = \frac{25}{45} = \frac{5}{9}$

5. If $\frac{20}{x} = \frac{y}{14}$, what is the value of xy?
   a) 300
   b) 280
   c) 200
   d) 210

   Answer: (B)
   Cross multiply: $20 \times 14 = xy = 280$

6. If $\frac{6}{q} = \frac{3}{7}$, what is the value of q?
   a) 10
   b) 11
   c) 12
   d) 14

   Answer: (D)
   Cross multiply.
   $6 \times 7 = 3 \times q \rightarrow q = 14$

Medium

7. Every Monday through Friday after school, John spends 1.5 hours playing tennis with his school team and 1.5 hours practicing violin for the school orchestra. What fraction of the total number of hours in these five days did he spend on his after school activities?

   a) $\frac{1}{5}$

   b) $\frac{1}{6}$

   c) $\frac{1}{8}$

   d) $\frac{1}{9}$

   Answer: (C)
   $$\frac{Part}{Whole} = \frac{1.5 + 1.5}{24} = \frac{3}{24} = \frac{1}{8}$$

8. An integer is divided by 3 more than itself. If the fraction is equal to $\frac{5}{6}$, what is the value of this integer?

   a) 12

   b) 15

   c) 18

   d) 20

   Answer: (B)
   $$\frac{x}{x+3} = \frac{5}{6}$$
   $6x = 5(x + 3)$ *(Cross multiply)*
   $x = 15$

9. If $x = -\frac{1}{2}$, what is the value of $\frac{1}{x} - \frac{1}{x+1}$?

   a) 2

   b) –2

   c) 4

   d) –4

   Answer: (D)
   $$\frac{1}{-\frac{1}{2}} - \frac{1}{-\frac{1}{2}+1} = -2 - 2 = -4$$

Hard

10. Sean needs to finish reading his book in four days. He read $\frac{1}{3}$ of the book on the first day, $\frac{1}{4}$ of the book on the second day, $\frac{1}{5}$ of the book on the third day. If he has 13 pages to finish on the fourth day, how many pages are there in the book?

    a) 40

    b) 42

    c) 50

    d) 60

    Answer: (D)
    Find out the last portion of pages.
    The last portion of pages: $1 - \frac{1}{3}$
    $$-\frac{1}{4} - \frac{1}{5} = \frac{13}{60} = \frac{13}{Total},$$
    Total Number of Pages = 60

III. ALGEBRAIC FACTORING

Factoring out Common Factors

A **common factor** is a non-negative number other than 1 (or an expression) that can divide into every term. For instance, the common factors of $2x^5, 4x^4, 6x^2, 2x$ are $2, x$, and $2x$.

Example: Factor $2x^2 + 14x$.
Solution: Take out the common factors $2x$.
$$2x^2 + 14x = 2x(x + 7)$$

Example: Factor $3x^2y + 9xy^2 + 6xy$.
Solution: Take out the common factors $3xy$.
$$3x^2y + 9xy^2 + 6xy = 3xy(x + 3y + 2)$$

Factoring by Grouping

Sometimes not all the terms in an expression have a common factor but we can still do some factoring. One strategy of factoring is to factor "in pairs". To factor "in pairs," split the expression into two pairs of terms, and then factor the pairs separately.

Example: Factor $12x^2 + 3x + 4xy + y$.
Solution: First, group in pairs.
$$(12x^2 + 3x) + (4xy + y)$$
Then, factor out the common factor from each pair.
$$(12x^2 + 3x) + (4xy + y) = 3x(4x + 1) + y(4x + 1) = (4x + 1)(3x + y)$$

Factoring by the Difference of Two Squares

An expression which has one square subtracted by another square can be factored into the sum of the two variables multiplied by the difference of the two variables.

$$x^2 - y^2 = (x + y)(x - y)$$

Example: Factor $x^2 - 1$.
Solution: $x^2 - 1 = x^2 - 1^2 = (x + 1)(x - 1)$.

Factoring Trinomials

To factor $x^2 + bx + c$ where b and c are integers:
First, by using FOIL we know that $(x + m)(x + n) = x^2 + (m + n)x + mn$. Therefore, by using backwards logic, in order to factorize $x^2 + bx + c$, numbers m and n must be found to satisfy the equations $m + n = b$ and $mn = c$.

To factor $ax^2 + bx + c$ where a, b and c are integers and $a \neq 1$:
a) Set $ax^2 + bx + c$ equal to $a(x + \frac{d_1}{a})(x + \frac{d_2}{a})$ where d_1 and d_2 are two numbers whose product is $a \times c$ and whose sum is b.
b) Factor a into two numbers, a_1 and a_2, so that $a_1 \times \frac{d_1}{a}$ and $a_2 \times \frac{d_2}{a}$ are two integers.

Example: Factor $4x^2 - 4x - 3$.

Solution: First, find two numbers whose product is –12 and sum is –4. The two numbers are –6 and 2.

$$4x^2 - 4x - 3 = 4(x + \tfrac{2}{4})(x - \tfrac{6}{4}) \rightarrow \text{Simplify into } 4(x + \tfrac{1}{2})(x - \tfrac{3}{2}).$$

$$4\left(x + \tfrac{1}{2}\right)\left(x - \tfrac{3}{2}\right) = \left(2x + 2 \times \tfrac{1}{2}\right)\left(2x - 2 \times \tfrac{3}{2}\right) = (2x + 1)(2x - 3)$$

Perfect Square of Trinomial

A **trinomial** is an expression with three unlike terms such as $x^2 + 2x + 3$. **Perfect square formulas** are two of the most important formulas in algebra that are worth remembering:

$$x^2 + 2xy + y^2 = (x + y)^2$$

$$x^2 - 2xy + y^2 = (x - y)^2$$

A quadratic equation can be solved with by creating a perfect square using the perfect square formula. A perfect square has the form $a^2 + 2ab + b^2$ where a and b can be any algebraic expression or integer.

Example: Solve for x if $x^2 - 2x - 2 = 0$.

Solution: $x^2 - 2x - 2 = 0$

$x^2 - 2x = 2$ add 1 to both sides to make a perfect square on the left

$x^2 - 2x + 1 = 2 + 1$

$(x - 1)^2 = 3$ take the square root on both sides

$x - 1 = \pm\sqrt{3}$

$x = 1 \pm \sqrt{3}$

Problem Solving Skills

Easy

1. If $c = 5$, which of the following is the equivalent to $cx^2 + cx + c$?

   a) $(5x^3 + 5)$
   b) $5(x + 1)^2$
   c) $(x^2 + 1)$
   d) $5(x^2 + x + 1)$

   Answer: (D)
   Replace c with the value 5.
   $5x^2 + 5x + 5 = 5(x^2 + x + 1)$

2. Which of the following is a factor of $x^2 + x - 20$?

   a) $x + 4$
   b) $x - 5$
   c) $x - 4$
   d) $x + 6$

   Answer: (C)
   $x^2 + x - 20 = (x + 5)(x - 4) = 0$

3. If $xy = 5$ and $x - y = 3$, then $x^2y - xy^2 =$?

   a) 3
   b) 5
   c) 10
   d) 15

   Answer: (D)
   Factor out the common factors.
   $x^2y - xy^2 = xy(x - y) = 5 \times 3 = 15$

4. Which of the following is the greatest common factor of $15x^3y^5$ and $27x^2y^4z$?

   a) $3xyz$
   b) $3x^2y^3$
   c) $3x^2y^4$
   d) $5x^2y^3$

   Answer: (C)
   Find the GCF of 15 and 27, which is 3. Find the GCF of two like variables, always take the smallest power.
   Therefore, the answer is $3x^2y^4$.

5. Which of the following is a factor of $2x^2 + 5x - 12$?

   a) $2x - 3$
   b) $2x - 4$
   c) $x - 4$
   d) $x - 6$

   Answer (a)
   First, find two numbers whose product is –24 and sum is 5. These two numbers are –3 and 8.
   $2x^2 + 5x - 12 = 2(x + \frac{8}{2})(x - \frac{3}{2})$
   $\rightarrow 2(x + 4)(x - \frac{3}{2})$
   $= (x + 4)\left(2x - 2 \times \frac{3}{2}\right)$
   $= (x + 4)(2x - 3)$

Medium

6. If $x^2 - y^2 = 15$, and $x - y = 3$, what is the value of $x + y$?
    a) 1
    b) 3
    c) 5
    d) 10

Answer: (C)
$x^2 - y^2 = (x - y)(x + y)$
$3(x + y) = 15$
$x + y = 5$

7. If $x^2 + y^2 = 128$ and $xy = 36$, find the value of $(x - y)^2 =$?
    a) 56
    b) 92
    c) 108
    d) 200

Answer: (A)
$(x - y)^2 = x^2 + y^2 - 2xy$
$128 - 2 \times 36 = 56$

Hard

8. If x and y are positive integers and $x^2 - y^2 = 5$, what is the value of x?
    a) 1
    b) 2
    c) 3
    d) 4

Answer: (C)
$x^2 - y^2 = (x - y)(x + y) = 5$
$5 = 1 \times 5$
$x - y = 1$
$x + y = 5$
$2x = 6$
$x = 3$

9. Which of the following is the expression $x^2 + 3xy + 5x^3 + 15x^2y$ in fully factored form?
    a) $xy(1 + 5x)(x + 3)$
    b) $(x + 5x^2)(x + 3y)$
    c) $x(1 + 5x)(x + 3y)$
    d) $(1 + 5x)(x + 3y)$

Answer: (C)
$x^2 + 3xy + 5x^3 + 15x^2y$
$= x(x + 3y) + 5x^2(x + 3y)$
$= (x + 5x^2)(x + 3y)$
$= x(1 + 5x)(x + 3y)$

10. If $x^2 - y^2 = 55$ and $x + y = 11$, find the value of y.
    a) 1
    b) 3
    c) 5
    d) 7

Answer: (B)
$x^2 - y^2 = (x - y)(x + y)$
$55 = (x - y) \times 11$
$x - y = 5$
$x + y = 11$
$y = 3$

IV. FUNCTIONS

Functions
A function is a set of data that has a single output for each input. Functions describe the relationship between an input and its output.

Here are some of the common words associated with input and output:
- **Input:**
  - ○ x-value
  - ○ **independent variable**
  - ○ **domain** – the possible value(s) of the function's input
  - ○ For a real function, input values could be restricted because of the nature of the function itself. For instance, x cannot be equal to zero when $f(x) = \frac{1}{x}$ because $f(x)$ would become undefined. Apply the following rules when checking possible values of x:
    1) The denominator cannot be zero.
    2) Values inside a square root or an even radical must be nonnegative.

    Example 1: What value(s) of x are not possible for the function $f(x) = \frac{2}{x-3}$?
    Answer: Apply rule 1), the denominator cannot be zero; therefore, x cannot be 3.

    Example 2: What are the possible values of x when the function $f(x) = \sqrt{x+3}$?
    Answer: Apply rule 2), the values inside a square root must be nonnegative.
    $x + 3 \geqq 0$
    $x \geqq -3$
    x could be any number greater than or equal to -3.

- **Output:**
  - ○ y-value
  - ○ **dependent variable**
  - ○ **range** – the possible value(s) that the function's output can take on

    Example: Determine the domain and range of the function $y = x^2$
    Answer: Domain: all real numbers
    Range: all numbers greater than or equal to 0

Graphs of Functions
- Every point (x, y) on the graph of $y = f(x)$ satisfies $y = f(x)$.
- **Vertical Line Test:** A test to determine whether the graph is a graph of a function. If any vertical line intersects the graph at more than one point, then the graph is not a graph of a function.

The domain of a function encompasses all the possible inputs (also referred to as the independent variable, often denoted as the x variable).

For a real function,
- The value inside a square root must be greater or equal to zero.
- Denominators CANNOT be zero.

The range of a function refers to all the possible outputs(often denoted as the y variable). For square root functions or absolute value functions, the values are always greater than or equal to zero.

Examples: Find the domain and range for each of the following functions:

a) $f(x) = \frac{5}{x-3}$

Domain: $\{x \mid -\infty < x < 3 \ \cup \ 3 < x < \infty\}$

Range: all real numbers

b) $f(x) = \sqrt{16 - x^2}$

$16 - x^2 \geq 0$

$x^2 - 16 \leq 0$

$(x - 4)(x + 4) \leq 0$

$-4 \leq x \leq 4$

Domain: $\{x \mid -4 \leq x \leq 4\}$

Range: $0 \leq f(x) \leq 4$

c) $f(x) = 3|x - 4| - 2$

Domain: all real numbers

Range: $f(x) \geq -2$

Composition of Functions

When the results of a function $g(x)$ are plugged into a function $f(x)$ to create a new function, the result is called the composition of $f(x)$ and $g(x)$. The notation used for the composition of functions is

$$(f \circ g)(x) = f(g(x))$$

Example: If $f(x) = x^2 - 4$ and $g(x) = x + 2$, evaluate $(f \circ g)(x)$.

Solution: $(f \circ g)(x) = f(g(x)) = (x + 2)^2 - 4 = x^2 + 4x + 4 - 4 = x^2 + 4x$

Problem Solving Skills

Easy

x	−1	3	j
$f(x)$	1	j	k

1. In the table above, if $f(x) = 3x + 4$, what is the value of k?
   a) 19
   b) 25
   c) 37
   d) 43

Answer: (D)
Plug x = 3 into the function.
$y = 3 \times 3 + 4 = 13 = j$
When x = j = 13,
$y = 3 \times 13 + 4 = 43 = k$

2. If $f(x) = \frac{x+3}{x}$ and $g(x) = x^2 - 10$, what is the difference between $f(x)$ and $g(x)$ when $x = 3$?

Answer: 3
Substitute 3 for x in both functions. The difference between f(3) and g(3) is f(3) – g(3).
$\frac{3+3}{3} - [(3)^2 - 10] = 2 - (-1) = 3$

3. If $f(x) = 2x - 1$ and $g(x) = \sqrt{x^2 - 8}$, what is the value of $f(g(3))$?

Answer: 1
$g(3) = \sqrt{3^2 - 8} = \sqrt{1} = 1$
$f(g(3)) = f(1) = 2(1) - 1 = 1$

4. The number of water lilies in a pond has doubled every four years since time $t = 0$. This relation is given by $y = (x) \times 2^{\frac{t}{4}}$, where t is in number of years, y is the number of water lilies in the pond at time t, and x is the original number of water lilies. If there were 600 water lilies in this pond 8 years after $t = 0$, then what was the original number of water lilies?

Answer: 150
Plug in t = 8 and y = 600 in the function.
$600 = (x) \times 2^{(8/4)} = x \times 2^2 = 4x$
$x = 150$

5. Which of the following is a graph of a function?

   a)

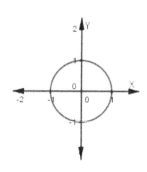

   Answer: (D)
   Apply Vertical Line Test.
   A function has at most one
   intersection with any vertical line.

   b)

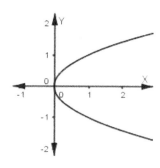

   c)

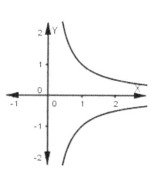

   d)

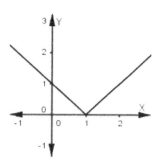

6. The amount of money A, in dollars, earned from a school fundraiser by selling x cookies is given by $A(x) = 1.5x - 80$. How many cookies must the event sell in order to raise 220 dollars?

   Answer: 200
   Set A(x) equal to 220.
   $1.5x - 80 = 220$
   $x = 200$

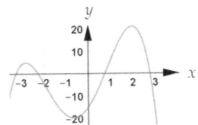

7. The figure above shows the graph of $y = f(x)$. For what value of x in this interval does the function f have its highest value between $x = -3$ to $x = 3$?

    a) –1
    b) 0
    c) 1
    d) 2

Answer: (D)
Maximum value is the value of y at the highest point, which occurs when $x = 2$.

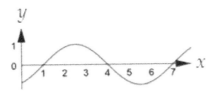

8. According to the graph above of the function f, what are the values of x where $f(x)$ is negative?

    a) $1 < x < 4$
    b) $0 < x < 1$ or $4 < x < 7$
    c) $x < 1$ or $x > 7$
    d) $1 < x < 4$ or $7 < x$

Answer: (B)
There are two regions which have negative values of $f(x)$, which are $0 < x < 1$ and $4 < x < 7$.

9. If $g(x) = 5x - 10$, then at what value of x does the graph of $g(x)$ cross the x-axis?

    a) – 6
    b) –3
    c) 0
    d) 2

Answer: (D)
The value of x where $g(x)$ crosses the x-axis is the value of x where $g(x)$ is equal to 0.
$0 = 5x - 10$
$x = 2$

$$f(x) = \sqrt{x^2 - 1}$$

10. Which of the following values of x makes $f(x)$ undefined?

    a) –2
    b) 0
    c) 2
    d) 1

Answer: (B)
The value under the square root must be greater than or equal to zero.

11. The domain of the function $y = \frac{x-2}{(x-1)(x+3)}$ consists of all real numbers except?

    a) $x \neq 1$
    b) $x \neq 2$
    c) $x \neq 1,\ x \neq 2,$ and $x \neq -3$
    d) $x \neq 1$ and $x \neq -3$

Answer: (D)
This function is defined everywhere except when the denominator is equal to zero.

Medium

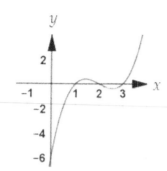

12. The graph of $y = f(x)$ is shown above. If $f(3) = a$, which of the following could be the value of $f(a)$?

    a) -2
    b) -4
    c) -6
    d) 2

Answer: (C)
As seen from the graph above, $f(3) = 0$, hence $a = 0$.
$f(a) = f(0) = -6$ (from graph above)

13. At what value(s) of x does the function $f(x) = x^2 - 9$ cross the x-axis?

    a) 0 only
    b) 3 only
    c) -3 only
    d) -3 and 3

Answer: (D)
"$f(x)$ crosses the x-axis" means $f(x) = 0$.
$x^2 - 9 = 0,\quad x = \pm 3$

x	0	1	2	4
$f(x)$	-5	-3	-1	3

14. The table above shows input values as x and the output values of the linear function $f(x)$. Which of the following is the expression for $f(x)$?

    a) $f(x) = \frac{1}{2}x - 5$
    b) $f(x) = -\frac{1}{2}x - 5$
    c) $f(x) = 2x - 5$
    d) $f(x) = -2x - 5$

Answer: (C)
$f(x) - y_o = m(x - x_0)$
m (the slope) $= \frac{-3 - (-5)}{1 - 0} = 2$
$f(x) + 5 = 2(x - 0)$
$f(x) = 2x - 5$

15. If $f(x) = x^2 - 1$ and $g(x) = \frac{1}{x}$, write the expression $f(g(x))$ in terms of x.

   a) $\dfrac{(1+x)(1-x)}{x^2}$

   b) $\dfrac{(1+x)}{x^2}$

   c) $\dfrac{(1-x)}{x^2}$

   d) $\dfrac{1}{x^2}$

Answer: (A)

$f(g(x)) = \left(\frac{1}{x}\right)^2 - 1$

$= \dfrac{1-x^2}{x^2}$

$= \dfrac{(1+x)(1-x)}{x^2}$

Hard

16. If $f(x) = x + 7$ and $f(g(2)) = 3$, which of the following functions could be $g(x)$?

   a) $x - 6$

   b) $x + 6$

   c) $3x - 1$

   d) $2x - 1$

Answer: (A)

$f(g(2)) = g(2) + 7 = 3$

$g(2) = -4$

Only (a) satisfies this condition.

17. The monthly cost of renting an apartment increases every year by 5%. John paid $600 per month this year on his rental. What is the monthly cost for John's rental n years from now?

   a) 600×0.05^n

   b) $600 \times 1.05 \times n$

   c) 600×1.05^n

   d) $600^n \times 1.05$

Answer: (C)

Increasing every year by 5% is to multiply $\left(1 + \frac{5}{100}\right)$ for each additional year.

$C(n) = (1.05)^n \times 600$

$\qquad = 600 \times (1.05)^n$

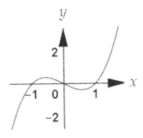

18. The figure above shows the graph of $y = f(x)$. If the function g is defined by $g(x) = f\left(\frac{x}{3}\right) - 2$, what is the value of $g(3)$?

   a) -2

   b) -1

   c) 0

   d) 1

Answer: (A)

$g(3) = f\left(\frac{3}{3}\right) - 2 = f(1) - 2$

From the graph above, $f(1) = 0$

$g(3) = 0 - 2 = -2$

V. COMPLEX NUMBERS

A **complex number** is a number of the form $a + bi$, where a and b are real numbers and i is the imaginary unit.

$$i = \sqrt{-1}$$
$$i^2 = -1$$
$$i^3 = -i$$
$$i^4 = 1$$

When two complex numbers are equal, their real parts are equal and their imaginary parts are also equal. For example, if $a + bi = c + di$, it must be true that $a = c$ and $b = d$.

Example: $3x + yi = 2x + 2 + 3i$
$$3x = 2x + 2 \rightarrow x = 2$$
$$yi = 3i \rightarrow y = 3$$

The expressions $a + bi$ and $a - bi$ are called **complex conjugates**. Multiplying a complex number by its complex conjugate will give you a real number.
$$(a + bi) \times (a - bi) = a^2 + b^2$$

Example: $(3 + 4i) \times (3 - 4i) = 3^2 + 4^2 = 25$

Rationalizing the Complex Number

We can rationalize a fraction involving a complex number, such as $\frac{1}{1 + 2i}$, by making the denominator a real number. **Complex conjugates** are used to simplify the fraction when the denominator is a complex number.

Example: $\frac{1}{1+2i} = \frac{1}{1+2i} \times \frac{1-2i}{1-2i} = \frac{1(1-2i)}{1^2+2^2} = \frac{1-2i}{5} = \frac{1}{5} - \frac{2}{5}i$

Operations on Complex Numbers

Let $z_1 = a + bi$ and $z_2 = c + di$. Then,
$$z_1 + z_2 = (a + c) + (b + d)i$$
$$z_1 - z_2 = (a - c) + (b - d)i$$
$$z_1 \times z_2 = (a + bi) \times (c + di) = (ac - bd) + (ad + bc)i$$
$$\frac{z_1}{z_2} = \frac{a+bi}{c+di} = \frac{a+bi}{c+di} \times \frac{c-di}{c-di} = \frac{ac+bd}{c^2+d^2} + \frac{bc-ad}{c^2+d^2}i \quad \text{where } z_2 \neq 0$$

Example: If $z = 3 - 2i$, what is the value of z^2?

$$z^2 = (3 - 2i)(3 - 2i) = 3^2 - 2^2 - 6i - 6i = 5 - 12i$$

Example: Write $\frac{i}{2-i}$ as a standard form complex number.

$$\frac{i}{2-i} = \frac{i}{2-i} \times \frac{2+i}{2+i} = \frac{2i-1}{2^2-i^2} = \frac{2i-1}{4-(-1)} \quad -\frac{1}{5} + \frac{2}{5}i$$

Example: Find $(1 + i)^8$.

$$(1+i)^2 = 1 - 1 + 2i = 2i$$
$$(1+i)^8 = [(1+i)^2]^4 = (2i)^4 = 2^4 = 16$$

Powers of *i* have a repeating pattern:

$$i = i = \sqrt{-1} \rightarrow i^{4n+1} = i$$
$$i^2 = -1 \qquad \rightarrow i^{4n+2} = -1$$
$$i^3 = -i \qquad \rightarrow i^{4n+3} = -i$$
$$i^4 = 1 \qquad \rightarrow i^{4n} = 1$$

Example: $i^{2012} + i^{2013} + i^{2015} = ?$

$$i^{2012} = i^{4(503)} = 1$$
$$i^{2013} = i^{4(503)+1} = i$$
$$i^{2015} = i^{4(503)+3} = -i$$
$$i^{2012} + i^{2013} + i^{2015} = 1$$

Complex numbers can be represented as a two-dimensional complex plane where the **horizontal axis** is **real component** and the **vertical axis** is the **imaginary component**. In the following figure, the complex number ***a + bi*** can be identified with the *point (a, b)* in the complex plane.

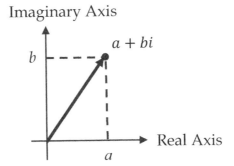

The Complex Plane

The magnitude of $a + bi$, denoted by $|a + bi|$, is equal to $\sqrt{a^2 + b^2}$.

Example: What is $|4 + 3i|$?

$$|4 + 3i| = \sqrt{4^2 + 3^2} = \sqrt{25} = 5$$

Problem Solving Skills

Easy

1. What is the value of $(2 - i)(2 + i)$?
   a) 5
   b) $4i$
   c) 3
   d) $2i$

   Answer: (A)
   $(2 - i)(2 + i) = 2^2 - (i)^2 = 4 - (-1) = 5$

2. What is the magnitude of $4 + 3i$?
   a) 4
   b) 5
   c) 6
   d) 7

   Answer: (B)
   $|4 + 3i| = \sqrt{4^2 + 3^2} = 5$

3. If $i = \sqrt{-1}$ and n is a positive integer, which of the following statements is FALSE?
   a) $i^{4n} = 1$
   b) $i^{4n+1} = -i$
   c) $i^{4n+2} = -1$
   d) $i^{n+4} = i^n$

   Answer: (B)
   If you don't remember the pattern, you can try plugging in n = 0 into each of the choices.
   $i = \sqrt{-1} \rightarrow i^{4n+1} = i$
   $i^2 = -1 \rightarrow i^{4n+2} = -1$
   $i^3 = -i \rightarrow i^{4n+3} = -i$
   $i^4 = 1 \rightarrow i^{4n} = 1$

4. $(3 - \sqrt{-4} + (5 - 2\sqrt{-9})) =$
   a) $8i$
   b) 8
   c) $8 - 8i$
   d) $8 + 8i$

   Answer: (C)
   $(3 - \sqrt{-4} + (5 - 2\sqrt{-9}))$
   $= 3 - 2\sqrt{-1} + 5 - 6\sqrt{-1}$
   $= 8 - 8i$

5. $(2 - 5i) - (5 + 2i) =$
   a) 0
   b) $10i$
   c) $3 + 7i$
   d) $-3 - 7i$

   Answer: (D)
   $(2 - 5i) - (5 + 2i)$
   $= (2 - 5) + (-5 - 2)i$
   $= -3 - 7i$

6. If $i^n = 1$, what could n be?
   a) 7
   b) 8
   c) 9
   d) 10

   Answer: (B)
   n must be a multiple of 4.

7. If $a - bi = i(3 - 7i)$, what is the value of $a + b$?

   Answer: 4
   $a - bi = i(3 - 7i) = 3i - 7i^2$
   $= 7 + 3i$
   $a = 7$ and $b = -3 \rightarrow a + b = 4$

8. $i^{24} + i^{25} + i^{26} + i^{27} = ?$
    a) 1
    b) i
    c) 0
    d) $-i$

Answer: (C)
$i = \sqrt{-1} \quad \rightarrow i^{4n+1} = i$
$i^2 = -1 \quad \rightarrow i^{4n+2} = -1$
$i^3 = -i \quad \rightarrow i^{4n+3} = -i$
$i^4 = 1 \quad \rightarrow i^{4n} = 1$
$i^{24} + i^{25} + i^{26} + i^{27}$
$= 1 + i - 1 - i = 0$

9. $(3 - 3i)^4 = ?$
    a) 324
    b) -324
    c) $18i$
    d) $-18i$

Answer: (B)
$(3 - 3i)^2 = 9 - 2 \times 3 \times 3i + (3i)^2$
$= -18i$
$(3 - 3i)^4 = [(3 - 3i)^2]^2$
$= (-18i)^2 = -324$

10. Which of the following is the fraction $\frac{1}{2-i}$ equivalent to?
    a) $-2i$
    b) $2 + i$
    c) $\frac{2-i}{3}$
    d) $\frac{2+i}{5}$

Answer: (D)
Rationalize the denominator.
$\frac{1}{2-i} \times \frac{2+i}{2+i} = \frac{2+i}{4-i^2} = \frac{2+i}{5}$

Medium

11. Which of the following is the equivalent of $\frac{3-2i}{4+3i}$?
    a) $\frac{12-4i}{7}$
    b) $\frac{6+17i}{25}$
    c) $\frac{6-10i}{7}$
    d) $\frac{6-17i}{25}$

Answer: (D)
Rationalize the denominator.
$\frac{3-2i}{4+3i} \times \frac{4-3i}{4-3i} = \frac{(3-2i)(4-3i)}{16+9} =$
$\frac{6-17i}{25}$

12. In $a + bi$ form, the reciprocal of $2 + 5i$ is
    a) $\frac{2}{29} - \frac{5}{29}i$
    b) $\frac{-2}{21} + \frac{5}{21}i$
    c) $\frac{1}{29} + \frac{5}{29}i$
    d) $\frac{2}{21} - \frac{5}{21}i$

Answer: (A)
The reciprocal of $(2 + 5i)$ is $\frac{1}{2+5i}$.
Rationalize the denominator.
$\frac{1}{2+5i} \times \frac{2-5i}{2-5i} = \frac{2-5i}{4+25} = \frac{2-5i}{29}$

13. What is the value of $|4 - 3i|$?
   a) 5
   b) $5\sqrt{2}$
   c) $2\sqrt{5}$
   d) $4 - 3i$

Answer: (A)

$|4 - 3i| = \sqrt{4^2 + 3^2} = \sqrt{25} = 5$

14. $i^{2016} + i^{2017} + i^{2018} = ?$
   a) -1
   b) 1
   c) $-i$
   d) i

Answer: (D)

$i^{2016} = i^{4(508)} = 1$
$i^{2017} = i^{4(508)+1} = i$
$i^{2018} = i^{4(508)+2} = -1$
$i^{2016} + i^{2017} + i^{2018} = i$

Hard

15. If $a - bi = \frac{2+i}{1-i}$ which of the following is true?
   a) $a = 1, b = 3$
   b) $a = -\frac{1}{2}, b = -\frac{3}{2}$
   c) $a = \frac{3}{2}, b = \frac{1}{2}$
   d) $a = \frac{1}{2}, b = -\frac{3}{2}$

Answer: (D)
Rationalize the denominator.

$\frac{2+i}{1-i} \times \frac{1+i}{1+i} = \frac{1+3i}{1+1} = \frac{1}{2} + \frac{3}{2}i$
$a - bi = \frac{1}{2} + \frac{3}{2}i$
$a = \frac{1}{2}$ and $b = -\frac{3}{2}$

16. If $a + bi = \frac{2+i}{1+i}$, what is the value of $a + b$?
   a) $3i$
   b) $\frac{1}{2}$
   c) 1
   d) $\frac{3}{2}$

Answer: (C)
Rationalize the denominator.

$\frac{2+i}{1+i} = \frac{(2+i)(1-i)}{(1+i)(1-i)} = \frac{3-i}{2} = \frac{3}{2} - \frac{1}{2}i = a + bi$
$a = \frac{3}{2}$ and $b = -\frac{1}{2}$
$a + b = \frac{3}{2} + \left(-\frac{1}{2}\right) = 1$

VI. QUADRATIC FUNCTIONS AND EQUATIONS

Quadratic functions are functions of the form $(x) = ax^2 + bx + c$, where $a \neq 0$.

Important Properties of Quadratic Functions

- The vertex of a quadratic function is located at coordinate $(\frac{-b}{2a}, \frac{-b^2 + 4ac}{4a})$.
- The axis of symmetric of $f(x)$ is $= -\frac{b}{2a}$.
- If $a > 0$, the quadratic function opens upwards and has a minimum value at the vertex.
- If $a < 0$, the quadratic function opens downwards and has a maximum value at the vertex.
- The domain of a quadratic function is $(-\infty, \infty)$.
- The range of a quadratic function is
  - $\left(\frac{-b^2 + 4ac}{4a}, \infty\right)$ when $a > 0$.
  - $\left(-\infty, \frac{-b^2 + 4ac}{4a}\right)$ when $a < 0$.

Quadratic Equations

A quadratic equation is an equation where the greatest exponent of the variable is 2. It can be converted into standard form, which is expressed as $ax^2 + bx + c = 0$, where a, b, and c are real number coefficients, $a \neq 0$, and x is the variable.

Zero-Product Rule: If the product of two or more terms is zero, at least one of the terms has to be zero. For instance, $(x - 1)(x - 2) = 0$, so either $(x - 1) = 0 \rightarrow x = 1$ or $(x - 2) = 0 \rightarrow x = 2$. Both 1 and 2 are the two roots of x.

Solving a Quadratic Equation Method 1: Factoring

$x^2 - 3x + 2 = 0$
$(x - 1)(x - 2) = 0$ *(trinomial factoring)*
$x = 1$ or 2 *(zero-product rule)*

Solving a Quadratic Equation Method 2: Complete the Square

$x^2 + 4x - 5 = 0$
$x^2 + 4x = 5$
$x^2 + 4x + 2^2 = 5 + 2^2$ *(add 2^2 on both side to make left hand side a perfect square)*
$(x + 2)^2 = 9$
$x + 2 = \pm 3$
$x = -2 \pm 3$
$x = 1$ or -5

Solving a Quadratic Equation Method 3: Quadratic Formula $x = \frac{-b \pm \sqrt{b^2 - 4ac}}{2a}$

$2x^2 - 7x + 3 = 0$
$x = \frac{-(-7) \pm \sqrt{(-7)^2 - 4 \times (2) \times (3)}}{2 \times 2} = \frac{7 \pm \sqrt{49 - 24}}{4} = \frac{7 \pm 5}{4}$
$x = 3$ or $\frac{1}{2}$

The Discriminant of Quadratic Equations: For a quadratic equation in standard form ($ax^2 + bx + c = 0$), the **discriminant Δ** is equal to $b^2 - 4ac$. The discriminant gives information about the roots.

- If $\Delta > 0$, then this quadratic equation has two real roots.
- If $\Delta = 0$, then this quadratic equation has one real double root (i.e., two roots have the same real value.)
- If $\Delta < 0$, then this quadratic equation has two complex roots with imaginary parts.

Problem Solving Skills

Easy

1. What are the solutions of x for which $(x - 1)(x + 2) = 0$?
   a) -1
   b) -2
   c) 1 and -2
   d) -1 and 2

   Answer: (C)
   $(x - 1)(x + 2) = 0$
   $x - 1 = 0,\ x = 1\ $ or
   $x + 2 = 0,\ x = -2$

2. If $x^2 - 5x - 6 = 0$, what are the possible values of x?
   a) $-1, 6$
   b) $1, -6$
   c) $-1, -6$
   d) $2, -3$

   Answer: (A)
   Use trinomial factoring.
   $x^2 - 5x - 6 = (x - 6)(x + 1) = 0$
   $x = 6\ $ or $\ -1$

3. How many points does the graph of function, $f(x) = x^2 - 1$, cross the x-axis?
   a) 0
   b) 1
   c) 2
   d) 3

   Answer: (C)
   The graph of f(x) intersects the x-axis when f(x) = 0.
   $0 = x^2 - 1$
   $x = \pm 1$

4. If $x^2 - 64 = 0$, which of the following could be a value of x?
   a) -4
   b) -8
   c) 2
   d) 4

   Answer: (B)
   $x^2 - 64 = 0$
   $x^2 = 64$
   $x = \pm 8$

5. If $x^2 = 16$ and $2y^3 = -16$, which of the following could be true?
   I. $x = 4$
   II. $y = 2$
   III. $x + y = 2$
   a) I only
   b) II only
   c) I and III only
   d) I, II, and III

   Answer: (C)
   Solve for x first.
   $x^2 = 16\ \rightarrow\ x = \pm 4$
   $2y^3 = -16$
   $y^3 = -8\ \rightarrow\ y = -2$
   Only I and III are correct.

6. If $x(x - 4) = -4$, what is the value of $x^2 + 3x - 5$?
   a) 3
   b) 5
   c) 1
   d) 0

Answer: (B)
$x^2 - 4x + 4 = 0$
$(x - 2)^2 = 0$
$x = 2$
$x^2 + 3x - 5 = 2^2 + 3 \times 2 - 5 = 5$

7. The axis of symmetry for $f(x) = x^2 + 3x - 2$ is $x = ?$
   a) 3
   b) -1
   c) 1
   d) -1.5

Answer: (D)
The axis of symmetry is $= -\frac{b}{2a}$.
$x = -\frac{3}{2} = -1.5$

8. Equation $(x + 2)(x + a) = x^2 + 4x + b$ where a and b are constants. If the equation is true for all values of x, what is the value of b?
   a) 8
   b) 6
   c) 4
   d) 2

Answer: (C)
This is an identity equation question.
The two expressions have the same coefficients for corresponding terms.
$(x + 2)(x + a) = x^2 + (2 + a)x + 2a$
By comparison: $2 + a = 4$ *and* $2a = b$
$a = 2$ *and* $b = 4$

9. Which of the following is one of the values of x if $x^2 - 2x - 2 = 0$?
   a) $1 - \sqrt{3}$
   b) $1 - \sqrt{2}$
   c) $\sqrt{3} - 1$
   d) $\sqrt{2} - 1$

Answer: (A)
Complete the square.
$x^2 - 2x - 2 = 0$
$x^2 - 2x = 2$ *add 1 to both sides to make a perfect square on the left*
$x^2 - 2x + 1 = 2 + 1$
$(x - 1)^2 = 3$ *take the square root on both sides*
$x - 1 = \pm\sqrt{3} \rightarrow x = 1 \pm \sqrt{3}$

Medium

10. At what points the graph of $y = x^2 + 2x - 8$ cuts the x-axis?
    a) $(-2, 0)$ and $(0, 0)$
    b) $(0, 0)$ and $(2, 0)$
    c) $(2, 0)$ and $(-4, 0)$
    d) $(4, 0)$ and $(2, 0)$

Answer: (C)

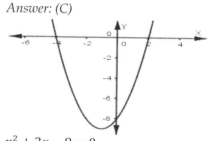

$x^2 + 2x - 8 = 0$
$(x - 2)(x + 4) = 0$
The graph intersects the x-axis at
$(2, 0)$ *and* $(-4, 0)$.

11. Which of the following is one of the values of x if
$2x^2 + 3x - 1 = 0$?
   a) 0.8
   b) 0.48
   c) 1.78
   d) −1.78

Answer: (D)
Since the equation set to 0, we can solve this using quadratic formula,
$$x = \frac{-b \pm \sqrt{b^2 - 4ac}}{2a}$$
$$a = 2, b = 3, c = -1$$
$$\frac{-3 \pm \sqrt{3^2 - 4ac}}{2a} = \frac{-3 \pm \sqrt{3^2 - 4(2)(-1)}}{2(2)}$$
$$= \frac{-3 \pm \sqrt{17}}{4} = -1.78 \text{ or } 0.28$$

12. If $x < 2$ and $a(x - 2)(x - 3) = 0$, what is the value of a?
   a) 3
   b) 2
   c) 1
   d) 0

Answer: (D)
Solve for x by zero-product rule.
$a(x - 2)(x - 3) = 0$
One of the terms a, (x− 2), and (x − 3) must be equal to zero.
Given that x < 2, only a can be equal to zero.

13. If $x - 2$ is a factor of $x^2 - kx - 8$, what is the value of k ?
   a) 1
   b) 4
   c) −3
   d) −2

Answer: (D)
$x^2 - kx - 8 = 0$
$(x - 2)(x + 4) = 0$
$x^2 + 2x - 8 = x^2 - kx - 8 = 0$
$-k = 2 \rightarrow k = -2$

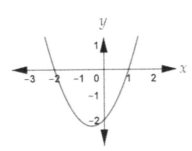

14. Which of the following equations best describes the curve in the figure above?
   a) $y = x^2 - 2$
   b) $y = x^2 + 2$
   c) $y = x^2 + x + 2$
   d) $y = x^2 + x - 2$

Answer: (D)
From the graph above, there are two roots, −2 and 1.
y = (x + 2) (x − 1) = x² + x −2

15. What is the x value at the minimum point of the equation $f(x) = x^2 + 4x + 2$?
    a) 7.75
    b) 2.25
    c) 0
    d) −2

Answer: (D)
The vertex of a quadratic function is $(\frac{-b}{2a}, \frac{-b^2+4ac}{4a})$.
If $a > 0$, $f(x)$ opens upwards and has a minimum value at the vertex. If $a < 0$, $f(x)$ opens downwards and has a maximum value at the vertex.
The equation $f(x) = x^2 + 4x + 2$ has a minimum value of x equal to $\frac{-b}{2a} = \frac{-4}{2} = -2$.

16. A baseball is hit and flies into a field at a trajectory defined by the equation $d = -1.2t^2 + 100$, where t is the number of seconds after the impact and d is the horizontal distance from the home plate to the outfield fence. How many seconds have passed if the ball is 50 meters away from the outfield fence?

Answer: 6.45
$50 = -1.2t^2 + 100$
$t = 6.45$

Hard

17. If $h(x) = 6 + \frac{x^2}{4}$ and $h(2m) = 5m$, what is one possible value of m?

Answer: 2, 3
Substitute 2m for x solve for m.
$h(2m) = 6 + \frac{(2m)^2}{4} = 5m$
$6 + m^2 = 5m$
$m^2 - 5m + 6 = 0$
$(m - 2)(m - 3) = 0$
$m = 2, \text{ or } 3$

18. If the function f is defined by $f(x) = ax^2 + bx + c$, where $a < 0$, $b > 0$, and $c > 0$, which of the following could be the graph of $f(x)$?

Answer: (D)
The leading coefficient of a quadratic function −1 means the curve goes downwards; the positive constant c means y-intercept is positive. The value of b is positive, so x-coordinate of the maximum point is positive. Only (d) meets all these conditions.

a)

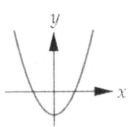

b)

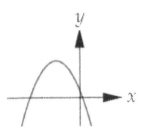

c)

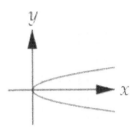

d)

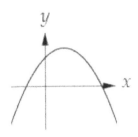

19. Which of the following could be a graph of the equation $y = ax^2 + bx + c$, where $b^2 - 4ac = 0$?

a)

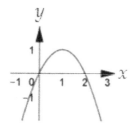

b)

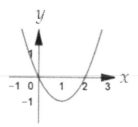

c)

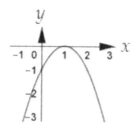

d)

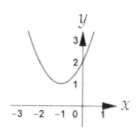

Answer: (C)

The discriminant, $b^2 - 4ac$, of a quadratic equation reveals the type of its roots.

- *When $b^2 - 4ac = 0$, the quadratic equation two equal, real roots.*
- *When $b^2 - 4ac > 0$, the quadratic equation has two unequal, real roots.*
- *When $b^2 - 4ac < 0$, the quadratic equation has no real roots.*

VII.   EXPONENTS AND ROOTS

The Power Rules For Exponents

-   $x^a x^b = x^{a+b}$

-   $(x^a)^b = x^{ab}$

-   $x^a y^a = (xy)^a$

-   $\dfrac{x^a}{x^b} = x^{a-b}$

-   $x^0 = \dfrac{x^a}{x^a} = x^{a-a} = 1$

-   $x^{-a} = \dfrac{x^0}{x^a} = \dfrac{1}{x^a}$

-   **Same Base**: Keep the same base and add the exponents when multiplying. Keep the same base but subtract the exponents when dividing.
    Examples:
    $$x^4 \times x^3 = x^{4+3} = x^7 \qquad x^4 \div x^3 = x^{4-3} = x^1$$

-   "$x^3 \times x^2$" denotes $(x \times x \times x)$ being multiplied by $(x \times x)$. There are 5 copies of x being multiplied together, which means that $x^3 \times x^2 = x \times x \times x \times x \times x = x^5$.

-   Same exponent but different base: Keep the same exponent but combine the bases.
    Examples:
    $$x^3 \times y^3 = (x \times y)^3 \qquad x^3 \div y^3 = \left(\frac{x}{y}\right)^3$$

-   "$\dfrac{x^5}{x^2}$" is equal to 5 copies of x divided by 2 copies of x. This is equal to only 3 copies of x multiplied together, which is also x^3.
    $$\frac{x^5}{x^2} = x^{5-2} = x^3$$

Raising One Power to Another (Raising an Exponent to Ano: To raise an exponent to another exponent, multiply their exponents.
Example:
$$(x^4)^3 = x^{4 \times 3}$$

Multiplying a Decimal Number by 10^n: If n is a positive integer, then this operation will move the decimal point n places to the right. If n is a negative integer, then this operation will move the decimal point $|n|$ places to the left.

Taking the Square Root
Taking the **square root** of a number is the inverse operation of squaring the number. The square root of a number is a value that can be multiplied by itself to give the original number.
Examples:
$$\sqrt{y} \times \sqrt{y} = y \quad \text{and} \quad \sqrt{4} \times \sqrt{4} = 4$$

A square root of a variable represents the variable's exponent being divided by 2.
Examples:

$$\sqrt{x} = x^{\frac{1}{2}} \quad \text{and} \quad \sqrt{x^4} = x^{\frac{4}{2}} = x^2$$

Multiplying and Dividing Radicals

When multiplying or dividing two variables **with the same radical**, multiply or divide two variables and keep the original radical.
Examples:

$$\sqrt{x} \times \sqrt{y} = \sqrt{xy} \quad \text{and} \quad \frac{\sqrt{x}}{\sqrt{y}} = \sqrt{\frac{x}{y}}$$

When multiplying or dividing two radicals **with same variable**, add or subtract their exponents.
Examples:

$$\sqrt{x} \times \sqrt[3]{x} = x^{\frac{1}{2}} \times x^{\frac{1}{3}} = x^{\frac{1}{2}+\frac{1}{3}} = x^{\frac{5}{6}}$$

$$\frac{\sqrt{x}}{\sqrt[3]{x}} = \frac{x^{\frac{1}{2}}}{x^{\frac{1}{3}}} = x^{\frac{1}{2}-\frac{1}{3}} = x^{\frac{1}{6}} = \sqrt[6]{x}$$

Only numbers with the same radicals can be combined through multiplication or division. The product of two radicals is equal to the radical of the product. The quotient of two radicals is equal to the radical of the quotient.
Examples:

$$\sqrt{2} \times \sqrt{6} = \sqrt{2 \times 6} = \sqrt{12} \qquad \frac{\sqrt{6}}{\sqrt{2}} = \sqrt{\frac{6}{2}} = \sqrt{3}$$

Adding and Subtracting Radicals

Adding and Subtracting Radicals only apply when both the root and the base are the same (when the terms are like terms).
Example:

$$2\sqrt{3} + 3\sqrt{3} = 5\sqrt{3}$$

Consider $\sqrt{3}$ as a unit. 2 units plus 3 units of $\sqrt{3}$ is equal to 5 units of $\sqrt{3}$. Therefore simply add the coefficients of like terms.

Simplify a Square Root

To simplify a square root, factor out all perfect squares and place its square root outside.
Example:

$$\sqrt{18} = \sqrt{3^2 \times 2} = 3\sqrt{2}$$

Similar steps apply to different radicals. To simplify a cube root, factor out cubes (factors with an exponent of 3) and place its cube root (base) outside.
Example:

$$\sqrt[3]{54} = \sqrt[3]{3^3 \times 2} = 3\sqrt[3]{2}$$

Rationalize a Denominator with a Square Root: multiply the top and bottom of the fraction by the square root in the denominator to get a rational denominator.

Example 1:

$$\frac{\sqrt{12}}{\sqrt{2}} = \frac{\sqrt{12} \times \sqrt{2}}{\sqrt{2} \times \sqrt{2}} = \frac{\sqrt{24}}{2} = \frac{\sqrt{2^2 \times 6}}{2} = \frac{2\sqrt{6}}{2} = \sqrt{6}$$

Example 2: Rationalize a denominator with a square root by using the conjugate.

$$\frac{2 + \sqrt{2}}{1 - \sqrt{2}} = \frac{(2 + \sqrt{2})(1 + \sqrt{2})}{(1 - \sqrt{2})(1 + \sqrt{2})} = \frac{2 + 3\sqrt{2} + 2}{1^2 - (\sqrt{2})^2} = -4 - 3\sqrt{2}$$

Problem Solving Skills

Easy

1. If $2^{x+1} = 8$, then what is the value of x?
   a) 0
   b) 1
   c) 2
   d) 3

   Answer: (C)
   Change both sides of equation to the same base 2.
   $2^{(x+1)} = 2^3$
   $x + 1 = 3 \rightarrow x = 2$

2. Which of the following is equal to 0.00126691?
   a) 1.26691×10^{-3}
   b) 1.26691×10^{-2}
   c) 1.26691×10^{-1}
   d) 12.6691×10^{-2}

   Answer: (A)
   1.26691 multiplied by 10^{-3} will move its decimal point 3 places to the left.
   $1.26691 \times 10^{-3} = 0.00126691$

3. If $n > 0$, what is the value of $4^n + 4^n + 4^n + 4^n$?
   a) $4^{(n+4)}$
   b) $4^{(n+1)}$
   c) $4^{(4n+1)}$
   d) $4^{(4n+3)}$

   Answer: (B)
   $4^n + 4^n + 4^n + 4^n = 4 \times 4^n = 4^{(n+1)}$

4. If $xyz \neq 0$, then $\frac{x^2 y^4 z^8}{x^6 y^4 z^2} = ?$
   a) xyz
   b) $\frac{z^3}{x^3}$
   c) $\frac{z^4}{x^3}$
   d) $\frac{z^6}{x^4}$

   Answer: (D)
   Apply exponent rules.
   $\frac{x^2 y^4 z^8}{x^6 y^4 z^2} = \left(\frac{x^2}{x^6}\right)\left(\frac{y^4}{y^4}\right)\left(\frac{z^8}{z^2}\right) = \frac{z^6}{x^4}$

5. $(-2x^2 y^6)^3 = ?$
   a) $4x^5 y^9$
   b) $-8x^6 y^{18}$
   c) $4x^6 y^{18}$
   d) $8x^6 y^{18}$

   Answer: (B)
   Raise power for each term inside the parentheses and apply the $(x^a)^b = x^{ab}$ rule.
   $(-2x^2 y^6)^3 = (-2)^3 (x^2)^3 (y^6)^3$
   $= -8x^6 y^{18}$

6. If $a^x \cdot a^4 = a^{16}$ and $(a^3)^y = a^{12}$, what is the value of $x + y$?
   a) 17
   b) 16
   c) 15
   d) 13

   Answer: (B)
   $a^x \cdot a^4 = a^{(x+4)} = a^{16}$
   $(a^3)^y = a^{3y} = a^{12}$
   $x = 12$
   $y = 4$
   $x + y = 16$

7. If x and y are positive integers and $5^2x + 5^2y = 100$, what is the value of $x + y$?
   a) 1
   b) 2
   c) 4
   d) 8

Answer: (C)
$5^2x + 5^2y = 25(x + y) = 100$
$x + y = 4$

8. If x is a positive integer, then $(5 \times 10^{-x}) + (2 \times 10^{-x})$ must be equal to?
   a) $\dfrac{10}{10^x}$
   b) $\dfrac{1}{10^x}$
   c) $\dfrac{7}{10^{-x}}$
   d) $\dfrac{7}{10^x}$

Answer: (D)
$(5 \times 10^{-x}) + (2 \times 10^{-x}) = 7 \times 10^{-x}$
$7 \times 10^{-x} = \dfrac{7}{10^x}$

9. If m is a positive number, which of the following is equal to $m^3 \times m^{-3}$?
   a) 0
   b) 1
   c) m^{-6}
   d) m

Answer: (B)
Except the number 0, any numbers raised to the power of 0 is equal to 1.
$m^3 \times m^{-3} = m^0 = 1$

10. If $4 + \sqrt{k} = 7$, then $k =$?
    a) 3
    b) 6
    c) 9
    d) $\sqrt{3}$

Answer: (C)
If $4 + \sqrt{k} = 7$, then $\sqrt{k} = 3$.

Square both sides: $k = 9$

11. If $\sqrt{x} = 2$ then $x + 4 = $?
    a) 2
    b) 4
    c) 8
    d) 80

Answer: (C)
Square both sides of the radical equation.
$\sqrt{x} = 2$
$\left(\sqrt{x}\right)^2 = 2^2;\ x = 4;\ x + 4 = 8$

12. If $\sqrt{2x} - 4 = 2$, then $x =$?
    a) -9
    b) -18
    c) 27
    d) 18

Answer: (D)
$\sqrt{2x} - 4 = 2$
$\sqrt{2x} = 2 + 4 = 6$
$\left(\sqrt{2x}\right)^2 = 6^2$
$2x = 36 \rightarrow x = 18$

13. If $x^{\frac{1}{3}} = 2$, what is the value of x?
    a) 2
    b) 4
    c) 6
    d) 8

Answer: (D)
$x^{\frac{1}{3}} = 2$
$x = 2^3 = 8$

Medium

14. If x, y and z are different positive integers and $2^x \times 2^y \times 2^z = 64$, then $x + y + z$?
    a) 12
    b) 3
    c) 4
    d) 6

Answer: (D)
$2^x \times 2^y \times 2^z = 2^{(x+y+z)} = 64 = 2^6$
$x + y + z = 6$

15. Positive integers x, y, and z satisfy the equations $x^{-\frac{1}{2}} = \frac{1}{2}$ and $y^z = 8$, $z > y$, what is the value of $x + y + z$?
    a) 5
    b) 7
    c) 9
    d) 11

Answer: (C)
$x^{-\frac{1}{2}} = \frac{1}{2}$, $x = (\frac{1}{2})^{-2} = 2^2 = 4$
$8 = 2^3 = y^z$
$y = 2$ and $z = 3$
$x + y + z = 2 + 3 + 4 = 9$

16. If $\frac{\sqrt{x} + y}{\sqrt{x} + 5} = 1$, then $y = $?
    a) 1
    b) 3
    c) 5
    d) 8

Answer: (C)
$\sqrt{x} + y = \sqrt{x} + 5$ $\rightarrow$ $y = 5$

17. If $7 = m^x$, then $7m^2 = $?
    a) m^{2x}
    b) m^{7x}
    c) m^{x+2}
    d) m^{x+7}

Answer: (C)
$7m^2 = m^x \times m^2 = m^{(x+2)}$

18. If $81 = a^x$, where a and x are both positive integers and $x > a$, what is the value of x^a?
    a) 16
    b) 27
    c) 64
    d) 81

Answer: (C)
$a = 3$ and $x = 4$

$4^3 = 64$

19. If $3^{7x+6} = 27^{3x}$, what is the value of x?
    a) 1
    b) 2
    c) 3
    d) 4

Answer: (C)
When solving the equation, convert both sides to the same base.
$3^{7x+6} = 27^{3x} = [(3)^3]^{3x} = 3^{9x}$
$7x + 6 = 9x$ $\rightarrow$ $x = 3$

20. If $3^4 = x$, which of the following expressions is equal to 3^{10}?

   a) $3x^2$
   b) $9x^2$
   c) $27x^2$
   d) x

   Answer: (B)
   $3^{10} = 3^2 \times (3^4)^2 = 9x^2$

21. If $x^{\frac{1}{4}} = \sqrt{3}$, then what is the value of x^2?
   a) 81
   b) 72
   c) 36
   d) 27

   Answer: (A)
   $(x^{\frac{1}{4}})^8 = x^2$
   $(\sqrt{3})^8 = 81$

22. If $\frac{5\sqrt{3}}{\sqrt{5}} = 2x$, then what is the value of x?

   a) $\sqrt{\dfrac{15}{2}}$

   b) $\sqrt{15}$

   c) $\dfrac{\sqrt{15}}{2}$

   d) $5\sqrt{3}$

   Answer: (C)
   Rationalize a denominator with a square root.
   $\frac{5\sqrt{3}}{\sqrt{5}} = \frac{5\sqrt{3}\times\sqrt{5}}{\sqrt{5}\times\sqrt{5}} = \frac{5\sqrt{3\times5}}{5} = \sqrt{15} = 2x$
   $x = \frac{\sqrt{15}}{2}$

23. If $x^{\frac{3}{2}} = \dfrac{1}{27}$, then what does x equal?
   a) -9
   b) -3
   c) $\dfrac{1}{9}$
   d) $-\dfrac{1}{9}$

   Answer: (C)
   Tips:
   $x^{\frac{3}{2}} = \frac{1}{27}$
   $x = (\frac{1}{27})^{\frac{2}{3}}$
   $\frac{1}{27} = 3^{-3}$
   $x = (3^{-3})^{\frac{2}{3}} = 3^{-2} = \frac{1}{9}$

24. $\dfrac{5}{\sqrt{3}} + \dfrac{4}{\sqrt{2}} = ?$

   a) $\dfrac{15}{\sqrt{5}}$

   b) $\dfrac{9\sqrt{6}}{\sqrt{6}}$

   c) $\dfrac{5\sqrt{2}+4\sqrt{3}}{\sqrt{3}+\sqrt{2}}$

   d) $\dfrac{5\sqrt{3}+6\sqrt{2}}{3}$

   Answer: (D)
   $\frac{5}{\sqrt{3}} + \frac{4}{\sqrt{2}} = \frac{5\sqrt{2}}{\sqrt{3}\times\sqrt{2}} + \frac{4\sqrt{3}}{\sqrt{2}\times\sqrt{3}} =$
   $\frac{5\sqrt{2}+4\sqrt{3}}{\sqrt{6}} = \frac{(5\sqrt{2}+4\sqrt{3})\times\sqrt{6}}{\sqrt{6}\times\sqrt{6}} =$
   $\frac{5\sqrt{12}+4\sqrt{18}}{6} = \frac{10\sqrt{3}+12\sqrt{2}}{6} = \frac{5\sqrt{3}+6\sqrt{2}}{3}$

25. If x and y are positive integers and $(x^{\frac{1}{6}} y^{\frac{1}{6}})^3 = 8$, what is the value of xy?
   a) 8
   b) 32
   c) 64
   d) 128

   Answer: (C)
   $(x^{\frac{1}{6}} y^{\frac{1}{6}})^3 = (xy)^{\frac{1}{2}}$
   $(xy)^{\frac{1}{2}} = 8$
   $xy = 64$

Hard

26. $10^{xy} = 1{,}000$, where x and y are positive integers and $x >$ y, what is one possible value of x?

    a) 3
    b) 4
    c) 5
    d) 7

Answer: (A)
Change both sides to the base 10.
$10^{xy} = 10^3 \rightarrow xy = 3$
Since both x and y are positive integers, both x and y can only be equal to 1 or 3.
$x > y \rightarrow x = 3$

Questions 27 – 28 refer to the following information:
    Compound interest is the interest added to the principal of a deposit so that the interest earned also earns interest continuously. A formula for calculating annual compound interest is as follows:

$$A = P\left(1 + \frac{r}{100}\right)^t$$

    A is the amount of money, in dollars, generated after t years by a principal amount P in a bank account that pays an annual interest rate of $r\%$, compounded annually.

27. If Bill deposits $1,000 in his bank account today with an annual interest rate of 3% compounded annually, what will be the amount of money in his bank account after 5 years? (Round your answer to the nearest dollar and ignore the dollar sign when gridding your response.)

Answer: 1159
$A = 1{,}000(1 + 0.03)^5 = \$1{,}159$

28. What is the fewest whole number of years that he will have $2,000 or more in the bank?

Answer: 24
$1{,}000(1 + 0.03)^t \geq 2{,}000$
$1.03^t \geq 2$
With calculator, the first whole number value of t that satisfies above inequality is 24.
Therefore, the fewest number of years required for him to accrue $2,000 is 24.

Questions 29 – 30 refer to the following information:
    In chemistry, a chemical reaction proceeds at a rate dependent on the concentration of its reactant. For reactant A, the rate of a reaction is defined as:

$$Rate = k\,[A]^n$$

    k is a constant and $[A]$ is the concentration of A. The order of reaction of a reactant A is the exponent n to which its concentration term in the rate equation is raised.

29. When n is equal to -1, it is called an order (-1) with espect to reactant A. Which of the following graphs depicts an order (-1) with respect to concentration A and reaction rate?

a)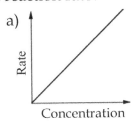

b)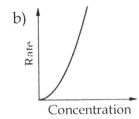

c)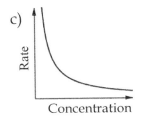

d)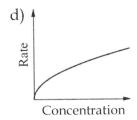

Answer: (C)
Rate $= k[A]^{-1}$
Rate $\times [A] = k$
When $n = -1$, the rate of the reaction is inversely proportional to the concentration A.
Only graph c) represents the inversely proportional relationship.

30. If the graph below shows the reaction rate versus the concentration of reactant A, what is the most likely order of reactant A?

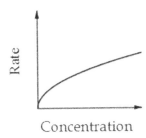

a) 1st order
b) 2nd order
c) $\frac{1}{2}$ order
d) 0th order

Answer: (C)
The graph is an exponential function with exponent less than 1 and greater than zero.
Only c) is the possible choice.

Chapter 3   Problem-Solving And Data Analysis

I.   UNIONS AND INTERSECTIONS OF SETS

Union and Intersection
The **Union** of two sets, denoted by $A \cup B$, is the set of elements which are in **either** set. It is similar to the "OR" logic among the sets.

Example: Let set $A = \{1, 2, 3\}$ and set $B = \{3, 4, 5\}$, the union of sets A and B is the set of elements that are included in **A or B**, i.e. $A \cup B = \{1, 2, 3, 4, 5\}$.

The **Intersection** of two sets, denoted by $A \cap B$, is the set of elements which are in **both** sets. It is similar to the "AND" logic among the sets.

Example: The intersection of set A and set B, as the example above, is the set of elements that are included in A and B, i.e. $A \cap B = \{3\}$.

Venn Diagram

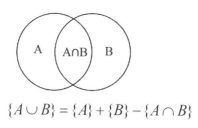

$$\{A \cup B\} = \{A\} + \{B\} - \{A \cap B\}$$

Example: In a class of 50 students, 18 students take chemistry, 26 students take biology, and 2 students take both chemistry and biology.

   a) How many students in the class are enrolled in either chemistry or biology?

      Solution: {Enrolled in either chemistry or biology} = {Enrolled in chemistry} + {Enrolled in biology} – {Enrolled in both chemistry and biology}
      = 18 + 26 – 2 = 42

   b) How many students in the class are **not** enrolled in either chemistry or biology?

      Solution: {**Not** enrolled in either chemistry or biology} = Total Students – {Enrolled in either chemistry or biology} = 50 – 42 = 8

Problem Solving Skills

Easy

Set X = {21, 22, 23}
Set Y = {22, 23, 24, 25, 26}

1. Sets X and Y are shown above. How many numbers are in the intersection of set X and set Y?
   a) Two
   b) Three
   c) Four
   d) Seven

Answer: (A)
Only 22 and 23 are both in set X and set Y.

2. Set A contains all odd positive numbers less than 10 and set B contains all prime numbers less than 20. What is the difference between the number of elements in the union of the two sets and the number of elements in their intersection?

Answer: 7
Union of two sets:
{1, 2, 3, 5, 7, 9, 11, 13, 17, 19}
Intersect of two sets: { 3, 5, 7 }

10 – 3 = 7

3. If A is the set of positive integers, B is the set of odd integers, and C is the set of integers multiple of 3, which of the following will be in all three sets?
   a) 24
   b) 18
   c) 15
   d) –21

Answer: (C)
The only odd positive integer that is also a multiple of 3 is 15.

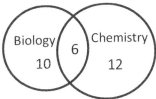

4. The Venn diagram above shows the distribution of 28 students in a class who took biology, chemistry, or both. If there are total 30 students in this class, what percent of the students did not take either chemistry or biology?
   a) 5%
   b) 6.7%
   c) 9%
   d) 10%

Answer: (B)
30 – (10 + 12 + 6) = 2
$\frac{2}{30}$ *= 0.067 = 6.7%*

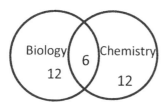

5. The Venn diagram above shows the distribution of 30 students in a class who took biology, chemistry, or both. If there are total 30 students in this class, what percent of the students studied chemistry?
   a) 30%
   b) 40%
   c) 50%
   d) 60%

Answer: (D)
Among the total 30 students, there were (6 + 12) students studied chemistry.

$\frac{18}{30} = 0.6 = 60\%$

Medium

6. What is the intersection of X and Y if X is the set of positive multiples of 3 and Y is the set of positive multiples of 4?
   a) the set of all positive integers
   b) the set of all positive real numbers
   c) the set of positive multiples of 12
   d) the set of positive multiples of 4

Answer: (C)
The common multiples of 3 and 4 will be the multiples of 12.

7. Set A contains all odd positive numbers less than 10 and set B contains all prime numbers less than 20. What is the difference between the number of elements in the union of the two sets and the number of elements in their intersection?

Answer: 7
Union of two sets:
{1, 2, 3, 5, 7, 9, 11, 13, 17, 19}
Intersect of two sets: { 3, 5, 7 }

10 – 3 = 7

Hard

8. If set A = {1, 3, 7, 10, 15} and set B consists of all the odd positive integers less than or equal to 13, how many elements are in the union of the two sets?
   a) 0
   b) 3
   c) 8
   d) 9

Answer: (D)
A ∪ B = A + B – (A ∩ B)
A = {1, 3, 7, 10, 15}
B= {1, 3, 5, 7, 9, 11, 13}
A ∩ B = { 1, 3, 7}
Number of Elements in (A ∪ B) =
5 + 7 – 3 = 9

II. Ratios, Proportions, and Rates

Setting up a Ratio
- A **ratio** is a comparison between two numbers or two measures with the same unit.
- Ratios can be expressed as a fraction. For example, $1 : 2$ can be written as $\frac{1}{2}$.
- Ratios can be reduced like a fraction. For example, $6 : 9$ can be reduced to $2 : 3$.

Setting up a Proportion
- A **proportion** is an equation relating two fractions or ratios.
- The phrase "a to b is equal to c to d" can be converted into an equation using ratios $(a : b = c : d)$ or fractions $(\frac{a}{b} = \frac{c}{d})$, both of which can be solved by cross-multiplication.

Example 1: The proportion of x in $\frac{2}{3}$ is equal to $\frac{1}{3}$. What is x?

Answer: $\dfrac{x}{\frac{2}{3}} = \dfrac{1}{3}$ (apply cross-multiplication)

$$3x = \frac{2}{3}$$
$$x = \frac{2}{9}$$

Example 2: What proportion of $\frac{2}{3}$ is $\frac{1}{3}$?

Answer: $x \times \dfrac{2}{3} = \dfrac{1}{3}$

$$x = \frac{3}{2} \times \frac{1}{3} = \frac{1}{2}$$

Two variables are **directly proportional** if an increase in one is directly correlated with an increase in another. For example, in the following

$$\frac{x_1}{y_1} = k \text{ (coefficient of proportionality)}$$

- x_1 and y_1 are directly proportional, and their ratio is called the coefficient of proportionality. If we do not change the coefficient of proportionality, then if we increase or decrease x_1, we increase or decrease y_1 respectively by the same factor.

Two variables are **inversely proportional** if an increase in one is directly correlated with a decrease in another. For example, in the following

$$x \times y = k \text{ (coefficient of inverse proportionality)}$$

Solve a Proportion
To solve a problem involving ratios, you can often write as a proportion and solve it by **cross_multiplication**. For example, what proportion to10 is equal to the

proportion of 3 out of 5? This problem can be written as $x : 10 = 3 : 5$. Changing the ratios to a fraction gives you $\frac{x}{10} = \frac{3}{5}$. Applying cross-multiplication gives you $5x = 30$. Solving for x gives you $x = 6$.

To solve conversions between units or scales, you can use ratios. Write the conversion's ratios so that you can cross out the unwanted unit.

Example: How many feet is 18 inches?

Answer:

$$\frac{1\ foot}{12\ inches} = \frac{x\ feet}{18\ inches}$$

$$\frac{18\ inches}{12\ inches} = \frac{x\ feet}{1\ foot}$$

$x = 1.5$ (18 inches × 1 foot/12 inches = 1.5 feet)

Rate and Work
A **rate** is a ratio that compares two different kinds of numbers, such as miles per hour or dollars per pound.

$$\textbf{Rate Formula}:\ Rate = \frac{Distance}{Time}$$

Example 1: Bob walks up and down a hill to get to school. He walks at 3 miles per hour up a hill and 4 miles per hour down a hill. The hill is 1 mile upwards and 1 mile downwards. What is his average rate?

Hint: If you get a question about the average rate traveled over several trips at different rates, you need to find the total distance and divide by the total time. Most people will think that they can average the two rates, 3.5 in this case – this does not work because you spend less time walking downhill and so you spend more than 50% of the time walking the slower rate.

Solution: The total distance traveled is obviously 2 miles (1 mile up and 1 mile down). The total time spent traveling is

$$1\ mile \times \frac{1\ hour}{3\ miles} + 1\ mile \times \frac{1\ hour}{4\ miles} = \frac{7}{12}\ hours$$

If we traveled 2 miles in $\frac{7}{12}$ hours, then we have traveled an average rate of

$$\frac{2\ miles}{\frac{7}{12}\ hours} = \frac{24}{7}\ miles\ per\ hour = 3.43\ miles\ per\ hour$$

(Applying rate formula: $Rate = \frac{Distance}{Time}$)

So the average rate is **less** than the arithmetic average between the two rates (3.43 < 3.5). This is because we spend more time traveling the slower rate.

Example 2: A plane travels from New York to San Francisco at 500 miles per hour. However, there is a headwind (a wind blowing against the direction of motion) of 100 miles per hour. When the plane flies back from San Francisco to New York, the same wind is now a tailwind (a wind blowing in the direction of motion) of 100 miles per hour. Each trip is 3000 miles. What speed does the plane actually travel at for both trips? What is the combined rate of travel for the entire trip?

Hint: If there are currents or winds involved, add the speed of the current or wind when it is moving along the direction of motion and subtract the speed of the current or wind when it is moving against the direction of motion.

Answer: The speed of the plane flying from New York to San Francisco is

$$500\ mph - 100\ mph = 400\ mph$$

The speed of the plane flying from San Francisco to New York is

$$500\ mph + 100\ mph = 600\ mph$$

Using the technique we used in the previous example to calculate the average rate. First, we find the total distance traveled, which is 3000 × 2 = 6000 miles. Then, we find the time traveled:

$$3000\ miles \times \frac{1\ hour}{400\ miles} + 3000\ miles \times \frac{1\ hour}{600\ miles} = 12.5\ hours$$

So the average rate is

$\frac{6000\ miles}{12.5\ hours} = 480\ mph$ (Applying rate formula: $Rate = \frac{Distance}{Time}$)

Total Time Worked $= \frac{1}{Rate\ of\ Work}$. If there is more than one person working, then the total rate is equal to the sum of each person's rate.

Example 1: It took Joe 5 hours to paint a house. What is his rate of painting?
Answer: Rate of painting $= \frac{x\ house}{1\ hour} = \frac{1\ house}{5\ hours}$, applying cross multiplication to find x.
$x = \frac{1}{5}$ houses per hour
Example 2: Once again, Joe takes 5 hours to paint a house. How much of a house can he paint in 1 hour?

Hint: Set up a fractional equation and then cross multiply.

Answer: $\frac{5\ hours}{1\ house} = \frac{1\ hour}{x\ houses}$, applying cross multiplication to find x.

$x = \frac{1}{5}$ houses per hour.

Example 3: Joe's friend Bob joins him in painting a house. Bob takes 3 hours to paint a house. What is their total rate of painting?

Hint: If there is more than one person painting, then the total rate is equal to the sum of each person's rate.

Answer: We calculate the total rate by adding two persons' rates:

Joe: $\frac{1}{5}$ houses per hour

Bob: $\frac{1}{3}$ houses per hour

Total rate: $\frac{1}{5} + \frac{1}{3} = \frac{8}{15}$ houses per hour

If some objects must be counted as whole numbers, then their total should be the multiple of the sum of the ratios. For example, if the ratio is $1 : 2 : 3$ for different colors of marbles in the bag, then the total number of marbles in the bag must be a multiple of $(1 + 2 + 3)$.

Example: The ratio of boys to girls in Ms. Johnson's class is 5 to 6. Which of the following CANNOT be the number of students in her class?
      a) 11
      b) 22
      c) 33
      d) 45

Answer: Since the ratio of boys to girls is 5 : 6, the total number of students must be a multiple of 11, $(5 + 6)$. Only choice *(d)* is not the multiple of 11. Answer is *(d)*.

Problem Solving Skills

Easy

1. How many pounds of flour are needed to make 15 rolls of bread if 20 pounds of flour are needed to make 100 rolls of bread?
   a) 3
   b) 4
   c) 5
   d) 3.5

   Answer: (A)
   20 pounds : 100 rolls = x : 15 rolls
   $$\frac{20\ pounds}{100\ rolls} = \frac{x\ pounds}{15\ rolls}$$
   Cross multiply: $100x = 20 \times 15$
   $x = 3$ pounds

2. A certain graph chart shows ♥ = 500 viewers in a particular TV show. Approximately how many viewers are represented by the symbols ♥♥♥♥?
   a) 1,000
   b) 2,000
   c) 3,500
   d) 4,500

   Answer: (B)
   4♥ = 4 × 500 = 2,000 viewers

3. John takes 8 minutes to bike 3 miles. At this rate, how many minutes will it take him to bike 4.5 miles?

   Answer: 12
   8 minutes : 3 miles = x minutes : 4.5 miles
   $x = 12$

4. If 60 pounds of force can stretch a spring 5 inches, how many inches will the spring be stretched by a force of 84 pounds? Assume the force needed to stretch a spring varies directly with its stretch distance.
   a) 10
   b) 9
   c) 7
   d) 6

   Answer: (C)
   $$\frac{60\ pounds}{5\ inches} = \frac{84\ pounds}{X\ inches}$$
   $x = 7$ inches

5. How many toy parts can a machine make in 10 minutes if this machine can make 36 toy parts in 1 hour?
   a) Two
   b) Three
   c) Five
   d) Six

   Answer: (D)
   36 parts : 60 minutes = x parts : 10 minutes
   $60x = 36 \times 10 = 360$
   $x = 6$

6. For a certain type of heater, the increase in gas bills is directly proportional to the temperature setting (in Fahrenheit). If the gas bills increased by $20 when the temperature setting is increased by 4 degrees Fahrenheit, by how much will expenses increase when the temperature setting is increased by 10 degrees Fahrenheit?

   a) $35
   b) $40
   c) $50
   d) $60

Answer: (C)
$20 : 4° F = $x : 10° F
$4x = 200$
$x = 50

7. On a map, $\frac{1}{3}$ of an inch represents 18 miles. If a river is 45 miles long, what is its length, in inches, on the map?

   a) $\frac{5}{6}$
   b) $\frac{1}{2}$
   c) $\frac{1}{3}$
   d) 1

Answer: (A)
$\frac{1}{3}$ inches : 18 miles
= x inches : 45 miles
$\frac{\frac{1}{3}\ inches}{18\ miles} = \frac{x\ inches}{45\ miles}$
$x = \frac{15}{18} = \frac{5}{6}$ inches

8. If y is inversely proportional to x and y is equal to 12 when x is equal to 8, what is the value of y when $x = 24$?

   a) $\frac{1}{6}$
   b) $\frac{1}{4}$
   c) 4
   d) 2

Answer: (C)
$8 \times 12 = y \times 24$
$y = 4$

9. If y is directly proportional to x and y is equal to 40 when x is equal to 6, what is the value of y when $x = 9$?

   a) 60
   b) 55
   c) 50
   d) 45

Answer: (A)
$\frac{40}{6} = \frac{y}{9}$
$y = 60$

Medium

10. In a mixture of flour and sugar, the ratio of flour to sugar is 5 to 3 when measured by cups. How many cups of sugar will be used for 4 cups of this mixture?

Answer: 1.5
$\frac{Sugar}{Total} = \frac{3}{5+3} = \frac{x}{4}$
$8x = 12$
$x = 1.5$ cups

11. Sam drove from home at an average speed of 50 miles per hour to her working place and then returned along the same route at an average speed of 40 miles per hour. If the entire trip took her 2.25 hours, what is the entire distance, in miles, for the round trip?

Answer: 100
Let one trip have x miles.
Time = 2.25 = $t_1 + t_2 = \frac{x}{50} + \frac{x}{40}$
2.25 = $x(\frac{1}{50} + \frac{1}{40})$
x = 50
Total Distance = 2 × 50 = 100

12. To make fruit punch, grapefruit juice, orange juice, and lemonade are mixed in with a ratio of 5:3:2 by volume, respectively. In order to make 5 liters of this drink, how much orange juice, in liters, is needed?
    a) 1
    b) 1.5
    c) 2
    d) 2.5

Answer: (B)
Every 10 liters, (2 + 3 + 5), of drink, 3 liters of orange juice will be needed. So 5 liters of this drink, we need $\frac{3}{10}$ × 5 of orange juice.
Orange Juice = 0.3 × 5 = 1.5 liters

13. If $x \neq 0$ and x is inversely proportional to y, which of the following is directly proportional to $\frac{1}{x^3}$?
    a) $\frac{1}{y^3}$
    b) $-\frac{1}{y^3}$
    c) y^3
    d) y^2

Answer: (C)
If "x is inversely proportional to y", then xy = k.
Raise power of 3 on both sides:
$(xy)^3 = k^3$
$x^3y^3 = k^3 \rightarrow y^3 = k^3 \left(\frac{1}{x^3}\right)$
So $\frac{1}{x^3}$ directly proportional to y^3

14. If Planet X is 20,000 billion meters away from the Sun, what is its orbital period, in Earth years? (Round your answer to the nearest whole number.)

Answer: 1546
$\frac{(Orbital\ Period)^2}{20000^3} = \frac{1^2}{149.6^3}$
Orbital Period =
1546 Earth years

Hard

Questions 16 – 17 refer to the following information:
The fluid dynamics continuity model states that the rate at which mass enters a system is equal to the rate at which mass leaves the system. The rate of mass at any cross section in a pipe is the product of the cross sectional area and the speed of the fluid.

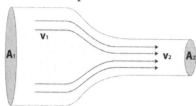

15. If water runs through a pipe with cross sectional area 0.4 m² at a speed of 6 m/s, calculate the speed of the water in the pipe when the pipe tapers off to a cross sectional area of 0.3 m².
    a) 8.0 m/s
    b) 7.5 m/s
    c) 7.0 m/s
    d) 5.5 m/s

Answer: (A)
$A_1 V_1 = A_2 V_2$
$0.4 \times 6 = 0.3 \times V_2$
$V_2 = 8 \ m/s$

16. If water enters a certain type of garden hose with a diameter of 1.5 cm at a speed of 5 m/s, calculate the speed of water when it travels to the nozzle, which has diameter 0.7 cm.
    a) 30.66 m/s
    b) 22.96 m/s
    c) 17.23 m/s
    d) 14.21 m/s

Answer: (B)
$A_1 V_1 = A_2 V_2$
$\pi \left(\frac{1.5}{2}\right)^2 \times 5 = \pi \left(\frac{0.7}{2}\right)^2 \times V_2$
$V_2 = 22.96 \ m/s$

III. PERCENTAGES

A percentage is a ratio of a part to a whole expressed as a fraction of 100. To calculate the percentage that a part represents in the whole, use the percent formula:

$$\text{Percentage} = \frac{Part}{Whole} \times 100\%$$

- Identify the part and the whole and then set up an equation using the percent formula.
- If you are performing **operations on percentages**, convert them into fractions first.

Example: A baseball pitcher won 28 out of 35 games he pitched. How many percent of his games did he win?

Answer: the percentage of winning = $\frac{28}{35} \times 100\% = 80\%$

Changing Decimals to Percentages
Multiply a decimal by 100 to get the equivalent percentage.

$$\text{Percentage} = \text{Decimal} \times 100\%$$

Example: 0.25 is equal to 0.25×100%, which is equal to 25%?

Changing Fractions to Percentages
Change a fraction into a decimal by dividing the denominator into numerator. Then convert the decimal into a percentage.

Example: Write $\frac{2}{5}$ as a percent.

Solution: $\frac{2}{5} = 0.4$ and $0.4 \times 100\% = 40\%$

Therefore, $\frac{2}{5}$ is equal to 40%.

Changing Percentages to Decimals
Divide the percentage by 100 and get rid of the percent sign (%).

The easy way to divide a number by 100 is to move the decimal point two places to the left.

Example: Convert 35% to a decimal.

Solution: 35 (without the % sign) divided by 100 is equal to 0.35. The easy way to divide 35 by 100 is to move the decimal point two places to the left. 35.0 is equivalent to 0.35.

Changing Percentages to Fractions

Write the percent as a fraction out of 100 and reduce the fraction.

$$\text{Fraction} = \frac{The\ Percent\ (without\ the\ \%\ sign)}{100}$$

Example: Change 40% into a fraction.

Answer: Fraction = $\frac{40}{100} = \frac{2 \times 20}{5 \times 20} = \frac{2}{5}$

Percent Change (Percent Increase and Percent Decrease)

The percent change is defined as the percent of the initial value that was gained or lost.

$$\text{Percent Change} = \frac{Final\ Value - Initial\ Value}{Initial\ Value} \times 100\%$$

- Percent Change > 0 → Percent Increase
- Percent Change < 0 → Percent Decrease

Example: The population of a small town was 1200 in last year and became 1260 this year. What was its population percent change from last year to this year?

Answer: Percent Change = $\frac{This\ Year's\ Population - Last\ Year's\ Population}{Last\ Year's\ Population} \times 100\%$

$= \frac{1260 - 1200}{1200} \times 100\% = 5\%$

Keywords: When dealing with percent problems, the following keywords usually translate to the following actions:

- Percent in decimal form → divide by 100
- Decimal in percent form → multiply by 100
- 'is' → =
- 'of' → × *(multiplication)*
- 'what' or 'a number' → x (the value you are solving for)

Example 1: 5 is what percent of 20?

Answer: 5 = x × 20

$x = \frac{5}{20} = 0.25$

0.25 × 100% = 25%

Changing 0.25 into a percent is equal to 25%.

Therefore, *5 is 25% of 20.*

Example 2: What is 15% of 60?

Answer: $x = \frac{12}{100} \times 60 = 9$

Example 3: 20% of what number is 16?

Answer: $\frac{20}{100} \times x = 16,\quad x = 80$

Example 4: What percent of 20 is 5?

Answer: $\frac{x}{100} \times 20 = 5$

$x = \frac{5 \times 100}{20} = 25\%$

Example 5: If 40 percent of 20 percent of a number is 20, what is the number?

Answer: Changing 40% into decimal form gives you 0.4. Changing 20% into decimal form gives you 0.2.

$0.4 \times 0.2 \times x = 20$

$x = \frac{20}{0.4 \times 0.2} = 250$

Discount: You might be asked a question that gives you two of the following: discount rate of an item, the original price of the item, and/or the total amount of money saved from purchasing the item at a discount, and asked to find the third term. To do this, you should use the discount formula:

Total Discount = Original Price × Discount Rate

Or if you are solving for or given the sale price of the item, you can either subtract the discount from the original price to get the sale price:

Original Price – Original Price × Discount Rate = Sale Price

Or multiply the original price by (1 – Discount Rate):

Sale Price = Original Price × (1 – Discount Rate)

Example 1: In a department store, a $50 T-shirt is marked "20% off." What is the sale price of the T-shirt?

Answer: Converting 20% to a decimal gives you 0.2.

Total Discount = $50×0.2 = $10

Sale Price of the T−shirt = $50 − $10 =$40

Example 2: An object that regularly sells for $125 is marked down to $100. What is the discount percentage?

Answer: Total Discount = $125 − $100 = $25

$25 = $125 × Discount Rate

Discount Rate = $\frac{25}{125} = 0.2$

Changing 0.2 to percent gives you 20%.

The discount rate is equal to 20%.

Simple Interest

When you put money in a bank, you usually earn something called interest. This is money the bank pays you for leaving money (principal) with them. Simple interest can be calculated with the simple interest formula:

Total Interest Earned = Interest Rate × Principal × Time

When you are using the interest formula, be careful of units and make sure your time units match with your interest rate units!

Example: A bank is offering its customers 3% simple interest rate annually on savings accounts. If a customer deposits $2,500 in the account, without cashing out, how much money will be in his saving account after 4 years?

Answer: Changing 3% to decimal gives you 0.03.
   Total Interest Earned = *0.03×$2,500× 4 =$300*
   Money in Account = *$2,500 + $300 = $2,800*
   After 4 years, his saving account will have *$2,800.*

Compound Interest

Compound interest is the interest added to the principal of a deposit so that the interest earned also earns interest continuously. A formula for calculating annual compound interest is as follows:

$$A = P\left(1 + \frac{r}{100}\right)^t$$

A is the amount of money, in dollars, generated after *t* years by a principal amount *P* in a bank account that pays an annual interest rate of *r*%, compounded annually.

Example: How much would you need to deposit in your bank account today with an annual interest rate of 3% compounded annually in order to get $10,000 in your back account after 10 years? (Round your answer to the nearest dollar and ignore the dollar sign when gridding your response.)

Answer: $10000 = P\left(1 + \frac{3}{100}\right)^{10}$
   $10000 = P \times (1.3439)$
   $P = \$7,441$

Problem Solving Skills

Easy

1. If 70 percent of x is 28, then what is 30 percent of x?

    Answer: 12
    $\frac{70}{100} \times x = 28$
    $x = 40$
    $40 \times 0.3 = 12$ *(Note: 30% = 0.3)*

2. If 60 percent of 30 percent of a number is 36.54, what is the number?

    Answer: 203
    This can be translated into 0.6 ×
    0.3 × A = 36.54.
    $A = \frac{36.54}{0.6 \times 0.3} = 203$

3. 50 percent of 210 is the same as 35 percent of what number?
    a) 340
    b) 300
    c) 350
    d) 275

    Answer: (B)
    This sentence can be translated
    into: $\frac{50}{100} \times 210 = \frac{35}{100} \times A$
    $A = \frac{50}{35} \times 210 = 300$

4. If John earns \$3,000 a month and he saves \$600 out of his salary, what percent of John's earnings is his monthly savings?
    a) 15%
    b) 20%
    c) 25%
    d) 30%

    Answer: (B)
    $Percent = \frac{Part}{Whole} \times 100$
    $\frac{600}{3000} \times 100 = 20$

5. A printer that regularly sells for \$150 is marked down to \$100. What is the discount percentage?
    a) 33%
    b) 42%
    c) 45%
    d) 50%

    Answer: (A)
    Discount = \$150 − \$100 = \$50
    \$50 = \$150 × Discount Rate
    Discount Rate = $\frac{50}{150} = 0.33$
    Changing 0.33 to percent gives you
    33%.

Auto Sales

6. According to the circle graph above, how many types of automobiles show less than 30 percent of the total sales?
    a) 0
    b) 1
    c) 2
    d) 3

    Answer: (C)
    30% is slightly more than $\frac{1}{4}$ (25%)
    of the whole graph.
    From the graph above, two types
    of automobiles make up less than $\frac{1}{4}$
    of the whole graph.

7. The percent increase from 6 to 15 is equal to the percent increase from 12 to what number?
   a) 20
   b) 22
   c) 24
   d) 30

Answer: (D)
$\frac{15-6}{6} = \frac{x-12}{12}$ *(cross multiply)*
$9 \times 12 = 6(x - 12)$
$18 = x - 12$
$x = (18 + 12) = 30$

8. Based on Mrs. Johnson's grading policies, if a student answers 90 to 100 percent of the questions correctly in a math test, she will receive a letter grade of A. If there are 60 questions on the final exam, what is the minimum number of questions the student would need to answer correctly to receive a grade of A?
   a) 34
   b) 38
   c) 42
   d) 54

Answer: (D)
$90\% = \frac{Correct\ Answers}{Total\ Questions}$
$\frac{x}{60} = \frac{90}{100}$ *(cross multiply)*
$x = \frac{90 \times 60}{100} = 54$

9. The price of a pair of shoes was first increased by 10 percent and then decreased by 25 percent. The final price was what percent of the original price?
   a) 80%
   b) 82.5%
   c) 85%
   d) 87.5%

Answer: (B)
Let the original price be 100, then the final price is $100 \times (1 + 0.1) \times (1 - 0.25) = 82.5$.

10. A bank is offering its customers 2% simple interest rate annually on savings accounts. If a customer deposits $1,500 in the account, without cashing out, how much money will be in his saving account after 5 years?

Answer: 1650
Changing 2% to decimal gives you 0.02.
Total Interest Earned = $0.02 \times \$1,500 \times 5 = \$150$
Money in Account = $\$1,500 + \$150 = \$1,650$
After 5 years, his saving account will have $1,650.

Medium

11. $\frac{1}{5}$ of 100 is equal to what percent of 400?
   a) 5 %
   b) 10 %
   c) 15 %
   d) 20 %

Answer: (A)
$\frac{1}{5}$ *of* $100 \rightarrow \frac{1}{5} \times 100 = 20$
$20 = \frac{x}{100} \times 400$
$20 = 4x \rightarrow x = 5$
Therefore, $\frac{1}{5} \times 100 = 20$ *is equal to* $400 \times 5\% = 20$

12. In a certain year at Lion High School, exactly 68 out of the 400 students are taking AP Chemistry. What percent of students are NOT taking AP Chemistry that year?
    a) 15
    b) 17
    c) 50
    d) 83

Answer: (D)
Percentage of people taking AP Chemistry: $\frac{68}{400} \times 100 = 17\%$
Percentage NOT taking AP Chemistry: 100% − 17% = 83%

13. A family spent $350 on utilities in January. Due to the weather, they spent 20% more in February. How much did they spend on utilities in February?

Answer: 420
"20% more of 350" $\rightarrow 350 \times (1 + 0.2) = 420$
x = 420

Questions 14 − 15 refer to the following information:
According to research, 90 percent of 20 to 36 month-old children in the United States need to have received measles vaccination in order to achieve herd immunity. In 2013, California did not meet the vaccination goal and Colorado, Ohio, and West Virginia had 86 percent of 20 to 36 month-olds received the vaccination.

14. If 89 percent of 20 to 36 month-olds received the measles vaccination in California in 2013 and the total number of 20-36 month-olds in California in 2013 is 1.41 million, which of the following could be the number of 20-36 month-olds who have received the measles vaccination in California in 2013?
    a) 1.24 million
    b) 1.25 million
    c) 1.26 million
    d) 1.27 million

Answer: (B)
The measles vaccination percentage in California is 89%. The number of 20 to 36 month-olds who had received measles vaccination in California need to be 1.41 million × 0.89 = 1.2549 million.

15. If the total number of 20 to 36 month-olds in Ohio in 2013 is 0.235 million, how many of 20 to 36 month-olds in Colorado have received the measles vaccination in 2013?
    a) 224,600
    b) 205,100
    c) 202,100
    d) 145,300

Answer: (C)
0.235 million × 0.86 = 0.2021 million = 202,100

16. A car salesman's monthly pay consists of $1000 plus 2% of his sales. If he got paid $3,000 in a certain month, what was the dollar amount, in thousands, of his sales for that month?

Answer: 100
Let his car sales be $x, then
3000 = 1000 + 0.02 × x
3000 − 1000 = 0.02x
x = $100,000

Hard

Questions 17 – 18 refer to the following information:
The unemployment rate is officially defined as the percentage of unemployed individuals divided by all individuals currently willing to work. To count as unemployed, a person must be 16 or older and have not held a job during the week of the survey. According to the Bureau of Labor Statistics, below is a comparison of the seasonally adjusted unemployment rates for certain states for the months of August and September 2015.

State	Rate (August 2015)	Rate (September 2015)
Nebraska	2.8	2.9
Hawaii	3.5	3.4
Texas	4.1	4.2
Wisconsin	4.5	4.3
Connecticut	5.3	5.2
New Jersey	5.7	5.6
Oregon	6.1	6.2
Alaska	6.6	6.4

17. Among those states shown in the table above, how many states have their unemployment rate drop from August 2015 to September 2015?
    a) 5
    b) 4
    c) 3
    d) 2

Answer: (A)
5 states, Hawaii, Wisconsin, Connecticut, New Jersey, and Alaska, have unemployment rate drop among those states shown above.

18. If about 251,400 residents of New Jersey were unemployed in September 2015, approximately how many New Jersey residents were willing to work in September 2015?
    a) 44,900
    b) 1,407,800
    c) 3,251,600
    d) 4,489,200

Answer: (D)
Let the number of residents who were willing to work be x.

$$\frac{251,400}{x} = 5.6\%$$
$$5.6x = 25,140,000$$
$$x = 4,489,286 \approx 4,489,200$$

IV. Averages

Average

The average of a set of values is equal to the sum of all values in that set divided by the number of values.

$$Average = \frac{Sum\ of\ Terms}{Number\ of\ Terms} \quad \text{(the average formula)}$$

The key to solving arithmetic average problems is using the average formula.

Example: John has the following scores on his math tests this semester: 80, 85, 89, and 90. What is his average score on his math tests that semester?

Answer: John's Average $= \frac{80 + 85 + 89 + 90}{4} = 86$

The average score of all of John's math tests is 86.

Sum of All Values in the Set

If you are given an average and asked to find the sum of all values in the set, multiply the average by the number of terms in the set.

$$\text{Sum of Terms = Average × Number of Terms}$$

Number of Terms in the Set

On the other hand, if you are given an average and a sum and asked to find the number of terms in the set, divide the sum by the average to get the number of terms.

$$\text{Number of Terms} = \frac{Sum\ of\ Terms}{Average}$$

Example: The average score of a math quiz in a class is 81 and the sum of the scores is 1215. How many students are in this class?

Answer: Number of Students $= \frac{1215}{81} = 15$

Finding the Missing Number

If you know the average of a set, the number of items in that set, and the sum of all but one of the values, then you can find the value in that set missing from the sum by subtracting the sum from the average times the number of items.

Example: There were 4 tests in Joe's Algebra class. So far he received the following scores on his tests: 83, 93, and 87. What score does he need on the last test in order to get an average score of 90 and above?

Hint: The current sum (with one score missing) is 83 + 93 + 87 = 263. He wants an average of 90 or above.

Answer: 90 × 4 − 263 = 360 − 263 = 97.

Joe needs to get at least an 87 to get an average of 90 or above.

Mean, Median, and Mode

- **Mean:** The usual arithmetic average of a set.

    Example: The mean of the set {2, 6, 4, 5, 3} is $\dfrac{2 + 6 + 4 + 5 + 3}{5} = 4$.

- **Median:** The middle element (or average of two middle elements) when a set is sorted from least to greatest. If the set has an odd number of elements, the median is the middle element. If the set has an even number of elements, the median is the average of the two middle elements.

    Example 1: What is the median of the set {3, 11, 6, 5, 4, 7, 12, 3, 10}?
    Hint: Sort the numbers in order first: {3, 3, 4, 5, 6, 7, 10, 11, 12}
    Answer: There are 9 numbers in the set, so the median is the middle element in the sorted set. The median is 6.

    Example 2: What is the median of the set {3, 11, 6, 5, 4, 7, 12, 3, 10, 12}?
    Hint: Sort the numbers in order: {3, 3, 4, 5, 6, 7, 10, 11, 12, 12}
    Answer: There are 10 numbers in the set, so the median number is the average of the two middle numbers, 6 and 7. The median is 6.5.

- **Mode:** The value(s) that appear most often in the set.

    Example: What is the mode of the set {7, 13, 18, 24, 9, 3, 18}?
    Hint: Sort the numbers in order: {3, 7, 9, 13, 18, 18, 24}
    Answer: The number which occurs most often is 18. Therefore, the mode is 18.

Problem Solving Skills

Easy

1. The average (arithmetic mean) of 5, 14, and x is 15. What is the value of x?
    a) 25
    b) 26
    c) 27
    d) 28

Answer: (B)
The average of these three numbers is 15, so the sum will be $3 \times 15 = 45$.
$5 + 14 + x = 45$
$x = 45 - 19 = 26$

2. If the average (arithmetic mean) of 2, X, and Y is 3, what is the value of X + Y?
    a) 4
    b) 5
    c) 7
    d) 8

Answer: (C)
$X + Y + 2 = 3 \times 3 = 9$
$X + Y = 7$

3. Mary has the following scores on 7 quizzes in Algebra class: 84, 79, 83, 87, 81, 94, and 87. What was the median score of all of her Algebra quizzes?
    a) 81
    b) 84
    c) 85
    d) 86

Answer: (B)
Sort the scores in order.
79, 81, 83, 84, 87, 87, 94
The median is 84.

4. If the sum of 4 numbers is between 61 and 63, then the average (arithmetic mean) of the 4 numbers could be which of the following?
    a) 15
    b) 15.2
    c) 15.5
    d) 16

Answer: (C)
$\frac{61}{4} < Average < \frac{63}{4}$
$15.25\ Average < 15.75$

5. Which of the following could be the sum of 8 numbers if the average of these 8 numbers is greater than 9 and less than 10?
    a) 85
    b) 83
    c) 82
    d) 79

Answer: (D)
Sum = Number of Elements × Average
$9 \times 8 < Sum < 10 \times 8$
$72 < Sum < 80$

6. When the average (arithmetic mean) of a list of grades is multiplied by the number of students, the result is *n*. What does *n* represent?
   a) the number of the grades
   b) the average of the grades
   c) the sum of the grades
   d) the range of the list of the grades

   Answer: (C)
   This is the definition of "sum."

7. Let A represents the average of all winter monthly heating bills for John's family. What is the result of multiplying A by the number of months in winter?
   a) The average of all heating expenses for John's family in the year.
   b) The highest monthly heating bill for John's family that winter.
   c) The sum of the eating expenses for the whole year for John's family.
   d) The sum of the heating expenses in winter for John's family.

   Answer: (D)
   Multiplying the average by the number of elements (months) in the set gives you the sum of all the elements.

8. The median of a set of 13 consecutive integers is 35. What is the greatest of these 13 integers?
   a) 37
   b) 38
   c) 40
   d) 41

   Answer: (D)
   The median is the 7th number of 13 consecutive integers. That means there are 6 integers less than the median and 6 integers greater than the median. The greatest integer is the 6th consecutive integer after 35.
   35 + 6 = 41

9. If the average of 3*a*, 4*a*, and 5*a* is equal to 8, what is *a* equal to?

   Answer: 2
   The average of 3a, 4a and 5a is equal to 4a.
   4a= 8 → a = 2

Medium

10. The average score of John's 5 math tests is 75. If the teacher decides not to count his lowest score, which is 55, what will be John's new average score?
    a) 78
    b) 79
    c) 80
    d) 81

    Answer: (C)
    John's original average is 75 for 5 tests.
    5 × 75 = 375 (sum of 5 tests)
    375 − 55 = 320 (sum of 4 tests)
    $\frac{320}{4}$ *= 80 (average of 4 tests)*

11. On a certain test, the highest possible score is 100 and the lowest is 0. If the average score of 5 students is 82, what is the lowest possible score of the fifth student?
    a) 0
    b) 5
    c) 7
    d) 10

Answer: (D)
The lowest possible score is equal to the lowest score a student can get if each of other four students got the highest possible score (otherwise we can always increase another student's score and decrease the lowest score). Thus, each of other four students must get 100.
Total Score = 5 × 82 = 410
Lowest Score = 410 − 400 = 10

Math Midterm	
Scores	Number of Students
100	1
95	3
90	5
85	8
80	3

12. The scores of the math midterm for every student in Sam's class are shown in the table above. Sam, who was the only student absent, will take the test next week. If Sam receives a score of 95 on the test, what will be the median score for the test?
    a) 75
    b) 82.5
    c) 85
    d) 87.5

Answer: (C)
For an odd set, the median is the score in the middle when scores listed in order.
If we include Sam, the median will be the 11th highest score which is 85.

13. On an Algebra final exam, class A has an average score of 90 with 10 students. Class B has an average score of 85 with 20 students. When the scores of class A and B are combined, what is the average score of class A and B?
    a) 82
    b) 82.5
    c) 83
    d) 86.7

Answer: (D)
*This is **not** the average of the averages since the classes have different number of students! The final average is the sum of all students' scores divided by the total number of students.*
We know that the sum of all the students' scores in one class is just the average multiplied by the number of students.
Average = $\frac{10 \times 90 + 20 \times 85}{10 + 20} = 86.67$

Hard

14. On a biology test with total of 100 points, a class of 21 students had an average of 93. If 5 of the students had a perfect score, what was the average score for the remaining students?
    a) 89
    b) 90
    c) 91
    d) 91.5

Answer: (C)
Once again, the average gives a way to calculate the total score of all the students. Deduct from that sum the sum of the test scores that were perfect and divide by the remaining number of students.
Average: $\frac{Sum}{21}$ = 93
Sum of all scores: 21 × 93 = 1953
Deduct 5 perfect scores:
1953 − 500 = 1453
New Average = $\frac{1453}{21-5}$ = 90.8 ~ 91

15. If the average (arithmetic mean) of x, y, and z is k, which of the following is the average of w, x, y and z?
    a) $\frac{k+w}{2}$
    b) $\frac{2k+w}{3}$
    c) $\frac{3k+w}{3}$
    d) $\frac{3k+w}{4}$

Answer: (D)
$k = \frac{x+y+z}{3}$
$x + y + z = 3k$
Average: $\frac{x+y+z+w}{4} = \frac{3k+w}{4}$

V. DATA ANALYSIS

Reading and Interpreting Graphs, Charts, and Tables

SAT data analysis questions use graphs, charts, and tables to organize information.

Bar graphs use horizontal or vertical bars to represent data.

Example: The bar graph below shows the number of students taking honors and AP classes. For math classes, there are 20 students taking math honors and 15 students taking AP math.

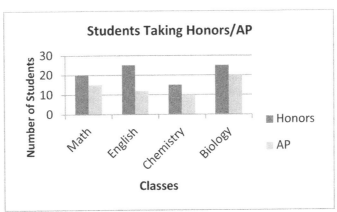

Pictographs use pictures to represent data. There is usually a scale provided that gives you an idea of what each picture represents.

Example: The pictograph below shows the car sales data from 1971 to 2010. The scale clearly states that each car represents 2 million cars. In the pictograph, we can see that the years 2001-2010 are drawn with four cars, which represents a total of 8 million cars sold. In the years 1981-1990, the pictograph shows $2\frac{1}{2}$ cars sold, which represents 5 million cars.

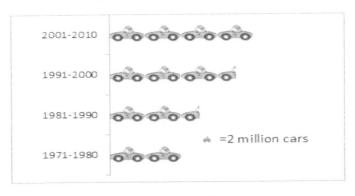

Car Sales from 1971 to 2010

Pie graphs use a circle (or pie) to display data. Pie graphs can be used to determine the proportion of an item out of a whole as well as ratios of different items to each other.

Example: The pie graph below shows Ellen's family's monthly expenses and the proportion of each expense out of all of their expenditures.

As we can see from the graph, food takes up about $\frac{1}{4}$ of all expenditures, and utilities take up about $\frac{1}{5}$ of all expenditures. The ratio of food expenditures to taxes is about 1:1.

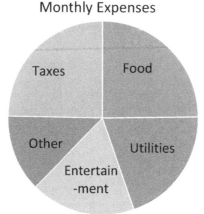

Monthly Expenses

Sometimes you are asked to the value of a sector given the total value. You can figure out the proportion of the sector in the pie and solve for the missing value:

$$\text{Proportion of Sector in Pie} = \frac{Value\ of\ the\ Sector}{Total\ Value}$$

Example: If the Ellen's family's total expenses are $6000 per month, approximately how much do they pay in taxes per month?

Solution: Taxes take up around $\frac{1}{4}$ of the total pie.
$$\frac{1}{4} = \frac{Taxes}{6000}$$

$$Taxes = \$1500$$

Tables represent data in rows and columns. Tables are simple to understand. The top entry of a column usually explains the contents of that column. Elements are corresponded to all the other elements in the same row.

Example: The table below shows the number of students taking AP classes in school. The entry that contains a '1' under 'Number of APs' corresponds to the entry that contains a '6' under 'Number of Students.' In other words, there are 6 students taking 1 AP class.

Students Taking AP Classes	
Number of Aps	Number of Students
1	6
2	4
3	5
4	4

Line graphs record a change in data. Usually this change is graphed over time. Time is usually graphed on the *x*-axis.

Example: The line graph below records car sales (in millions) over four years.

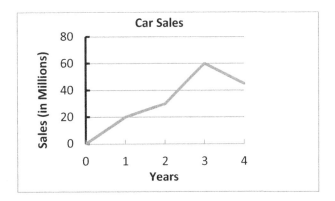

Scatterplots are similar to line graphs, but show the individual data points instead of connecting them with a line. Like line graphs, scatterplots show trends in the data.

Example: The scatterplot below shows the wolf population in a safari every 5 years.

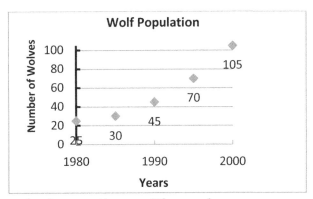

Tips to solve data analysis questions with graphs:
- Always look through the question first to check what the question is asking.
- Read the titles and axes to see what the graph is trying to show.
- Collect information from the graph as needed.
- Perform operations on the data you collected.

Problem Solving Skills

Easy

1. From the graph below, John sold how many more cars in year 3 than the sum of cars sold in years 1 and 2?

   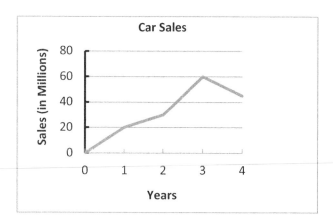

   Answer: (A)
   Year 1 + Year 2 = 20 + 30 = 50 cars
   Year 3 = 60 cars
   60 − 50 = 10 cars

   a) 10
   b) 15
   c) 20
   d) 25

2. According to the graph below, how many students are taking honors classes altogether?

   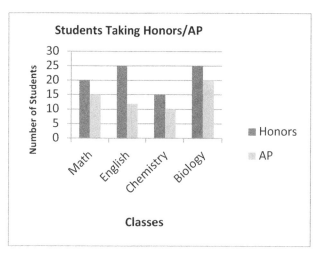

   Answer: (C)
   Total = (20 + 25 + 15 + 25) = 85

   a) 75
   b) 80
   c) 85
   d) 90

3. Of the following, which is the closest approximation of the cost per ticket when one purchases a book of 6?

Answer: (A)

$\dfrac{\$40}{6\,Tickets} = \$6.67\ per\ ticket$

Bus Ticket Price	
Number of Bus Tickets	Price
1	7.5
Book of 6	40
Book of 12	75

a) $6.67
b) $6.75
c) $6.83
d) $6.90

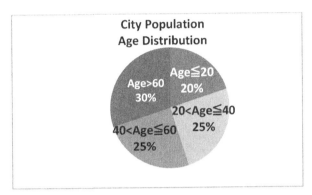

4. Town A has a population of 25,000 and the chart above shows their age distribution. How many people are 40 years or younger?
    a) 5,000
    b) 8,000
    c) 10,000
    d) 11,250

Answer: (D)
The number of population 40 years or younger:
$(25\% + 20\%) \times 25,000$
$= 45\% \times 25,000 = 0.45 \times 25,000$
$= 11,250$

5. What is the percent increase of sales from the third to the fourth year in the chart below?

a) 40%
b) 55%
c) 65%
d) 67%

Answer: (D)
Percent increase =
$\dfrac{4^{th}\ Year\ Sales - 3^{rd}\ Year\ Sales}{3^{rd}\ Year\ Sales}$
$\times 100\%$
From the graph, sales in the 3rd year is 6 million and sales in the 4th year is 10 million.
Percent Increase = $\dfrac{10 - 6}{6} \times$
$100\% = 67\%$

6. According to the graph below, how many employees have salary less than or equal to $40,000?

a) 100
b) 150
c) 250
d) 300

Monthly Expenses

7. The pie graph above shows Ellen's family's monthly expenses and the proportion of each expense out of all of their expenditures. If the family's total expenses are $3,000 per month, approximately how much do they pay on taxes per month?

a) $500
b) $600
c) $700
d) $750

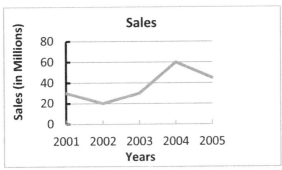

8. Which of the following is closest to the decrease in sales in millions between 2004 and 2005 according to the graph above?

    a) 10
    b) 12
    c) 15
    d) 20

Answer: (C)
2004 Sales = 60 million units
2005 Sales = 45 million units
60 − 45 = 15 million units

Questions 9 − 10 refer to the chart below:

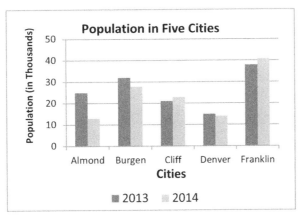

9. Which of the following cities had a population in 2014 that was approximately 50% less than its population in 2013?

    a) Almond
    b) Burgen
    c) Cliff
    d) Denver

Answer: (A)
Almond's population in 2014 is around double its population in 2013.

10. The total population in all five cities increased by approximately what percent from 2013 to 2014?

    a) 10%
    b) 9%
    c) −10%
    d) −9%

Answer: (D)
Total Population in 2013 = 25 + 32 + 21 + 15 + 37 = 130 thousand.
Total Population in 2014 = 13 + 28 + 22 + 14 + 41 = 118 thousand. $\frac{118 - 130}{130} \times 100\%$
= −9.2% ~ −9%

Medium

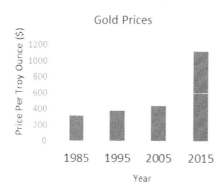

Gold Prices

Annual Average Gold Price from 1985 to 2015
(U.S. dollars per troy ounce)

11. The figure above shows the change of the annual average gold price between 1985 and 2015, in U.S. dollars per troy ounce. A troy ounce is a traditional unit of gold weight. In 1985, a troy ounce of gold had an annual average price of around $317. Based on the information shown, which of the following conclusions is valid?

 a) A troy ounce of gold cost more in 1995 than in 2005.

 b) The price more than doubled between 2005 and 2015.

 c) The percent increase from 1985 to 2015 is more than 300%.

 d) The overall average gold price between 1985 and 2015 is around US $555.

Answer: (D)

Percent Change: $\frac{1100-310}{310} \times 100\% \approx 255\%$

Overall Average:
$\frac{310+390+420+1100}{4} = \$555$

Questions 12 − 13 refer to the following information:

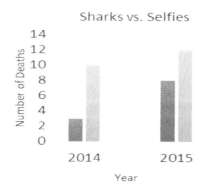

Sharks vs. Selfies

■ Shark-Related Deaths ■ Selfie-Related Deaths

News outlet *Reuters* reports that taking a selfie is actually a dangerous endeavor, and that many people have been injured or died while taking a selfie. The figure above shows that more people around the world have died by taking selfies than by shark attacks in the years of 2014 and 2015. There have been twelve recorded selfie deaths in 2015 compared to eight people dying from shark attacks. The most common selfie-related deaths have been due to falling or being hit by a moving vehicle.

12. What is the percent change of total deaths of selfie-related and shark-related from 2014 to 2015?
    a) 54%
    b) 72%
    c) 100%
    d) 233%

Answer: (A)
Total deaths of 2014: 10 + 3 = 13
Total deaths of 2015: 12 + 8 = 20
Percent Increase = $\frac{20-13}{13} \times$
100% = 54%

13. What is the difference between the percent changes of shark-related deaths and selfie-related deaths from 2014 to 2015?
    a) 20%
    b) 147%
    c) 167%
    d) 187%

Answer: (B)
Percent change of selfie-related deaths: $\frac{12-10}{10} \times 100\% = 20\%$
Percent change of shark-related deaths: $\frac{8-3}{3} \times 100\% = 167\%$
Difference: 167% − 20% = 147%

14. The table below, describing number of students who passed or failed the Algebra I final exam, is partially filled in. Based on the information in the table, how many females have failed?

Algebra I Final Exam Results			
	Pass	Fail	Total
Male	125		
Female			145
Total	230		305

Answer: 40
The Number of Students Passing = the Number of Males Passing + the Number of Females Passing
230 = 125 + the Number of Females Passing
The Number of Females Passing = 105
Total Number of Females = Number of Females Passing + Number of Females Failing
The Number of Females Failing = 145 − 105 = 40

Age Distributions

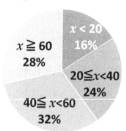

15. If there are 4,180 residents ranging in age from 40 to 59 in Green Village County according to the graph above, approximately how many residents are under the age of 20?
    a) 2,000
    b) 2,100
    c) 2,200
    d) 2,300

Answer: (B)
This is a proportion problem.
Percent of residents 40 to 59 years old: 32%.
Percent of residents under 20: 16%
32% : 4180 = 16% : x
x = 2090

Hard

Number of Hours of TV Watched

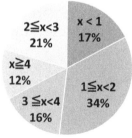

16. The graph above shows breakdown of the average number of hours of TV watched per day. 1,000 people were surveyed, and all but 120 people surveyed responded to the question. If x is the number of hours spent, about how many respondents watch TV for more than 3 hours a day?
    a) 200
    b) 220
    c) 250
    d) 280

Answer: (C)
Watching TV for more than 3 hours a day includes those who answered with $3 \leqq x < 4$ and $4 \leqq x$, which make up around 28% (12% + 16%) of those who answered.
Total Respondents = 1000 − 120 = 880 people
880 × 28% = 246 ~ 250 people

17. The number of books that have been checked out of the town public library in a particular week was recorded in the table below. If the median number of books checked out for the whole week was 93, which of the following could have been the number of books checked out on Saturday and Sunday, respectively, of the same week?

Town Library Checkout Records	
Day of the Week	Number of Books Checked Out
Monday	87
Tuesday	91
Wednesday	92
Thursday	93
Friday	96

a) 88 and 92
b) 89 and91
c) 90 and 97
d) 94 and 97

Answer: (D)
If the median number of books checked out for the whole week was 93, the number of books checked out on both Saturday and Sunday should be more than 93.

18. According to the graphs above, the total number of full-time employees is how many more than the total number of part time employees at Oak Town High School?
   a) 20
   b) 40
   c) 50
   d) 60

Answer: (B)
Number of Full Time Employees = 15 + 45 + 60 = 120
Full time employees comprise of 60% of the total.
0.6 × Number of Employees = 120
Number of Employees = 200
Part Time Employees = 200 × 0.4 = 80
Full Time Employees – Part Time Employees = 120 − 80 = 40

VI. COUNTING AND PROBABILITY

Multiplication Principle of Counting

If an event A happens in p possible ways and an event B happens independently in q possible ways, and then the total number of possible ways that event A **AND** B happen is $p \times q$ ways.

Example: Suppose that there are 5 different main course items and 6 different side dishes. How many different orders can a customer buy one main course and one side dish?

Hint: Because the customer is ordering a main course AND a side dish, use the Multiplication Principle.

Answer: $5 \times 6 = 30$

Addition Principle of Counting

If an event A happens in p possible ways and an event B happens in q different ways, and then the total number of possible ways that either event A **OR** event B happens is $p + q$ ways.

Example: Suppose that there are 4 seafood main dishes and 6 chicken main dishes. How many different ways can a customer choose a main dish?

Hint: Because the customer can choose a seafood dish OR a chicken dish, use the Addition Principle.

Answer: $4 + 6 = 10$

Probability of an Event

Probability problems are very similar to counting problems. The **probability** of an event occurring is equal to the ratio of successful events to the total possible events.

$$\text{Probability of an Event} = \frac{Number\ of\ Successful\ Events}{Total\ Number\ of\ Possible\ Events}$$

Example: What is the probability of rolling a number less than 4 when you roll one dice?

Solution: Probability of Rolling a Number $< 4 = \frac{Rolling\ 1,2,or\ 3}{6} = \frac{3}{6} = \frac{1}{2}$

Sometimes probability problems take place over a multi-dimensional sample space. In these problems, use familiar geometric concepts to find the **geometric probability** of an event.

$$\text{Geometric Probability} = \frac{Size\ of\ Target\ Space}{Size\ of\ Sample\ Space}$$

where size could refer to the length, area, or volume of the space.

Example: The diagram below shows 2 concentric circles, with radii 1 and 3 respectively. What is the probability that a randomly selected point in the diagram will fall in the shaded region?

Solution: The shaded region is the target; therefore, the probability of falling in the shaded region is:

$$\frac{Size\ of\ the\ Target}{Total\ Size} = \frac{Size\ of\ Small\ Circle}{Size\ of\ Big\ Circle} = \frac{\pi(1)^2}{\pi(3)^2} = \frac{1}{9}$$

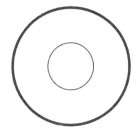

Problem Solving Skills

Easy

1. For every 20 cars sold by a dealer, 8 of them were red. What is the probability that a car sold that is selected at random would be red?

    a) $\frac{1}{5}$

    b) $\frac{2}{5}$

    c) $\frac{1}{3}$

    d) $\frac{2}{3}$

    Answer: (B)
    Probability =
    $$\frac{Number\ of\ Successful\ Events}{Total\ Number\ of\ Possible\ Events}$$

    $$\frac{8}{20} = \frac{2}{5}$$

2. There are 10 red boxes, 15 blue boxes, and 20 white boxes. If a blue marble is randomly placed into one of these boxes, what is the probability that it will be placed in a box that is the same color as it?

    a) $\frac{1}{4}$

    b) $\frac{2}{3}$

    c) $\frac{1}{3}$

    d) $\frac{1}{2}$

    Answer: (C)
    Probability =
    $$\frac{Number\ of\ Successful\ Events}{Total\ Number\ of\ Possible\ Events}$$
    $$\frac{15}{15 + 10 + 20} = \frac{1}{3}$$

3. For a salad dish, each customer can choose from 5 types of vegetables and 4 types of dressings. How many distinct salad dishes containing one type of vegetable and one dressing are there?

    a) 20
    b) 16
    c) 14
    d) 8

    Answer: (A)
    For one vegetable AND one dressing, use the Multiplication Principle.
    $5 \times 4 = 20$

4. A restaurant offers a choice of one side dish when a main course is ordered. Customers can choose from a list of 5 different main courses and 6 different side dishes. How many different combinations are there of one main course and one side dish?

    a) 11
    b) 16
    c) 20
    d) 30

    Answer: (D)
    Because the customer is ordering a main course AND a side dish, use the Multiplication Principle. Total number of choices: $5 \times 6 = 30$

5. There are four points A, B, C, and D on line *l*, and another four points W, X, Y, and Z on a different line parallel to line *l*. How many distinct lines can be drawn that include exactly two of these 8 points?

Answer: 16
Each of the four points on line l can be connected to each of the four points on the parallel line.
4 × 4 = 16

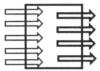

6. The figure above shows an indoor parking lot with the rectangular arrows indicating the different entrances and exits. What is the total number of distinct ways that a driver can enter and exit the parking lot?

    a) 9
    b) 5
    c) 4
    d) 20

Answer: (D)
Because cars entering the parking lot will also exit, so use the Multiplication Principle.
Total number of ways: 5 × 4 = 20

7. As a part of a vacation package, a travel agent offers 3 choices for the destination, 7 choices for the hotels and 2 choices for car rental companies. How many distinct vacation packages are there with a destination, hotel, and car rental company?

    a) 52
    b) 42
    c) 21
    d) 12

Answer: (B)
We want to find all distinct packages, so we want to solve for the total number of combinations. The total number of combinations of one hotel AND one car rental can be found by using the Multiplication Principle.
2   × 7 × 2 = 42

8. How many different positive four-digit integers can be formed if the digits 1, 2, 3, and 4 are each used exactly once?

    a) 10
    b) 12
    c) 14
    d) 24

Answer: (D)
4 × 3 × 2 × 1 = 24

9. A bag contains 15 tennis balls, 6 of which are yellow, 4 pink, and the rest blue. If one ball is randomly chosen from the bag, what is the probability that the ball is blue?

   a) $\frac{1}{2}$

   b) $\frac{1}{3}$

   c) $\frac{1}{4}$

   d) $\frac{3}{5}$

Answer: (B)
The number of blue balls:
$15 - 6 - 4 = 5$
Probability $= \frac{5}{15} = \frac{1}{3}$

10. In a high school pep rally, a student is to be chosen at random. The probability of choosing a freshman is $\frac{1}{8}$. Which of the following cannot be the total number of students in the pep rally?

    a) 20
    b) 24
    c) 32
    d) 80

Answer: (A)
The total number of students must be a multiple of 8. Note that the number of students must be a whole number.
Only (a) is not a multiple of 8.

11. At an intersection, a complete cycle of the traffic light takes 60 seconds. Within each cycle, the green light lasts for 30 seconds and the yellow light 10 seconds. If a driver arrives at the intersection at a random time, what is the probability that the light is red?

    a) $\frac{3}{4}$

    b) $\frac{2}{3}$

    c) $\frac{1}{3}$

    d) $\frac{1}{2}$

Answer: (C)
The red light takes 20 seconds.
$60 - 30 - 10 = 20$
Probability of Red Light $= \frac{20}{60} = \frac{1}{3}$

12. Bella has 5 blue pens, 6 black pens, and 5 red pens in her pencil case. She takes out a pen at random and puts it aside because the pen is not blue. She then takes out a second pen randomly from her pencil case. What is the probability that the second pen will be a blue pen?

    a) $\frac{1}{4}$

    b) $\frac{1}{2}$

    c) $\frac{2}{3}$

    d) $\frac{1}{3}$

Answer: (D)
After first taking, there are 5 blue pens and a total of 15 pens left in her pencil case.
Probability to get a blue pen:
$\frac{5}{15} = \frac{1}{3}$

Medium

13. How many different positive 2-digit integers are there such that the tens digit is less than 5 and the units digit is even?
    a) 20
    b) 16
    c) 14
    d) 12

Answer: (A)
There are 4 choices for the tens digit and 5 choices for the units digit.
$$3 \times 5 = 20$$

14. There are 5 red, 5 green, 5 blue, and 5 yellow letters, each of which is inside one of twenty identical, unmarked envelopes. What is the least number of envelopes that must be selected in order to have at least 3 letters of same color?
    a) 4
    b) 8
    c) 9
    d) 12

Answer: (C)
If 2 letters for each color have been picked, then the next pick has to make at least one color triple.
$2 \times 4 + 1 = 9$

15. There are four different games: Monopole, Good, Words with Ends, and Turner. Each of four friends wants to play a different game. How many different arrangements of who wants to play what are possible?

Answer: 24
The number of ways to arrange n distinct objects in order is n!.
$4! = 4 \times 3 \times 2 \times 1 = 24$

16. What is the total number of distinct line segments that must be drawn in the interior of the heptagon, as shown above, to connect all pairs of the vertices?
    a) 7
    b) 8
    c) 14
    d) 28

Answer: (C)
Each of the 7 vertices has to be connected to each of its 4 non-adjacent vertices, but this double counts the number of line segments needed because each line segment connects two vertices.
$(7 \times 4) \div 2 = 14$

17. The figure below shows a top view of a container with a square-shaped opening and which is divided into 5 smaller compartments. The side of the overall square is double the length of the side of the center square and the areas of compartments A, B, C, and D are all equal. If a baseball is thrown into the box at random, what is the probability that the baseball is found in compartment A?

a) $\dfrac{1}{4}$

b) $\dfrac{2}{15}$

c) $\dfrac{3}{16}$

d) $\dfrac{1}{8}$

Answer: (C)
Find the ratio of the total area to the area of A.
If the total area is 1, the small square area in the middle will be $\dfrac{1}{4}$.

Area of A $= \dfrac{1 - \frac{1}{4}}{4} = \dfrac{3}{16}$

Probability $= \dfrac{3}{16}$

18. A box contains red, blue and green pens. If one pen is chosen at random, the probability that a red pen will be chosen is two times the probability for a blue pen and three times the probability for a green pen. If there are 12 red pens in the box, how many pens are in the box?

a) 20
b) 22
c) 24
d) 28

Answer: (B)
Red : Blue : Green = $1 : \dfrac{1}{2} : \dfrac{1}{3}$
= 12 : 6 : 4
Total number of pens:
12 + 6 + 4 = 22

19. Linda's purse contains 4 quarters, 5 dimes, 2 nickels, and 4 pennies. If she takes out one coin at random, what is the probability that the coin is worth less than 10 cents?

Answer: $\dfrac{2}{5}$ *or .4*
If the coin is worth less than 10 cents, then the coin must be either a penny or a nickel.
Probability $= \dfrac{2 + 4}{4 + 5 + 2 + 4} = \dfrac{2}{5}$

20. Kat has some coins in her purse. Of the coins, 6 are pennies. If she randomly picks one of the coins from her purse, the probability of picking a penny is $\frac{1}{3}$. How many coins are in her purse?

Answer: 18
$\dfrac{6}{Total\ Coins} = \dfrac{1}{3}$
Total Coins = 18

Hard

21. How many combinations of three dishes can be prepared if you have the recipes for 10 dishes?

Answer: 120
This is combination. The number of ways to select m objects from n objects ($n \geq m$), where order does not matter: $(C_m^n = \frac{n!}{m!(n-m)!})$
To choose 3 from 10: $C_3^{10} = 120$

22. The center of a circle is the origin of a rectangular coordinate plane. If (−4, 0), (0, 4), and (4, 0) are three points on the circumference of the circle, what is the probability that a randomly picked point inside the circle would fall inside the triangle formed by those three points?

    a) $\frac{1}{2}$
    b) $\frac{1}{3}$
    c) $\frac{1}{\pi}$
    d) $\frac{2}{\pi}$

Answer: (C)
Radius of the Circle = 4
Area of the Circle = $\pi (4)^2 = 16\pi$
Area of the Triangle = $\frac{1}{2} \times 4 \times 8$
= 16
Probability = $\frac{16}{16\pi} = \frac{1}{\pi}$

23. A bag contains red, blue, and green marbles. The probability of pulling out a red marble randomly is $\frac{1}{4}$ and the probability of pulling out a blue marble randomly is $\frac{1}{5}$. Which of the following could be the total number of marbles in the bag?

    a) 10
    b) 12
    c) 18
    d) 20

Answer: (D)
The total number of marbles should be a common multiple of 4 and 5.
The LCM of 4 and 5 is 20, so the total number of marbles has to be a multiple of 20.

24. If there are 7 points in a plane, no three of which are collinear, how many distinct lines can be formed by connecting two of these points?

    a) 18
    b) 20
    c) 21
    d) 22

Answer: (C)
This is combination. The number of ways to select m objects from n objects ($n \geq m$), where order does not matter: $C_m^n = \frac{n!}{m!(n-m)!}$
To choose any two points among the 7 points: $C_2^7 = 21$

Chapter 4 Geometry And Trigonometry

I. LINES AND ANGLE

Vertical Angles Are Congruent

In the figure below, ∠1 and ∠3 are vertical angles, and ∠2 and ∠4 are vertical angles. Thus, $m∠1 = m∠3$ and $m∠2 = m∠4$.

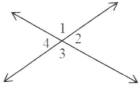

Lines

- Only one distinct line can pass through any two distinct points.
- Two different lines can intersect at most one point.
- If two lines intersect at right angles, they are **perpendicular**.

Parallel Lines and Their Transversals

- Two lines on the same plane that never intercept each other are **parallel** lines.
- If two distinct lines on the same plane are both perpendicular to another line, the two lines must be parallel.

If lines l and m are parallel and line n crosses both lines, line n is a **transversal** of lines l and m. Then the following holds:

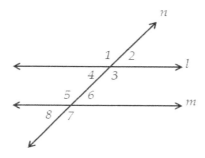

- **Corresponding angles** are congruent: pairs of corresponding angles include ∠1 and ∠5, ∠2 and ∠6, ∠4 and ∠8, and ∠3 and ∠7.
- **Alternate interior angles** are congruent: pairs of alternate interior angles include ∠3 and ∠5, and ∠4 and ∠6.
- **Consecutive interior angles** are supplementary: pairs of consecutive interior angles include ∠3 and ∠6, and ∠4 and ∠5.
- **Alternate exterior angles** are congruent: pairs of alternate exterior angles include ∠1 and ∠7, and ∠2 and ∠8.
- Pairs of **vertical angles** are always congruent, such as ∠1 and ∠3, and ∠6 and ∠8.

Example: From the graph below, if l_1 is parallel to l_2 and $x = 50$, what are the values of a, b, c, and d?

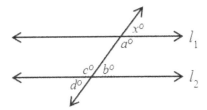

Answer: $b = 50$ (Corresponding angles x and b are congruent.)

$d = 50$ (Alternate exterior angles d and x are congruent.)

$a = 130$ (Consecutive interior angles a and b are supplementary.)

$c = 130$ (Alternate interior angles a and c are congruent.)

Problem Solving Skills

Easy

1. In the figure below, lines l_1 and l_2 are parallel. What is the value of $-y$?

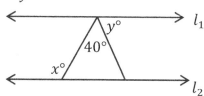

Answer: 40
$40 + y = x$
$x - y = 40$

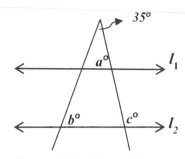

2. In the figure above, if $l_1 \parallel l_2$ and $c = 110$, what is the value of b, in degrees?
   a) 70
   b) 75
   c) 80
   d) 85

Answer: (B)
Corresponding angles are congruent.
$a = 180° - c = 70°$
$a + b + 35° = 180°$
$b = 75°$

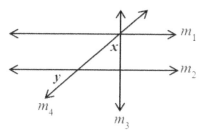

3. In the figure above, if m_1 is parallel to m_2 and m_3 is perpendicular to m_1, what is the sum of x and y, in degrees?
   a) 180°
   b) 120°
   c) 100°
   d) 90°

Answer: (D)

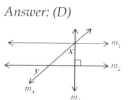

We are given that $m_1 \parallel m_2$, so if $m_1 \perp m_3$, then $m_2 \perp m_3$. x plus the vertical angle of y equals 90° since $m_2 \perp m_3$. Thus, $x + y = 90°$

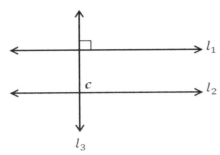

4. In the figure above, $l_1 \parallel l_2$ and $l_3 \perp l_1$. Which of the following must be true?
    a) $c < 90°$
    b) $c > 90°$
    c) $c = 90°$
    d) $l_1 \perp l_2$

Answer: (C)
∠C is the supplementary angle of a right angle.
$c = 90°$

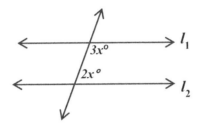

5. In the figure above $l_1 \parallel l_2$, what is the value of x?
    a) 36
    b) 40
    c) 45
    d) 54

Answer: (A)
Consecutive interior angles are supplementary.
$2x + 3x = 180$
$x = 36$

6. In the figure below, lines l_1 and l_2 are parallel. What is the value of y?

Answer: 150
$x = 50$
$180 - 100 - 50 = 30$
$y = 180 - 30 = 150$

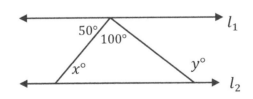

Medium

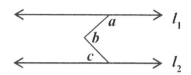

7. In the figure above, $l_1 \parallel l_2$, $a = 130°$, and $c = 40°$. What is the value of b?

    a) 50°
    b) 60°
    c) 70°
    d) 90°

Answer: (D)
Draw an auxiliary line extending to l_2:

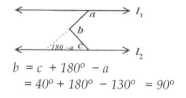

$b = c + 180° - a$
$\quad = 40° + 180° - 130° = 90°$

8. In the figure below, $l_1 \parallel l_2$. What is the value of x?

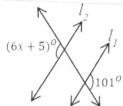

$(6x + 5)°$ $101°$

    a) 15
    b) 16
    c) 17
    d) 18

Answer: (B)
$6x + 5 = 101$
$x = 16$

9. In the figure below, $l_1 \parallel l_2$ and $b = 2a + 6$. What is the value of a, in degrees?

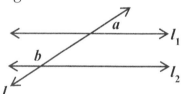

Note: Figure not drawn to scale.

Answer: 58
$a + b = 180°$
$2a + 6 + a = 180°$
$3a = 174$
$a = 58°$

Hard

10. In the figure below, $l_1 \parallel l_2$. Which of the following statements must be true?

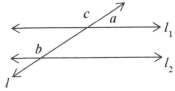

Note: Figure not drawn to scale.

I. $a + c = 180°$
II. $b + c = 180°$
III. $a + b = 180°$

a) I only
b) I and II only
c) I and III only
d) I, II, and III

Answer: (C)
$a + c = 180°$
$c = 180° - a$
$a + b = 180°$
$a = 180° - b$
$c = 180° - (180° - b)$
$b = c$

11. In the figure below, $l_1 \parallel l_2$ and $a = b$. Which of the following statements must be true?

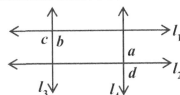

Note: Figure not drawn to scale.

I. l_1 and l_2 are parallel
II. l_3 and l_1 are perpendicular
III. $c = d$

a) I only
b) I and II only
c) III only
d) I, II, and III

Answer: (C)
*Two angles placed adjacently make a straight angle, these two angles are **supplementary angles**. The sum of two supplementary angles is $180°$.*
$a + d = 180°$
$b + c = 180°$
If $a = b$ then $c = d$

II. TRIANGLE

Sum of Interior Angles Theorem: The sum of the three interior angles of a triangle is 180°.

Example: Find the value of x.

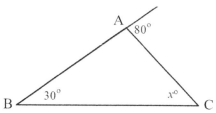

Answer: $80^o + \angle BAC = 180^o = 30 + x + \angle BAC$
$80^o = 30^o + x^o \rightarrow x = 50$

An **equilateral triangle** is a triangle with three equal sides and three equal interior angles measuring 60°.

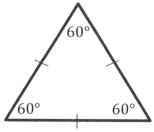

An **isosceles triangle** is a triangle with two equal sides and congruent corresponding base angles. If two sides of a triangle are equal in length, their opposite angles must be congruent as well.

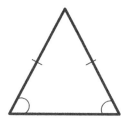

NOTE: The height of an isosceles triangle always bisects the triangle, creating two equal right triangles.

A **right triangle** is a triangle with a 90° angle. The two perpendicular sides are called legs and the side opposite the right angle is called the hypotenuse.

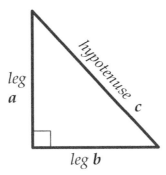

Pythagorean Theorem for right triangles: $a^2 + b^2 = c^2$

Special Right Triangles: Two special right triangles you need to get familiar with: 45°-45°-90° and 30°-60°-90° right triangles.

- The ratio of the sides of a 45-45-90 right triangle is $1 : 1 : \sqrt{2}$.
- The ratio of the sides of a 30-60-90 right triangles is $1 : \sqrt{3} : 2$.

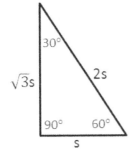

30-60-90 right triangle

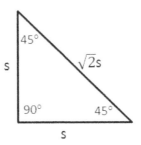

45-45-90 right triangle

Example: Find the values of x and y.

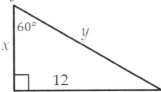

Answer: This is a 30-60-90 special right triangle. The ratio of sides is $1 : \sqrt{3} : 2$.

$$\frac{1}{x} = \frac{\sqrt{3}}{12} = \frac{2}{y}$$

Therefore, $x = 4\sqrt{3}$ and $y = 8\sqrt{3}$.

Similar Triangles

When two triangles are similar, their corresponding angles are congruent and their corresponding sides are proportional.

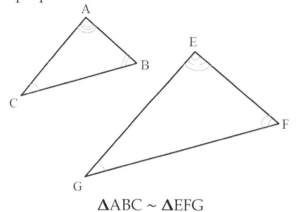

$$\Delta ABC \sim \Delta EFG$$
$$m\angle A = m\angle E, \ m\angle B = m\angle F, \ m\angle C = m\angle G$$
$$\frac{AB}{EF} = \frac{AC}{EG} = \frac{BC}{FG}$$

Problem Solving Skills

Easy

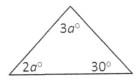

Note: Figure not drawn to scale.

1. Based on the figure above, what is the value of a?
   a) 25
   b) 30
   c) 35
   d) 40

Answer: (B)
Sum of Interior Angles = 180º
3a + 2a + 30 = 180
a = 30

2. In a triangle, one angle is double the size of another angle. If the measure of the third angle is 30 degrees, what is the measure of the largest angle in degrees?
   a) 70°
   b) 80°
   c) 90°
   d) 100°

Answer: (D)
Let x and 2x be two unknown angles.
30 +2x + x = 180°
x = 50°
The largest angle is 2 × 50 = 100°.

3. In the figure below, if $a = 3c$, and $b = 2a$, what is the value of c?

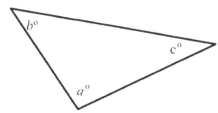

Note: Figure not drawn to scale.

   a) 18
   b) 20
   c) 28
   d) 34

Answer: (A)
a + b + c = 180
3c + 6c + c = 180
c = 18

Answer: (C)

4. What is the length of the third side in the triangle above?
   a) 8
   b) 9
   c) 10
   d) 12

Isosceles triangle with base angles of 60° is an equilateral triangle.
The two angles at the base must be equal, so this triangle must be an equilateral triangle. This means that the third side has length 10.

5. A 24-foot-long ladder is placed against a building to form a triangle with the sides of the building and ground. If the angle between ladder and ground is 60°, how far is the bottom of the ladder to the base of the building?
   a) 10
   b) $10\sqrt{3}$
   c) 12
   d) $12\sqrt{3}$

Answer: (C)
Since the building makes a 90° angle with the ground, the triangle must be a 30−60−90 special right triangle. The ladder itself is the hypotenuse and the bottom of the ladder to the base of the building is across from the 30° angle. Therefore, the distance between the bottom of the ladder and the base of the building is one half of the length of the ladder.

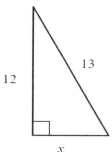

6. In the right triangle above, what is the value of x?

Answer: 5
Use the Pythagorean Theorem.
$x^2 + 12^2 = 13^2$
$x = 5$

7. A square and an equilateral triangle have equal perimeter. If the square has an area of 36 square feet, what is the length of one side of the triangle, in feet?
   a) 4
   b) 6
   c) 8
   d) 10

Answer: (C)
The length of a side of the square: $\sqrt{36}$ = 6. The perimeter of this square is 4 × 6 = 24. Let x be the length of one side of the triangle. The perimeter of the triangle is 3x.
$3x = 24 \rightarrow x = 8$

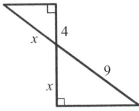

8. In the figure above, what is the value of x?
    a) 9
    b) 8
    c) 6
    d) $3\sqrt{5}$

Answer: (C)
The two triangles are similar by
the AA Similarity Theorem.
$\frac{x}{9} = \frac{4}{x}$
$x^2 = 36$
$x = 6$

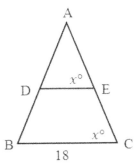

9. In the figure above, if $\overline{AD} = \overline{DB}$, what is the length of $\overline{DE}$?
    a) 6
    b) 9
    c) $9\sqrt{2}$
    d) 12

Answer: (B)
$\triangle ABC$ and $\triangle ADE$ are similar by
the AA Similarity Thoerem.
$\frac{AD}{AB} = \frac{1}{2} = \frac{DE}{BC}$
$\frac{1}{2} = \frac{DE}{18}$
$DE = 9$

Medium

10. In the figure below, $\triangle ABC$ is an equilateral triangle. What is the value of $x + y$ in degrees?

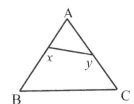

Answer: 240
The sum of the interior angles of a
quadrilateral triangle is 360°.
$60° + 60° + x + y = 360°$
$x + y = 240°$

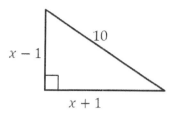

11. The figure above is a right triangle. If $x > 1$, what is the value of x?
    a) 6
    b) 7
    c) 8
    d) 9

Answer: (B)
Use the Pythagorean Theorem.
$(x-1)^2 + (x+1)^2 = 10^2$
$x^2 - 2x + 1 + x^2 + 2x + 1 = 100$
$2x^2 + 2 = 100$
$x^2 = 49$
$x = 7$

12. In the figure below shows $\triangle ABC$ and its exterior angle $\angle DAC$. What is the value of a?

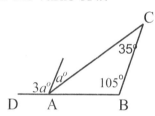

Answer: 35
$3a + a = 35 + 105 = 140$
$4a = 140$
$a = 35$

13. The three interior angle measures of a triangle have the ratio $3 : 4 : 5$. What is the sum of the measures, in degrees, of the smallest and largest angles?
    a) 100°
    b) 110°
    c) 120°
    d) 140°

Answer: (C)
We can define the measures of the three angles to be 3x, 4x, and 5x.
$3x + 4x + 5x = 180°$
$x = 15°$
$3x + 5x = 8x = 8 \times 15 = 120°$

14. The three angles of a triangle have measures $x°$, $2x°$, and $4y°$, where $x > 56$. If x and y are integers, what is one possible value of y?

Answer: 1 or 2
$x + 2x + 4y = 180$
$4y = 180 - 3x$
$4y < 180 - 3 \times 56$
$4y < 12 \rightarrow y < 3$
$y = 1, 2$

Hard

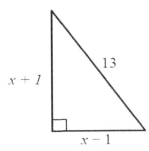

15. In the figure shown above, we assume that $x > 1$. What is the value of $2x^2 + 1$?

    a) 166
    b) 167
    c) 168
    d) 169

Answer: (C)
Use the Pythagorean Theorem.
$(x - 1)^2 + (x + 1)^2 = 13^2$
$x^2 - 2x + 1 + x^2 + 2x + 1 = 169$
$2x^2 + 1 = 168$

16. The lengths of the sides of a right triangle are consecutive even integers, and the length of the shortest side is x. Which of the following equations could be used to find x?

    a) $x^2 + (x + 1)^2 = (x + 2)^2$
    b) $x^2 + (x + 2)^2 = (x + 4)^2$
    c) $x + x + 2 = x + 4$
    d) $x^2 = (x + 2)(x + 4)$

Answer: (B)
Consecutive even integers can be written as x, $x + 2$, and $x + 4$. The longest side, $x + 4$, is the hypotenuse.
Apply the Pythagorean Theorem.
$x^2 + (x + 2)^2 = (x + 4)^2$

III.   CIRCLES

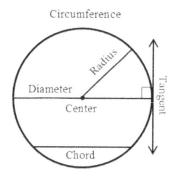

Segments of a Circle

The **radius** is a line segment that connects the center of a circle with any point on the circle. The lengths of all the radii of a circle are equal. A **chord** is a line segment that connects any two points on a circle. The **diameter** is a chord that passes through the center of the circle. The diameter is the longest chord in the circle and has length equal to twice the radius. A **tangent** line is a line that intersects the circle at exactly one point. A radius that touches the point of the tangent is perpendicular to the tangent line.

A radius that is perpendicular to a chord bisects the chord:

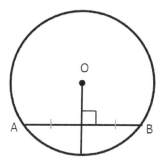

Arc Length and Circumference of the Circle

An **arc** is a curved segment of the circle. Connecting two endpoints of the arc to the center of the circle forms a **central angle**. An arc with a central angle less than 180° is called **minor arc** while an arc with a central angle greater than 180° is called **major arc**. A diameter divides its circle into two equal arcs of 180° known as **semicircles**.

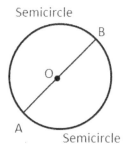

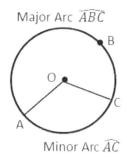

Circumference of a Circle

The **circumference** of a circle is equal to $2\pi r$, where r is the radius of the circle.

Example: Find the circumference of the circle below.

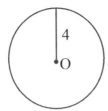

Answer: $r = 4$

$2\pi r = 2\pi \times 4 = 8\pi$

Length of an Arc

A whole circle has $360°$. An arc with a central angle of θ is $\dfrac{\theta}{360}$ of a whole circle, so the

length of the arc is equal to : $\dfrac{\theta}{360} \times 2\pi r$

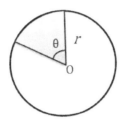

Example: Find the length of arc AB in the figure below.

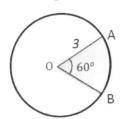

Answer: $r = 3$, so the length of arc $AB = \dfrac{\theta}{360} \times 2\pi r = \dfrac{60}{360} \times 2\pi(3) = \pi.$

Area of a Circle

The area of a circle is πr^2, where r is the radius of the circle.

Example: Find the area of the circle below.

Answer: $r = 5$

$\pi r^2 = \pi \times 5^2 = 25\pi$

Area of a Sector

A **sector** with a central angle of θ is $\dfrac{\theta}{360}$ of a whole circle, so the area of the sector is $\dfrac{\theta}{360}\pi r^2$.

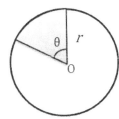

Example: Find the area of sector with the central angle $60°$ in the figure below.

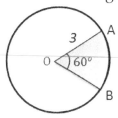

Answer: $\dfrac{\theta}{360}\pi r^2 = \dfrac{60}{360}\pi(3)^2 = \dfrac{3}{2}\pi$

Equations of Circles

A circle is the set of all points on a plane that are a fixed distance from a point, its center. The fixed distance is the radius of the circle. Any equation that can be written in the form of $(x - h)^2 + (y - k)^2 = r^2$ is a graph of the circle with radius r and center at point (h, k).

Example: Find the center and radius of the circle given by the equation
$$(x - 2)^2 + (y + 1)^2 = 4.$$
Answer: According to the standard equation of a circle, the center of this circle is $(2, -1)$ and the radius is 2.

Example: Find the center and radius of the circle given by the equation $x^2 + y^2 - 4x + 2y = 20$.
Answer: Rewrite the original equation into the standard equation of a circle:
$$x^2 + y^2 - 4x + 2y = 20$$
$$(x^2 - 4x + 2^2) + (y^2 + 2y + 1^2) = 20 + 2^2 + 1^2 = 25$$
$$(x - 2)^2 + (y + 1)^2 = 5^2$$
The center of the circle is $(2, -1)$ and the radius is 5.

Problem Solving Skills

Easy

1. The diameter of a semi-circle is 4. What is its perimeter?
   a) $2\pi + 2$
   b) $2\pi + 4$
   c) $2\pi + 6$
   d) $\pi + 2$

   Answer: (B)
   The perimeter of semicircle is the sum of half of the circumference of a circle plus the length of the diameter.
   Perimeter = $\frac{1}{2}(2\pi r) + 2r$
   $= \frac{1}{2} \times 2\pi \times 2 + 2 \times 2 = 2\pi + 4$

2. A chord of a circle is 2 inches away from the center of the circle at its closest point. If the circle has a 3-inch radius, what is the length of this chord, in inches?
   a) 1
   b) $\sqrt{5}$
   c) 2
   d) $2\sqrt{5}$

   Answer: (D)

   $x = \sqrt{3^2 - 2^2} = \sqrt{5}$
   Length of Chord = $2\sqrt{5}$ inches

3. Point O is the center of the circle in the figure below. If angle ∠PQO = 65°, what is the measure of the center angle ∠POQ in degrees?

   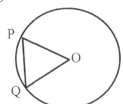

   Answer: 50
   Triangle PQO is an isosceles triangle with base angles 65°.
   $2 \times m\angle PQO + m\angle POQ = 180°$
   $m\angle PQO = 65°$
   $m\angle POQ = 180 - 2 \times 65 = 50°$

   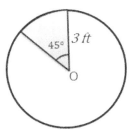

4. In the figure above, the circle has a center O and radius of 3 ft. What is the area of the shaded portion, in square feet?
   a) $\frac{3}{4}\pi$
   b) $\frac{9}{8}\pi$
   c) $\frac{11}{8}\pi$
   d) 1.5π

   Answer: (B)
   The area of the shaded portion is $\frac{45}{360}$ of the area of the whole circle.
   Shaded Area = $\frac{45}{360} \times \pi \times 3^2 = \frac{9}{8}\pi$

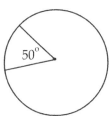

5. In the figure above, a piece with a 50° center angle has been cut out of an 18-ounce pie. How many ounces was the piece of pie that was cut out?

Answer: 2.5
Weight of Pie : 360° = Weight of Piece : 50°
18 : 360° = x : 50°
$\frac{18}{360} = \frac{x}{50}$ → *x = 2.5 ounces*

6. In the figure below, points A and B lie on circle O. If ∠AOB = y°, what is the value of x in term of y?

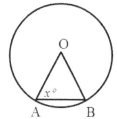

Answer : (D)
ΔOAB is an isosceles Δ.
2 × x + y = 180
$x = \frac{1}{2}(180 - y) = 90 - \frac{1}{2}y$

a) y
b) 90 – y
c) 180 – y
d) $90 - \frac{1}{2}y$

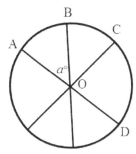

Note: Figure not drawn to scale.

7. In the figure above, O is the center of the circle, $\widehat{AB} = \widehat{BC}$, and $\widehat{AC} = \widehat{CD}$. What is the value of a, in degrees?

Answer: 45
$\widehat{AB}$ is half of $\widehat{AC}$ so it is $\frac{1}{4}$ of $\widehat{AD}$.
$A = \frac{1}{4} × 180°$
a = 45°

8. In the circle below, hexagon ABCDEF is equilateral. What is the ratio of the length of arc ABCD to the length of arc AFE?

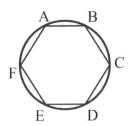

a) 1 to 2
b) 2 to 3
c) 3 to 2
d) 4 to 5

Answer: (C)
The arc ABCD is 3 times the arc AB and arc AFE is 2 times the arc AB (since the polygon is regular).
ABCD : AFE = 3 : 2

9. The area of circle A is 9 times the area of circle B. What is the ratio of the diameter of circle A to the diameter of circle B?
a) $9:1$
b) $6:1$
c) $3:1$
d) $3:2$

Answer: (C)
The ratio of the diameter of two circles is the square root of the ratio of their areas.
Ratio = $\sqrt{9} : \sqrt{1}$ = 3 : 1

10. What is the difference, in degrees, between an arc that is $\frac{3}{8}$ of a circle and an arc that is $\frac{1}{3}$ of a circle?
a) $20°$
b) $18°$
c) $15°$
d) $12°$

Answer: (C)
$\left(\frac{3}{8}-\frac{1}{3}\right) \times 360° = 15°$

11. Segment $\overline{AB}$ is the diameter of a circle with center O. Another point C lies on circle O. If AC = 6 and BC = 8, what is the area of circle O?
a) 25π
b) 50π
c) 100π
d) 200π

Answer: (A)
ΔABC is a right triangle.
$AB^2 = AC^2 + BC^2$
$AB = \sqrt{6^2 + 8^2} = 10$
$Radius = \frac{1}{2}(10) = 5$
$Area = \pi \times 5^2 = 25\pi$

12. One circle has a radius of 3 and another circle has a radius of 2. What is the ratio of the area of the larger circle to the area of the smaller circle?
a) $3:2$
b) $9:4$
c) $3:1$
d) $4:1$

Answer: (B)
The ratio of the areas of two circles is equal to the square of the ratio of their radius.
$3^2 : 2^2 = 9 : 4$

Medium

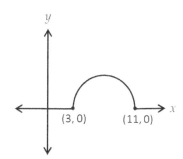

13. The figure above shows a circle with center O. Segments AB and CD are perpendicular and AB passes through point O. If the length of AB is 10 and length of CD is 8, what is the distance of O to line CD?

a) 2
b) 3
c) 4
d) 5

Answer: (B)

$$Distance = \sqrt{\overline{OC}^2 - \left(\frac{CD}{2}\right)^2}$$
$$= \sqrt{5^2 - 4^2} = 3$$

14. In the figure above, what is the sum of the x and y coordinates of the highest point on the above semicircle?

a) 6
b) 8
c) 9
d) 11

Answer: (D)
The highest point is at the middle of semicircle.

y-Coordinate = Radius = $\frac{11-3}{2}$ = 4
x-Coordinate = $\frac{1}{2}$ (3 + 11) = 7
x-Coordinate + y-Coordinate = 11

15. In the figure below, the two circles are tangent at point P and OQ = 9. If the area of the circle with center O is four times the area of the circle with center Q, what is the length of OP?

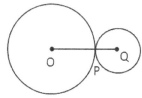

a) 2
b) 4
c) 6
d) 8

Answer: (C)
Since the area of circle O is four times the area of circle Q, the radius of circle O is $\sqrt{4}$ times of the radius of circle Q.
If PQ = r, OP = 2r, then r + 2r = 9.
R = 3 = PQ
OP = 9 – 3 = 6

16. In the figure above, O is the center of the two circles. If the bigger circle has a radius of 5 and the smaller circle has a radius of 4, what is the area of shaded region?

    a) 2π
    b) π
    c) $\frac{9}{8}\pi$
    d) $\frac{1}{2}\pi$

Answer: (C)

Area $= \frac{45}{360}(\pi \times 5^2 - \pi \times 4^2) = \frac{9}{8}\pi$

Hard

17. In the figure below, rectangle ABOC is drawn in circle O. If OB = 3 and OC = 4, what is the area of the shaded region?

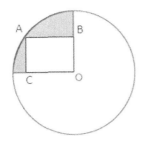

    a) $6\pi - 3$
    b) $\frac{25\pi}{4} - 12$
    c) $25\pi - 12$
    d) $\frac{25\pi}{4} - 3$

Answer: (B)

OA is the radius of the circle and the shaded area is the area of the quarter circle minus the area of the rectangle.

Radius $= \sqrt{OB^2 + OC^2} = \sqrt{3^2 + 4^2} = 5$

Shaded Area = Area of $\frac{1}{4}$ Circle – Area of Rectangle =

$\frac{1}{4}(\pi \times 5^2) - 4 \times 3$

$= \frac{1}{4} \times 25\pi - 12$

$= \frac{25\pi}{4} - 12$

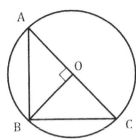

18. In the figure above, a circle O with diameter $\overline{AC}$ has an area of 16π. What is the length of segment $\overline{AB}$?
    a) 4
    b) 6
    c) $6\sqrt{2}$
    d) $4\sqrt{2}$

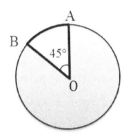

19. The circle above has an area of 16π. What is the perimeter of the shaded region?
    a) $8 - \frac{1}{3}\pi$
    b) $8 + 7\pi$
    c) $8 + \frac{2}{3}\pi$
    d) $8 + \frac{1}{3}\pi$

IV.   AREAS AND VOLUMES

CONCEPT OVERVIEWS

Area of a Triangle

$$Area\ of\ a\ Triangle = \frac{Base \times Height}{2}$$

The **height** of a triangle is the perpendicular distance from the **base** to the opposite vertex.

Some different triangles with different bases and heights are shown below:

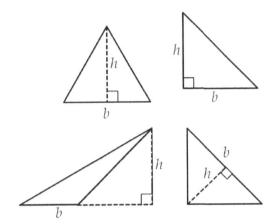

Area of an Equilateral Triangle = $\frac{\sqrt{3}}{4} s^2$, where s is the length of a side.

Example: Find the area of this triangle.

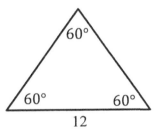

Solution: This is an equilateral triangle with equal side length of 12.
The easy way to solve this problem is to apply the formula for finding the area of an equilateral.

$$A = \frac{\sqrt{3}}{4}s^2 = \frac{\sqrt{3}}{4} \times 12^2 = 36\sqrt{3}$$

If the ratio of the corresponding sides of two similar triangles is $a : b$, then the ratio of their areas is $a^2 : b^2$.

Example: Find the area of triangle B if the triangles A and B are similar.

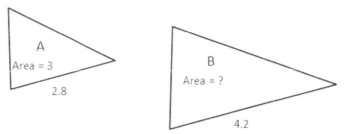

Solution: In two similar triangles, the ratio of their areas is equal to the square of the ratio of their sides.

Let the area of B be x.

Set up the proportion: $\left(\dfrac{2.8}{4.2}\right)^2 = \dfrac{3}{x} \rightarrow \dfrac{0.44}{1} = \dfrac{3}{x}$

Cross multiply: $0.44x = 3 \rightarrow x = 6.82$

Area of a Parallelogram: Base × Height

$$A = b \times h$$

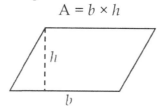

Area of a Rectangle: Length × Width

$$A = l \times w$$

Area of a Square:
- Side × Side = (Side)²
- $\dfrac{1}{2}$ × (Diagonal)²

$$A = s^2 = \frac{1}{2}d^2$$

Area of a Rhombus: $\frac{1}{2} \times$ Diagonal 1 $\times$ Diagonal 2

$$A = \frac{1}{2} \times d_1 \times d_2$$

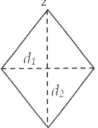

Area of a Trapezoid: $\frac{1}{2} \times$ (Base 1 + Base 2) $\times$ Height

$$A = \frac{1}{2} \times (b_1 + b_2) \times h$$

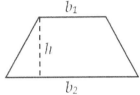

Volumes of 3-D Figures
Cubes
Surface area: $6a^2$
Volume: a^3

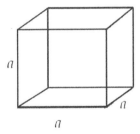

Rectangular Prisms
Surface area: $2(w \times h + l \times w + l \times h)$
Volume: $l \times w \times h$
Diagonal of a rectangular prism: $d = \sqrt{h^2 + l^2 + w^2}$

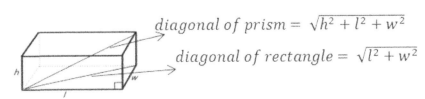

$$\text{diagonal of prism} = \sqrt{h^2 + l^2 + w^2}$$
$$\text{diagonal of rectangle} = \sqrt{l^2 + w^2}$$

Cylinders
Surface area: $2\pi r^2 + 2\pi rh$
Volume: $\pi r^2 h$

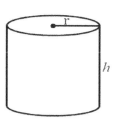

Cones
Volume: $\frac{1}{3}$ (Area of Base) × (Height) = $\frac{1}{3} \pi r^2 h$

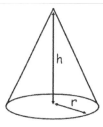

Pyramids
Volume: $\frac{1}{3}$ (Area of Base) × (Height) = $\frac{1}{3} l \times w \times h$

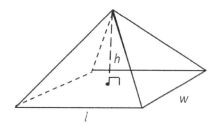

Problem Solving Skills

Easy

1. A rectangular storage room has a volume of 9,375 cubic feet. If its length is 75 feet and its height is 5 feet, what is the width of the room?

Answer: 25
Volume = Length × Height × Width
9375 = 75 × 5 × Width
Width = 25 feet

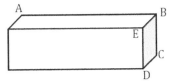

2. In the rectangular solid above, the area of BCDE is 10 and $\overline{AB}$ = 12. What is the volume of this solid?
   a) 120
   b) 180
   c) 240
   d) 90

Answer: (A)
Volume = Area of Base × Height =
10 × 12 = 120

3. A truck has a container with dimensions 40 × 12 × 8 feet. How many cubic boxes with side length of 2 feet can fit into the container?

Answer: 480
Total Number of Boxes =
$\frac{40}{2} \times \frac{12}{2} \times \frac{8}{2}$ = 480 boxes

4. A rectangular box is 24 inches long, 18 inches wide, and 12 inches high. What is the least number of cubic boxes that can be stored perfectly in this box?
   a) 12
   b) 18
   c) 24
   d) 36

Answer: (C)
Cubic boxes' length, width, and height have the same length, so the number of cubic boxes must be a common factor of 24, 18, and 12. To find the minimum number of boxes, we need to find the GCF (greatest common factor) of these three numbers.
The GCF of 24, 18 and 12 is 6, so there are $\frac{24}{6} \times \frac{18}{6} \times \frac{12}{6}$ cubic boxes.
$\frac{24}{6} \times \frac{18}{6} \times \frac{12}{6} = 24$

Answer: 432

5. The dimensions of the rectangular storage box shown on the above left are 2 feet by 2 feet by 1 foot. What is the maximum number of Lego blocks (shown on the right) that can fit inside the storage box if each Lego block has dimensions 4 inches by 4 inches by 1 inch?

2 feet by 2 feet by 1 foot = 24 inches by 24 inches by 12 inches
$\frac{24}{4} \times \frac{24}{4} \times \frac{12}{1}$ = 432 Legos

Medium

6. The cube shown above has side length a. What is the length of its diagonal as drawn?
   a) a
   b) $2a$
   c) $\sqrt{2}a$
   d) $\sqrt{3}a$

Answer: (D)

Diagonal $= \sqrt{a^2 + a^2 + a^2} = \sqrt{3}a$

7. What is the volume of a cube if its total surface area is 96 square units?

Answer: 64
Let a be the length of one side of the cube.
Surface Area $= 6 \times a^2 = 96$
$a = 4$
Volume $= a^3 = 4^3 = 64$

Hard

Questions 8 – 9 refer to the following information:
   Density describes how compact or concentrated a material is. It is defined as the ratio between mass and volume, or mass per unit volume. The formula to calculate the density is:

$$Density = \frac{Mass}{Volume}$$

8. The kilobar of gold is 1,000 grams in mass. If the density of the gold bar is 19.3 grams per cm^3, what would be the volume of the kilobar, in cm^3? (Round your answer to the nearest tenth)

Answer: 51.8
Density $= \frac{Mass}{Volume}$
$19.3 = \frac{1000}{Volume}$
Volume $= \frac{1000}{19.3} = 51.8 \ cm^3$

9. If a cylinder gold block has a diameter of 2 centimeters and height of 10 centimeters, what would be its mass, in grams? (Round your answer to the nearest whole number.)

Answer: 606
Volume $= \pi r^2 h = \pi \times 1^2 \times 10$
Mass $= 19.3 \times 10\pi = 606.3$

V.   Trigonometric Functions

Concept Overviews

Right Triangle Trigonometry

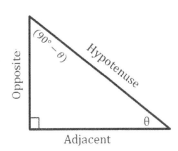

SOH CAH TOA

$$sin(\theta) = \frac{Opposite}{Hypotenuse} = cos(90° - \theta)$$

$$cos(\theta) = \frac{Adjacent}{Hypotenuse} = sin(90° - \theta)$$

$$tan(\theta) = \frac{Opposite}{Adjacent} = cot(90° - \theta)$$

Pythagorean Theorem: $Hypotenuse^2 = Adjacent^2 + Opposite^2$

Example: If $0 < \theta < 90°$ and $sin(\theta) = \frac{3}{5}$, what are the values of $cos(\theta)$ and $tan(\theta)$?

Solution: If $sin(\theta) = \frac{3}{5}$, we can represent $sin(\theta)$ as the following triangle:

According to the Pythagorean Theorem, the length of the adjacent side is $\sqrt{5^2 - 3^2} = 4$. Therefore, $cos(\theta) = \frac{4}{5}$ and $tan(\theta) = \frac{3}{4}$

Example: What is the height of the tree according to the following figure?

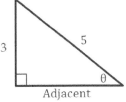

Solution: $tan(40°) = \frac{h}{50}$

$h = 50 \times tan(40°) = 50 \times 0.8391 = 41.95$ ft.

A unit circle is a circle with a radius of 1 centered at the origin on the coordinate plane as shown in the figure below.

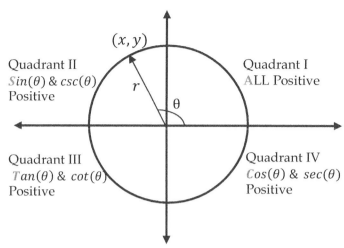

Use the mnemonic *"All Students Take Calculus!"*

$$sin(\theta) = \frac{y}{r} \qquad cos(\theta) = \frac{x}{r} \qquad tan(\theta) = \frac{y}{x}$$
$$csc\,(\theta) = \frac{r}{y} \qquad sec\,(\theta) = \frac{r}{x} \qquad cot\,(\theta) = \frac{x}{y}$$

There are two **special right triangles** that you need to remember:

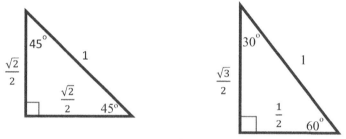

Some important angles, $0°, 30°, 45°, 60°,$ and $90°,$ and their sine, cosine, and tangent values are summarized below:

θ	$sin(\theta)$	$cos(\theta)$	$tan(\theta)$
0°	0	1	0
30°	$\frac{1}{2}$	$\frac{\sqrt{3}}{2}$	$\frac{\sqrt{3}}{3}$
45°	$\frac{\sqrt{2}}{2}$	$\frac{\sqrt{2}}{2}$	1
60°	$\frac{\sqrt{3}}{2}$	$\frac{1}{2}$	$\sqrt{3}$
90°	1	0	undefined

A **cofunction** is a trigonometric function whose value for the complement of a given angle is equal to the value of a trigonometric function of the angle itself. Pairs of cofunctions are sine and cosine, tangent and cotangent, and secant and cosecant.

$$sin(\theta) = cos(90° - \theta) \qquad cos(\theta) = sin(90° - \theta)$$
$$tan(\theta) = cot(90° - \theta) \qquad cot(\theta) = tan(90° - \theta)$$
$$sec(\theta) = csc(90° - \theta) \qquad csc(\theta) = sec(90° - \theta)$$

Example: One angle measures x, where $sin(x) = \frac{2}{3}$. What is $cos(90° - x)$?

Solution: $cos(90° - x) = sin(x) = \frac{2}{3}$

Radians and **degrees** are two units for measuring angles. A full circle has a total angle of 360 degrees or 2π radians.

The formulas to convert between degrees and radians are:
$$\text{Degrees} = \frac{180}{\pi} \times \text{Radians}$$
$$\text{Radians} = \frac{\pi}{180} \times \text{Degrees}$$

Example: What is the angle $225°$ in radians?

Solution: $\text{Radians} = \frac{\pi}{180} \times 225 = \frac{5}{4}\pi$

Example: Convert 2.36 radians to degrees.

Solution: $\text{Degrees} = \frac{180}{\pi} \times 2.36 = 135°$

Problem Solving Skills

Easy

1. If $0 < \theta < 90°$ and $cos(\theta) = \frac{5}{13}$, what is the value of $sin(\theta)$?

   a) $\frac{12}{13}$

   b) $\frac{5}{13}$

   c) $\frac{4}{5}$

   d) $\frac{5}{12}$

   Answer: (A)

   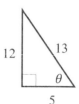

   $sin(\theta) = \frac{12}{13}$

2. A seven feet long ladder leans against a wall and makes an angle of $60°$ with the ground. How high up the wall does the ladder reach?

   a) $\frac{2\sqrt{3}}{7}$

   b) $\frac{7\sqrt{3}}{2}$

   c) $\frac{\sqrt{3}}{14}$

   d) $7\sqrt{3}$

   Answer: (B)

   $sin(60°) = \frac{Height}{7} = \frac{\sqrt{3}}{2}$

   $Height = 7 \times \frac{\sqrt{3}}{2} = \frac{7\sqrt{3}}{2}$

   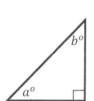

3. In the triangle above, the sine of $b°$ is 0.8. What is the cosine of $a°$?

   a) 0.8

   b) 0.6

   c) 0.4

   d) 0.2

   Answer: (A)
   Use the value of $sin(b°)$ and the Pythagorean Theorem to find the ratio of lengths of sides of the right

   triangle.
   $cos(a°) = sin(90° - a°) = 0.8$
   Or $cos(a°) = \frac{8}{10} = 0.8$

4. If $sin(\frac{\pi}{2} - x) = 0.35$, what is $cos\ x$?

   a) 0.35

   b) 0.43

   c) 0.45

   d) 0.53

   Answer: (A)
   Cofuntion: The value of a trigonometric function of an angle is equal to the value of the cofunction of the complement of that angle.
   $sin(\theta) = cos(90° - \theta)$
   $cos(\theta) = sin(90° - \theta)$

5. If $a + b = 90°$, which of the following must be true?
    a) $cos(a) = cos(b)$
    b) $sin(a) = sin(b)$
    c) $sin(a) = cos(b)$
    d) $sin(a) = -cos(b)$

Answer: (C)
Cofuntion: The value of a trigonometric function of an angle is equal to the value of the cofunction of the complement of that angle.
$sin(\theta) = cos(90° - \theta)$
$cos(\theta) = sin(90° - \theta)$

6. $45°$ is equivalent to an angle measure of
    a) $\frac{1}{4}$ radians
    b) $\frac{\pi}{4}$ radians
    c) $\frac{\pi}{3}$ radians
    d) $\frac{\pi}{2}$ radians

Answer: (B)
$Radians = \frac{\pi}{180} \times 45 = \frac{\pi}{4}$

7. How many degrees are in 1.65 radians?
    a) 94.54
    b) 78.56
    c) 10.88
    d) 0.029

Answer: (A)
$Degrees = \frac{180}{\pi} \times 1.65 = 94.54$

8. Which of the following trigonometric functions is (are) positive in the third Quadrant?
    a) $sin(x)$
    b) $cos\ (x)$
    c) $tan(x)$
    d) All of the above

Answer: (C)
Use the mnemonic "All Students Take Calculus!!"

9. Which of the following cofunctions is (are) true?
    a) $sin(90° - x) = cos(x)$
    b) $cos(90° - x) = sin(x)$
    c) $tan(90° - x) = cot(x)$
    d) All of the above

Answer: (D)
Cofuntion: The value of a trigonometric function of an angle is equal to the value of the cofunction of the complement of that angle.

10. A shaft, pivoted at one end, spins through $\frac{4\pi}{3}$ radians. If the shaft is 15 centimeters long, what is the distance (in cm) that the shaft travels?
    a) 5π
    b) 10π
    c) 15π
    d) 20π

Answer: (D)
Find the length of the arc.
$l = r\theta = 15 \times \frac{4\pi}{3} = 20\pi$

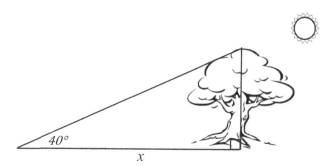

11. When the Sun is 40° above the horizon, how long is the shadow cast by a tree which is 55 feet tall? (Round your answer to the nearest tenth.)

Answer: 65.5

$tan(40°) = \frac{55}{x}$

$x = \frac{55}{tan(40°)} = \frac{55}{0.8391} = 65.5$

12. If an angle θ measured counter-clockwise from the positive x-axis terminates in the third Quadrant, which of the following is true?
    a) Both of $sin(\theta)$ and $cos(\theta)$ are negative.
    b) Both of $sin(\theta)$ and $cos(\theta)$ are positive.
    c) $sin(\theta)$ is negative and $cos(\theta)$ is positive.
    d) $sin(\theta)$ is positive and $cos(\theta)$ is negative.

Answer: (A)
Use the mnemonic "All Students Take Calculus!!"

Medium

13. In triangle ABC, the measure of $\angle C$ is $90°$, $AB = 15$, and $BC = 12$. Triangle XYZ is similar to triangle ABC, where vertices X, Y, and Z correspond to vertices A, B, and C, respectively. If each side of triangle XYZ is $\frac{1}{3}$ the length of the corresponding side of triangle ABC, what is the value of $sin(X)$?

Answer: $\frac{4}{5}$ or 0.8

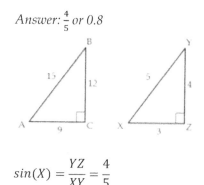

$sin(X) = \frac{YZ}{XY} = \frac{4}{5}$

14. A ramp is 60 meters long and set at a 25° angle of inclination. If you walk up to the top of the ramp, how high off the ground will you be?
    a) 25.357 meters
    b) 26.561 meters
    c) 27.91 meters
    d) 28.13 meters

Answer: (A)

$sin(25°) = \frac{x}{60}$
$x = sin(25°) \times 60$
$x = 25.357$

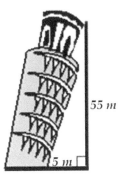

15. If the Leaning Tower of Pisa is 55 meters tall and the top edge of the tower leans 5 meters out from the bottom edge, what is *sine* of the angle created between the ground and the tower?

    a) 1

    b) 0.091

    c) 0.993

    d) 0.996

Answer: (D)
Use the Pythogoream Theorm to find the hypotenuse.
$Hypotenuse = \sqrt{55^2 + 5^2} = 55.23\ m$
$sin(\theta) = \dfrac{55}{55.23} = 0.996$

Hard

Note: Figures not drawn to scale.

16. The angles shown above are acute, and $sin(x^o) = cos(y^o)$. If $x = 3k - 11$ and $y = 2k - 9$, what is the value of k?

    a) 12

    b) 22

    c) 23.5

    d) 27.5

Answer: (B)
$(3k - 11) + (2k - 9) = 90$
$k = 22$

Chapter 5   Ten Math Mock Tests

Math Mock Test 1
22 QUESTIONS

DIRECTIONS

The questions in this section address a number of important math skills.

Use of a calculator is permitted for all questions.

o **Check the answers after the Module 1 test. If there are more than 8 questions answered incorrectly in Module 1, take the Easy part of Module 2. Otherwise, take the Hard part of Module 2.**

NOTES

Unless otherwise indicated:
- All variables and expressions represent real numbers.
- Figures provided are drawn to scale.
- All figures lie in a plane.
- The domain of a given function f i s the set of all real numbers x for which f(x) is a real number.

REFERENCE

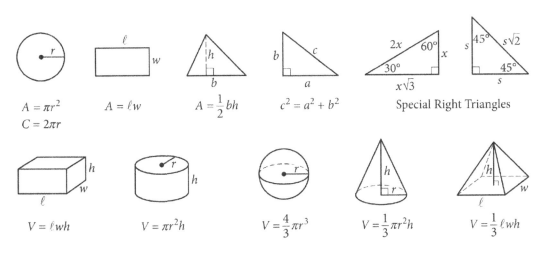

$A = \pi r^2$ $A = \ell w$ $A = \dfrac{1}{2}bh$ $c^2 = a^2 + b^2$ Special Right Triangles

$C = 2\pi r$

$V = \ell w h$ $V = \pi r^2 h$ $V = \dfrac{4}{3}\pi r^3$ $V = \dfrac{1}{3}\pi r^2 h$ $V = \dfrac{1}{3}\ell w h$

The number of degrees of arc in a circle is **360**.

The number of radians of arc in a circle is 2π.

The sum of the measures in degrees of the angles of a triangle is **180**.

For multiple-choice questions, solve each problem, choose the correct answer from the choices provided, and then circle your answer in this book. Circle only one answer for each question. If you change your mind, completely erase the circle. You will not get credit for questions with more than one answer circled, or for questions with no answers circled.

For student-produced response questions, solve each problem and write your answer next to or under the question in the test book as described below.

- Once you've written your answer, circle it clearly. You will not receive credit for anything written outside the circle, or for any questions with more than one circled answer.
- If you find **more than one correct answer**, write and circle only one answer. Your answer can be up to 5 characters for a **positive** answer and up to 6 characters (including the negative sign) for a **negative** answer, but no more.
- If your answer is a **fraction** that is too long (over 5 characters for positive, 6 characters for negative), write the decimal equivalent.
- If your answer is a **decimal** that is too long (over 5 characters for positive,
- 6 characters for negative), truncate it or round at the fourth digit.
- If your answer is a **mixed number** (such as $3\frac{1}{2}$, write it as an improper fraction (7/2) or its decimal equivalent (3.5).
- Don't include symbols such as a percent sign, comma, or dollar sign in your circled answer.

$$x + y = 21$$
$$x - 2y = -3$$

1. According to the system of equations above, what is the value of x?
   - a) 6
   - b) 8
   - c) 13
   - d) 15

2. If $\sqrt{k + 3} - 6 = 0$, k is a constant. What is the value of k?
   - a) 1
   - b) 3
   - c) 9
   - d) 33

3. Which of the following is an equation of the line in the xy-plane that has a slope of $\frac{1}{2}$ and passes through the point $(0, -2)$?
   - a) $y = -\frac{1}{2} + 2$
   - b) $y = -2x - 2$
   - c) $y = 2x - 2$
   - d) $y = \frac{1}{2}x - 2$

4. If $3a - 2b = 5$ and $a + 2b = 23$, then $a + b$?
   - a) −5
   - b) 5
   - c) 10
   - d) 15

5. Which of the following represents the graph of the function $f(x) = |-2x + 3|$ in the xy-plane?

   a)

   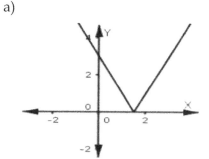

b)

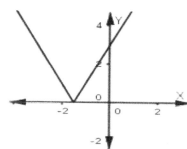

c)

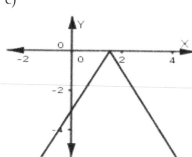

d)

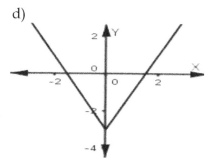

6. The function $j \triangledown k = \left(\frac{j}{k}\right)^j$. If $j \triangledown k = -8$ when $j = -3$, what is the value of k?

7. If $5x = 4y^2 = 20$, what is the value of xy^2?

8. If $x > 0$ and $x^y x^{\frac{1}{2}} = x^{\frac{1}{4}}$, what is the value of y?

     a) $\frac{1}{2}$

     b) $\frac{1}{4}$

     c) $-\frac{1}{4}$

     d) $-\frac{1}{2}$

9. If $|x - 2| = p$, where $x < 2$, then $x - p =$

     a) 2

     b) 2−2p

     c) 2p−2

     d) 2p + 2

10. It takes between 6 and 8 minutes for Joe to run one mile up to the hill during a marathon. The amount of time it takes for him to run a mile down the hill is 2 to 3 minutes shorter than the time it takes him to run up the hill. What is the range of possible times it would take Joe to run one mile down the hill?

     a) 4 and 5 minutes

     b) 3 and 6 minutes

     c) 5 and 7 minutes

     d) 6 and 8 minutes

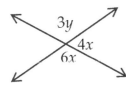

11. In the figure above, what is the value of $2x + y$?

     a) 60

     b) 72

     c) 85

     d) 100

12. In the xy-coordinate plane, lines m and n are perpendicular. If line m contains the points $(0, 0)$ and $(2, 1)$, and line n contains the points $(2, 3)$ and $(-1, a)$, what is the value of a?

     a) 6

     b) 9

     c) 0

     d) −9

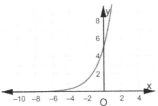

13. The graph of the function f is shown in the xy-plane above. The equation that describes $f(x) = ab^x$, where a and b are integers. What is the value of a?

14. If $r > 0$ and $\sqrt[3]{\frac{9r}{2}} = \frac{1}{2}r$, what is the value of r?

15. $a, b, x,$ and y are positive numbers. If $x^{-\frac{2}{3}} = a^{-2}$ and $y^{\frac{2}{3}} = b^4$, what is $(xy)^{-\frac{1}{3}}$ in terms of a and b?

     a) ab

     b) $a^{-1}b^{-2}$

     c) a^2b^2

     d) $a^{-2}b^{-2}$

16. If $3x + 1 = a$, then $6x + 1$?

     a) $a + 3$

     b) $a - 3$

     c) $2a - 1$

     d) $2a + 1$

17. The table below shows the number of cars sold by a certain brand of car dealerships for the first quarter of 2016 in five different locations. Based on the information in the table, what is the approximately probability of a car sold that is from the region II?

Number of Cars Sold in Five Locations

Locations	Months		
	Jan.	Feb.	Mar.
I	80	75	65
II	76	48	52
III	90	82	68
IV	52	68	72
V	64	62	60

   a) 6.4%
   b) 10.8%
   c) 17.4%
   d) 21.2 %

18. A rectangular solid has dimensions of $a \times b \times c$ where a, b and c are positive integers. Its volume is v and its surface area is s. If v is odd, which of the following must be true?

   I. a is odd.
   II. Both b and c are odds
   III. s is even.

   a) I only
   b) I and II only
   c) I and III only
   d) I, II, and III

19. Which of the following expressions is equivalent to $(4x^3)^{\frac{2}{3}}$?

   a) $2x^3\sqrt[3]{2}$
   b) $x^3\sqrt[3]{16}$
   c) $2x^2\sqrt[3]{2}$
   d) $2x^2\sqrt[3]{16}$

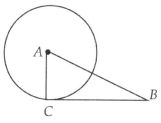

Note: Figure not drawn to scale.

20. In the figure above, the circle has center A, and line segment CB is tangent to the circle at point C. If $AB = 1.0$ and $CB = 0.6$, what is the length of the diameter of the circle?

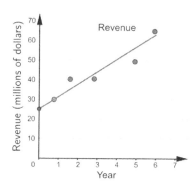

21. The scatterplot above shows the revenue, in millions of dollars, that a company earned over several years and a line of best fit for the data. In year 5, the difference between the actual revenue and the predicted revenue is n million dollars, where n is a positive integer. What is the value of n? Round your answer to the nearest whole number. (Disregard the $ sign when gridding your answer.)

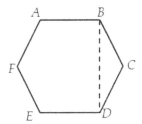

22. In the regular hexagon as shown above, if length of $\overline{AB}$ is 6, what is the length of $\overline{BD}$?

    a) 12
    b) 9
    c) $6\sqrt{3}$
    d) $6\sqrt{2}$

Math Mock Test 1
22 QUESTIONS

DIRECTIONS

The questions in this section address a number of important math skills.
Use of a calculator is permitted for all questions.

NOTES

Unless otherwise indicated:
- All variables and expressions represent real numbers.
- Figures provided are drawn to scale.
- All figures lie in a plane.
- The domain of a given function f i s the set of all real numbers x for which f(x) is a real number.

REFERENCE

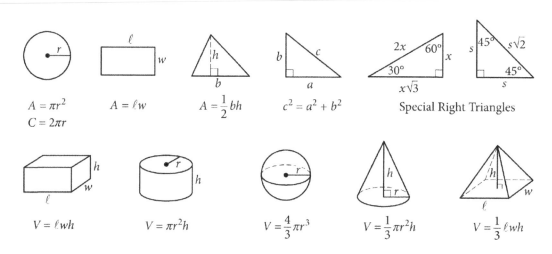

$$A = \pi r^2$$
$$C = 2\pi r$$

$$A = \ell w$$

$$A = \frac{1}{2}bh$$

$$c^2 = a^2 + b^2$$

Special Right Triangles

$$V = \ell wh$$

$$V = \pi r^2 h$$

$$V = \frac{4}{3}\pi r^3$$

$$V = \frac{1}{3}\pi r^2 h$$

$$V = \frac{1}{3}\ell wh$$

The number of degrees of arc in a circle is **360**.
The number of radians of arc in a circle is 2π.
The sum of the measures in degrees of the angles of a triangle is **180**.

For multiple-choice questions, solve each problem, choose the correct answer from the choices provided, and then circle your answer in this book. Circle only one answer for each question. If you change your mind, completely erase the circle. You will not get credit for questions with more than one answer circled, or for questions with no answers circled.

For student-produced response questions, solve each problem and write your answer next to or under the question in the test book as described below.

- Once you've written your answer, circle it clearly. You will not receive credit for anything written outside the
- circle, or for any questions with more than one circled answer.
- If you find **more than one correct answer**, write and circle only one answer. Your answer can be up to 5 characters for a **positive** answer and up to 6 characters (including the negative sign) for a **negative** answer, but no more.
- If your answer is a **fraction** that is too long (over 5 characters for positive, 6 characters for negative), write the decimal equivalent.

- If your answer is a **decimal** that is too long (over 5 characters for positive,
- 6 characters for negative), truncate it or round at the fourth digit.
- If your answer is a **mixed number** (such as $3\frac{1}{2}$, write it as an improper fraction (7/2) or its decimal equivalent (3.5).
- Don't include symbols such as a percent sign, comma, or dollar sign in your circled answer

1. Which of the lines described by the following equations best fits those points above?

   a) $y = \frac{1}{4}x + \frac{1}{2}$

   b) $y = \frac{1}{4}x + 1$

   c) $y = -\frac{1}{4}x - \frac{1}{2}$

   d) $y = -\frac{1}{2}x + \frac{1}{2}$

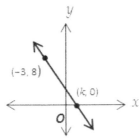

2. In the figure above, the slope of the line through points $(-3, 8)$ and $(k, 0)$ is -2. What is the value of k?

   a) 4

   b) 3

   c) 2

   d) 1

3. A car rental company charges $50 per day for the first 5 days, and $45 a day for each day after that. How much will Tom be charged if he rents a car for two weeks?

   a) $455

   b) $525

   c) $555

   d) $655

$$\begin{cases} \frac{1}{2}x = 6 \\ \frac{1}{6}x - \frac{1}{2}y = 1 \end{cases}$$

4. The system of equations above have solution (x, y). What is the value of y?

   a) 1

   b) 2

   c) −1

   d) −2

5. A cheetah can run at a maximum speed of 123 kilometers per hour. What is the cheetah's maximum speed, to the nearest mile per hour? (1 mile is approximately 1.61 kilometers.)

   a) 56

   b) 76

   c) 123

   d) 197

6. Mrs. Alan's class of 23 students will have a 3-day educational camp. Each student is expected to use one pack of index card each day. If index cards are bought as a box of six packs, how many boxes will Mrs. Alan have to buy?

7. At an intersection, a complete cycle of the traffic light takes 70 seconds. Within each cycle, the red light lasts for 30 seconds and the yellow light 10 seconds. If a driver arrives at the intersection at a random time, what is the probability that the light is green?

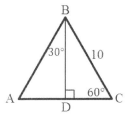

8. In $\triangle ABC$ above, what is the length of $\overline{AD}$?
   a) 3
   b) 5
   c) $5\sqrt{2}$
   d) 10

9. An analysis of a random sample of a type of laptop computer battery estimated that the mean working time was 4.5 hours with a margin of error of 0.5 hours. Which of the following is the most appropriate conclusion based on this analysis?
   a) This type of laptop computer battery has a mean working time of at least 4.5 hours
   b) This type of laptop computer battery has a mean working time of at least 5.0 hours.
   c) This type of laptop computer battery has a mean working time of between 4.0 and 5.0 hours.
   d) This type of laptop computer battery has a mean working time of between 0.0 and 0.5 hours.

1, 2, 3, 4 , 5, 6

10. A three-digit integer is to be formed from the digits listed above. If the first digit must be even, either the second or the third digit must be 5, and no digit may be repeated, how many such integers are possible?
    a) 12
    b) 15
    c) 18
    d) 24

11. In normal weather conditions, a particular type of jet burns an average of 2.5 gallons of fuel per nautical mile flown. The distance from New York to Los Angeles is about 2,200 nautical miles. Approximately how many gallons of fuel will the jet burn for a trip from New York to Los Angeles in normal weather conditions?
    a) 2,200
    b) 2,500
    c) 5,000
    d) 5,500

2x , y , 2y

12. If the average (arithmetic mean) of the three numbers above is $3x$ and $x \neq 0$, what is y in terms of x?
    a) $2x$
    b) $3x$
    c) $\frac{5x}{2}$
    d) $\frac{7x}{3}$

13. If $f(x) = \frac{x^2+35}{x^2-10}$, what is the value of $f(5)$?

14. The difference of two consecutive numbers is equal to k. What is the value of k?

15. A rectangular box has dimensions $36 \times 14 \times 18$. Without wasting any space, which of the following could be the dimensions of the smaller boxes which can be packed into the rectangular box?
    a) $2 \times 5 \times 6$
    b) $7 \times 9 \times 12$
    c) $3 \times 5 \times 6$
    d) $4 \times 5 \times 6$

16. Which of the following expressions is equivalent to $(16x^9y^3)^{\frac{1}{2}}$, where $x \geq 0$ *and* $y \geq 0$?

    a) $4x^3y^{\frac{1}{2}}$

    b) $4x^{\frac{9}{2}}y^{\frac{3}{2}}$

    c) $8x^3y^3$

    d) $8x^{\frac{9}{2}}y^3$

17. If $f(x + 1) = x^2 - 1$, then $f(x) = $?

    a) $x^2 - 2x + 1$

    b) $x^2 + 2x + 1$

    c) $x^2 - 2x$

    d) $x^2 + 2x$

18. If x and y are non-zero integers, what is x percent of y percent of 2000?

    a) xy

    b) $5xy$

    c) $10xy$

    d) $\frac{1}{5}xy$

19. The kinetic energy of an object is calculated by the following formula:

    $$K_e = \frac{1}{2}mv^2$$

    where K_e is the kinetic energy, m is the mass, and v is the velocity. If the mass of an object is a constant, which of the following graphs best represents the possible relationship between the kinetic energy (K_e) and the velocity (v) of the object?

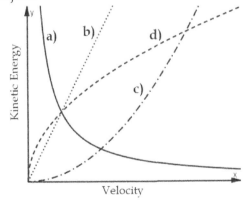

20. A circle in the xy-plane has a diameter with endpoints $(-2, 3)$ and $(8, 3)$. If the point $(0, b)$ lies on the circle and $b > 0$, what is the value of b ?

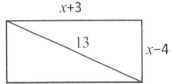

21. The figure above is a rectangle. What is the value of x?

    a) 9

    b) 8

    c) $5\sqrt{2}$

    d) 6

22. A "square-root-factor" is an integer greater than 1 with exactly three positive integer factors: itself, its square root, and 1. Which of the following is a square-root-factor?

    a) 128

    b) 81

    c) 64

    d) 49

Math Mock Test 1
22 QUESTIONS

DIRECTIONS
The questions in this section address a number of important math skills.
Use of a calculator is permitted for all questions.

NOTES
Unless otherwise indicated:
• All variables and expressions represent real numbers.
• Figures provided are drawn to scale.
• All figures lie in a plane.
• The domain of a given function f is the set of all real numbers x for which f(x) is a real number.

REFERENCE

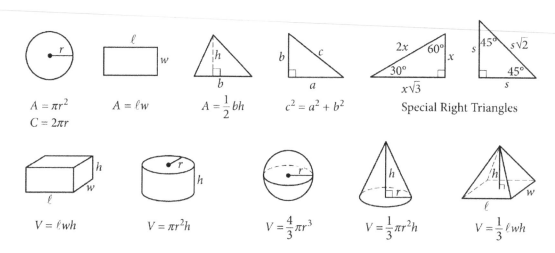

$A = \pi r^2$

$C = 2\pi r$

$A = \ell w$

$A = \frac{1}{2}bh$

$c^2 = a^2 + b^2$

Special Right Triangles

$V = \ell wh$

$V = \pi r^2 h$

$V = \frac{4}{3}\pi r^3$

$V = \frac{1}{3}\pi r^2 h$

$V = \frac{1}{3}\ell wh$

The number of degrees of arc in a circle is **360**.
The number of radians of arc in a circle is 2π.
The sum of the measures in degrees of the angles of a triangle is **180**.

For multiple-choice questions, solve each problem, choose the correct answer from the choices provided, and then circle your answer in this book. Circle only one answer for each question. If you change your mind, completely erase the circle. You will not get credit for questions with more than one answer circled, or for questions with no answers circled.

For student-produced response questions, solve each problem and write your answer next to or under the question in the test book as described below.
• Once you've written your answer, circle it clearly. You will not receive credit for anything written outside the circle, or for any questions with more than one circled answer.
• If you find **more than one correct answer,** write and circle only one answer. Your answer can be up to 5 characters for a **positive** answer and up to 6 characters (including the negative sign) for a **negative** answer, but no more.
• If your answer is a **fraction** that is too long (over 5 characters for positive, 6 characters for negative), write the decimal equivalent.
• If your answer is a **decimal** that is too long (over 5 characters for positive,
• 6 characters for negative), truncate it or round at the fourth digit.
• If your answer is a **mixed number** (such as $3\frac{1}{2}$, write it as an improper fraction (7/2) or its decimal equivalent (3.5).
• Don't include symbols such as a percent sign, comma, or dollar sign in your circled answer.

1. In the xy-plane, the graph of line l has slope 3. Line k is parallel to line l and contains the point $(3, 6)$. Which of the following is an equation of line k ?

   a) $y = -\frac{1}{3}x + 6$

   b) $y = \frac{1}{3}x + 9$

   c) $y = 3x - 3$

   d) $y = 3x + 2$

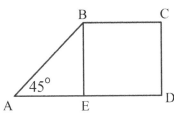

2. In the figure above, BCDE is a square and its area is 16. The points A, E and D are on the same line. What is the length of $\overline{AB}$?

   a) 4

   b) $4\sqrt{2}$

   c) $4\sqrt{3}$

   d) 6

3. How much money was originally in Sue's checking account if she withdrew m dollars, deposited n dollars, and now has l dollars in her checking account?

   a) $l + m - n$

   b) $l - m - n$

   c) $m + n - l$

   d) $m + n + l$

4. The number of DVDs that have been checked out of the local public library in a particular week was recorded in the table below. If the median number of DVDs checked out for the whole week was 83, which of the following could have been the number of DVDs checked out on Saturday and Sunday, respectively, of the same week?

Local Library Checkout Records	
Day of the Week	Number of DVDs Checked Out
Monday	77
Tuesday	81
Wednesday	82
Thursday	83
Friday	86

   a) 78 and 82

   b) 79 and 81

   c) 80 and 87

   d) 84 and 87

5. Each term in a sequence of numbers, except for the first term, is 2 less than the square root of the previous term. If the third term of this sequence is 1, what is the first term?

   a) 4

   b) 9

   c) 121

   d) 81

6. The scatter plot below shows the wolf population in a safari every 5 years. If w is the number of wolves present in the park and t is the number of years since the study began in 1980, which of the following equations best represents the wolf population in the safari?

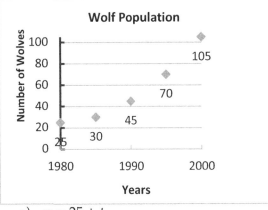

   a) $w = 25 + t$

   b) $w = 25 + 5t^2$

   c) $w = 25 + 0.2t^2$

   d) $w = (25)(0.2)^{(t/5)}$

7. If $2x - y$ is equal to 60% of $5y$, what is the value of $\frac{y}{x}$?

    a) $\frac{1}{4}$

    b) $\frac{1}{3}$

    c) $\frac{1}{2}$

    d) $\frac{2}{3}$

8. The monthly cost of renting an apartment increases every year by 3%. John paid $500 per month this year on his rental. What is the monthly cost for John's rental n years from now?

    a) 500×0.03^n

    b) $500 \times 1.03 \times n$

    c) 500×1.03^n

    d) $500 \times 1.03^{n-1}$

9. A sample of seawater is 4% salt by mass and contains 1,000 grams of salt. Which of the following is closest to the mass, in grams, of the sample of seawater?

    a) 27,500

    b) 25,000

    c) 19,600

    d) 13,500

10. Which of the following scatterplots is the best representation of a function, $f(x) = a \log_b x$ where a is a positive number and b is greater than 1?

    a)

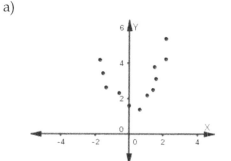

b)

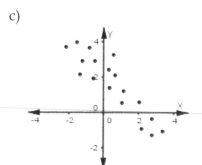

c)

d)

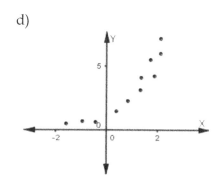

11. Five erasers cost as much as 3 pencils. If Matt bought one eraser and one pencil for $1.60, how much does one pencil cost in dollars?

    a) 0.50

    b) 0.60

    c) 1.00

    d) 1.10

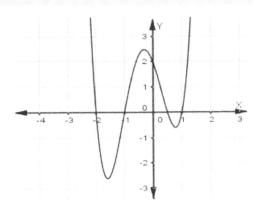

12. The function $f(x) = 2x^4 + 3x^3 - 4x^2 - 3x + 2$ was graphed in the xy-plane above. How many real solutions are there if $f(x) = 3x$?
    a) 1
    b) 2
    c) 3
    d) 4

13. A ramp is 20 meters long and set at a 30° angle of inclination. If you walk up to the top of the ramp, how high off the ground (in meters) will you be?

14. In a toy factory production line, every 9th toy has their electronic parts checked and every 12th toy will have their safety features checked. In the first 180 toys, what is the probability that a toy will have both its electronic parts and safety features checked?

15. Plant A is currently 20 centimeters tall, and Plant B is currently 15 centimeters tall. The ratio of the heights of Plant A to Plant B is equal to the ratio of the heights of Plant C to Plant D. If Plant C is 60 centimeters tall, what is the height of Plant D, in centimeters?
    a) 32
    b) 45
    c) 60
    d) 75

16. What is the remainder of 2013^{2014} divided by 10?
    a) 1
    b) 3
    c) 7
    d) 9

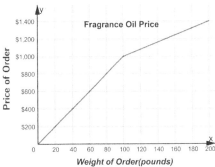

17. The graph above shows the price that a chemical company charges for an order of fragrance oil, depending on the weight of the order. Based on the graph, which of the following statements must be true?
    a) The company charges more per pound for orders greater than 100 pounds than for orders less than 100 pounds.
    b) The company charges less per pound for orders greater than 100 pounds than for orders less than 100 pounds.
    c) The company charges less per pound for orders greater than 1,000 pounds than for orders less than 1,000 pounds.
    d) The company charges the same price per pound, regardless of order size.

18. If John gives Sally $5, Sally will have twice the amount of money that John will have. Originally, there was a total of $45 between the two of them. How much money did John initially have?
    a) 25
    b) 20
    c) 18
    d) 15

19. The kinetic energy of an object is calculated by the following formula:
$$K_e = \frac{1}{2}mv^2$$
where K_e is the kinetic energy, m is the mass, and v is the velocity. If the mass of an object is a constant, which of the following graphs best represents the possible relationship between the kinetic energy (K_e) and the velocity (v) of the object?

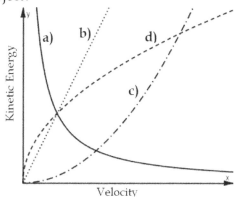

20. In the xy-plane, the circle with radius 5 and center $(6, 4)$ contains the point $(w, 0)$. what is one possible value of w?

21. A data set consists of the values 230, 300, 410, 450, 700, and 20, 160. If the outlier is removed, what will happen to the value of the mean of the data set?
    a) The mean will remain the same.
    b) The mean will decrease.
    c) The mean will increase.
    d) There is not enough information to determine how the mean will change.

$$x^2 + y = 7$$
$$x - y = 5$$

22. Which value is a y-coordinate of a solution to the system of equations above?
    a) -8
    b) -3
    c) -2
    d) 6

Mock Test 1

Module 1 Keys

1. (C)	2. (D)	3. (D)	4. (D)	5. (A)	6. 6	7. 20	8. (C)
9. (B)	10. (B)	11. (B)	12. (B)	13. 5	14. 6	15. (B)	16. (C)
17. (C)	18. (D)	19. (C)	20. 1.6	21. 5	22. (C)		

Module 2 Easy Keys

1. (A)	2. (D)	3. (D)	4. (B)	5. (B)	6. 12	7. $\frac{3}{7}$ or .428	8. (B)
9. (C)	10. (D)	11. (D)	12. (D)	13. 4	14. 1	15. (B)	16. (B)
17. (D)	18. (D)	19. (C)	20. 7	21. (A)	22. (D)		

Module 2 Hard Keys

1. (C)	2. (B)	3. (A)	4. (D)	5. (C)	6. (C)	7. (C)	8. (C)
9. (B)	10. (B)	11. (C)	12. (B)	13. 10	14. $\frac{1}{36}$	15. (B)	16. (D)
17. (B)	18. (B)	19. (C)	20. 3 or 9	21. (D)	22. (C)		

Mock Test 1

Module 1 Answers

1. *Answer: (C)*
    $x + y = 21 \quad --(1)$
    $x - 2y = -3 \quad --(2)$
    $(1) - (2):$
    $3y = 24 \to y = 8$
    $x = 21 - y = 13$

2. *Answer: (D)*
    $\sqrt{k + 3} - 6 = 0$
    $k + 3 = 36$
    $k = 33$

3. *Answer: (D)*
    Slope Intercept Form
    $y = mx + b$
    Slope = $\frac{1}{2}$ and y-intercept = -2
    $y = \frac{1}{2}x - 2$

4. *Answer: (D)*
    It is easier to use the method of elimination for this question.
    $3a - 2b = 5 \qquad (1)$
    $a + 2b = 23 \qquad (2)$
    Add equations (1) and (2) to eliminate b.
    $(1) + (2) \to 4a = 28$
    $a = 7$
    $3 \times 7 - 2b = 5$
    $b = 8$
    $a + b = 15$

5. *Answer: (A)*
    f(x) should have its vertex at $\left(\frac{3}{2}, 0\right)$ and all positive. The answer is (a).

6. *Answer: 6*
    $J = -3$
    $(\frac{-3}{k})^{-3} = -8$
    $(\frac{-3}{k})^{3} = \frac{1}{-8}$
    $\frac{-3}{k} = \sqrt[3]{\frac{1}{-8}} = \frac{-1}{2} \to k = 6$

7. *Answer: 20*
    $x = \frac{20}{5} = 4 \; ; \; y^2 = \frac{20}{4} = 5$
    $xy^2 = 4 \times 5 = 20$

8. *Answer: (C)*
    $x^y x^{\frac{1}{2}} = x^{(y + \frac{1}{2})} = x^{\frac{1}{4}}$
    $y + \frac{1}{2} = \frac{1}{4} \quad \to \quad y = -\frac{1}{4}$

9. *Answer: (B)*
    $|x - 2| = p$
    If $x < 2$, then $|x - 2| = -(x - 2) = 2 - x$
    $2 - x = p$
    $x = 2 - p$
    $x - p = 2 - p - p = 2 - 2p$

10. *Answer: (B)*
    Running down the hill saves 2 to 3 minutes. Therefore, the minimum amount of time would be 6 – 3 = 3 minutes and the maximum amount of time would be 8 – 2 = 6 minutes.

11. *Answer: (B)*
    $4x + 6x = 180° \quad and \quad 3y = 6x$
    $10x = 180$
    $x = 18°$
    $3y = 6x = 6 \times 18 = 108$
    $y = 36°$
    $2x + y = 36 + 36 = 72°$

12. *Answer: (B)*
    If two lines are perpendicular, then the product of their slopes is -1.
    $\frac{1-0}{2-0} \times \frac{3-a}{2-(-1)} = -1$
    $3 - a = -6 \quad \to \quad a = 9$

13. *Answer: 5*
    When $x = 0$, $f(0) = 5 = a(b)^0 = a$

14. *Answer: 6*
    $\left(\sqrt[3]{\frac{9r}{2}}\right)^3 = \left(\frac{1}{2}r\right)^3$
    $\frac{9r}{2} = \frac{1}{8}r^3 \to r = \sqrt{\frac{(9)(8)}{2}} = 6$

15. *Answer: (B)*
    $x^{-\frac{2}{3}} = a^{-2}$
    $x = (a^{-2})^{(-3/2)} = a^3$
    $y^{\frac{2}{3}} = b^4, \quad y = (b^4)^{(3/2)} = b^6$
    $(xy)^{-\frac{1}{3}} = (a^3 b^6)^{(-\frac{1}{3})} = a^{-1}b^{-2}$

16. *Answer: (C)*
    $3x = a - 1$
    $6x = 2 \times (3x) = 2 \times (a - 1) = 2a - 2$
    $6x + 1 = 2a - 2 + 1 = 2a - 1$

17. *Answer: (C)*
    The total number of cars sold: 1,014
    The probability that the car sold from the region II:
    $76 + 48 + 52 = 176$
    probability $= \frac{176}{1014} = 0.174 = 17.4\%$

18. *Answer: (D)*
    $v = abc$
    If v is odd, then a, b, and c must be all odd numbers.
    $s = 2(ab + bc + ca)$
    s is always an even number if a, b, and c are positive integers.

19. *Answer: (C)*
    $(4x^3)^{\frac{2}{3}} = (2^2)^{\frac{2}{3}}\left(x^{\frac{9}{2}}\right)$
    $= 2^{\frac{4}{3}}x^2 = 2\sqrt[3]{2}x^2$

20. *Answer: 1.6*
    $AC \perp BC$
    $AC^2 + BC^2 = AB^2$
    $AC = \sqrt{1^2 - 0.6^2} = 0.8 = r$
    r is the radius of this circle:
    Diameter $= 2r = 1.6$

21. *Answer: 5*
    From the graph:
    Actual Revenue $= 50$
    Predicted Revenue $= 55$
    The difference is $55 - 50 = 5.$

22. *Answer: (C)*

$\frac{(6-2) \times 180}{6} = 120$ *(each interior angle)*
ΔBGC *is a 30–60–90 special right triangle.*
$BG = BC \times \frac{\sqrt{3}}{2} = 6 \times \frac{\sqrt{3}}{2} = 3\sqrt{3}$
$BD = 2BG = 6\sqrt{3}$

Module 2 Easy Answers

1. *Answer: (A)*
   Slope $= \frac{Rise}{Run} = \frac{1 - \frac{1}{2}}{2 - 0} = \frac{1}{4}$
   y-intercept $= \frac{1}{2}$
   $y = \frac{1}{4}x + \frac{1}{2}$

2. *Answer: (D)*
   Slope $= \frac{Rise}{Run} = \frac{0 - 8}{k - (-3)} = -2$
   $-2k = -2, \quad k = 1$

3. *Answer: (D)*
   Two weeks have 14 days.
   $50 \times 5 + 45 \times 9 = 655$

4. *Answer: (B)*
   $\frac{1}{2}x = 6 \rightarrow x = 12$
   $\frac{1}{6}(12) - \frac{1}{2}y = 1$
   $2 - \frac{1}{2}y = 1$

   $-\frac{1}{2}y = -1 \rightarrow y = 2$

5. *Answer: (B)*
   $123 \, km \times \frac{1 \, mile}{1.61 \, km} = 76 \, miles$

6. *Answer: 12*
   The total number of boxes of index cards needed is
   $23 \times 3 = 69.$
   Since index cards are bought in 6-pack boxes,
   $69 \div 6 = 11.5$
   12 boxes will be needed for the entire camp.

7. *Answer:* $\frac{3}{7}$ *or .428 or .429*
   The green light takes 30 seconds.
   $70 - 30 - 10 = 30$
   Probability of Green Light $= \frac{30}{70} = \frac{3}{7}$

8. *Answer: (B)*
   $\triangle ABC$ is equilateral ard both $\triangle ABD$ and $\triangle BCD$ are $30° - 60° - 90°$ special triangles. $\overline{AD}$ is opposite to the angle $30°$. Therefore,
   $\overline{AD} = \frac{1}{2}\overline{AB} = \frac{1}{2} \times 10 = 5$

9. *Answer: (C)*
   Let x be the mean working time.
   $4.5 - 0.5 \le x \le 4.5 + 0.5$
   $4.0 \le x \le 5.0$
   The answer is c).

10. *Answer: (D)*
    1st *digit must be even: 3 choices*
    If 2nd digit is 5, then 2nd digit has 1 choice, and 3rd digit has 4 choices.
    If 2nd digit is not 5, then 3rd digit is 5: 2nd digit has 4 choices and 3rd digit has 1 choice.
    $3 \times 1 \times 4 + 3 \times 4 \times 1 = 24$

11. *Answer: (D)*
    $2.5 \times 2200 = 5500$

12. *Answer: (D)*
    $3x = \frac{2x+y+2y}{3}$
    $9x = 2x + 3y$
    $7x = 3y$
    $y = \frac{7x}{3}$

13. *Answer: 4*
    Plug the number 5 into the function.
    $f(5) = \frac{5^2 + 35}{5^2 - 10}$
    $\frac{60}{15} = 4$

14. *Answer: 1*
    Let the two consecutive numbers be x and (x + 1).
    $(x + 1) - x = k$
    $k = 1$

15. *Answer: (B)*
    The number 5 is not a factor of 14, 36 or 18; therefore, answers (a), (c), (d) are not possible. Only (b)'s dimensions could be packed into the rectangular box without wasting space.
    $\frac{14}{7} \times \frac{36}{12} \times \frac{18}{9} = 12$

16. *Answer: (B)*
    $(16x^9y^3)^{\frac{1}{2}} = (16)^{\frac{1}{2}}(x)^{\frac{9}{2}}(y)^{\frac{3}{2}} = 4(x)^{\frac{9}{2}}(y)^{\frac{3}{2}}$

17. *Answer: (D)*
    $f(x + 1) = x^2 - 1$
    $f(x) = f\big((x + 1) - 1\big)$
    $= (x - 1)^2 - 1$
    $= x^2 - 2x + 1 - 1 = x^2 - 2x$

18. *Answer: (D)*
    x percent of y percent of 2000 $\rightarrow$
    $\frac{x}{100} \times \frac{y}{100} \times 2000 = \frac{xy}{5}$

19. *Answer: (C)*
    Since $\frac{1}{2}m$ is a constant, $K_e \propto v^2$

20. *Answer: 7*
    $Center: \frac{(-2,3)+(8,3)}{2} = (3,3)$
    $Radius: \frac{\sqrt{\left(8-(-2)\right)^2 + (3-3)^2}}{2} = 5$
    The equation of circle: $(x - 3)^2 + (y - 3)^2 = 5^2$
    $x = 0 \rightarrow 3^2 + (y - 3)^2 = 25$
    $y - 3 = \pm 4 \rightarrow y = 7 \text{ or } -1$

21. *Answer: (A)*
    Use the Pythagorean Theorem.
    $(x + 3)^2 + (x - 4)^2 = 13^2$
    $x^2 + 6x + 9 + x^2 - 8x + 16 = 169$
    $2x^2 - 2x = 144$
    $x^2 - x - 72 = 0$
    $(x + 8)(x - 9) = 0$
    $x = 9 \text{ or } -8 \text{ (not applicable)}$

22. *Answer: (D)*
    The square root of the number must be a prime number.
    Only $\sqrt{49}$ is a prime number.

Module 2 Hard Answers

1. *Answer: (C)*
   The equation of line k: $y = 3x + b$
   Plug in (3, 6):
   $6 = 3 \times 3 + b$
   $b = -3$
   Therefore, the equation of line k: $y = 3x - 3$

2. *Answer: (B)*
   $\triangle ABE$ *is a 45-45-90 right triangle.*
   $\overline{BE} = \sqrt{16} = 4$
   $\overline{AB} = \sqrt{2} \times 4$

3. *Answer: (A)*
   If there were x dollars in the account originally, then the total dollars now is:
   $l = x - m + n$
   $x = l + m - n$

4. *Answer: (D)*
   If the median number of DVDs checked out for the whole week was 83, the number of DVDs checked out on either Saturday or Sunday should be more than 83.

5. *Answer: (C)*
   If first term is x, then second term is $\sqrt{x} - 2$ *and the third term is* $\sqrt{\sqrt{x} - 2} - 2$.
   $\sqrt{\sqrt{x} - 2} - 2. = 1$
   $\sqrt{x} - 2 = 3^2$
   $\sqrt{x} = 11$
   $x = 121$

6. *Answer: (C)*
   Plot numbers into your calculator and test:
   Year 1980, t = 0, w = 25
   Year 1985, t = 5, w = 30
   Only (a) and (c) satisfy, but (a) is a linear equation which contradicts the shape of the graph.

7. *Answer: (C)*
   $2x - y = .6 \times 5y$
   $2x - y = 3y$
   $2x = 4y \rightarrow \frac{y}{x} = \frac{2}{4} = \frac{1}{2}$

8. *Answer: (C)*
   Increasing every year by 3% is to multiply $(1 + \frac{3}{100})$
   for each additional year.
   $C(n) = (1.03)^n \times 500 = 500(1.03)^n$

9. *Answer: (B)*
   $\frac{4}{100} = \frac{1000}{x}$
   $x = 25,000$

10. *Answer: (B)*
    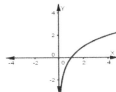
    The graph of $f(x) = \log_2 x$: *So, answer is (b).*

11. *Answer: (C)*
    Let the price of one eraser be x and the price of one pencil be y. The price of 6 erasers = The price of 3 pencils.
    $5x = 3y, x = \frac{3}{5}y$
    $x + y = 1.60$
    $\frac{3}{5}y + y = 1.60$
    Solve for y to get the price of one pencil $1.00.

12. *Answer: (B)*
    Use your graphing calculator.
    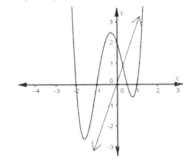
    There are two intersections between $y = 3x$ *and* $y = 2x^4 + 3x^3 - 4x^2 - 3x + 2$

13. *Answer: 10*
    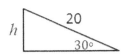
    $h = 20 \times \sin(30^o) = 20 \times 0.5 = 10$

14. *Answer:* $\frac{1}{36}$
The LCM of 9 and 12 is 36.
The every 36th toy will have both of their electronic parts and safety features checked.
There are 5 such toys (180 divided by 36).
$$\frac{5}{180} = \frac{1}{36}$$

15. *Answer: (B)*
$$\frac{20}{15} = \frac{60}{D}$$
$$D = 45$$

16. *Answer: (D)*
2013^1 has units digit of 3
2013^2 has units digit of 9 ($3 \times 3 = 9$)
2013^3 has units digit of 7 ($3 \times 9 = 27$)
2013^4 has units digit of 1 ($3 \times 7 = 21$)
2013^5 has units digit of 3 ($3 \times 1 = 3$)
Only the units digit needs to be concerned.
So every fourth power of 2013 repeats its units digit.
$2014 \div 4$ has remainder of 2
2013^{2014} has the same units digit as 2013^2, which is 9.

17. *Answer: (B)*
    After ordering 100 pounds of fragrance oil,
    the slope of the line becomes smaller.
    The answer is b).

18. *Answer: (B)*
Let J be the amount of money John initially had and S be the amount of money Sally initially had. Together, they originally had \$45.
$J + S = 45$
$J = 45 - S$
After John gives Sally \$5, John will have J – 5 dollars and Sally will have S + 5 dollars. Therefore,
$S + 5 = 2(J - 5)$.
$S + 5 = 2(45 - S - 5) = 80 - 2S$
$S = 25$
Plug $J = 45 - S$ into the equation above to get $J = \$20$.

19. *Answer: (C)*
Since $\frac{1}{2}m$ is a constant, $K_e \propto v^2$

20. *Answer: 3 or 9*
The standard equation of the circle:
$(x - 6)^2 + (y - 4)^2 = 25$
Plug in the point $(w, 0) \rightarrow (w - 6)^2 + 16 = 25$
$w - 6 = \pm 3 \rightarrow w = 9$ or 3

21. *Answer: (D)*
It is not clear which outlier, 700 or 20, will be removed.

22. *Answer: (C)*
Solve the system of the equations:
$x^2 + x - 12 = 0$
$x = 3$ or -4
$y = -2$ or -9

Math Mock Test 2

22 QUESTIONS

DIRECTIONS

The questions in this section address a number of important math skills.

Use of a calculator is permitted for all questions.

o **Check the answers after the Module 1 test. If there are more than 8 questions answered incorrectly in Module 1, take the Easy part of Module 2. Otherwise, take the Hard part of Module 2.**

NOTES

Unless otherwise indicated:

• All variables and expressions represent real numbers.

• Figures provided are drawn to scale.

• All figures lie in a plane.

• The domain of a given function f i s the set of all real numbers x for which f(x) is a real number.

REFERENCE

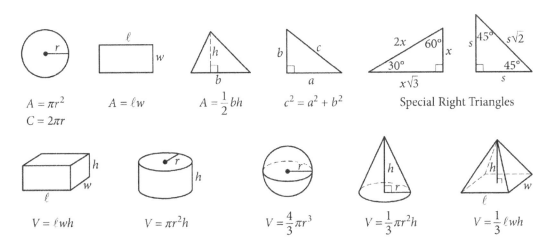

$A = \pi r^2$
$C = 2\pi r$

$A = \ell w$

$A = \frac{1}{2}bh$

$c^2 = a^2 + b^2$

Special Right Triangles

$V = \ell wh$

$V = \pi r^2 h$

$V = \frac{4}{3}\pi r^3$

$V = \frac{1}{3}\pi r^2 h$

$V = \frac{1}{3}\ell wh$

The number of degrees of arc in a circle is **360**.

The number of radians of arc in a circle is 2π.

The sum of the measures in degrees of the angles of a triangle is **180**.

For multiple-choice questions, solve each problem, choose the correct answer from the choices provided, and then circle your answer in this book. Circle only one answer for each question. If you change your mind, completely erase the circle. You will not get credit for questions with more than one answer circled, or for questions with no answers circled.

For student-produced response questions, solve each problem and write your answer next to or under the question in the test book as described below.

• Once you've written your answer, circle it clearly. You will not receive credit for anything written outside the circle, or for any questions with more than one circled answer.

• If you find **more than one correct answer**, write and circle only one answer. Your answer can be up to 5 characters for a **positive** answer and up to 6 characters (including the negative sign) for a **negative** answer, but no more.

• If your answer is a **fraction** that is too long (over 5 characters for positive, 6 characters for negative), write the decimal equivalent.

• If your answer is a **decimal** that is too long (over 5 characters for positive,

• 6 characters for negative), truncate it or round at the fourth digit.

• If your answer is a **mixed number** (such as $3\frac{1}{2}$, write it as an improper fraction (7/2) or its decimal equivalent (3.5).

• Don't include symbols such as a percent sign, comma, or dollar sign in your circled answer.

1. If $3x - 1 = 3$, then $12x - 4 =$?
    a) 6
    b) 8
    c) 12
    d) 16

2. If $c = 3$, which of the following is the equivalent to $cx^2 + cx + c$?
    a) $(3x^3 + 5)$
    b) $3(x + 1)^2$
    c) $(x^2 + 1)$
    d) $3(x^2 + x + 1)$

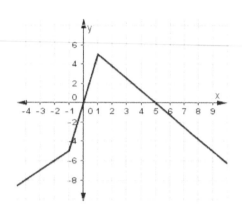

3. $f(x)$ is graphed in the figure above. For what values of x does $f(x)$ have a negative slope?
    a) $x > -1$
    b) $-1 < x < 1$
    c) $x > 1$
    d) $x > 0$

4. If x is a positive integer, then $3 \times 10^{-x} + 10^{-x}$ must be equal to?
    a) $\frac{1}{10^x}$
    b) $\frac{2}{10^x}$
    c) $\frac{3}{10^{-x}}$
    d) $\frac{4}{10^x}$

$$c = 80h + 100$$

5. The equation above gives the amount c, in dollars, an electrician charges for a job that takes h hours. Ms. Sanchez and Mr. Roland each hired this electrician. The electrician worked 2 hours longer on Ms. Sanchez's job than on Mr. Roland's job. How much more did the electrician charge Ms. Sanchez than Mr. Roland?
    a) $80
    b) $140
    c) $160
    d) $200

6. If $3x^2 = 5y = 15$, what is the value of x^2y?

7. The three angles of a triangle have measures $x°$, $2(x+1)°$ and $4y°$, where $x > 55$. If x and y are integers greater than zero, what is one possible value of y?

8. If $x^2 - 16 = 0$, which of the following could be a value of x?
    a) -4
    b) -8
    c) 2
    d) 8

9. What values of x satisfy $x^2 + 5x + 6 = 9x + 3$
    a) 1 and 3
    b) 1 and -3
    c) 2 and 3
    d) 2 and -3

10. In the xy-plane, the point $(2, 6)$ lies on the graph of $y = \frac{k}{x}$, where k is a constant. Which of the following points must also lie on the graph?
    a) $(1, 3)$
    b) $(1, 4)$
    c) $(3, 3)$
    d) $(3, 4)$

11. What is the solution to the equation shown?

$$\frac{x-2}{3} = \frac{x+1}{2}$$

   a) -5
   b) -7
   c) 1
   d) 3

12. A number a is multiplied by $\frac{1}{3}$. The product is then multiplied by 27, which results in 81. What is the value of a?

   a) 3
   b) 6
   c) 9
   d) 18

13. A bag contains only red, white, and blue marbles. If randomly choosing a blue marble is three times as likely as randomly choosing a white marble, and randomly choosing a red marble is twice as likely as randomly choosing a blue marble, then what is the smallest possible number of marbles in the bag?

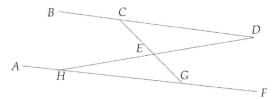

14. In the figure above, $\overline{AF} \parallel \overline{BD}$, and $\overline{CG}$ and $\overline{DH}$ intersect at E. If $HE = 16$, $ED = 24$ and $CG = 20$, what is the length of $\overline{EG}$?

15. If $x + y = 9$, $y = z - 3$, and $z = 2$, then what is the value of x?

   a) -8
   b) -6
   c) 10
   d) 3

16. Which of the following is a solution to the equation $4x^2 + 8x - 5 = 0$?

   a) -1.5
   b) 0.5
   c) 1
   d) 2

17. By 7 AM, $\frac{1}{4}$ of all students were in school. Half an hour later, 100 more students arrived, raising the attendance to $\frac{3}{4}$ of the total students. How many students are in this school?

   a) 240
   b) 220
   c) 200
   d) 180

18. If $\frac{4x+4x+4x}{5} = 12$, what is the value of x ?

   a) 10
   b) 8
   c) 5
   d) 1

19. An integer is divided by 2 more than itself. If the fraction is equal to $\frac{3}{4}$, what is the value of this integer?

   a) 2
   b) 5
   c) 6
   d) 8

20. Megan has 7 blue cards, 3 black cards, and 5 red cards in her pocket. She takes out a card at random and puts it aside because the card is not blue. She then takes out a second card randomly from her pocket. What is the probability that the second card will be a blue card?

$$3xi + 2i^6 = 6i + 4i^{13} + 5y$$

22. In the equation above, x and y are real numbers and $i = \sqrt{-1}$. Which of the following ordered pair could be the solution for this equation?

a) $(\frac{10}{3}, -\frac{2}{5})$

b) $(-\frac{2}{5}, -\frac{10}{3})$

c) $(\frac{10}{3}, \frac{2}{5})$

d) $(-\frac{2}{5}, \frac{10}{3})$

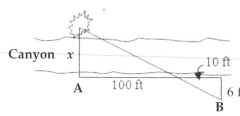

21. A wild fire is sighted on the other side of a canyon at points A and B as shown in the figure above. Find the width, in feet, of the canyon.

Math Mock Test 2
22 QUESTIONS

DIRECTIONS
The questions in this section address a number of important math skills.
Use of a calculator is permitted for all questions.

NOTES
Unless otherwise indicated:
• All variables and expressions represent real numbers.
• Figures provided are drawn to scale.
• All figures lie in a plane.
• The domain of a given function f is the set of all real numbers x for which f(x) is a real number.

REFERENCE

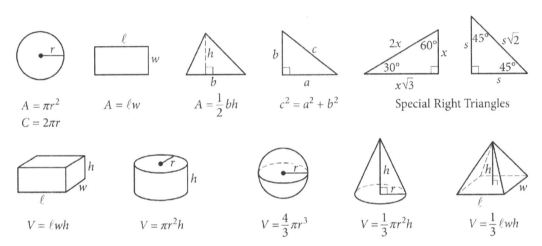

$A = \pi r^2$ $A = \ell w$ $A = \frac{1}{2}bh$ $c^2 = a^2 + b^2$ Special Right Triangles
$C = 2\pi r$

$V = \ell wh$ $V = \pi r^2 h$ $V = \frac{4}{3}\pi r^3$ $V = \frac{1}{3}\pi r^2 h$ $V = \frac{1}{3}\ell wh$

The number of degrees of arc in a circle is **360**.
The number of radians of arc in a circle is 2π.
The sum of the measures in degrees of the angles of a triangle is **180**.

For multiple-choice questions, solve each problem, choose the correct answer from the choices provided, and then circle your answer in this book. Circle only one answer for each question. If you change your mind, completely erase the circle. You will not get credit for questions with more than one answer circled, or for questions with no answers circled.

For student-produced response questions, solve each problem and write your answer next to or under the question in the test book as described below.
• Once you've written your answer, circle it clearly. You will not receive credit for anything written outside the
• circle, or for any questions with more than one circled answer.
• If you find **more than one correct answer**, write and circle only one answer. Your answer can be up to 5 characters for a **positive** answer and up to 6 characters (including the negative sign) for a **negative** answer, but no more.
• If your answer is a **fraction** that is too long (over 5 characters for positive, 6 characters for negative), write the decimal equivalent.

• If your answer is a **decimal** that is too long (over 5 characters for positive,
• 6 characters for negative), truncate it or round at the fourth digit.
• If your answer is a **mixed number** (such as $3\frac{1}{2}$, write it as an improper fraction (7/2) or its decimal equivalent (3.5).
• Don't include symbols such as a percent sign, comma, or dollar sign in your circled answer

1. A gravel company had 30 tons of gravel in stock at the end of the day on Monday. On Tuesday the company shipped 10 tons of gravel and received no deliveries. On Wednesday the company made no shipments and received a delivery of 20 tons of gravel. On Thursday the company made no shipments and received no deliveries. On Friday the company shipped 20 tons of gravel and received no deliveries. Which of the following represents the number of tons of gravel the company had in stock at the end of each day?

a)

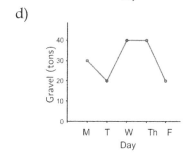

b)

c)

d)

$$f(x) = 2x + 1$$
2. The function f is defined above. What is the value of $f(-2)$?
   a) -3
   b) -5
   c) 3
   d) 5

3. How many pounds of flour are needed to make 18 rolls of bread if 20 pounds of flour are needed to make 120 rolls of bread?
   a) 3
   b) 4
   c) 5
   d) 3.5

$$\sqrt{x^2} = x$$
4. Which of the following values of x is NOT a solution to the equation above?
   a) -4
   b) 0
   c) 1
   d) 3

5. If $x > 0$, then $(9^x)(27^x) =$?
   a) 3^{9x}
   b) 3^{8x}
   c) 3^{6x}
   d) 3^{5x}

$$s(p) = 10000 - 4.4p$$
6. The function s above gives the remaining free space, in megabytes (MB), on a 10,000 MB memory card that is storing p photos, each with a size of 4.4 MB. If there are 1,200 photos on the card, how many MB of free space remain on the card?

$$p = 9n - (2n + k)$$

7. The profit p, in dollars, from producing and selling n units of a certain product is given by the equation above, where k is a constant. If 200 units are produced and sold for a profit of $1,275, what is the value of k?

8. A box in the shape of a right rectangular prism has a volume of 60 cubic inches. If the dimensions of the box are 3 inches by 5 inches by h inches, what is the value of h?

    a)   3
    b)   4
    c)   5
    d)   6

Personal Finance Seminar Enrollment

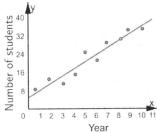

9. The number of students enrolled in a personal finance seminar for each of 10 years is shown in the scatterplot above. A line of best fit is also drawn. For how many of these 1 0 years was enrollment in the seminar less than predicted by this line of best fit?

    a) 2
    b) 4
    c) 6
    d) 8

10. According to the bar graph below, the total population in all five cities increased by approximately what percent from 2012 to 2013?

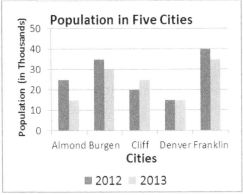

    a)   11%
    b)   10%
    c)   −10%
    d)   −11%

$$t = (3r - 6)$$
$$w = (3r + 6)$$

11. The equation above define t and w in terms of r, what is $\frac{tw}{9}$ in terms of r?

    a) $r^2 - 4$
    b) $r^2 - 9$
    c) $4r^2 - 4$
    d) $4r^2 - 16$

12. John's monthly salary increases every year by 4%. If he gets paid $2500 per month this year, what would be his monthly salary in n years from now?

    a) 2500×0.04^n
    b) $2500 \times 1.04 \times n$
    c) 2500×1.04^n
    d) $2500 \times 1.04^{n-1}$

13. The numbers of people, in millions, who visited Amusement Park A and Amusement Park B in 2015 through 2019 are listed in the table below. What is the positive difference between the mean number of people, in millions, who visited Amusement Park B and the mean number of people, in millions, who visited Amusement Park A during those years? (Round your answer to the nearest tenth.)

Location	2015	2016	2017	2018	2019
Amusement Park A	15.7	15.2	14.4	14.1	12.3
Amusement Park B	15.9	16.0	16.1	16.0	16.2

	English Courses	
Gender	Honor	AP
Male		
Female		
Total	60	20

14. The incomplete table above summarizes the number of students who take English Honor and English AP classes by gender for the Springfield High School. There are 4 times as many English Honor female students as there are AP English female students, and there are 2 times as many as Honor English male students as there are AP English male students. If there is a total of 20 AP English students and 60 Honor English students in the school, which of the following is closest to the probability that an English AP student selected at random is female?

$$3x + 2y = 13$$
$$2x + y = 9$$

15. In the system of equations above, what is the value of $x + y$?
    a) 5
    b) 4
    c) 3
    d) 2

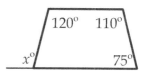

Note: Figure not drawn to scale.

16. What is the value of x in the figure above?
    a) 90
    b) 100
    c) 125
    d) 120

17. United States Consumption of Certain Types of Renewable Energy since 2003

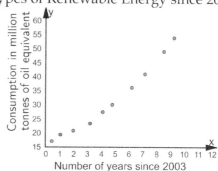

Which of the following equations best models the relationship between the variables in the scatterplot above?
    a) $y = 16(60)^x$
    b) $y = 16(0.8)^x$
    c) $y = 16(1.14)^x$
    d) $y = 16(20)^x$

18. In the figure below, what is the value of $a - b$?

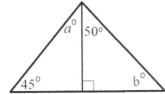

Note: Figure not drawn to scale.

a) 0
b) 5
c) 10
d) 15

19. A group of 10 students played a certain game. Every player received a score equal to an integer from 1 to 10, inclusive. For the 10 players, the mean score was 5. If more than half of the players received a score greater than 6, which of the following is true about the mean score of the remaining players?
    a) It must be less than 5.
    b) It must be equal to 5.
    c) It must be between 5 and 6.
    d) It must be greater than 6.

20. An arc of a circle measures 2.4 radians. To the nearest degree, what is the measure, in degrees, of this arc? (Disregard the degree sign when gridding your answer.)

$$f(x) = x(x + 1)$$

21. The function f is defined above. If the function g is defined by $g(x) = f(x) + 3$, what is the value of $g(3)$?
    a) 9
    b) 15
    c) 22
    d) 27

22. If x and y are positive and $3x^2y^{-1} = 27x$, what is y^{-1} in term of x?
    a) $\dfrac{x}{9}$
    b) $\dfrac{9}{x}$
    c) $\dfrac{x^2}{9}$
    d) $\dfrac{x}{3}$

Math Mock Test 2
22 QUESTIONS

DIRECTIONS
The questions in this section address a number of important math skills.
Use of a calculator is permitted for all questions.

NOTES
Unless otherwise indicated:
• All variables and expressions represent real numbers.
• Figures provided are drawn to scale.
• All figures lie in a plane.
• The domain of a given function f i s the set of all real numbers x for which f(x) is a real number.

REFERENCE

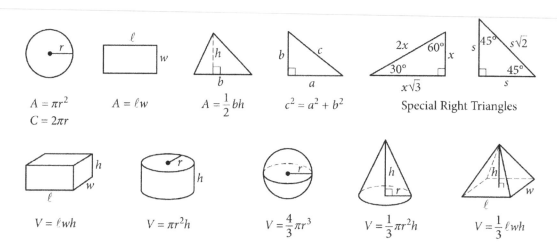

$A = \pi r^2$ $A = \ell w$ $A = \frac{1}{2}bh$ $c^2 = a^2 + b^2$ Special Right Triangles
$C = 2\pi r$

$V = \ell wh$ $V = \pi r^2 h$ $V = \frac{4}{3}\pi r^3$ $V = \frac{1}{3}\pi r^2 h$ $V = \frac{1}{3}\ell wh$

The number of degrees of arc in a circle is **360**.
The number of radians of arc in a circle is 2π.
The sum of the measures in degrees of the angles of a triangle is **180**.

For multiple-choice questions, solve each problem, choose the correct answer from the choices provided, and then circle your answer in this book. Circle only one answer for each question. If you change your mind, completely erase the circle. You will not get credit for questions with more than one answer circled, or for questions with no answers circled.

For student-produced response questions, solve each problem and write your answer next to or under the question in the test book as described below.
• Once you've written your answer, circle it clearly. You will not receive credit for anything written outside the circle, or for any questions with more than one circled answer.
• If you find **more than one correct answer**, write and circle only one answer. Your answer can be up to 5 characters for a **positive** answer and up to 6 characters (including the negative sign) for a **negative** answer, but no more.
• If your answer is a **fraction** that is too long (over 5 characters for positive, 6 characters for negative), write the decimal equivalent.
• If your answer is a **decimal** that is too long (over 5 characters for positive,
• 6 characters for negative), truncate it or round at the fourth digit.
• If your answer is a **mixed number** (such as $3\frac{1}{2}$, write it as an improper fraction (7/2) or its decimal equivalent (3.5).
• Don't include symbols such as a percent sign, comma, or dollar sign in your circled answer.

1. If 15% of x is equal to 10% of y, which of the following is equivalent to y?
   a) 200% of x
   b) 150% of x
   c) 100% of x
   d) 75% of x

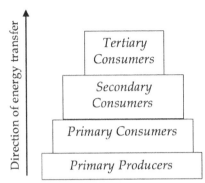

2. The energy pyramid below shows four trophic levels in an ecosystem and the direction of energy transfer between those levels. On average, 15% of the net energy of one trophic level is transferred to the next trophic level in an ecosystem. Based on the energy pyramid, if primary producers have 4,000 joules (J) of energy, approximately how much of this energy, in calories, is transferred to the secondary consumers in this ecosystem? (1 calorie = 4.18 J)
   a) 21.50
   b) 35.90
   c) 69.60
   d) 82.70

3. Of the following, which is the closest approximation of the cost per ticket when one purchases 8 tickets?

Bus Ticket Price	
Number of Bus Tickets	Price
1	7.5
Book of 6	40
Book of 12	75

   a) $6.67
   b) $6.70
   c) $6.80
   d) $6.90

4. If $-3 \le x \le 7$ and $-2 \le y \le 3$, which of the following gives the set of all possible values of xy?
   a) $-9 \le xy \le 14$
   b) $0 \le xy \le 21$
   c) $-21 \le xy \le 5$
   d) $-14 \le xy \le 21$

5. Jenn had to pay off her student loan $24,000 on a twelve-year payment plan. The amount she paid each year for the first six years is three times as much as the amount she paid each of her remaining years. How much did she pay the first year?
   a) $3,000
   b) $2,000
   c) $1,500
   d) $1,000

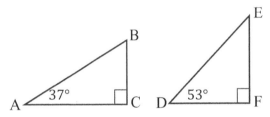

6. $\triangle ABC$ and $\triangle DEF$ are shown above. Which of the following is equal to the ratio $\frac{BC}{AC}$?
   a) $\frac{EF}{DE}$
   b) $\frac{DF}{EF}$
   c) $\frac{DE}{DF}$
   d) $\frac{DF}{DE}$

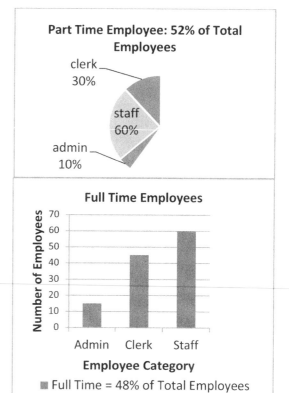

7. John runs 4 miles on each of eighteen days. The scatterplot above shows his average running speed and corresponding heart rate after each run. The line of best fit for the data is also shown. For the running speed of 8 miles per hour, John's actual heart rate was about how many beats per minutes less than the rate predicted by the line of best fit?

     a) 5
     b) 9
     c) 12
     d) 14

8. Sam drove from home at an average speed of 40 miles per hour to her working place and then returned along the same route at an average speed of 30 miles per hour. If the entire trip took her 2.1 hours, what is the entire distance, in miles, for the round trip?

     a) 36
     b) 72
     c) 84
     d) 90

9. Among the 12 colleges Helen applied to, 3 are her top schools. How many admissions would Helen have to receive to guarantee that she can get into at least one of her top schools?

     a) 8
     b) 9
     c) 10
     d) 11

10. According to the graphs above, how many part time administrators at Oak Town High School?

     a) 10
     b) 12
     c) 13
     d) 20

11. An economist thinks that the price of an investment will increase at an annual rate of 5%. If the current price of the investment is \$100, which of the following equations models the price, p, after t years?

     a) $p = 100(1.05t)$
     b) $p = 100(0.05^t)$
     c) $p = 100(1.05^t)$
     d) $p = 100(t^{0.05})$

12. In the xy-plane, the point $(1, 2)$ is the minimum of the quadratic function $f(x) = x^2 + ax + b$. What is the value of $|a-b|$?
    - a) 2
    - b) 3
    - c) 4
    - d) 5

13. Monday morning, Jason starts out with a certain amount of money that he plans to spend throughout the week. Every morning after that, he spends exactly $\frac{1}{3}$ the amount he has left. 6 days later, on Sunday morning, he finds that he has $64 left. How many dollars did Jason originally have on Monday morning?

14. Gisela would owe $23,750 in taxes each year if she were not eligible for any tax deductions. This year, Gisela is eligible for tax deductions that reduce the amount of taxes she owes by $2,850.00. If these tax deductions reduce the taxes Gisela owes this year by d%, what is the value of d ?

15. Which of the following is an equation of the circle in the xy-plane that has center $(0,0)$ and radius 4?
    - a) $x^2 + y^2 = 4$
    - b) $x^2 + y^2 = 8$
    - c) $x^2 + y^2 = 16$
    - d) $x^2 + y^2 = 64$

16. A company sells boxes of marbles in red and green. Helen purchased a box of marbles in which there were half as many green marbles in the box as red ones and 15 marbles were green. How many marbles were in Helen's box?

a) 30
b) 40
c) 45
d) 50

Roof Type			
	Asphalt Shingle	Slate	Cedar Shake	Total
Single-Story	8	4	3	15
Two-Story	21	10	2	33
Total	29	14	5	48

17. The table above shows the distribution of single-story and two-story houses in a neighborhood classified according to roof type. If one of the houses is selected at random, what is the probability that it will be a single-story house with a slate roof?
    - a) $\frac{1}{12}$
    - b) $\frac{4}{15}$
    - c) $\frac{4}{14}$
    - d) $\frac{7}{24}$

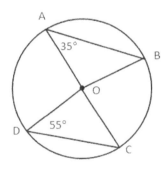

Note: Figure not drawn to scale.

18. In the graph shown above, what is the value of m∠AOD + m∠BOC?
    - a) 180
    - b) 150
    - c) 110
    - d) 100

19. A car rental company calculates the price of renting a car by adding the fixed rental fee with an additional charge for every 10 miles traveled. If the charge to rent a car and drive 50 miles is $120 and the charge to rent a car and drive 200 miles is $165, what would be the price, in dollars, to rent a car and travel 300 miles?
    a) 178
    b) 186
    c) 195
    d) 225

20. An arc of a circle measures 2.4 radians. To the nearest degree, what is the measure, in degrees, of this arc? (Disregard the degree sign when gridding your answer.)

21. In the xy-plane, line l passes through the origin and is perpendicular to the line $3x + 2y = 2b$, where b is a constant. If the two lines intersect at the point $(2a, a - 1)$, what is the value of b?
    a) –13
    b) −12
    c) −6
    d) 12

22. Let the function f be defined by $f(x) = x^2 + 27$. If $f(3y) = 3f(y)$, what is the one possible value of y?
    a) −1
    b) 1
    c) 2
    d) −3

Mock Test 2

Module 1 Keys

1. (C)	2. (D)	3. (C)	4. (D)	5. (C)	6. 15	7. 1, 2, 3	8. (A)
9. (A)	10. (D)	11. (B)	12. (C)	13. 10	14. 8	15. (C)	16. (B)
17. (C)	18. (C)	19. (C)	20. $\frac{1}{2}$ or .5	21. 60	22. (A)		

Module 2 Easy Keys

1. (D)	2. (A)	3. (A)	4. (A)	5. (D)	6. 4720	7. (125)	8. (B)
9. (B)	10. (D)	11. (A)	12. (C)	13. 1.7	14. $\frac{1}{2}$	15. (B)	16. (C)
17. (C)	18. (B)	19. (A)	20. 137 or 138	21. (B)	22. (B)		

Module 2 Hard Keys

1. (B)	2. (A)	3. (D)	4. (D)	5. (A)	6. (B)	7. (A)	8. (B)
9. (C)	10. (C)	11. (C)	12. (D)	13. 729	14. 12	15. (C)	16. (C)
17. (A)	18. (A)	19. (C)	20. 137 or 138	21. (A)	22. (D)		

Mock Test 2

Module 1 Answers

1. *Answer: (C)*
   $3x - 1 = 3$
   $12x - 4 = 4(3x - 1) = 4 \times 3 = 12$

2. *Answer: (D)*
   Replace c with value 3.
   $3x^2 + 3x + 3 = 3(x^2 + x + 1)$

3. *Answer: (C)*
   A line with a negative slope descends from left to right. According to the graph above, only when x > 1 does the line have a negative slope.

4. *Answer: (D)*
   $(3 \times 10^{-x}) + (1 \times 10^{-x}) = 4 \times 10^{-x}$
   $4 \times 10^{-x} = \frac{4}{10^x}$

5. *Answer: (C)*
   It costs $80 for every one additional hour of work.
   $2 \times 80 = \$160$

6. *Answer: 15*
   $x^2 = \frac{15}{3} = 5$
   $y = \frac{15}{5} = 3$
   $x^2 y = 5 \times 3 = 15$

7. *Answer: 1, 2, 3*
   $x + 2x + 2 + 4y = 180$
   $4y = 178 - 3x$
   $4y < 178 - 3 \times 55$
   $4y < 13$
   $0 < y < 3.25$
   $y = 1, 2, or 3$

8. *Answer: (A)*
   $x^2 - 16 = 0$
   $x^2 = 16 \rightarrow x = \pm 4$

9. *Answer: (A)*
   $x^2 + 5x + 6 = 9x + 3$
   $x^2 - 4x + 3 = 0$
   $(x - 1)(x - 3) = 0$
   $x = 1 \, or \, 3$

10. *Answer: (D)*
    The point (2, 6) lies on the graph of $y = \frac{k}{x}$.
    $6 = \frac{k}{2} \rightarrow k = 12$
    $y = \frac{k}{x} \rightarrow xy = 12$
    Therefore answer is d) where $x = 3$, $y = 4$ satisfy $xy = 12$.

11. *Answer: (B)*
    Cross multiply.
    $\frac{x-2}{3} = \frac{x+1}{2}$
    $2x - 4 = 3x + 3$
    $x = -7$

12. *Answer: (C)*
    $a \times \frac{1}{3} \times 27 = 81$
    $a = 9$

13. *Answer: 10*
    Blue: White = 3: 1
    Red : Blue = 2 : 1
    Red : Blue : White = 6 : 3 : 1
    The smallest possible number of marbles in the bag is 10.

14. *Answer: 8*
    $\Delta CED \sim \Delta GEH$
    $\frac{HE}{EG} = \frac{ED}{CE}$
    $\frac{16}{EG} = \frac{24}{20-EG}$
    $320 - 16EG = 24EG$
    $EG = 8$

15. *Answer: (C)*
    If $z = 2$, then $y = 2 - 3 = -1$.
    $x + (-1) = 9 \rightarrow x = 10$

16. *Answer: (B)*
    $4x^2 + 8x - 5 = 0$
    $(2x - 1)(2x + 5) = 0$
    $x = 0.5, or \, 2.5$

17. *Answer: (C)*
Let m be the total number of students in the school.
$(\frac{1}{4} \times m)$ *students arrive by 7 AM and 100 students arrive half an hour later. The total number of students that have arrived would be*
$\frac{1}{4} \times m + 100 = \frac{3}{4} \times m$.
$m = 200$ *students*

18. *Answer: (C)*
$\frac{4x+4x+4x}{5} = 12$
$12x = 60$
$x = 5$

19. *Answer: (C)*
$\frac{x}{x+2} = \frac{3}{4}$
$4x = 3(x + 2) \rightarrow x = 6$

20. *Answer:* $\frac{1}{2}$ *or .5*
After first taking, there are 7 blue cards and a total of 14 cards left in her pocket.
Probability to get a blue card : $\frac{7}{14} = \frac{1}{2}$

21. *Answer: 60*
The two triangles are similar; therefore, their corresponding sides are proportional.
$\frac{x}{100} = \frac{6}{10}$
$x = 60\ feet$

22. *Answer: (A)*
$3xi + 2i^6 = 6i + 4i^{13} + 5y$
$3xi - 2 = 6i + 4i + 5y$
$3xi - 2 = 10i + 5y$
$-2 + (3x - 10)i = 5y + 0i$
$5y = -2$ *and* $3x - 10 = 0$
$y = -\frac{2}{5}$ *and* $x = \frac{10}{3}$

Module 2 Easy Answers

1. *Answer: (D)*
Mon.: 30
Tue.: 20
Wed.: 40
Thur.: 40
Fri.: 20
The answer is d)

2. *Answer: (A)*
$f(-2) = 2(-2) + 1 = -3$

3. *Answer: (A)*
20 pounds : 120 rolls = x : 18 rolls
$\frac{20\ pounds}{120\ rolls} = \frac{x\ pouns}{18\ rolls}$
$120x = 20 \times 18$ *(Cross multiply)*
$x = 3\ pounds$

4. *Answer: (A)*
$\sqrt{x^2} \geq 0$
$\sqrt{x^2} = x \geq 0$

5. *Answer: (D)*
Convert to the same base before performing multiplication.
$(9^x)(27^x) = (3^2)^x(3^3)^x$
$= 3^{2x} \times 3^{3x} = 3^{5x}$

6. *Answer: 4720*
$s = 10000 - 4.4(1200) = 4720\ MB$

7. *Answer: (125)*
$1275 = 9(200) - (2 \times 200 + k)$
$k = 125$

8. *Answer: (B)*
Volume = $l \times w \times h = (3)(5)(h) = 60$
$h = 4\ inches$

9. *Answer: (B)*
There are 4 dots below the line.

10. *Answer: (D)*
Percent Increase = $\frac{2013\ Population - 2012\ Population}{2012\ Population} \times 100\%$
Total Population in 2012 = 25 + 35 + 20 + 15 + 40 = 135 thousand.
Total Population in 2013 = 15 + 30 + 25 + 15 + 35 = 120 thousand.
$\frac{120-135}{135} \times 100\% = -11.1\% \sim -11\%$

11. *Answer: (A)*
$\frac{tw}{9} = \frac{(3r-6)(3r+6)}{9} = \frac{9(r^2-4)}{9} = r^2 - 4$

12. *Answer: (C)*
Increasing every year by 4% is to multiply $(1 + \frac{4}{100})$
for each additional year.
$C(n) = (1.04)^n \times 2500 = 2500(1.04)^n$

13. *Answer: 1.7*
$Mean_A = \frac{15.7+15.2+14.4+14.1+12.3}{5} = 14.34$
$Mean_B = \frac{15.9+16.0+16.1+16.0+16.2}{5} = 16.04$
Difference $= 16.04 - 14.34 = 1.7$

14. *Answer:* $\frac{1}{2}$

Gender	English Courses	
	Honor	AP
Male	2y	y
Female	4x	x
Total	60	20

$\begin{cases} x + y = 20 \\ 2y + 4x = 60 \end{cases}$
By solving the system of equations, we find x = 10 and y = 10.
Probability $= \frac{10}{20} = \frac{1}{2}$

15. *Answer: (B)*
$(3x + 2y) - (2x + y) = 13 - 9$
$x + y = 4$

16. *Answer: (C)*
The sum of a quadrilateral's interior angles is equal to 360°.
$120 + 110 + 75 + (180 - x) = 360$
$x = 125$

17. *Answer: (C)*
It is an exponential growth model according to the graph.
$y = ab^x$, *where a is the initial value.*
$y = 16(b)^x$
Plug in one point (9, 55)
$55 = 16(b)^9$
$b = \left(\frac{55}{16}\right)^{\frac{1}{9}} = 1.14$
$y = 16(1.14)^x$

18. *Answer: (B)*
$a = 45$ *and* $b = 40$
$a - b = 5$

19. *Answer: (A)*
The average is 5. If one part is greater than 5, the other part must be less than 5. The answer is a).

20. *Answer: 137 or 138*
$\frac{2.4}{2\pi} \times 360 = 137.6$

21. *Answer: (B)*
$g(3) = f(3) + 3 = 3(3 + 1) + 3 = 15$

22. *Answer: (B)*
Divide by $3x^2$ *on both sides of the equation* $3x^2y^{-1} = 27x$.
$y^{-1} = \frac{27x}{3x^2} = \frac{9}{x}$

Module 2 Hard Answers

1. *Answer: (B)*
$\frac{15}{100}x = \frac{10}{100}y$
$y = \frac{15}{10}x = \frac{3}{2}x = 1.5\ x = 150\%\ x$

2. *Answer: (A)*
It is two levels up from primary producers to secondary consumers.
$(4000)(0.15)(0.15) \times \frac{1}{4.18}$
$= 21.5$ *calories*

3. *Answer: (D)*
$\frac{\$40 + 2 \times 7.5}{8\ tickets} = \$6.875$ *per ticket*

4. *Answer: (D)*
Try out different combinations of x and y.
$-14 \le xy \le 21$

5. *Answer: (A)*
Let the first year payment be \$x and each of her last 6 years be \$y.
$x = 3y$ *and* $6x + 6y = 24000$
$18y + 6y = 24000$
$y = 1000$
$x = 3000$
The first year payment is \$3000.

6. *Answer: (B)*
ΔABC and ΔDEF are similar triangles by AA similarity (right triangles)
$\frac{BC}{AC} = \frac{DF}{EF}$

7. *Answer: (A)*
According to the graph, at 8 miles/hour, the predicted heart rate is about 157 beats per minute and the actual heart rate is about 152 beats per minute.
The difference is $157 - 152 = 5$ beats/minute.

8. *Answer: (B)*
Let one trip have x miles.
Time $= 2.1 = t_1 + t_2 = \frac{x}{30} + \frac{x}{40}$
$2.1 = x(\frac{1}{30} + \frac{1}{40})$
$x = 36$
Entire Distance $= 2 \times 36 = 72$

9. *Answer: (C)*
$12 - 3 = 9$
She applied to 9 schools that are not her top choices. If all 9 of these schools accept Helen, then the 10th school which accepts her must be one of her top schools.
$9 + 1 = 10$

10. *Answer: (C)*
Number of Full Time Employees $= 15 + 45 + 60 = 120$ employees.
Full time employees comprise of 48% of the total.
$0.48 \times$ Total Employees $= 120$ employees
Total Employees $= 250$ employees
Part Time Employees $= 250 \times 0.52 = 130$ employees
$130 \times 0.1 = 13$ part time administrators

11. *Answer: (C)*
This is a compound interest formula.
$p = p_0(1 + r)^t = 100(1.05)^t$

12. *Answer: (D)*
The vextex of the quadratic function $f(x) = x^2 + ax + b$ is $(-\frac{a}{2}, f(-\frac{a}{2}))$
$-\frac{a}{2} = 1 \rightarrow a = -2$
$2 = (1)^2 - 2(1) + b \rightarrow b = 3$
$|a - b| = |-2 - 3| = 5$

13. *Answer: 729*
Jason spends $\frac{1}{3}$ of his money each day, so he has $\frac{2}{3}$ of his money left next morning.
Let Jason have \$x on Monday. On Sunday, he will have:$(\frac{2}{3} \times \frac{2}{3} \times \frac{2}{3} \times \frac{2}{3} \times \frac{2}{3} \times \frac{2}{3})x$ dollars left.
$\frac{2^6 x}{3^6} = 64$
$x = 3^6 = 729$ dollars

14. *Answer: 12*
$\frac{2850}{23750} \times (100\%) = 12\%$

15. *Answer: (C)*
Standard equation of a circle:
$(x - h)^2 + (y - k)^2 = r^2$
$(x - 0)^2 + (y - 0)^2 = 4^2$

16. *Answer: (C)*
Let g be the number of green marbles and r be the number of red marbles.
Translate "half as many green marbles as red ones" into an algebraic statement: $g = \frac{1}{2}r$
Plug $g = 15$ into the equation to get $r = 30$
Therefore, $15 + 30 = 45$.

17. *Answer: (A)*
$p = \frac{single\ house\ and\ slate\ roof}{total\ house} = \frac{4}{48} = \frac{1}{12}$

18. *Answer: (A)*
$m\angle AOD + m\angle BOC = 360 - m\angle DOC - m\angle AOB$
$m\angle AOB = 180 - 2 \times 35 = 110$
$m\angle DOC = 180 - 2 \times 55 = 70$
$m\angle AOD + m\angle BOC = 360 - 110 - 70 = 180$

19. *Answer: (C)*
Let initial charge be \$x, and the fee for every 10 miles be \$y.
$x + 5y = 120$
$x + 20y = 165$
$15y = 45, \quad y = 3, \quad x = 105$
For traveling 300 miles, the total charge is $105 + 30 \times 3 = 195$.

20. *Answer: 137 or 138*
$\frac{2.4}{2\pi} \times 360 = 137.6$

21. *Answer: (A)*

The line of $3x + 2y = 2b$ has a slope of $\frac{-3}{2}$.

Line l is perpendicular, so it should have a slope of
$\frac{2}{3}$. We also know that it passes through the origin.

$y = \frac{2}{3}x$

$a - 1 = \frac{2}{3}(2a)$

$3a - 3 = 4a \quad \rightarrow \quad a = -3$

point (−6 , −4) passing through $3x + 2y = 2b$ →

$-6 \times 3 - 4 \times 2 = -26 = 2b$

$b = -13$

22. *Answer: (D)*

$f(3y) = (3y)^2 + 27 = 3f(y) = 3(y^2 + 27)$

$9y^2 + 27 = 3y^2 + 3 \times 27$

$6y^2 = 54, \quad y^2 = 9, \quad y = \pm 3$

Math Mock Test 3
22 QUESTIONS

DIRECTIONS

The questions in this section address a number of important math skills.

Use of a calculator is permitted for all questions.

○ **Check the answers after the Module 1 test. If there are more than 8 questions answered incorrectly in Module 1, take the Easy part of Module 2. Otherwise, take the Hard part of Module 2.**

NOTES

Unless otherwise indicated:

• All variables and expressions represent real numbers.

• Figures provided are drawn to scale.

• All figures lie in a plane.

• The domain of a given function f i s the set of all real numbers x for which f(x) is a real number.

REFERENCE

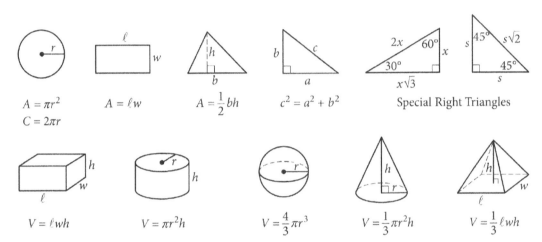

$A = \pi r^2$ $A = \ell w$ $A = \frac{1}{2}bh$ $c^2 = a^2 + b^2$ Special Right Triangles

$C = 2\pi r$

$V = \ell wh$ $V = \pi r^2 h$ $V = \frac{4}{3}\pi r^3$ $V = \frac{1}{3}\pi r^2 h$ $V = \frac{1}{3}\ell wh$

The number of degrees of arc in a circle is **360**.

The number of radians of arc in a circle is 2π.

The sum of the measures in degrees of the angles of a triangle is **180**.

For multiple-choice questions, solve each problem, choose the correct answer from the choices provided, and then circle your answer in this book. Circle only one answer for each question. If you change your mind, completely erase the circle. You will not get credit for questions with more than one answer circled, or for questions with no answers circled.

For student-produced response questions, solve each problem and write your answer next to or under the question in the test book as described below.

• Once you've written your answer, circle it clearly. You will not receive credit for anything written outside the circle, or for any questions with more than one circled answer.

• If you find **more than one correct answer**, write and circle only one answer. Your answer can be up to 5 characters for a **positive** answer and up to 6 characters (including the negative sign) for a **negative** answer, but no more.

• If your answer is a **fraction** that is too long (over 5 characters for positive, 6 characters for negative), write the decimal equivalent.

• If your answer is a **decimal** that is too long (over 5 characters for positive,

• 6 characters for negative), truncate it or round at the fourth digit.

• If your answer is a **mixed number** (such as $3\frac{1}{2}$, write it as an improper fraction (7/2) or its decimal equivalent (3.5).

• Don't include symbols such as a percent sign, comma, or dollar sign in your circled answer.

1. Larry spent a total of $200 to lease snowboard equipment at Winter Mountain during his vacation. Each day of his vacation, he purchased a lift ticket for $44. If Larry purchased t lift tickets, how much money, in dollars, did Larry spend during his vacation at Winter Mountain on snowboard equipment and lift tickets?
    a) $44t$
    b) $44t - 200$
    c) $200 + 44t$
    d) $200 - 44t$

2. Jenna has practiced a total of 150 hours for her sport this year. If Jenna practices exactly 10 hours each week, which of the following equations can be solved to find the total number of weeks, x, she practiced this year?
    a) $10x = 150$
    b) $\frac{x}{10} = 150$
    c) $\frac{10}{x} = 150$
    d) $x(x - 10) = 150$

 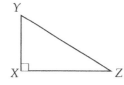

3. Right triangle ABC and XYZ above are similar. What is the tangent of angle Z?
    a) $\frac{3}{5}$
    b) $\frac{3}{4}$
    c) $\frac{4}{3}$
    d) $\frac{5}{3}$

4. Let $wx^2 = y$, where $wxy \neq 0$. If both x and y are multiplied by 3, then w is
    a) multiplied by $\frac{1}{3}$
    b) multiplied by $\frac{1}{9}$
    c) multiplied by $\frac{1}{18}$
    d) multiplied by $\frac{1}{27}$

5. If $(x - 1)^2 - 6(x - 1) + 9 = 0$, what is the value of x?
    a) 2
    b) 4
    c) 5
    d) 7

6. The total amount of registration fees paid by participants at a conference was $12,400. each participant who registered on the day of the conference paid a $150 fee, and each participant who registered in advance paid a $125 fee. If 74 participants registered in advance, how many participants registered on the day of the conference?

7. There are four points A, B, C, D and E on line l, and another four points W, X, Y, and Z on a different line parallel to line l. How many distinct lines can be drawn that include exactly two of these 9 points?

$$\frac{4}{x - 2} + \frac{2}{x} = \frac{8}{x^2 - 2x}$$

8. What value of x satisfies the equation above?
    a) 0
    b) 2
    c) 14
    d) No value of x satisfies the equation.

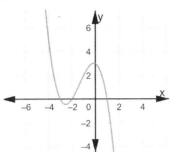

9. The graph of function f, where $y = f(x)$, is shown in the xy-plane. What is the value of $f(0)$?

     a) -2
     b) 0
     c) 1
     d) 3

$$4x - 2y > 8$$

10. Which of the following ordered pairs (x, y) are in the solution set for the inequality above?

     I. $(-1, -10)$
     II. $(2, 0)$
     III. $(1, -2)$
     a) I only
     b) II only
     c) III only
     d) I and II only

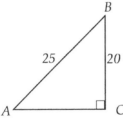

11. In the right triangle above, the tangent of $\angle A$ is $\frac{4}{3}$. What is the sine of $\angle B$?

     a) $\frac{3}{5}$
     b) $\frac{3}{4}$
     c) $\frac{4}{5}$
     d) $\frac{5}{3}$

12. If $0 > a > b$, which of the following must be less than $\frac{a}{b}$?

     a) 1
     b) 2
     c) ab
     d) $\frac{a}{2b}$

13. In the complex number system, what is the value of the expression $6i^4 - 5i^2 + 4$? (Note: $i = \sqrt{-1}$)

14. Kat has some coins in her purse. Of the coins, 5 are pennies. If she randomly picks one of the coins from her purse, the probability of picking a penny is $\frac{1}{4}$. How many coins are in her purse?

15. Which of the following CANNOT affect the value of the median in a set of nonzero unique numbers with more than two elements?

     a) Decrease each number by 3
     b) Increase the largest number only
     c) Increase the smallest number only
     d) Decrease the largest number only

16. If the average (arithmetic mean) of a and b is m, which of the following is the average of a, b, and $4m$?

     a) $2m$
     b) $\frac{5m}{2}$
     c) $3m$
     d) $\frac{7m}{3}$

17. If $g(x) = 3x - 6$, then at what value of x does the graph of $g(x)$ cross the x-axis?
    a) -6
    b) -3
    c) 0
    d) 2

18. Let $*m$ be defined as $*m = m^2 + 4$ for all values of m. If $*x = 3x^2$, which of the following could be the value of x?
    a) -2
    b) 1
    c) 2
    d) $-\sqrt{2}$

19. In the xy-plane, the points $(2, 4)$ and $(-2, -4)$ are the endpoints of a diameter of a circle. Which of the following is an equation of the circle?
    a) $(x - 2)^2 + (y + 4)^2 = 80$
    b) $(x - 2)^2 + (y + 4)^2 = 20$
    c) $x^2 + y^2 = 80$
    d) $x^2 + y^2 = 20$

20. Alice is ordering desktop computers for her company. The desktop computers cost $500 each, and tax is an additional 8% of the total cost of the computers. If she can spend no more than $50,000 on the desktop computers, including tax, what is the maximum number of computers that Alice can purchase?

21. In the figure below, point P is the center of the circle. What is the value of x?

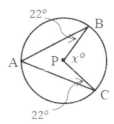

22. Which statement describes the solution to the equation above?

$$\frac{6}{x^2 - 9} = \frac{2}{x - 3} + \frac{1}{x + 3}$$

    a) 1 is the only solution.
    b) -1 is the only solution.
    c) 1 and -1 are both solutions.
    d) There are no solutions.

Math Mock Test 3
22 QUESTIONS

DIRECTIONS
The questions in this section address a number of important math skills.
Use of a calculator is permitted for all questions.

NOTES
Unless otherwise indicated:
- All variables and expressions represent real numbers.
- Figures provided are drawn to scale.
- All figures lie in a plane.
- The domain of a given function f i s the set of all real numbers x for which f(x) is a real number.

REFERENCE

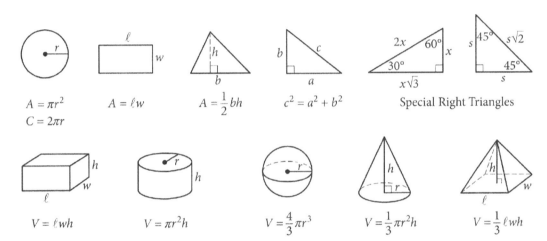

$A = \pi r^2$ $A = \ell w$ $A = \frac{1}{2}bh$ $c^2 = a^2 + b^2$ Special Right Triangles
$C = 2\pi r$

$V = \ell wh$ $V = \pi r^2 h$ $V = \frac{4}{3}\pi r^3$ $V = \frac{1}{3}\pi r^2 h$ $V = \frac{1}{3}\ell wh$

The number of degrees of arc in a circle is **360**.
The number of radians of arc in a circle is 2π.
The sum of the measures in degrees of the angles of a triangle is **180**.

For multiple-choice questions, solve each problem, choose the correct answer from the choices provided, and then circle your answer in this book. Circle only one answer for each question. If you change your mind, completely erase the circle. You will not get credit for questions with more than one answer circled, or for questions with no answers circled.

For student-produced response questions, solve each problem and write your answer next to or under the question in the test book as described below.
- Once you've written your answer, circle it clearly. You will not receive credit for anything written outside the
- circle, or for any questions with more than one circled answer.
- If you find **more than one correct answer**, write and circle only one answer. Your answer can be up to 5 characters for a **positive** answer and up to 6 characters (including the negative sign) for a **negative** answer, but no more.
- If your answer is a **fraction** that is too long (over 5 characters for positive, 6 characters for negative), write the decimal equivalent.

- If your answer is a **decimal** that is too long (over 5 characters for positive,
- 6 characters for negative), truncate it or round at the fourth digit.
- If your answer is a **mixed number** (such as $3\frac{1}{2}$, write it as an improper fraction (7/2) or its decimal equivalent (3.5).
- Don't include symbols such as a percent sign, comma, or dollar sign in your circled answer.

1. If $n > 0$, what is the value of $4^n + 4^n + 10 \times 4^n + 4^{n+1}$?
   a) 4^{4n}
   b) $4^{(n+4)}$
   c) $4^{(n+1)}$
   d) $4^{(n+2)}$

2. Cahill purchased 6.75 gallons of gasoline, for which she paid $15.40. Which of the following is closest to the price, in dollars, Cahill paid per gallon of gasoline?
   a) $2.04
   b) $2.10
   c) $2.20
   d) $2.28

3. If $10 = 2x + 14$, which of the following must be true?
   a) $4x = 8$
   b) $10x = 16$
   c) $8x = -16$
   d) $12x = -144$

4. Gina sold boxes of cookies and bags of candy. The ratio of the number of boxes of cookies she sold to the number of bags of candy she sold was 2 to 1. If Gina sold 8 boxes of cookies, how many bags of candy did she sell?
   a) 4
   b) 8
   c) 10
   d) 16

5. There are 18 boxes of apples in the storage room. Each box has at least 23 apples, and at most 25 apples. Which of the following could be the total number of apples in the storage room?
   a) 300
   b) 350
   c) 400
   d) 425

6. In the thirty days of June, for every day it rained, it did not rain for four days. The number of days it rained in June was how many days less than the number of days it did not rain?

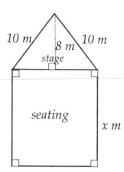

7. The figure above is the floor plan drawn by an architect for a small concert hall. The stage has depth 8 meters (m) and two walls each of length 10 m. If the seating portion of the hall has an area of 180 square meters, what is the value of x?

$$6ax - 2 = 16$$

8. Based on the equation above, what is the value of $3ax - 1$?
   a) 3
   b) 6
   c) 8
   d) 12

9. If y is directly proportional to x and y is equal to 30 when x is equal to 4, what is the value of y when $x = 8$?
   a) 15
   b) 45
   c) 60
   d) 70

10. Sandy rode her bike 6 miles in 45 minutes. At this rate, how long would it take her to ride her bike 20 miles?

    a) 2 hours and 5 minutes
    b) 2 hours and 20 minutes
    c) 2 hours and 30 minutes
    d) 2 hours and 50 minutes

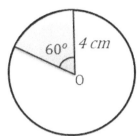

11. In the figure above, the circle has a center O and radius of 4 cm. What is the area of the shaded portion, in square centimeters?

    a) $\frac{1}{2}\pi$

    b) $2\frac{2}{3}\pi$

    c) $2\frac{3}{4}\pi$

    d) 3π

12. The Rockville Reservoir had an original storage capacity of 500,000 acre-feet at the end of 1950, the year in which it was built. Starting in 1951, sediment carried downstream by the Rockville River collected in the reservoir and began reducing the reservoir s storage capacity at the approximate rate of 1,000 acre-feet per year. If the reservoir s capacity x years after 1951 was between 490,000 and 492,000 acre-feet, which of the following must be true?

    a) $x < 4$
    b) $4 < x < 6$
    c) $6 < x < 8$
    d) $8 < x < 10$

$$\frac{1}{2}x = a$$
$$x + y = 5a$$

13. In the system of equations above, a is a constant such that $0 < a < \frac{1}{3}$. If (y, x) is a solution to the system of equations, what is one possible value of y?

14. If the lengths of the edges of a cube are increased by 20%, the volume of the cube will increase by how many percent? (Round your answer to the nearest tenth)

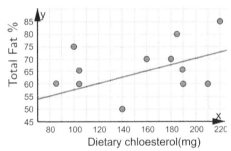

15. The scatterplot above shows the relationship between the amount of dietary cholesterol, in milligrams (mg), and the amount of total fat, in grams (g), in the 12 sandwiches offered by a certain restaurant. The line of best fit predicts the amount of total fat a sandwich has based on the amount of dietary cholesterol in the sandwich. How many grams of total fat are in the sandwich for which this prediction is the most accurate?

    a) 140
    b) 115
    c) 85
    d) 60

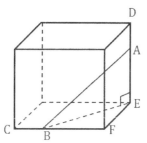

16. The cube shown above has edges of length 5. If $\overline{CB} = \overline{AD} = 2$, what is the length of $\overline{AB}$?

    a) $\sqrt{33}$

    b) $\sqrt{38}$

    c) $\sqrt{43}$

    d) $\sqrt{50}$

17. The electric charge of a single electron is called the electron charge and can be measured in coulombs (C). The table below shows four measurements of the electron charge made in the early 1900s.

Electron Charge (C)
-1.639×10^{-19}
-1.641×10^{-19}
-1.647×10^{-19}
-1.641×10^{-19}

What is the mean of these measurements, in coulombs?

    a) -4.118×10^{-20}
    b) -1.641×10^{-19}
    c) -1.642×10^{-19}
    d) -1.568×10^{-19}

18. If $2 \times 2^x + 2^x + 2^x = 2^6$, what is the value of x?

    a) 4
    b) 3
    c) 2
    d) 1

19. Which of the following is an equation of a line in the xy-plane that is parallel to the line with equation $2x + 3y = 18$?

    a) $2x + 3y = 12$
    b) $2x - 3y = 10$
    c) $3x + 2y = 9$
    d) $3x - 2y = 4$

1.313113111311113...

20. The decimal number above consists of only 1s and 3s. The first 3 is followed by one 1, the second 3 is followed by two 1s, and the third 3 is followed by three 1s. If such a pattern goes on, how many 1s are between the 94th 3 and the 98th 3?

21. If $(x^{24})^a = (x^2)^4$, and $x > 1$, what is the value of a?

    a) $\frac{1}{4}$
    b) $\frac{1}{3}$
    c) $\frac{1}{2}$
    d) 2

$$kx + y = 1$$
$$y = -x^2 + k$$

22. In the system of equations above, k is a constant. When the equations are graphed in the xy-plane, the graphs intersect at exactly two points. Which of the following CANNOT be the value of k?

    a) 3
    b) 2
    c) 1
    d) 0

Math Mock Test 3
22 QUESTIONS

DIRECTIONS

The questions in this section address a number of important math skills.
Use of a calculator is permitted for all questions.

NOTES

Unless otherwise indicated:
• All variables and expressions represent real numbers.
• Figures provided are drawn to scale.
• All figures lie in a plane.
• The domain of a given function f i s the set of all real numbers x for which f(x) is a real number.

REFERENCE

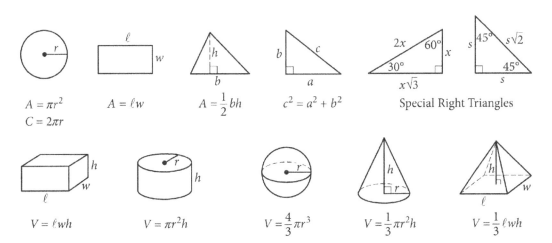

$A = \pi r^2$ $A = \ell w$ $A = \frac{1}{2}bh$ $c^2 = a^2 + b^2$ Special Right Triangles

$C = 2\pi r$

$V = \ell wh$ $V = \pi r^2 h$ $V = \frac{4}{3}\pi r^3$ $V = \frac{1}{3}\pi r^2 h$ $V = \frac{1}{3}\ell wh$

The number of degrees of arc in a circle is **360**.
The number of radians of arc in a circle is 2π.
The sum of the measures in degrees of the angles of a triangle is **180**.

For multiple-choice questions, solve each problem, choose the correct answer from the choices provided, and then circle your answer in this book. Circle only one answer for each question. If you change your mind, completely erase the circle. You will not get credit for questions with more than one answer circled, or for questions with no answers circled.

For student-produced response questions, solve each problem and write your answer next to or under the question in the test book as described below.
• Once you've written your answer, circle it clearly. You will not receive credit for anything written outside the circle, or for any questions with more than one circled answer.
• If you find **more than one correct answer**, write and circle only one answer. Your answer can be up to 5 characters for a **positive** answer and up to 6 characters (including the negative sign) for a **negative** answer, but no more.
• If your answer is a **fraction** that is too long (over 5 characters for positive, 6 characters for negative), write the decimal equivalent.
• If your answer is a **decimal** that is too long (over 5 characters for positive,
• 6 characters for negative), truncate it or round at the fourth digit.
• If your answer is a **mixed number** (such as $3\frac{1}{2}$, write it as an improper fraction (7/2) or its decimal equivalent (3.5).
• Don't include symbols such as a percent sign, comma, or dollar sign in your circled answer.

1. △ABC is an equilateral triangle with side length of 8. What is the area of △ABC?
   a) 64
   b) 32
   c) $16\sqrt{3}$
   d) $16\sqrt{2}$

2. A rectangular frame with a 1-inch margin is placed around a rectangular picture with dimensions of 6 inches by 8 inches. What is the area of the frame itself in square inches?
   a) 80
   b) 48
   c) 32
   d) 24

3. Sam drove from home at an average speed of 60 miles per hour to her working place and then returned along the same route at an average speed of 40 miles per hour. If the entire trip took her 2 hours, what is the entire distance, in miles, for the round trip?
   a) 48
   b) 96
   c) 100
   d) 108

4. A restaurant offers a choice of one side dish when a main course is ordered. Customers can choose from a list of 3 different main courses and 4 different side dishes. How many different combinations are there of one main course and one side dish?
   a) 7
   b) 12
   c) 16
   d) 2

5. In the figure below, the vertices of an isosceles right triangle, an equilateral triangle, and a regular pentagon intersect at one point. What is the value of $a + b + c$?

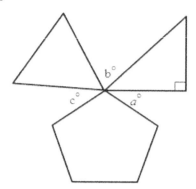

   a) 90
   b) 100
   c) 135
   d) 147

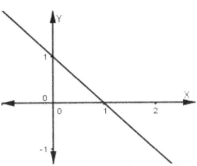

6. The figure above shows the graph of the line $y = mx + b$, where m and b are constants. Which of the following best represents the graph of the line $y = -2mx + b$?

a)

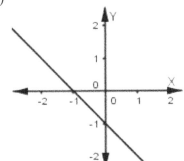

b)

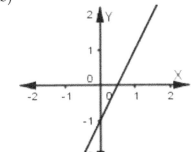

c)

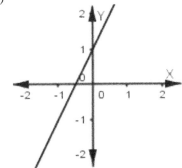

d)

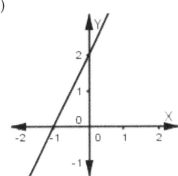

7. The following are coordinates of points on the xy-plane. Which of these points is nearest to the origin?

    a) $(0, -1)$

    b) $(-\frac{1}{2}, 0)$

    c) $(-\frac{1}{2}, -\frac{1}{2})$

    d) $(\frac{1}{2}, \frac{1}{2})$

$$h(x) = -16x^2 + 100x + 10$$

8. The quadratic function above models the height above the ground h, in feet, of a projectile x seconds after it had been launched vertically. If $y = h(x)$ is graphed in the xy-plane, which of the following represents the real-life meaning of the positive x-intercept of the graph?

    a) The initial height of the projectile

    b) The maximum height of the projectile

    c) The time at which the projectile reaches its maximum height

    d) The time at which the projectile hits the ground

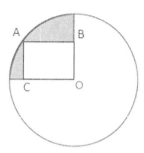

9. In the figure above, rectangle ABOC is drawn in circle O. If OB = 6 and OC = 8, what is the area of the shaded region?

     a) $24\pi - 24$

     b) $25\pi - 24$

     c) $25\pi - 48$

     d) $\frac{25\pi}{2} - 48$

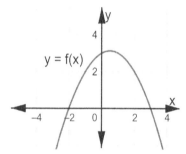

10. The graph of function f is shown in the xy–plane above, and selected values for the function g are shown in the table. For which of the following values of x is $g(x) > f(x)$?

     a) 0

     b) 1

     c) 2

     d) 3

11. The efficiency of an engine is the proportion of its fuel energy that the engine can convert into motion x energy. The equation $E = 1 - \frac{x}{p}$ relates an engine's efficiency, E ,to its exhaust temperature x , in kelvins, and its operating temperature p , in kelvins. A particular automobile

engine has an operating temperature of 480 kelvins and an exhaust temperature of 250 kelvins. Based on the engine's efficiency, about how many joules of motion energy can the engine obtain from 50,000,000 joules of fuel energy?

     a) 15,200,000

     b) 24,000,000

     c) 64,600,000

     d) 105,000,000

12. A biologist grows a culture of bacteria as part of an experiment. At the start of the experiment, there are 100 bacteria in the culture. The biologist observes that the population of bacteria doubles every 20 minutes. Which of the following equations best models the number, n, of bacteria t hours after the start of the experiment?

     a) $n = 100(2)^{\frac{t}{20}}$

     b) $n = 100(1 + \frac{t}{20})$

     c) $n = 100(2)^{\frac{10t}{3}}$

     d) $n = 100(1 + \frac{10t}{3})$

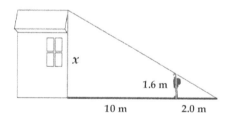

13. Jon walks 10 meters away from a wall outside his school building as shown in the figure above. At the point he stands, he notices that his shadow reaches to the same spot as the shadow of the school. If Jon is 1.6 meters tall and his shadow is 2 meters long, how high is the school building, in meters?

14. Gina drove at an average of 40 miles per hour from her house to a bookstore. Along the same route, she returned at an average of 60 miles per hour. If the entire trip took her 1 hour, how many miles did Gina drive in total?

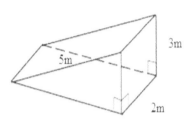

15. Find the surface area in square meter of the half of a rectangular solid as shown above.
    a) 44
    b) 36
    c) 34
    d) 32

16. If $x = \sqrt{12} + \sqrt{48}$, what is the value of x^2
    a) 124
    b) 120
    c) 108
    d) 84

$$h(t) = -16t^2 + 320t + h_o$$

17. At time $t = 0$, a rocket was launched from a height of h_o feet above the ground. Until the rocket hit the ground, its height, in feet, after t seconds was given by the function h above. For which of the following values of t did the rocket have the same height as it did when $t = 5$.
    a) 10
    b) 15
    c) 18
    d) 20

18. If N has a remainder of 2 when divided by 3, 4, 5, or 6 and N is a three-digit number, what is the largest possible value for N?
    a) 360
    b) 362
    c) 720
    d) 722

19. Based on Mrs. Johnson's grading policies, if a student answers 90 to 100 percent of the questions correctly in a math test, she/he will receive a letter grade of A. If there are 50 questions on the final exam, what is the minimum number of questions the student would need to answer correctly to receive a grade of A?
    a) 36
    b) 40
    c) 42
    d) 45

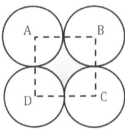

20. The figure above consists of four congruent, tangent circles with radius 2. What is the area of the shaded region? (Round your answer to the nearest hundredth)

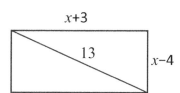

21. The figure above is a rectangle. What is the value of *x*?
    a) 9
    b) 8
    c) $5\sqrt{2}$
    d) 6

22. 36 marbles, all of which are red, blue, or green, are placed in a bag. If a marble is picked from the bag at random, the probability of getting a red marble is $\frac{1}{4}$ and the probability of getting a blue marble is $\frac{1}{2}$. How many green marbles are in the bag?
    a) 9
    b) 10
    c) 12
    d) 15

Mock Test 3

Module 1 Keys

1. (C)	2. (A)	3. (B)	4. (A)	5. (B)	6. 21	7. 20	8. (D)
9. (D)	10. (A)	11. (A)	12. (D)	13. 15	14. 20	15. (B)	16. (A)
17. (D)	18. (D)	19. (D)	20. 92	21. 88	22. (A)		

Module 2 Easy Keys

1. (D)	2. (D)	3. (C)	4. (A)	5. (D)	6. 18	7. 15	8. (C)
9. (C)	10. (C)	11. (B)	12. (D)	13. $0 < y < 1$	14. 72.8	15. (D)	16. (C)
17. (C)	18. (A)	19. (D)	20. 382	21. (B)	22. (D)		

Module 2 Hard Keys

1. (C)	2. (C)	3. (B)	4. (B)	5. (D)	6. (C)	7. (B)	8. (D)
9. (C)	10. (D)	11. (B)	12. (A)	13. 9.6	14. 48	15. (B)	16. (C)
17. (B)	18. (D)	19. (D)	20. 3.43	21. (A)	22. (A)		

Mock Test 3

Module 1 Answers

1. Answer: (C)
   A linear model:
   $y = 44t + 200$

2. Answer: (A)
   (Hours per Week) × (Number of week) =
   Total Hours of Sport
   $10 × (x) = 150$

3. Answer: (B)
   $AC = \sqrt{10^2 - 6^2} = 8$
   $tan(c) = \frac{AB}{AC} = \frac{6}{8} = \frac{3}{4}$
   $\Delta ABC \sim \Delta XYZ$
   $m\angle C = m\angle Z$
   $tan(Z) = tan(C) = \frac{3}{4}$

4. Answer: (A)
   $w(3x)^2 = 3y$
   $w = \frac{3y}{9x^2} = \frac{1y}{3x^2}$

5. Answer: (B)
   Set $x - 1 = a \rightarrow a^2 - 6a + 9 = 0$
   $(a - 3)^2 = 0 \rightarrow a = 3$
   $x - 1 = 3 \rightarrow x = 4$

6. Answer: 21
   Let x be the participants registered on the day of the conference:
   $12400 = 74(125) + 150x$
   $x = 21$

7. Answer: 20
   Each of the five points on line l can be connected to each of the four points on the parallel line.
   $5 × 4 = 20$

8. Answer: (D)
   $\frac{4}{x-2} + \frac{2}{x} = \frac{4x + 2(x-2)}{x^2 - 2x} = \frac{6x - 4}{x^2 - 2x}$
   $\frac{6x - 4}{x^2 - 2x} = \frac{8}{x^2 - 2x}$
   $6x - 4 = 8$
   $x = 2$ but $x = 2$ can't be a solution because it makes the denominator of $\frac{4}{x-2}$ equal to zero.

9. Answer: (D)
   The value of $f(0)$ is the y-intercept which is 3.

10. Answer: (A)
    $4(-1) - 2(-10) > 8 \rightarrow ok$
    $4(2) - 2(0) > 8 \rightarrow wrong$
    $4(1) - 2(-2) > 8 \rightarrow wrong$
    Therefore, I is the only solution.

11. Answer: (A)
    $tan(A) = \frac{4}{3} = \frac{20}{AC} \rightarrow AC = 15$
    $sin(B) = \frac{AC}{AB} = \frac{15}{25} = \frac{3}{5}$

12. Answer: (D)
    $0 > a > b$
    If divided each sides by b, then change direction:
    $0 < \frac{a}{b} < 1.$
    Only (d) correct. $\frac{a}{2b} < \frac{a}{b}$

13. Answer: 15
    $6i^4 - 5i^2 + 4 =$
    $6(1) - 5(-1) + 4 = 15$

14. Answer: 20
    $\frac{5}{Total\ Coins} = \frac{1}{4}$
    Total Coins = 20

15. Answer: (B)
    The median of an odd-numbered set is the number in the middle when all numbers in the set have been sorted in numerical order. In an even-numbered set, it is the average of the two middle elements.
    We can change the median by:
        Changing the value of the median
        Changing order of numbers so that we have a new median
    Choices (a) change all values so the median will be changed. Choice (c) and (d) could result in a new median if the number changed becomes the new median. Choice (b) increases the element that is already the largest, and we know that there are more than 2 elements, so the median does not get changed.

16. Answer: (A)

The average of a, b, and $4m$ is equal to the sum of a, b, and $4m$ divided by 3.

$a + b = 2m$

$a + b + 4m = 2m + 4m = 6m$

Average: $\frac{6m}{3} = 2m$

17. *Answer: (D)*

The value of x where $g(x)$ crosses the x-axis is the value of x where $g(x)$ is equal to 0.

$0 = 3x - 6$

$x = 2$

18. *Answer: (D)*

*$x = x^2 + 4$

$x^2 + 4 = 3x^2$

$x^2 = 2 \rightarrow x = \pm\sqrt{2}$

19. *Answer: (D)*

$Center = \frac{(2,4)+(-2,-4)}{2} = (0,0)$

$Radius = \frac{\sqrt{(2+2)^2+(4+4)^2}}{2} = \sqrt{20}$

$x^2 + y^2 = \left(\sqrt{20}\right)^2 = 20$

20. *Answer: 92*

Let x be the maximum number of computer to purchase.

$500(x)(1 + 0.08) \leq 50000$

$x \leq 92.6$

The maximum of x is 92.

21. *Answer: 88*

$\frac{1}{2}x + (360 - x) + 22 + 22 = 360$

$-x = -88 \rightarrow x = 88$

22. *Answer: (A)*

$\frac{2}{x-3} + \frac{1}{+3} = \frac{2x+6+x-3}{(x+3)(x-3)} = \frac{3x+3}{x^2-9}$

$\frac{3x+3}{x^2-9} = \frac{6}{x^2-9}$

$6 = 3x + 3 \rightarrow x = 1$

Module 2 Easy Answers

1. *Answer: (D)*

$4^n + 4^n + 10 \times 4^n + 4 \times 4^n = 16 \times 4^n = 4^{(n+2)}$

2. *Answer: (D)*

$Price\ per\ Gallon = \frac{\$15.4}{6.75} = \$2.28/gal$

3. *Answer: (C)*

$10 = 2x + 14$

$x = -2$

$8x = -16$

4. *Answer: (A)*

Number of bags of candy is x:

$\frac{candies}{cookies} = \frac{1}{2} = \frac{x}{8}$

$x = 4$

5. *Answer: (D)*

Set up the inequality for the number of apples and then multiply the inequality by 18.

$(23 < x < 25) \times 18$

$414 < 15x < 450$

6. *Answer: 18*

Rain Days : Dry Days = 1 : 4

$\frac{The\ Number\ of\ Rain\ Days}{30\ Days} = \frac{1}{1+4}$

Apply cross multiplication.

The Number of Rain Days = 6

$30 - 6 = 24$

The Number of Dry Days = 24

$24 - 6 = 18$

7. *Answer: 15*

$a^2 + 8^2 = 10^2$

$a = 6$

The width of the seating portion is $2 \times 6 = 12$

$12x = 180 \rightarrow x = 15$

8. *Answer: (C)*

$6ax - 2 = 16$

$3ax - 1 = 8$

9. *Answer: (C)*
   $\frac{30}{4} = \frac{y}{8} \;\rightarrow\; y = 60$

10. *Answer: (C)*
    This is a proportion problem.
    $\frac{6 \; miles}{45 \; minutes} = \frac{20 \; miles}{x \; minutes}$
    $x = 150 \; min = 2 \; hours \; and \; 30 \; minutes$

11. *Answer: (B)*
    The area of the shaded portion is $\frac{60}{360}$ of the area of the whole circle.
    Shaded Area $= \frac{60}{360} \times \pi \times 4^2 = \frac{8}{3}\pi = 2\frac{2}{3}\pi$

12. *Answer: (D)*
    $49000 < -1000x + 500000 < 492000$
    $10000 > 1000x > 8000$
    $10 > x > 8$

13. *Answer: $0 < y < 1$*
    Solve the system of the equations:
    $x = 2a$
    $y = 3a$
    $0 < a < \frac{1}{3} \rightarrow 0 < 3a < 1$
    $0 < y < 1$

14. *Answer: 72.8*
    If the original lengths of the edges of the cube are 1. After increasing by 20%, its lengths become 1.2. The volume of the cube is equal to $(1.2)^3$ or 1.728. The volume of the cube increases 72.8%.

15. *Answer: (D)*
    From the graph, the closest distance between point and line is at 60% of fat.

16. *Answer: (C)*
    $BF = 5 - 2 = 3$
    $EF = 5$
    $EA = 5 - 2 = 3$
    $AB = \sqrt{EA^2 + EB^2} = \sqrt{BF^2 + EF^2 + EA^2}$
    $AB = \sqrt{3^2 + 5^2 + 3^2} = \sqrt{43}$

17. *Answer: (C)*
    $Mean = \frac{-1.639 - 1.641 - 1.647 - 1.641}{4} \times (10)^{-19}$
    $= 1.642 \times 10^{-19}$

18. *Answer: (A)*
    $2 \times 2^x = 2^x + 2^x$
    $2^x + 2^x + 2^x + 2^x = 4 \times 2^x = 2^6$
    $2^{x+2} = 2^6$
    $x = 4$

19. *Answer: (D)*
    $2x + 3y = 18$
    $y = -\frac{2}{3}x + 18$
    The perpendicular line has a slope of $\frac{3}{2}$.
    $y = \frac{3}{2}x + b$
    $2y - 3x = 2b \; or \; 3 - 2y = -2b$
    The answer should be d).

20. *Answer: 382*
    Following the pattern, find the number of 1s between the 94th 3 and the 98th 3.
    $94 + 95 + 96 + 97 = 382 \; ones$

21. *Answer: (B)*
    $(x^{24})^a = (x^2)^4 = x^{24a} = x^8$
    $24a = 8 \rightarrow a = \frac{1}{3}$

22. *Answer: (D)*
    $y = 1 - kx = -x^2 + kx$
    $x^2 - kx - (k - 1) = 0$
    Since the graphs intersect at exactly two points, its discriminant > 0.
    $(-k)^2 - 4(1)\big(-(k - 1)\big) > 0$
    $k^2 + 4k - 4 > 0$
    When $k = 0$, it does not satisfy this inequality. Therefore, the answer is d).

Module 2 Hard Answers

1. *Answer: (C)*

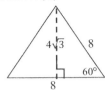

   30-60-90 special right triangle
   $\frac{1}{2} \times 8 \times 4\sqrt{3} = 16\sqrt{3}$

2. *Answer: (C)*
   Area WITH Frame and Picture = (6 + 2) × (8 + 2)
   = 80
   Area of Picture = 6 × 8 = 48
   Area of Frame = 80 – 48 = 32

3. *Answer: (B)*
   Let one trip have x miles.
   Time = 2 = $t_1 + t_2 = \frac{x}{60} + \frac{x}{40}$
   $2 = x(\frac{1}{60} + \frac{1}{40})$
   x = 48
   The Round-Trip Distance = 2 × 48 = 96

4. *Answer: (B)*
   Because the customer is ordering a main course AND a side dish, use the multiplication Principle.
   Total number of choices: 3 × 4 = 12

5. *Answer: (D)*
   The base angle of an isosceles right triangle is 45°, each interior angle of an equilateral triangle is 60°, and each interior angle of a regular pentagon is 108°.
   a + b + c + 45° + 60° + 108° = 360°
   a + b + c = 147°

6. *Answer: (C)*
   The graph of y = mx + b shows the slope equals −1 and y-intercept is 1.
   m = −1, b = 1
   y = −2mx + b = 2x + 1 with a positive slope and positive y-intercept.

7. *Answer: (B)*
   Distance to the Origin = $\sqrt{(x-0)^2 + (y-0)^2}$ = $\sqrt{x^2 + y^2}$
   (b) Has the shortest distance of $\frac{1}{2}$ from the origin.

8. *Answer: (D)*
   Let h = 0 to find its x-intercept.
   When h = 0, the projectile hits the ground.

9. *Answer: (C)*
   OA is the radius of the circle and the shaded area is the area of the quarter circle minus the area of the rectangle.
   Radius = $\sqrt{OB^2 + OC^2}$ = $\sqrt{6+8}$ = 10
   Shaded Area = Area of $\frac{1}{4}$ Circle – Area of Rectangle
   = $\frac{1}{4}(\pi \times 10^2) - 6 \times 8 = \frac{1}{4} \times 100\pi - 48 = 25\pi - 48$

10. *Answer: (D)*
    g(3) = 1 and f(3) = 0
    g(3) > f(3)

11. *Answer: (B)*
    $E = 1 - \frac{x}{p} = 1 - \frac{250}{480} = 0.48$
    Motion energy: 50000000 × 0.48 = 24,000,000

12. *Answer: (A)*
    $n = n_0(2)^{\# of double}$
    $n = 100(2)^{\frac{t}{20}}$

13. *Answer: 9.6*
    Let the height of the school building be x.
    The two triangles are similar; therefore, their corresponding sides are proportional.
    $\frac{2}{10+2} = \frac{1.6}{x}$
    x = 9.6 m

14. *Answer: 48*
    Let one trip have x miles
    Total Time = $t_{go} + t_{back}$
    $1 = \frac{x}{40} + \frac{x}{60} = x(\frac{1}{40} + \frac{1}{60}) \rightarrow x = 24$
    Total miles: 2 × 24 = 48 miles

15. *Answer: (B)*
    Surface Area = 2 × 3 + 2 × (½ × 3 × 4) + 4 × 2 + 5 × 2 = 36

16. *Answer: (C)*
    $(\sqrt{12} + \sqrt{48})^2 = 12 + 48 + 2\sqrt{12 \times 48} = 12 + 48 + 48 = 108$

17. *Answer: (B)*
$h(5) = -16(5)^2 + 320(5) + h_o = -16t^2 + 320t + h_o$
divided by 16
$-25 + 100 = -t^2 + 20t$
$t^2 - 20t + 75 = 0$
$(t - 5)(t - 15) = 0$
$t = 5$ or 15

18. *Answer: (D)*
The LCM of 3, 4, 5 and 6 is 360. The multiple of 360 that is three−digit value is 360 and 720. The largest possible value for N is 360 × 2 + 2 = 722

19. *Answer: (D)*
$90\% = \frac{Correct\ Answers}{Total\ Questions}$
$\frac{x}{50} = \frac{90}{100}$ *(cross multiply)*
$x = \frac{90 \times 50}{100} = 45$

20. *Answer: 3.43*
Area of Shaded Region = Area of Square – 4 × Area of a Quarter-Circle
$4^2 - \pi \times 2^2 = 16 - 4\pi = 3.43$

21. *Answer: (A)*
Use the Pythagorean Theorem.
$(x + 3)^2 + (x - 4)^2 = 13^2$
$x^2 + 6x + 9 + x^2 - 8x + 16 = 169$
$2x^2 - 2x = 144$
$x^2 - x - 72 = 0$
$(x + 8)(x - 9) = 0$
$x = 9$ or -8 *(not applicable)*

22. *Answer: (A)*
The probability of getting green marbles: $1 - \frac{1}{4} - \frac{1}{2}$
$= \frac{1}{4}$
$\frac{1}{4} = \frac{x}{36}, \quad x = 9$

Math Mock Test 4
22 QUESTIONS

DIRECTIONS

The questions in this section address a number of important math skills.

Use of a calculator is permitted for all questions.

○ **Check the answers after the Module 1 test. If there are more than 8 questions answered incorrectly in Module 1, take the Easy part of Module 2. Otherwise, take the Hard part of Module 2.**

NOTES

Unless otherwise indicated:

• All variables and expressions represent real numbers.

• Figures provided are drawn to scale.

• All figures lie in a plane.

• The domain of a given function f i s the set of all real numbers x for which f(x) is a real number.

REFERENCE

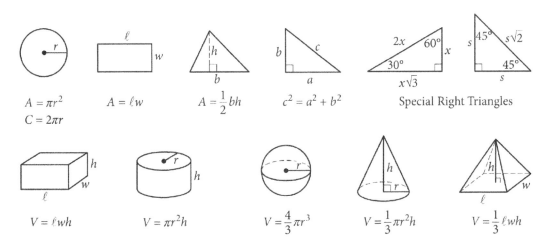

$A = \pi r^2$ $A = \ell w$ $A = \dfrac{1}{2}bh$ $c^2 = a^2 + b^2$ Special Right Triangles

$C = 2\pi r$

$V = \ell wh$ $V = \pi r^2 h$ $V = \dfrac{4}{3}\pi r^3$ $V = \dfrac{1}{3}\pi r^2 h$ $V = \dfrac{1}{3}\ell wh$

The number of degrees of arc in a circle is **360**.

The number of radians of arc in a circle is 2π.

The sum of the measures in degrees of the angles of a triangle is **180**.

For multiple-choice questions, solve each problem, choose the correct answer from the choices provided, and then circle your answer in this book. Circle only one answer for each question. If you change your mind, completely erase the circle. You will not get credit for questions with more than one answer circled, or for questions with no answers circled.

For student-produced response questions, solve each problem and write your answer next to or under the question in the test book as described below.

• Once you've written your answer, circle it clearly. You will not receive credit for anything written outside the circle, or for any questions with more than one circled answer.

• If you find **more than one correct answer,** write and circle only one answer. Your answer can be up to 5 characters for a **positive** answer and up to 6 characters (including the negative sign) for a **negative** answer, but no more.

• If your answer is a **fraction** that is too long (over 5 characters for positive, 6 characters for negative), write the decimal equivalent.

• If your answer is a **decimal** that is too long (over 5 characters for positive,

• 6 characters for negative), truncate it or round at the fourth digit.

• If your answer is a **mixed number** (such as $3\frac{1}{2}$, write it as an improper fraction (7/2) or its decimal equivalent (3.5).

• Don't include symbols such as a percent sign, comma, or dollar sign in your circled answer.

1. A triangle has a perimeter of 27. The medium-length side is 3 more than the length of the shortest side, and the longest side is twice the length of the shortest side. Find the length of the shortest side?
    a) 5
    b) 6
    c) 7
    d) 8

2. If $a + 3b = 2b$, which of the following must equal $6a + 6b$?
    a) 0
    b) 1
    c) b
    d) $2b$

3. If $a^2 + 11 = b^3$, and $3a = 12$, which of the following could be the value of b?
    a) 3
    b) 2
    c) 0
    d) −3

4. Mr. Jones has taught math for 5 years less than half as long as Miss Carter. If Mr. Jones has taught Math for m years, which of the following indicates the number of years that Miss Carter has taught?
    a) $2m + 5$
    b) $m + 5$
    c) $2m - 5$
    d) $2(m + 5)$

5. Which of the following is equivalent to $(2x + 4)^2 - 4x^2$?
    a) $16(x + 1)$
    b) $12(x + 1)$
    c) $8(2x + 1)$
    d) $4(4x + 1)$

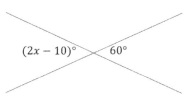

6. Two lines interest in the figure above. What is the value of x?

7. For a service visit, a technician charges a \$40 dollars fee plus an additional \$15 for every $\frac{1}{4}$ hour of work. If the technician's total charge was \$160 for how much time, in hours, did the technician charge?

$$\frac{1}{2}(x - 1) = x - 3$$

8. What value of x satisfies the equation above?
    a) $\frac{4}{3}$
    b) 3
    c) 5
    d) $\frac{16}{3}$

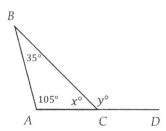

9. In triangle ABC above, side $\overline{AC}$ is extended to point D. What is the value of $y - 2x$?
    a) 60
    b) 75
    c) 100
    d) 110

10. If $3x + 1 = a$, then $6x + 1$?
    a) $a + 3$
    b) $a - 3$
    c) $2a - 1$
    d) $2a + 1$

11. Which of the following numbers could NOT be the remainder when a positive integer is divided by 5?
    a) 0
    b) 2
    c) 4
    d) 5

12. The square of the sum of x and 2 is equal to y. If y is the square of the difference of x and 3, what is the value of x?
    a) 2
    b) $\frac{1}{2}$
    c) $-\frac{1}{2}$
    d) $-\frac{1}{4}$

13. For a function f, $f(-1) = 5$ and $f(1) = 9$. If the graph of $y = f(x)$ is a line in the xy-plane, what is the slope of the line?

x	$f(x)$
8	10
12	18

14. The table above shows two pairs of values for the linear function f. The function can be written in the form $f(x) = ax + b$, where a and b are constants. What is the value of $a - b$?

15. In the xy-plane, line r passes through the origin and is perpendicular to line t and intersects at the point (2, 2). What is the slope of line t?
    a) -1
    b) -2
    c) 1
    d) 2

$$a = x(x + 2)$$
$$b = x(x + 1)$$
$$c = x(x - 1)$$

16. In the equations above, a, b ,and c are given in terms of x. Which of the following expressions is equivalent to $a - b + c$?
    a) x^2
    b) $x^2 + 2$
    c) $x^2 + 2x$
    d) $2 - x^2$

17. If $a^2 + b^2 = x$ and $2ab = y$, which of the following is equivalent to $4x + 4y$?
    a) $(a + b)^2$
    b) $(a + 2b)^2$
    c) $(2a + 2b)^2$
    d) $\left(\frac{1}{2}a + b\right)^2$

18. Which of the following expressions is equivalent to $(16x^2)^{\frac{1}{2}}$?
    a) $4|x|$
    b) $8|x|$
    c) $\sqrt{8x}$
    d) $16x$

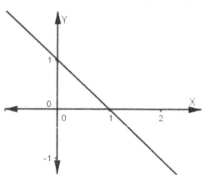

19. The figure above shows the graph of the line $y = mx + b$, where m and b are constants. Which of the following best represents the graph of the line $y = 2mx + b$?

   a)

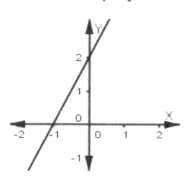

   b)

   c)

 d)

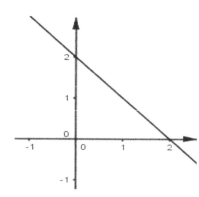

20. If $x > 1$ and $\frac{6}{\sqrt{x-1}} = 3$, what is the value of x?

21. The function f has the property that, for all x, $3f(x) = f(3x)$. If $f(6) = 12$, what is the value of $f(2)$?

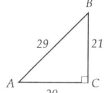

22. Triangles ABC and DEF above are similar. How much longer than segment EF is segment DE?
   a) 1
   b) 2
   c) 4
   d) 8

Math Mock Test 4
22 QUESTIONS

DIRECTIONS
The questions in this section address a number of important math skills.
Use of a calculator is permitted for all questions.

NOTES
Unless otherwise indicated:
- All variables and expressions represent real numbers.
- Figures provided are drawn to scale.
- All figures lie in a plane.
- The domain of a given function f i s the set of all real numbers x for which f(x) is a real number.

REFERENCE

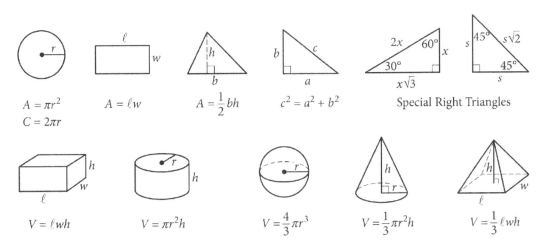

$A = \pi r^2$ $A = \ell w$ $A = \frac{1}{2}bh$ $c^2 = a^2 + b^2$ Special Right Triangles
$C = 2\pi r$

$V = \ell wh$ $V = \pi r^2 h$ $V = \frac{4}{3}\pi r^3$ $V = \frac{1}{3}\pi r^2 h$ $V = \frac{1}{3}\ell wh$

The number of degrees of arc in a circle is **360**.
The number of radians of arc in a circle is 2π.
The sum of the measures in degrees of the angles of a triangle is **180**.

For multiple-choice questions, solve each problem, choose the correct answer from the choices provided, and then circle your answer in this book. Circle only one answer for each question. If you change your mind, completely erase the circle. You will not get credit for questions with more than one answer circled, or for questions with no answers circled.

For student-produced response questions, solve each problem and write your answer next to or under the question in the test book as described below.
- Once you've written your answer, circle it clearly. You will not receive credit for anything written outside the
- circle, or for any questions with more than one circled answer.
- If you find **more than one correct answer**, write and circle only one answer. Your answer can be up to 5 characters for a **positive** answer and up to 6 characters (including the negative sign) for a **negative** answer, but no more.
- If your answer is a **fraction** that is too long (over 5 characters for positive, 6 characters for negative), write the decimal equivalent.
- If your answer is a **decimal** that is too long (over 5 characters for positive,
- 6 characters for negative), truncate it or round at the fourth digit.
- If your answer is a **mixed number** (such as $3\frac{1}{2}$, write it as an improper fraction (7/2) or its decimal equivalent (3.5).
- Don't include symbols such as a percent sign, comma, or dollar sign in your circled answer.

1. What value of x satisfies the equation $3x + 2 = 11$?
   a) 3
   b) 6
   c) -4
   d) -2

2. A jaguar can run at speeds up to 70 miles per hour. About how many miles can a jaguar run in 10 seconds?
   a) 0.1
   b) 0.2
   c) 0.3
   d) 0

3. For a certain type of heater, the increase in gas bills is directly proportional to the temperature setting (in Fahrenheit). If the gas bills increased by $20 when the temperature setting is increased by 5 degrees Fahrenheit, by how much will expenses increase when the temperature setting is increased by 9 degrees Fahrenheit?
   a) $30
   b) $36
   c) $40
   d) $45

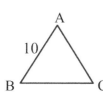

4. The perimeter of $\triangle ABC$ is equal to the perimeter of $\triangle XYZ$, which are shown above. If $\triangle ABC$ is equilateral, what is the value of x?
   a) 4
   b) 5
   c) 6
   d) 8

5. A teacher has signed up for a program that automatically delivers books for the classroom library. The classroom library currently consists of 40 books. If the program delivers 10 books a month, how many books will the classroom library consist of after 5 months?
   a) 90
   b) 100
   c) 110
   d) 120

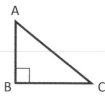

6. In the figure above, $\triangle ABC$ is a right triangle and $\overline{AB}$ has the length of 5. If the area of $\triangle ABC$ must be more than 25 but less than 35 and all three sides' lengths are positive integer, what is one possible value of AC?

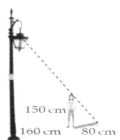

7. A girl who is 150 centimeters tall stands 160 centimeters away from a lamp post at night. If her shadow is 80 centimeters long, how high, in centimeters, is the lamp post?

8. The area enclosed by a circle is 36π square inches. What is the length, in inches, of the diameter of the circle?

    a) 3
    b) 5
    c) 6
    d) 12

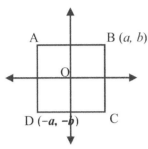

9. In the figure above, rectangle ABCD lies on the xy-coordinate plane. If the origin is located at the center of rectangle, which of the following could be the coordinates of point C?

    a) $(-a, b)$
    b) $(a, -b)$
    c) (a, b)
    d) $(-b, -a)$

10. A parallel circuit has two or more paths for current to flow through and has more than one resistor as shown below. In a house, there are many electrical appliances that connect in parallel so they would not affect each other when their switches are turned on or off.

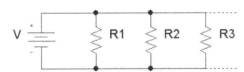

The total resistance, R_{Total}, in a parallel circuit can be calculated by the following formula:

$$\frac{1}{R_{Total}} = \frac{1}{R_1} + \frac{1}{R_2} + \frac{1}{R_3}$$

If three resistors are connected together in parallel and the resistors have values of 10 ohm, 15 ohm, and 30 ohm respectively, what is the total resistance of the circuit?

    a) 55 ohm
    b) 12 ohm
    c) 6 ohm
    d) 5 ohm

11. In all except one of the following, at least one of the coordinates of the ordered pair, when squared, is equal to the reciprocal of the other coordinate. For which ordered pair does this not hold true?

    a) $(1, 1)$
    b) $(-1, 1)$
    c) $(2, \frac{-1}{4})$
    d) $(4, \frac{-1}{2})$

12. Washington High School randomly selected freshman, sophomore, junior, and senior students for a survey about potential changes to next year's schedule. Of students selected for the survey, $\frac{1}{4}$ were freshmen and $\frac{1}{3}$ were sophomores. Half of the remaining selected students were juniors. If 336 students were selected for the survey, how many were seniors?

    a) 65
    b) 70
    c) 90
    d) 120

13. A ramp is 20 meters long and set at a 30° angle of inclination. If you walk up to the top of the ramp, how high off the ground (in meters) will you be?

$$(x + 3)^2 + (y - 1)^2 = 121$$

14. The graph of the equation above in the xy-plane is a circle. What is the length of the diameter of the circle?

$$g(x) = x^3 - 1$$

15. The function g is defined above. If $s = 4$, what is the value of $g(s + 1)$?
    a) 63
    b) 64
    c) 124
    d) 125

16. If the center of the circle defined by $x^2 + y^2 - 4x + 2y = 20$ is (a, b), then $a + b =$?
    a) 0
    b) 1
    c) 3
    d) 4

17. A cargo helicopter delivers only 100-pound packages and 120-pound packages. For each delivery trip, the helicopter must carry at least 10 packages, and the total weight of the packages can be at most 1,100 pounds. What is the maximum number of 120-pound packages that the helicopter can carry per trip?
    a) 2
    b) 4
    c) 5
    d) 6

18. A company purchased a machine valued at $100,000. The value of the machine depreciates by the same amount each year so that after 10 years the value will be $40,000. Which of the following equations gives the value, v, of the machine, in dollars, t years after it was purchased for $0 \le t \le 10$?
    a) $= 40000 - 6000t$
    b) $v = 100000 - 6000t$
    c) $v = 100000 + 6000t$
    d) $v = 100000 - 40000t$

19. The daily cost of phone services in a business building is $.25 per hour from 9 AM through 9 PM, and $.06 per hour at any other hours of the day. Which of the following expressions represents the cost, in dollars, of the phone service starting from 9 AM and lasting for 20 hours a day over 30 days?
    a) $30 \times 11(.25) + 30(20 - 11)(.6)$
    b) $30 \times 12(.25) + 30(20 - 12)(.6)$
    c) $30 \times 13(.25) + 30(20 - 13)$
    d) $30 \times 12(.25) + 30(.6)$

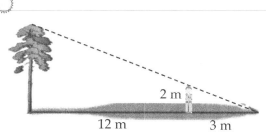

20. Sam walked 12 meters away from the base of a tree as shown in the figure above. At the point he was standing, he noticed that his shadow reached the same spot on the ground as the shadow of the tree. If Sam is 2 meters tall and his shadow is 3 meters long, how high is the tree, in meters?

21. If $2w + 4t = 14$ and $4w + 5t = 25$, what is the value of $2w + 3t$?
    a) 6
    b) 10
    c) 13
    d) 17

22. There are only two different percentages, 10% and 50%, of a chemical solution available in the chemical lab. A student needs to prepare a 100-ml solution including 25% this chemical solution. The volume of the 10% solution is x ml and the volume of the 50% solution is y ml. Which system of equations could be used to determine the values of x and y?

a) $\begin{cases} x + y = 100 \\ x + 5y = 100 \times 0.25 \end{cases}$

b) $\begin{cases} x + y = 100 \\ 0.1x + 0.5y = 100 \times 0.25 \end{cases}$

c) $\begin{cases} x + y = 25 \\ 0.1x + 0.5y = 100 \end{cases}$

d) $\begin{cases} x + y = 25 \\ x + 5y = 100 \end{cases}$

Math Mock Test 4
22 QUESTIONS

DIRECTIONS

The questions in this section address a number of important math skills.
Use of a calculator is permitted for all questions.

NOTES

Unless otherwise indicated:
- All variables and expressions represent real numbers.
- Figures provided are drawn to scale.
- All figures lie in a plane.
- The domain of a given function f is the set of all real numbers x for which f(x) is a real number.

REFERENCE

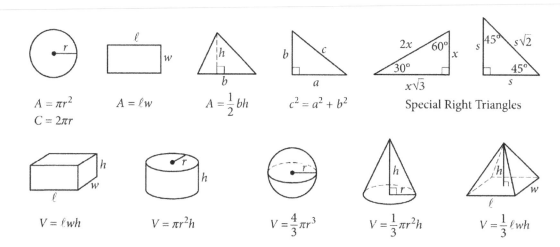

$A = \pi r^2$
$C = 2\pi r$

$A = \ell w$

$A = \frac{1}{2} bh$

$c^2 = a^2 + b^2$

Special Right Triangles

$V = \ell wh$

$V = \pi r^2 h$

$V = \frac{4}{3}\pi r^3$

$V = \frac{1}{3}\pi r^2 h$

$V = \frac{1}{3}\ell wh$

The number of degrees of arc in a circle is **360**.
The number of radians of arc in a circle is 2π.
The sum of the measures in degrees of the angles of a triangle is **180**.

For multiple-choice questions, solve each problem, choose the correct answer from the choices provided, and then circle your answer in this book. Circle only one answer for each question. If you change your mind, completely erase the circle. You will not get credit for questions with more than one answer circled, or for questions with no answers circled.

For student-produced response questions, solve each problem and write your answer next to or under the question in the test book as described below.
- Once you've written your answer, circle it clearly. You will not receive credit for anything written outside the circle, or for any questions with more than one circled answer.
- If you find **more than one correct answer**, write and circle only one answer. Your answer can be up to 5 characters for a **positive** answer and up to 6 characters (including the negative sign) for a **negative** answer, but no more.
- If your answer is a **fraction** that is too long (over 5 characters for positive, 6 characters for negative), write the decimal equivalent.
- If your answer is a **decimal** that is too long (over 5 characters for positive,
- 6 characters for negative), truncate it or round at the fourth digit.
- If your answer is a **mixed number** (such as $3\frac{1}{2}$, write it as an improper fraction (7/2) or its decimal equivalent (3.5).
- Don't include symbols such as a percent sign, comma, or dollar sign in your circled answer.

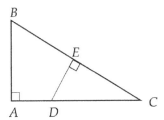

Note: Figure not drawn to scale.

1. In the figure above, triangle ABC and triangle EDC are right triangles. If $EC = 6\sqrt{3}$ and the cosine of angle ABC is $\frac{1}{2}$, what is the length of segment ED?
   a) 6
   b) $6\sqrt{3}$
   c) 12
   d) 18

2. To determine if gender and number of siblings are related to whether 9-year-old children like to read, Sarah selected a random sample of 40 boys with fewer than 3 siblings and a random sample of 30 girls with 3 or more siblings tram the 9-year-old children in her city. For each child, she recorded the child's age, gender, and whether the child reported liking to read. Why is it inappropriate for Sarah to draw a conclusion from her study?
   a) The two samples are not of equal size.
   b) The two samples should have been chosen from different cities.
   c) There is no upper bound on the number of siblings of the 30 girls.
   d) Sarah will not be able to tell whether a difference in liking to read is related to the difference in gender or to the difference in number of siblings.

3. The circumference of Earth is estimated to be 40,030 kilometers at the equator. Which of the following best approximates the diameter, in miles, of Earth's equator? (1 kilometer ≈ 0.62137 miles)
   a) 4,203 miles
   b) 7,917 miles
   c) 9,826 miles
   d) 12,705 miles

4. If a movie is 100 minutes long, what fraction of the movie has been completed 25 minutes after it begins?
   a) $\frac{1}{5}$
   b) $\frac{1}{6}$
   c) $\frac{1}{4}$
   d) $\frac{1}{3}$

5. Near the end of a US cable news show, the host invited viewers to respond to a poll on the show's website that asked, "Do you support the new federal policy discussed during the show?" At the end of the show, the host reported that 28% responded "Yes," and 70% responded "No." Which of the following best explains why the results are unlikely to represent the sentiments of the population of the United States?
   a) The percentages do not add up to 100%, so any possible conclusions from the poll are invalid.
   b) Those who responded to the poll were not a random sample of the population of the United States.
   c) There were not 50% "Yes" responses and 50% "No" responses.
   d) The show did not allow viewers enough time to respond to the poll.

2012 Graduates' Plans
Total Number of Graduates:400

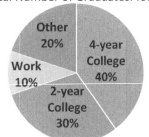

6. In 2012, how many graduates from
    Paterson High School chose to go to 2 or 4
    years of college to continue their
    education?
    a) 250
    b) 260
    c) 270
    d) 280

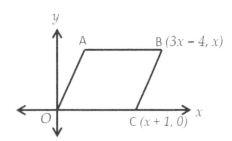

7. In the figure above, if the area of
   parallelogram OABC is 42, what is the
   value of x?
   a) 7
   b) 6
   c) −6
   d) −7

$$5x + y = a$$
$$3x - 2y = 5$$

8. In the system of equations above, a is a
   constant. What is the y-value of the
   solution to the system in terms of a ?
   a) $\frac{3a-25}{13}$
   b) $\frac{3a-1}{13}$
   c) $\frac{3a+5}{13}$
   d) $\frac{3a+5}{13}$

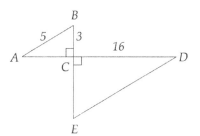

Note: Figure not drawn to scale.
9. In the figure above, $\angle B$ is congruent to $\angle E$.
   What is the value of $sin(D)$?
   a) $\frac{3}{5}$
   b) $\frac{4}{5}$
   c) $\frac{16}{5}$
   d) $\frac{16}{25}$

**Number of Hours of TV
Watched**

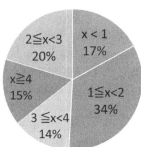

10. The graph above shows breakdown of the
    average number of hours of TV watched
    per day. 1000 people were surveyed, and
    all but 160 people surveyed responded to
    the question. If x is the number of hours
    spent, about how many respondents watch
    TV for more than 3 hours a day?
    a) 210
    b) 221
    c) 243
    d) 255

$$h(t) = -\frac{1}{175}t + 481$$

11. An archeologist estimates that, as a result of erosion, the height of the Great Pyramid of Giza has been decreasing at a constant rate since it was built. The function above is used by the archeologist to model the height $h(t)$, in feet, of the pyramid t years after it was built. According to the following statements is true?
    a) Every 1,750 years the height of the pyramid decreases by 10 feet.
    b) Every 175 years the height of the pyramid decreases by 0.1 feet.
    c) Every 100 years the height of the pyramid decreases by 1.75 feet.
    d) Every year the height of the pyramid decreases by 175 feet.

12. The table below shows the number of students in Mr. Jang's class that are taking 1, 2, 3, or 4 AP classes. After a new student joined the class (not shown in the table), the average (arithmetic mean) number of AP classes per student became equal to the median. How many AP classes is the new student taking?

Students Taking AP Classes	
Number of APs	Number of Students
1	6
2	4
3	5
4	4

    a) 5
    b) 4
    c) 3
    d) 2

13. If $f(x) = \frac{x^2+35}{x^2-10}$, what is the value of $f(5)$?

14. The estimated daytime population of Manhattan, New York, during a weekday is 4.1 million people. The area of Manhattan is approximately 24 square miles. Based on these estimates, what is the daytime population density, in millions of people per square mile, of Manhattan during a weekday, rounded to the nearest hundredth?

15. For all numbers j and k, let $j@k$ be defined by $j@k = (j + 1)^2 \times (2k - 2)^2$, what is the value of 6@3?
    a) 228
    b) 338
    c) 544
    d) 784

16. Biologists found a new species of pale shrimp at the world's deepest undersea vent, the Beebe Vent Field. The vent is 3.1 miles below the sea's surface. Approximately how many kilometers below the sea's surface is the vent? (1 kilometer ≈ 0.6214 miles)
    a) 2
    b) 3
    c) 4
    d) 5

17. The electric charge of a single electron is called the electron charge and can be measured in coulombs (C). The table below shows four measurements of the electron charge made in the early 1900s.

Electron Charge (C)
-1.639×10^{-19}
-1.641×10^{-19}
-1.647×10^{-19}
-1.641×10^{-19}

What is the mean of these measurements, in coulombs?
  a) -4.118×10^{-20}
  b) -1.641×10^{-19}
  c) -1.642×10^{-19}
  d) -1.568×10^{-19}

18. If $2 \times 2^x + 2^x + 2^x = 2^6$, what is the value of x?
  a) 4
  b) 3
  c) 2
  d) 1

19. Which of the following is an equation of a line in the xy-plane that is parallel to the line with equation $2x + 3y = 18$?
  a) $2x + 3y = 12$
  b) $2x - 3y = 10$
  c) $3x + 2y = 9$
  d) $3x - 2y = 4$

20. A circle in the xy-plane has a diameter with endpoints $(-2, 3)$ and $(8, 3)$. If the point $(0, b)$ lies on the circle and $b > 0$, what is the value of b?

21. If $2w + 4t = 14$ and $4w + 5t = 25$, what is the value of $2w + 3t$?
  a) 6
  b) 10
  c) 13
  d) 17

22. In the figure below, what is the value of $a + b + 2c + 2d$?

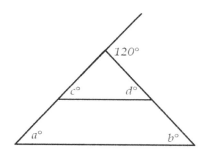

Note: Figure not drawn to scale.

  a) 240
  b) 300
  c) 360
  d) 380

Mock Test 4

Module 1 Keys

1. (B)	2. (A)	3. (A)	4. (D)	5. (A)	6. 35	7. 2	8. (C)
9. (A)	10. (C)	11. (D)	12. (B)	13. 2	14. 8	15. (A)	16. (A)
17. (C)	18. (A)	19. (C)	20. 5	21. 4	22. (B)		

Module 2 Easy Keys

1. (A)	2. (B)	3. (B)	4. (C)	5. (A)	6. 13	7. 450	8. (C)
9. (B)	10. (D)	11. (C)	12. (B)	13. 10	14. 22	15. (C)	16. (B)
17. (C)	18. (B)	19. (B)	20. 10	21. (C)	22. (B)		

Module 2 Hard Keys

1. (A)	2. (D)	3. (B)	4. (C)	5. (B)	6. (D)	7. (B)	8. (A)
9. (A)	10. (C)	11. (A)	12. (A)	13. 4	14. 0.17	15. (D)	16. (D)
17. (C)	18. (A)	19. (D)	20. 7	21. (C)	22. (C)		

Mock Test 4

Module 1 Answers

1. *Answer: (B)*
   Let the length of the shortest side be x.
   $27 = x + x + 3 + 2x$
   $x = 6$

2. *Answer: (A)*
   $a + 3b = 2b, \quad a + b = 0$
   $6a + 6b = 6(a + b) = 0$

3. *Answer: (A)*
   $3a = 12, \quad a = 4$
   $4^2 + 11 = b^3$
   $27 = b^3 = 3^3 \rightarrow b = 3$

4. *Answer: (D)*
   If Miss Carter has taught x years, then
   $m = \frac{1}{2}x - 5.$
   $m + 5 = \frac{1}{2}x$
   $x = 2(m + 5)$

5. *Answer: (A)*
   $(2x + 4)^2 - 4x^2$
   $= 4x^2 + 16x + 16 - 4x^2$
   $= 16x + 16$
   $= 16(x + 1)$

6. *Answer: 35*
   $2x - 10 = 60$
   $x = 35$

7. *Answer: 2*
   A linear model with initial value of 40 and slope of
   $15(4) = 60.$
   $y = 60x + 40 = 160$
   $x = 2 \; hours$

8. *Answer: (C)*
   $x - 1 = 2x - 6 \rightarrow x = 5$

9. *Answer: (A)*
   $x = 180 - 35 - 105 = 40^o$
   $y = 180 - x = 140$
   $y - 2x = 140 - 80 = 60^o$

10. *Answer: (C)*
    $3x = a - 1$
    $6x = 2 \times (3x) = 2 \times (a - 1) = 2a - 2$
    $6x + 1 = 2a - 2 + 1 = 2a - 1$

11. *Answer: (D)*
    The remainder of a number divided by 5 must be less than 5.

12. *Answer: (B)*
    $(x + 2)^2 = y$ and $y = (x - 3)^2$
    $(x + 2)^2 = (x - 3)^2$
    $x^2 + 4x + 4 = x^2 - 6x + 9$
    $10x = 5 \rightarrow x = \frac{1}{2}$

13. *Answer: 2*
    $Slope = \frac{9-5}{1-(-1)} = 2$

14. *Answer: 8*
    $Slope = a = \frac{18-10}{12-8} = 2$
    Plug in $(8, 12)$ *to* $f(x) = ax + b \rightarrow 10 = 2(8) + b$
    $b = -6$
    $a - b = 2 - (-6) = 8$

15. *Answer: (A)*
    The product of the slopes of two perpendicular lines must be −1.
    $Slope \; of \; r = \frac{2-0}{2-0} = 1$
    $Slope \; of \; t = -1$

16. *Answer: (A)*
    $a - b + c = x(x + 2) - x(x + 1) + x(x - 1) = x^2$

17. *Answer: (C)*
    $4x + 4y = 4(a^2 + b^2) + 4(2ab)$
    $= 4a^2 + 4b^2 + 8ab$
    $= (2a + 2b)^2$

18. *Answer: (A)*
    $(xy)^a = x^a y^b$
    $(16x^2)^{\frac{1}{2}} = (16)^{\frac{1}{2}}(x^2)^{\frac{1}{2}} = 4|x|$
    ($|x|$ *is because* $(x^2)^{\frac{1}{2}}$ *needed to be a positive but x is not necessary a positive)*

19. *Answer: (C)*
    From the graph, slope equals −1 and y-intercept is 1.
    $m = -1, \ b = 1$
    $y = 2mx + b = -2x + 1$
    (with negative slope and positive y-intercept)

20. *Answer: 5*
    Apply cross multiplication.
    $\dfrac{6}{\sqrt{x-1}} = \dfrac{3}{1}$
    $\sqrt{x-1} \times 3 = 6$
    $\sqrt{x-1} = 2$
    $x - 1 = 4$

$x = 5$

21. *Answer: 4*
    $3f(2) = f(3 \times 2) = f(6) = 12$
    $f(2) = 4$

22. *Answer: (B)*
    $\dfrac{29}{20} = \dfrac{DE}{5}$
    $DE = \dfrac{29}{4}$
    $\dfrac{21}{20} = \dfrac{EF}{5}$
    $EF = \dfrac{21}{4}$
    $\dfrac{29}{4} - \dfrac{21}{4} = \dfrac{8}{4} = 2$

Module 2 Easy Answers

1. *Answer: (A)*
    $3x + 2 = 11$
    $3x = 9$
    $x = 3$

2. *Answer: (B)*
    1 hour = 3600 seconds
    70 miles : 3600 seconds = x miles : 10 seconds
    $3600x = 70 \times 10; \ x = \dfrac{700}{3600} \sim 0.2 \ miles$

3. *Answer: (B)*
    $\$20 : 5^{\circ}F = \$x : 9^{\circ}F$
    $5x = 180$
    $x = \$36$

4. *Answer: (C)*
    The perimeter of $\triangle ABC$: $12 + 12 + x = 3 \times 10$
    $x = 6$

5. *Answer: (A)*
    $40 + (10) \times 5 = 90$

6. *Answer: 13*
    Area of $\triangle ABC = \dfrac{1}{2} AB \times BC$
    $\qquad\qquad = 2.5 \times BC$
    $25 < 2.5 \times BC < 35$
    $10 < BC < 14$
    Apply the Pythagorean Theorem.
    $AC^2 = AB^2 + BC^2 = 5^2 + BC^2$
    $AC = \sqrt{25 + BC^2}$
    See if BC equals 11, 12, or 13.
    $AC = \sqrt{25 + 12^2} = 13$

7. *Answer: 450*
    The two triangles are similar, so their corresponding sides are proportional.
    Let the height of the lamp post be x.
    $\dfrac{150}{x} = \dfrac{80}{80 + 160}$
    $x = 450 \ cm$

8. *Answer: (C)*
    $\pi r^2 = 36\pi$
    $r = 6$
    $d = 2r = 12$

9. *Answer: (B)*
    C is located in the quadrant IV which has positive x and negative y coordinates. (a, –b)

10. *Answer: (D)*
    $\dfrac{1}{R_{total}} = \dfrac{1}{10} + \dfrac{1}{15} + \dfrac{1}{30} = \dfrac{1}{5}$
    $R_{total} = 5 \ ohm$

11. *Answer: (C)*
    a) $1^2 = \dfrac{1}{1}$
    b) $(-1)^2 = \dfrac{1}{1}$
    c) $2^2 \neq \dfrac{1}{\frac{-1}{4}}$
    d) $\left(\dfrac{-1}{2}\right)^2 = \dfrac{1}{4}$

12. *Answer: (B)*

$$Juniors = \frac{\frac{3}{4} - \frac{1}{3}}{2} = \frac{\frac{5}{12}}{2} = \frac{5}{24}$$

$$Seniors = 1 - \frac{1}{3} - \frac{1}{4} - \frac{5}{24} = \frac{5}{24}$$

$$336 \times \frac{5}{24} = 70$$

13. *Answer: 10*

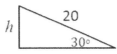

$$h = 20 \times sin(30^o) = 20 \times 0.5 = 10$$

14. *Answer: 22*
The radius of the circle is $\sqrt{121} = 11$
The diameter is 2(11) = 22.

15. *Answer: (C)*
$$g(4 + 1) = (5)^3 - 1 = 124$$

16. *Answer: (B)*
Rewrite to the equation in standard form.
$$x^2 - 4x + 4 + y^2 + 2y + 1 = 20 + 5$$
$$(x - 2)^2 + (y + 1)^2 = 5^2$$
The center of the circle is (2, −1) and the radius is 5.
$$a = 2, b = -1$$
$$a + b = 1$$

17. *Answer: (C)*
Let x be the number of 120-pound package and y be the number of 100-pound package.
$$x + y \geq 10$$
$$120x + 100y \leq 1100$$
By checking the number of x and y,
when x=6 and y=4, then
120(6) + 100(4) = 1120, which is greater than 1,100 pounds;

when x=5 and y=5, then
$$120(5) + 100(5) = 1100, \text{ which is equal}$$
to 1,100 pounds. Therefore, the answer is c).

18. *Answer: (B)*
This is a linear model.
$$Slope = \frac{40000 - 100000}{10} = -6000$$
The initial value is 100,000.
The equation is $v = -6000t + 100000$.

19. *Answer: (B)*
In order to find the daily price, add the cost from the rush hours, which is 12 (hours) × (.25), and the cost from the additional hours, which is (20 – 12)(hours) × (.6).
Multiply the daily cost by 30 to find the total cost for 30 days.

20. *Answer: 10*
Let the height of the tree be x.
The two triangles are similar; therefore, their corresponding sides are proportional.
$$\frac{3}{12 + 3} = \frac{2}{x}$$
$$x = 10 \ m$$

21. *Answer: (C)*
$$(2w + 4t) + (4w + 5t) = 14 + 25$$
$$6w + 9t = 39$$
$$2w + 3t = 13$$

22. *Answer: (B)*
Total Volume = 100
$$x + y = 100$$
Total chemical balance:
$$x \times 0.1 + y \times 0.5 = 100 \times 0.25$$

Module 2 Hard Answers

1. *Answer: (A)*
$$\Delta ABC \sim \Delta EDC \ ; \ cos(\angle ABC) = cos(\angle EDC) = \frac{1}{2} =$$
$$\frac{EC}{DC} ; \frac{1}{2} = \frac{6\sqrt{3}}{DC} \rightarrow DC = 12\sqrt{3}$$
$$ED = \sqrt{\left(12\sqrt{3}\right)^2 - \left(6\sqrt{3}\right)^2} = 6$$

2. *Answer: (D)*
There is only one control factor in the same research to isolate the effects of each factor.

3. *Answer: (B)*
$$2\pi r = 40030$$
$$2r = \frac{40030}{\pi} = 12742 \ km$$
$$12742 \times 0.62137 = 7917.70 \ miles$$

4. *Answer: (C)*
$$\frac{25}{100} = \frac{1}{4}$$

5. *Answer: (B)*
If the sample is not randomly selected, this sample can't represent the whole population.

6. *Answer: (D)*
30% + 40% = 70% of the total number of graduates go to 2 or 4 years of college.
0.7 × 400 =280 students

7. *Answer: (B)*
Area of OABC = Base × Height = (x + 1) × (x) = 42
$x^2 + x - 42 = 0; (x + 7)(x - 6) = 0$
x = 6 or x = −7(x must be positive)

8. *Answer: (A)*
Solve the system of equation.
$3(5x + y) - 5(3x - 2y)$
$= 3a - 25$
$13y = 3a - 25$
$y = \frac{3a-25}{13}$

9. *Answer: (A)*
$\Delta ABC \sim \Delta DEC$
$\sin(D) = \sin(A) = \frac{3}{5}$

10. *Answer: (C)*
Watching TV for more than 3 hours a day includes those who answered with $3 \leqq x < 4$ and $4 \leqq x$, which make up 29% (14% + 15%) of those who answered.
Total Respondents = 1000 – 160 = 840 people
840 × 29% = 243 people

11. *Answer: (A)*
This is a linear model.
Slope = $-\frac{1}{175}$
The height decreases 1 foot for every 175 years.
Every 1,750 years, the height decreases by 10 feet.

12. *Answer: (A)*
There are 20 students after a new student joined the class. If the student is taking 2 or less APs, the median is 2. If the student is taking more than 2 APs, the median is 2.5.
If median is 2 and the new average is 2, then the new student needs to take 20 × 2 − (6 × 1 + 4 × 2 + 5 × 3 + 4 × 4) = −5 AP classes (which is not possible). If the median is 2.5 and the new average is 2.5, then the new student needs to take 20 × 2.5 − (6 × 1 + 4 × 2 + 5 × 3 + 4 × 4) = 5 AP classes.

13. *Answer: 4*
Plug the number 5 into the function.
$f(5) = \frac{5^2 + 35}{5^2 - 10} \rightarrow \frac{60}{15} = 4$

14. *Answer: 0.17*
$Density = \frac{4.1}{24} = 0.17$

15. *Answer: (D)*
Replace j with 6 and k with 3.
$6@3 = (6 + 1)^2 (2 \times 3 - 2)^2 = 49 \times 16 = 784$

16. *Answer: (D)*
$\frac{1\,km}{0.6214\,miles} = \frac{x\,km}{3.1} \; ; x = 5$

17. *Answer: (C)*
$Mean = \frac{-1.639 - 1.641 - 1.647 - 1.641}{4} \times (10)^{-19}$
$= 1.642 \times 10^{-19}$

18. *Answer: (A)*
$2 \times 2^x = 2^x + 2^x$
$2^x + 2^x + 2^x + 2^x = 4 \times 2^x = 2^6$
$2^{x+2} = 2^6 \; ; x = 4$

19. *Answer: (D)*
$2x + 3y = 18 \rightarrow y = -\frac{2}{3}x + 18$
The perpendicular line has a slope of $\frac{3}{2}$.
$y = \frac{3}{2}x + b \;\; 2y - 3x = 2b \text{ or } 3 - 2y = -2b$
The answer should be d).]

20. *Answer: 7*
$Center: \frac{(-2,3)+(8,3)}{2} = (3,3)$
$Radius: \frac{\sqrt{(8-(-2))^2 + (3-3)^2}}{2} = 5$
The equation of circle: $(x - 3)^2 + (y - 3)^2 = 5^2$
$x = 0 \rightarrow 3^2 + (y - 3)^2 = 25$
$y - 3 = \pm 4 \rightarrow y = 7 \text{ or } -1$

21. *Answer: (C)*
$(2w + 4t) + (4w + 5t) = 14 + 25$
$6w + 9t = 39 \; ; 2w + 3t = 13$

22. *Answer: (C)*
$120 = c + d = a + b$
$a + b + 2(c + d) = 120 + 2 \times 120 = 360$

Math Mock Test 5

22 QUESTIONS

DIRECTIONS

The questions in this section address a number of important math skills.

Use of a calculator is permitted for all questions.

○ **Check the answers after the Module 1 test. If there are more than 8 questions answered incorrectly in Module 1, take the Easy part of Module 2. Otherwise, take the Hard part of Module 2.**

NOTES

Unless otherwise indicated:

• All variables and expressions represent real numbers.

• Figures provided are drawn to scale.

• All figures lie in a plane.

• The domain of a given function f is the set of all real numbers x for which f(x) is a real number.

REFERENCE

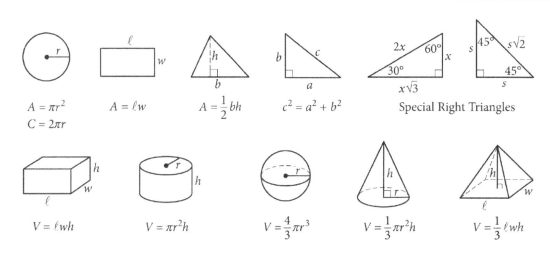

$A = \pi r^2$ $A = \ell w$ $A = \frac{1}{2}bh$ $c^2 = a^2 + b^2$ Special Right Triangles

$C = 2\pi r$

$V = \ell wh$ $V = \pi r^2 h$ $V = \frac{4}{3}\pi r^3$ $V = \frac{1}{3}\pi r^2 h$ $V = \frac{1}{3}\ell wh$

The number of degrees of arc in a circle is **360**.

The number of radians of arc in a circle is 2π.

The sum of the measures in degrees of the angles of a triangle is **180**.

For multiple-choice questions, solve each problem, choose the correct answer from the choices provided, and then circle your answer in this book. Circle only one answer for each question. If you change your mind, completely erase the circle. You will not get credit for questions with more than one answer circled, or for questions with no answers circled.

For student-produced response questions, solve each problem and write your answer next to or under the question in the test book as described below.

• Once you've written your answer, circle it clearly. You will not receive credit for anything written outside the circle, or for any questions with more than one circled answer.

• If you find **more than one correct answer**, write and circle only one answer. Your answer can be up to 5 characters for a **positive** answer and up to 6 characters (including the negative sign) for a **negative** answer, but no more.

• If your answer is a **fraction** that is too long (over 5 characters for positive, 6 characters for negative), write the decimal equivalent.

• If your answer is a **decimal** that is too long (over 5 characters for positive,

• 6 characters for negative), truncate it or round at the fourth digit.

• If your answer is a **mixed number** (such as $3\frac{1}{2}$, write it as an improper fraction (7/2) or its decimal equivalent (3.5).

• Don't include symbols such as a percent sign, comma, or dollar sign in your circled answer.

1. In the xy-plane, what is the y-intercept of the line with equations $y = 4x - 1$?
   a) 4
   b) $\frac{1}{4}$
   c) $-\frac{1}{4}$
   d) -1

$$5v - 3t = 1655$$

2. The equation above models the relationship between the speed of the sound v, in meters per second, in dry air, and temperature of the air t, in degree Celsius. Which of the following express v in terms of t?
   a) $v = \frac{3}{5}t + 331$
   b) $v = \frac{5}{3}t + 375$
   c) $t = \frac{3}{5}v + 331$
   d) $t = \frac{5}{3}v + 375$

3. Which of the following statements is true about the graph of the equation $2y - x = -4$ in the xy-plane?
   a) It has a negative slope and a positive y-intercept.
   b) It has a negative slope and a negative y-intercept.
   c) It has a positive slope and a positive y-intercept.
   d) It has a positive slope and a negative y-intercept.

4. If $x = -2$ is a solution of the equation $x^2 = -x + c$ where c is a constant, what is another value of x that satisfies the equation?
   a) 1
   b) 2
   c) 3
   d) 4

5. Which two lines are perpendicular to each other?
   a) $y = x - 2$; $x = 1$
   b) $y = x + 2$; $x = 1$
   c) $y = -x - 1$; $x = 1$
   d) $y = -5$; $x = 1$

6. The ratio of action movies to dramas in Albert's DVD collection is 4 to 3. If the total number of DVDs in the collection is greater than 20 but less than 30, what could be a possible number of DVDs in his collection?

7. Which of the When twice a number is reduced by 10, the result is 200. What is the number?

8. A chef plans to cook a maximum of 100 entrées for a dinner party; each entrée will include either chicken or fish. The cost of ingredients for each chicken entrée is $7, and the cost of ingredients for each fish entrée is $9. If no more than $850 can be spent on ingredients for the entrées and the chef cooks c chicken entrées and f fish entrées, which of the following systems best represents the constraints on c and f?
   a) $c + f = 16$; $7c + 9f \leq 100$
   b) $c + f \leq 100$; $7c + 9f > 850$
   c) $c + f \leq 100$; $7c + 9f \leq 850$
   d) $c + f = 100$; $7c + 9f < 850$

9. If $x = 2y^2 + 3y + 4$ and $z = -y - 1$, what is x in terms of z?
   a) $2z^2 - 7z - 9$
   b) $2z^2 - 7z + 9$
   c) $2z^2 + z + 3$
   d) $2z^2 - z + 3$

10. Every Saturday, Bob bakes loaves of bread to sell at the farmer's market. Each loaf costs him $2 to make, and he sells the loaves for $4 each. He also pays a vendor's fee of $75 every Saturday to set up his booth. What is the least number of loaves of bread Bob needs to sell every Saturday to cover the cost of the vendor's fee?
    a) 38
    b) 37
    c) 25
    d) 19

11. If $x^2 > 4$, which of the following must be true?
    a) $x > 4$
    b) $x > 2$
    c) $x < 2$
    d) $x > 2$ or $x < -2$

12. On the xy-plane, what is the equation of the line that is a reflection the line $y = -2x - 1$ across the y-axis?
    a) $y = -2x + 1$
    b) $y = -2x - 1$
    c) $y = 2x - 1$
    d) $y = 2x \div 1$

13. For every 20 cars sold by a dealer, 6 of them were red. What is the probability, in fraction, that a car sold that is selected at random would be red?

14. $4(p + 2) + 4(p - 1) = 10p$
    What value of p is the solution of the equation above?

15. The pressure exerted on an object under water increases by 1 atmosphere every 33 feet below the surface of the water. At sea level, the pressure is 1 atmosphere. Which equation gives the total pressure p, in atmospheres, exerted on an underwater object at a depth of f feet below sea level?
    a) $p = \frac{f}{33}$
    b) $p = 33 f$
    c) $p = 33f + 1$
    d) $p = \frac{f}{33} + 1$

$$\frac{x + 1}{x} = \frac{1}{x} - \frac{1}{x - 3}$$

16. What is the solution set of the equation above?
    a) { 1 }
    b) {0, 2}
    c) {2}
    d) {1, 2}

$$P(t) = 60(3)^{\frac{t}{4}}$$

17. The number of microscopic organisms in a petri dish grows exponentially with time. The function P above models the number of organisms after growing for t days in the petri dish. Based on the function, which of the following statements is true?
    a) The predicted number of organisms in the dish triples every four days.
    b) The predicted number of organisms in the dish doubles every three days.
    c) The predicted number of organisms in the dish triples every day.
    d) The predicted number of organisms in the dish doubles

18. If $y^2 = x\sqrt{7}$ and $x \neq 0$, what does x^2 equal in terms of y?
    a) $\frac{y}{7}$
    b) $7y^4$
    c) $\frac{49}{y^2}$
    d) $\frac{y^4}{7}$

19. If x, y, and z are all integers greater than 1 and $xy = 15$ and $yz = 21$, which of the following must be true?
    a) $z > x > y$
    b) $y > z > x$
    c) $y > x > z$
    d) $x > z > y$

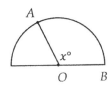

20. Segments $\overline{OA}$ and $\overline{OB}$ are radii of the semicircle above. Arc $\widehat{AB}$ has length 3π and $OA = 5$. What is the value of x?

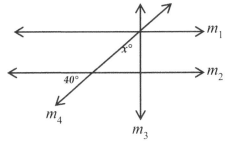

22. In the figure above, if m_1 is parallel to m_2 and m_3 is perpendicular to m_1, what is the value of x, in degrees?
    a) 40
    b) 45
    c) 50
    d) 55

21. The length of a rectangular piece of cardboard is 15 inches longer than its width. If a 5-inch square is cut from each corner of the cardboard, and the remaining piece is folded up to form a box, the volume of the box is 1,250 cubic inches. Find the sum of the length and the width, in inches, of the original cardboard.

Math Mock Test 5
22 QUESTIONS

DIRECTIONS

The questions in this section address a number of important math skills.
Use of a calculator is permitted for all questions.

NOTES

Unless otherwise indicated:
- All variables and expressions represent real numbers.
- Figures provided are drawn to scale.
- All figures lie in a plane.
- The domain of a given function f i s the set of all real numbers x for which f(x) is a real number.

REFERENCE

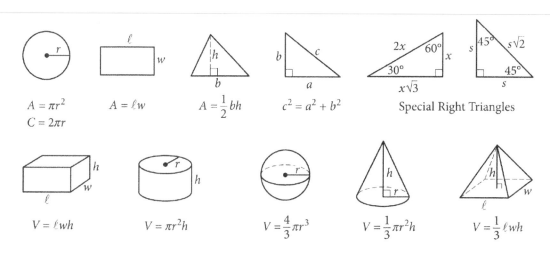

$A = \pi r^2$ $A = \ell w$ $A = \frac{1}{2} bh$ $c^2 = a^2 + b^2$ Special Right Triangles
$C = 2\pi r$

$V = \ell wh$ $V = \pi r^2 h$ $V = \frac{4}{3}\pi r^3$ $V = \frac{1}{3}\pi r^2 h$ $V = \frac{1}{3}\ell wh$

The number of degrees of arc in a circle is **360**.
The number of radians of arc in a circle is 2π.
The sum of the measures in degrees of the angles of a triangle is **180**.

For multiple-choice questions, solve each problem, choose the correct answer from the choices provided, and then circle your answer in this book. Circle only one answer for each question. If you change your mind, completely erase the circle. You will not get credit for questions with more than one answer circled, or for questions with no answers circled.

For student-produced response questions, solve each problem and write your answer next to or under the question in the test book as described below.

- Once you've written your answer, circle it clearly. You will not receive credit for anything written outside the
- circle, or for any questions with more than one circled answer.
- If you find **more than one correct answer**, write and circle only one answer. Your answer can be up to 5 characters for a **positive** answer and up to 6 characters (including the negative sign) for a **negative** answer, but no more.
- If your answer is a **fraction** that is too long (over 5 characters for positive, 6 characters for negative), write the decimal equivalent.

- If your answer is a **decimal** that is too long (over 5 characters for positive,
- 6 characters for negative), truncate it or round at the fourth digit.
- If your answer is a **mixed number** (such as $3\frac{1}{2}$, write it as an improper fraction (7/2) or its decimal equivalent (3.5).
- Don't include symbols such as a percent sign, comma, or dollar sign in your circled answer.

1. If the sum of three consecutive even integers is 108 and m represents the largest of the three integers, which of the following represents the statement above?
   a) $3m + 6 = 108$
   b) $m + 2 = 54$
   c) $m - 2 = 54$
   d) $m - 2 = 36$

2. Equation $(x + 3)(x + a) = x^2 + 4x + b$ where a and b are constants. If the equation is true for all values of x, what is the value of b?
   a) 8
   b) 6
   c) 4
   d) 3

3. If 20 percent of x is 50, what is x percent of 40?
   a) 50
   b) 100
   c) 150
   d) 200

4. If $\frac{2}{5}$ of a number is 30, what is $\frac{1}{15}$ of that number?
   a) 3
   b) 4
   c) 5
   d) 6

w, x, y, z

5. In the sequence above, if each term after the first is d more than the preceding term, what is the sum of w, x, y, and z in terms of w and d?
   a) $3w + 6d$
   b) $4w + 3d$
   c) $6w + 6d$
   d) $2(2w + 3d)$

$$\frac{1}{2}(2ax - 5) = 5$$

6. Based on the equation above, what is the value of $4ax$?

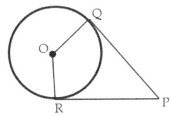

7. In the figure above, point O is the center of the circle, line segments PQ and PR are tangent to the circle at points Q and R, respectively, and the segments intersect at point P as shown. If the radius of the circle is 5 and the length of PQ is $5\sqrt{3}$, what is the area of minor sector $\overset{\frown}{RQ}$? (Round your answer to the nearest tenth.)

8. Which of the following is the expression that represents the statement that the value of the cube of y multiplied by the value of the square root of z, all subtracted from five–sevenths of the square of x equals x?
   a) $\frac{5x^2}{7} - y^3\sqrt{z} = x$
   b) $\frac{5x^2}{7} - y^2\sqrt{z} = x$
   c) $\frac{5x^2}{7} - \sqrt{y^3 z} = x$
   d) $\frac{5}{7}x^2 - y^3 z^2 = x$

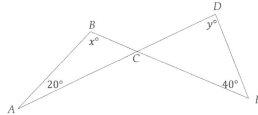

Note: Figure not drawn to scale.

9. In the figure above, $\overline{AD}$ intersects $\overline{BE}$ at C. If $x = 100$, what is the value of y?
   a) 100
   b) 90
   c) 80
   d) 60

10. The function g is defined as $g(x) = \frac{2x}{3} +$
    3 . What is the value of $g(-15)$?
    a) -27
    b) -15
    c) -7
    d) -3

Customer Purchases at a Gas Station

	Beverage Purchased	Beverage not Purchased	Total
Gasoline Purchased	60	25	85
Gasoline not Purchased	35	15	50
Total	95	40	135

11. On Tuesday, a local gas station had 135 customers. The table above summarizes whether or not the customers on Tuesday purchased gasoline, a beverage, both, or neither. Based on the data in the table, what is the probability that a gas station customer selected at random on that day did <u>not</u> purchase gasoline?
    a) $\frac{15}{50}$
    b) $\frac{15}{40}$
    c) $\frac{35}{50}$
    d) $\frac{50}{135}$

12. Which of the following is the graph of
    $y = -(x + 3)^2 - 2$
    a)
    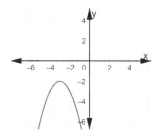

b)
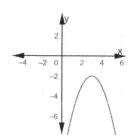

c)
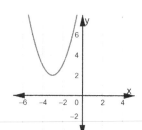

d)
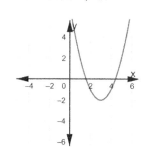

$$x + 2y = -5$$
$$2x - y = 3$$

13. If the solution to the system of equations above is (x, y), what is the value of $x - 3y$?

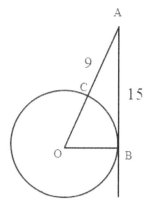

14. In the figure above, AB is tangent to circle O, $\overline{AB} = 15$, and $AC = 9$. What is the area of $\triangle OAB$?

15. When the number 99 is divided by the positive integer N, the remainder is 4. For how many different values of N is this true?
    a) One
    b) Two
    c) Three
    d) Four

16. Biologists found a new species of pale shrimp at the world's deepest undersea vent, the Beebe Vent Field. The vent is 3.1 miles below the sea's surface. Approximately how many kilometers below the sea's surface is the vent? (1 kilometer ≈ 0.6214 miles)
    a) 2
    b) 3
    c) 4
    d) 5

17. The three interior angle measures of a triangle have the ratio 3 : 4 : 5. What is the measure, in degrees, of the largest angles?
    a) 60°
    b) 70°
    c) 75°
    d) 85°

18. Segment $\overline{AB}$ is the diameter of a circle with center O. Another point C lies on circle O. If AC = 5 and BC = 12, what is the area of circle O?
    a) $\frac{169}{2}\pi$
    b) $\frac{169}{4}\pi$
    c) 100π
    d) 50π

19. Line m in the xy-plane contains the points (2, 4) and (0, 1). Which of the following is an equation of line m ?
    a) $= 2x + 3$
    b) $y = 2x + 4$
    c) $y = \frac{3}{2}x + 3$
    d) $y = \frac{3}{2}x + 1$

20. How many combinations of three dishes can be prepared if you have the recipes for 9 dishes?

21. A data set consists of the values 230, 300, 410, 450, 700, and 20, 160. If the outlier is removed, what will happen to the value of the mean of the data set?
    a) The mean will remain the same.
    b) The mean will decrease.
    c) The mean will increase.
    d) There is not enough information to determine how the mean will change.

$$x^2 + y = 7$$
$$x - y = 5$$

22. Which value is a y-coordinate of a solution to the system of equations above?
    a) -8
    b) -3
    c) -2
    d) 6

Math Mock Test 5
22 QUESTIONS

DIRECTIONS

The questions in this section address a number of important math skills.
Use of a calculator is permitted for all questions.

NOTES

Unless otherwise indicated:
- All variables and expressions represent real numbers.
- Figures provided are drawn to scale.
- All figures lie in a plane.
- The domain of a given function f is the set of all real numbers x for which f(x) is a real number.

REFERENCE

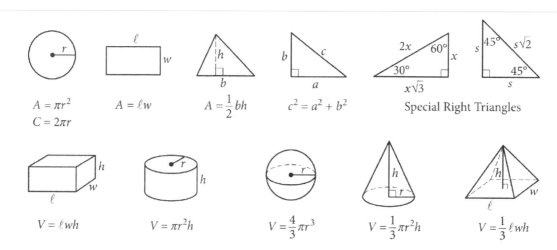

$$A = \pi r^2$$
$$C = 2\pi r$$

$$A = \ell w$$

$$A = \frac{1}{2}bh$$

$$c^2 = a^2 + b^2$$

Special Right Triangles

$$V = \ell w h$$

$$V = \pi r^2 h$$

$$V = \frac{4}{3}\pi r^3$$

$$V = \frac{1}{3}\pi r^2 h$$

$$V = \frac{1}{3}\ell w h$$

The number of degrees of arc in a circle is **360**.
The number of radians of arc in a circle is 2π.
The sum of the measures in degrees of the angles of a triangle is **180**.

For multiple-choice questions, solve each problem, choose the correct answer from the choices provided, and then circle your answer in this book. Circle only one answer for each question. If you change your mind, completely erase the circle. You will not get credit for questions with more than one answer circled, or for questions with no answers circled.

For student-produced response questions, solve each problem and write your answer next to or under the question in the test book as described below.
- Once you've written your answer, circle it clearly. You will not receive credit for anything written outside the circle, or for any questions with more than one circled answer.
- If you find **more than one correct answer**, write and circle only one answer. Your answer can be up to 5 characters for a **positive** answer and up to 6 characters (including the negative sign) for a **negative** answer, but no more.
- If your answer is a **fraction** that is too long (over 5 characters for positive, 6 characters for negative), write the decimal equivalent.
- If your answer is a **decimal** that is too long (over 5 characters for positive,
- 6 characters for negative), truncate it or round at the fourth digit.
- If your answer is a **mixed number** (such as $3\frac{1}{2}$, write it as an improper fraction (7/2) or its decimal equivalent (3.5).
- Don't include symbols such as a percent sign, comma, or dollar sign in your circled answer.

1. Every student at Oak Tree High School is required to study at least one language among Spanish, French, and Chinese, but no one may study more than two. If 150 students study Spanish, 110 study French, 90 study Chinese, and 40 study two languages, how many students are there at Oak Tree High School?
   a) 430
   b) 390
   c) 350
   d) 310

2. Set S is a set of consecutive integers whose sum is a positive even integer. If the smallest integer in the set is −5, what is the least possible number of integers in the set?
   a) 8
   b) 12
   c) 10
   d) 11

3. A recipe of a cake for 8 people requires 1.2 pounds of flour. Assuming the amount of flour needed is directly proportional to the number of people eating the cake, how many pounds of flour are required to make a big cake for 200 people?
   a) 20
   b) 25
   c) 30
   d) 35

4. In June, 24 people enrolled in a cooking class. In July, the number of people who enrolled increased 150%. How many people enrolled in the cooking class in July?
   a) 30
   b) 60
   c) 70
   d) 80

5. If $f(x) = \frac{2-x^2}{x}$ for all nonzero x, then $f(2) = ?$
   a) 1
   b) 2
   c) 3
   d) −1

6. How many positive factors does the number 72 have?
   a) 5
   b) 6
   c) 12
   d) 9

7. If no wallpaper is wasted, how many square feet of wall paper is needed to cover a rectangular wall that is 6 yards by 8 yards (1 yard = 3 feet)?
   a) 432 square feet
   b) 384 square feet
   b) 378 square feet
   d) 324 square feet

8. The gas mileage $M(s)$, in miles per gallon, of a car traveling s miles per hour is modeled by the function below, where $20 \le s \le 75$,
   $$M(s) = -\frac{1}{25}s^2 + 4s - 60$$
   According to the model, at what speed, in miles per hour, does the car obtain its greatest gas mileage?
   a) 45
   b) 47
   c) 50
   d) 55

$$y = x^2 - 6x - 16$$

9. The graph of the equation above in the xy-plane is a parabola. Which of the following equivalent forms of the equation includes the x- and y-coordinates of the vertex as constants?
   a) $y = (x-3)^2 - 25$
   b) $y = x(x-6) - 16$
   c) $y = x^2 - 2(3x+8)$
   d) $y + 16 = x(x-6)$

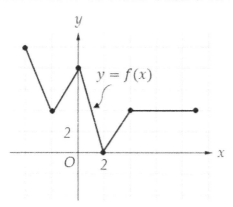

10. The complete graph of the function f is shown in the xy-coordinate plane above. Which of the following are equal to 4?

    I. $f(-2)$
    II. $f(3)$
    III. $f(5.5)$

    a)   I only
    b)   I and II only
    c)   I and III only
    d)   I, II, and III

11. If a and b are both positive integers and $\frac{a}{3} = \frac{8}{b}$, how many pairs of (a, b) is possible?

    a)   12
    b)   10
    c)   8
    d)   6

12. Given the set of integers that are greater than 0 and less than 1000, how many of the integers are multiples of either 2 or 5?

    a) 900
    b) 898
    c) 600
    d) 599

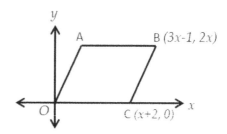

13. In the figure above, if the area of parallelogram OABC is 16, what is the value of x?

$$\frac{(x^2 + 17x + 66)}{x + 6}$$

14. If the expression above is equivalent to an expression of the form $x + a$, where $x \neq -6$, what will be the value of a ?

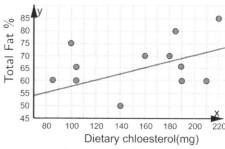

15. The scatterplot above shows the relationship between the amount of dietary cholesterol, in milligrams (mg), and the amount of total fat, in grams (g), in the 12 sandwiches offered by a certain restaurant. The line of best fit predicts the amount of total fat a sandwich has based on the amount of dietary cholesterol in the sandwich. How many grams of total fat are in the sandwich for which this prediction is the most accurate?

    a)   140
    b)   115
    c)   85
    d)   60

16. Which of the following expressions is equivalent to $(16x^9y^3)^{\frac{1}{2}}$, where $x \geq 0 \ and \ y \geq 0$?

   a) $4x^3y^{\frac{1}{2}}$

   b) $4x^{\frac{9}{2}}y^{\frac{3}{2}}$

   c) $8x^3y^3$

   d) $8x^{\frac{9}{2}}y^3$

17. United States Consumption of Certain Types of Renewable Energy since 2003

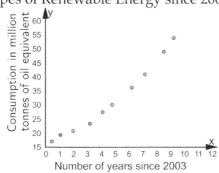

Number of years since 2003

Which of the following equations best models the relationship between the variables in the scatterplot above?

   a) $y = 16(60)^x$

   b) $y = 16(0.8)^x$

   c) $y = 16(1.14)^x$

   d) $y = 16(20)^x$

18. To determine if cooking with olive oil reduces the risk of heartburn for men, researchers interviewed a random sample of 5,500 men who had no history of heartburn. Study participants were identified as either regular or occasional olive oil users. Five years later, researchers interviewed the men again. They found that the proportion of men who experienced frequent heartburn was significantly lower for men identified as regular olive oil users Which of the following is the most appropriate conclusion of the study?

   a) Olive oil use causes a reduction in the risk of heartburn for men and women.

   b) Olive oil use causes a reduction in the risk of heartburn for men but not necessarily for women.

   c) There is an association between olive oil use and the risk of heartburn for men and women, but it is not necessarily a cause-and-effect relationship.

   d) There is an association between olive oil use and the risk of heartburn for men, but it is not necessarily a cause-and-effect relationship, and the association may not exist for women.

19. Line m in the xy-plane contains the points $(2, 4)$ and $(0, 1)$. Which of the following is an equation of line m ?

   a) $= 2x + 3$

   b) $y = 2x + 4$

   c) $y = \frac{3}{2}x + 3$

   d) $y = \frac{3}{2}x + 1$

$$\frac{3}{4}x - \frac{1}{2}y = 12$$
$$ax - by = 9$$

20. The system of equations above has no solutions. If a and b are constants, what is the value of $\frac{a}{b}$?

21. If the area of an equilateral triangle equals the area of a square multiplied by $\sqrt{3}$, what is the ratio of the length of a side of the triangle to the length of a side of the square?

   a) $2 : 1$

   b) $2 : 3$

   c) $1 : 2$

   d) $4 : 3$

22. There are only two different percentages, 10% and 50%, of a chemical solution available in the chemical lab. A student needs to prepare a 100-ml solution including 25% this chemical solution. The volume of the 10% solution is x ml and the volume of the 50% solution is y ml. Which system of equations could be used to determine the values of x and y?

a) $\begin{cases} x + y = 100 \\ x + 5y = 100 \times 0.25 \end{cases}$

b) $\begin{cases} x + y = 100 \\ 0.1x + 0.5y = 100 \times 0.25 \end{cases}$

c) $\begin{cases} x + y = 25 \\ 0.1x + 0.5y = 100 \end{cases}$

d) $\begin{cases} x + y = 25 \\ x + 5y = 100 \end{cases}$

Mock Test 5

Module 1 Keys

1. (D)	2. (A)	3. (D)	4. (A)	5. (D)	6. 21, 28	7. 105	8. (C)
9. (C)	10. (A)	11. (D)	12. (C)	13. $\frac{3}{10}$ or .3	14. 2	15. (D)	16. (C)
17. (A)	18. (D)	19. (A)	20. 108	21. 55	22. (C)		

Module 2 Easy Keys

1. (D)	2. (D)	3. (B)	4. (C)	5. (D)	6. 30	7. 26.2	8. (A)
9. (C)	10. (C)	11. (D)	12. (A)	13. 8	14. 60	15. (C)	16. (D)
17. (C)	18. (B)	19. (D)	20. (D)	21. (D)	22. (C)		

Module 2 Hard Keys

1. (D)	2. (B)	3. (C)	4. (B)	5. (D)	6. (C)	7. (A)	8. (C)
9. (A)	10. (C)	11. (C)	12. (D)	13. (B)	14. 11	15. (D)	16. (B)
17. (C)	18. (D)	19. (D)	20. $\frac{3}{2}$	21. (A)	22. (B)		

Mock Test 5

Module 1 Answers

1. Answer: (D)
    Slope intercept form $y = mx + b$

2. Answer: (A)
    $5v - 3t = 1655$
    $v = \frac{3}{5}t + 331$

3. Answer: (D)
    $2y - x = -4$
    $y = \frac{1}{2}x - 2$ with a positive slope and negative y-intercept

4. Answer: (A)
    Plug in $x = -2$
    $(-2)^2 = -(-2) + c \rightarrow c = 2$
    $x^2 = -x + 2$
    $x^2 + x - 2 = 0$
    $(x + 2)(x - 1) = 0$
    $x = -2$ or 1

5. Answer: (D)
    The value of the y coordinate is constant for a horizontal line.

6. Answer: 21, 28
    The total number should be a multiple of $(4 + 3)$.
    The numbers between 20 and 30 and a multiple of 7 are 21, and 28.

7. Answer: 105
    $2a - 10 = 200$
    $a = 105$

8. Answer: (C)
    Cost of chicken $= c$
    Cost of fish $= f$
    "maximum of 100 entrées" $\rightarrow c + f \leq 100$
    "If no more than \$850 can be spent" $\rightarrow 7c + 9f \leq 850$
    The answer is c).

9. Answer: (C)
    Plug in $y = -1 - z$ to the first equation and then apply FOIL method and the distributive law.
    $x = 2(-1-z)^2 + 3(-1-z) + 4$
    $= 2(1 + 2z + z^2) - 3 - 3z + 4$
    $= 2z^2 + z + 3$

10. Answer: (A)
    Cost = Earning
    x is the number of loaves of bread
    $75 + x(2) = 4(x)$
    $x = 37.5$
    Next integer of x is 38
    The answer is a).

11. Answer: (D)
    $x^2 > 2$
    $x^2 - 2 > 0$
    $(x - 2)(x + 2) > 0$
    The terms $(x - 2)$ and $(x + 2)$ must be both positive or both negative for $(x - 2)(x + 2)$ to be greater than 0.
    $x > 2$ or $x < -2$

12. Answer: (C)
    A reflection across the y-axis flips all y-coordinates from x to –x and keeps the y-coordinates unchanged.
    $y = -2(-x) -1$
    $y = 2x - 1$

13. Answer: $\frac{3}{10}$ or .3
    $\frac{6}{20} = \frac{3}{10}$

14. Answer: 2
    $4(p + 2) + 4(p - 1) = 10p$
    $4p + 8 + 4p - 4 = 10p$
    $8p + 4 = 10p$
    $2p = 4 \rightarrow p = 2$

15. Answer: (D)
    A linear equation:
    "increases by 1 atmosphere every 33 feet below" $\rightarrow$
    slope $= \frac{1}{33}$
    The pressure at water surface is 1atm $\rightarrow$ y-intercept is 1
    $p = \frac{1}{33}f + 1$

16. *Answer: (C)*

$$\frac{x+1}{x} = \frac{1}{x} - \frac{1}{x-3}$$

$$1 + \frac{1}{x} = \frac{1}{x} - \frac{1}{x-3}$$

$$-1 = \frac{1}{x-3}$$

$$x - 3 = -1$$

$$x = 2$$

17. *Answer: (A)*

The expression $(3)^{\frac{t}{4}}$ means the number triples every four days.

18. *Answer: (D)*

Divide by $\sqrt{7}$ on both sides of the equation $y^2 = x\sqrt{7}$.

$x = \frac{y^2}{\sqrt{7}}$ *(Then square both sides.)*

$$x^2 = \frac{y^4}{7}$$

19. *Answer: (A)*

The only common factor of 15 and 21 other than 1 is 3, so y = 3.

$$x = \frac{15}{3} = 5$$

$$z = \frac{21}{3} = 7$$

20. *Answer: 108*

$$\frac{\overline{AB}}{2\pi r} = \frac{x}{360}$$

$$\frac{3\pi}{2(5)\pi} = \frac{x}{360}$$

$$x = 3 \times 36 = 108$$

21. *Answer: 55*

If the width of the cardboard is x inches, the length of the carboard is $15 + x$ inches.
After 5-inch square is cut from each corner and the cardboard is folded to form a box, the width will be $x - 10$, the length will be $x + 5$, and the height will be 5 inches.
The volume of the box is given, so $(x - 10)(x + 5)(5) = 1250$.

$$x^2 - 5x - 50 = 250$$

$$x^2 - 5x - 300 = 0$$

$$(x + 15)(x - 20) = 0$$

$$x = 20 \text{ inches}$$

$$20 + (20 + 15) = 55$$

22. *Answer: (C)*

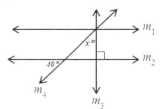

We are given that $m_1 \parallel m_2$, so if $m_1 \perp m_3$, then $m_2 \perp m_3$.
The vertical angles are equal and $m_2 \perp m_3$, thus $x + 40 = 90$.

$$x = 50$$

Module 2 Easy Answers

1. *Answer: (D)*

$$(m - 4) + (m - 2) + m = 108$$

$$3m - 6 = 108$$

$$m - 2 = 36$$

2. *Answer: (D)*

This is an identity equation question. The two expressions have the same coefficients for corresponding terms.

$(x +3)(x + a) = x^2+(3+a)x +3a$

By comparison, $3 + a = 4$ and $3a = b$

$a = 1$ and $b = 3$

3. *Answer: (B)*

Translate "20 percent of x is 50" into an algebraic equation: $\frac{20}{100} \times x = 50$

$$x = \frac{100 \times 50}{20} = 250$$

"x percent of 40" $= 40 \times \frac{250}{100} = 100$

4. *Answer: (C)*

Let the number be x.

$$\frac{2}{5}x = 30 \rightarrow x = 75$$

$$\frac{1}{15} \times 75 = 5$$

5. *Answer: (D)*

The four terms can be rewritten as w, w+d, w+2d, and w+3d

The Sum of the Sequence $= w + w + d + w + 2d + w + 3d = 4w + 6d = 2(2w +3d)$

6. *Answer: 30*

$\frac{1}{2}(2ax - 5) = 5$

$2ax = 15$

$4ax = 30$

7. *Answer: 26.2*

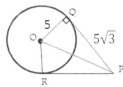

In the right triangle ΔOPQ, the ratio of $\frac{QP}{QO} = \sqrt{3}$;

therefore, $\angle QOP = 60^o$ and $\angle QOR = 120^o$

The area of the minor sector $\overparen{RQ} = \frac{120}{360} \times \pi \times 5^2 = 26.2$

8. *Answer: (A)*
Translate the expression to an algebraic equation.

9. *Answer: (C)*
$y + 40 = x + 20$
$y + 40 = 100 + 20 = 120$
$y = 80$

10. *Answer: (C)*
$g(-15) = \frac{2(-15)}{3} + 3$
$= -7$

11. *Answer: (D)*
$P = \frac{Gasoline\ Not\ Purchased}{Total} = \frac{50}{135}$

12. *Answer: (A)*
The vertex at $(-3, -2)$ and is an open-downward parabolic. The answer a).

13. *Answer: 8*
$(2x - y) - (x + 2y) = 3 - (-5)$
$x - 3y = 8$

14. *Answer: 60*
ΔABO is a right triangle with hypotenuse $\overline{AO}$, so use the Pythagorean Theorem to find OB.
OB and OC are radii and let their length be r.
$15^2 + r^2 = (9 + r)^2$
$225 + r^2 = 81 + 18r + r^2$
$144 = 18r$
$r = 8$
Area of $\Delta OAB = \frac{1}{2} \times 8 \times 15 = 60$

15. *Answer: (C)*
Find all the factors of $(99 - 4)$ that are greater than 4.
$95 = 5 \times 19$
The total number of factors of 95: $(1+1)(1+1) = 4$
N must be greater than 4, so we need to deduct factors that are smaller than or equal to 4 which are 1.
The total number of different values of N: $4 - 1 = 3$

16. *Answer: (D)*
$\frac{1\ km}{0.6214\ miles} = \frac{x\ km}{3.1}$
$x = 5$

17. *Answer: (C)*
We can define the measures of the three angles to be $3x$, $4x$, and $5x$.
$3x + 4x + 5x = 180^o \rightarrow x = 15^o$
$5 \times 15 = 75^o$

18. *Answer: (B)*
ΔABC is a right triangle.
$AB^2 = AC^2 + BC^2$
$AB = \sqrt{5^2 + 12^2} = 13$
Radius $= \frac{1}{2}(13) = 6.5$
Area $= \pi \times 6.5^2 = 42.25\ \pi = \frac{169}{4}\pi$

19. *Answer: (D)*
Slope $= \frac{4-1}{2-0} = \frac{3}{2}$
$y = \frac{3}{2}x + b$ *then plug in* $(0, 1)$
$b = 1$
The equation of line m:
$y = \frac{3}{2}x + 1$

20. *Answer: (D)*
This is combination. The number of ways to select m objects from n objects ($n \geq m$), where order does not matter: ($C_m^n = \frac{n!}{m!(n-m)!}$)
To choose 3 from 9: $C_3^9 = \frac{9!}{3! \times 6!} = 84$

21. *Answer: (D)*
It is not clear which outlier, 700 or 20, will be removed.

22. *Answer: (C)*
Solve the system of the equations:
$x^2 + x - 12 = 0$
$x = 3\ or\ -4$
$y = -2\ or\ -9$

Module 2 Hard Answers

1. *Answer: (D)*
    Total number of students is equal to the number of students who study one langue only plus number of students who study two languages.
    If number of students who only study Spanish is a, only study French is b and only study Chinese is c.
    The number of students who study Spanish and another langue is 150 – a
    The number of students who study French and another language is 110 – b
    The number of students who study Chinese and another language is 90 – c
    However, we count French/Spanish and Spanish/French twice. Therefore,
    (150 – a) + (110 – b) + (90 – c) = 40 × 2
    a + b + c = 150 + 110 + 90 – 80 = 270
    So the total number of students in high school is 270 + 40 = 310

2. *Answer: (B)*
    The last integer must be more than 5 and must be an even positive number. Because the integers in the set have to be consecutive, all positive integers less than or equal to 5 will cancel out their negative counterparts.
    The integer 6 is the first integer greater than 5. So we include the next integer, 6, to the set, which gives us a sum of 6, an even sum.
    Therefore, the integers in the set:
    {–5, –4, –3, –2, –1, 0, 1, 2, 3, 4, 5, 6}

3. *Answer: (C)*
    $\frac{8\,People}{1.2\,Pounds} = \frac{200\,People}{x\,Pounds}$
    $8x = 1.2 \times 200$
    x = 30 pounds of flour

4. *Answer: (B)*
    $24(1 + 1.5) = 60$

5. *Answer: (D)*
    Plug x = 2 into the function.
    $f(2) = \frac{2-(2)^2}{2} = \frac{-2}{2} = -1$

6. *Answer: (C)*
    $72 = 2^3 \times 3^2$
    Number of positive factors of 72:
    (3 + 1) × (2 + 1)= 12

7. *Answer: (A)*
    (3 × 6) × (3 × 8) = 432 square feet

8. *Answer: (C)*
    Vertex of the quadratic $y = ax^2 + bx + c$ is at the point when $x = -\frac{b}{2a}$.
    $s = -\frac{4}{2 \times \left(-\frac{1}{25}\right)} = 50$

9. *Answer: (A)*
    Vertex form of an quadratic function is $y = (x - h)^2 + k$.
    $y = x^2 - 6x + 9 - 25$
    $= (x - 3)^2 - 25$
    The answer is a).

10. *Answer: (C)*
    The function f is the set of points $(x, f(x))$
    y = 4 when x = –2, 1, or $4 \leq x \leq 9$

11. *Answer: (C)*
    $\frac{a}{3} = \frac{8}{b}$
    $ab = 24$
    The number of possible pairs of (a, b) is equal to the number of factors of 24.
    $24 = 3^1 \times 2^3$
    24 has (1 + 1) × (3 + 1) = 8 factors.

12. *Answer: (D)*
    Between 0 and 1000 (exclude), there are 499 ($\frac{998-2}{2}$ + 1) integers which are multiples of 2.
    Between 0 and 1000 (exclude), there are 199 ($\frac{995-5}{5}$ + 1) integers which are multiples of 5.
    LCM of 2 and 5 is 10.
    Between 0 and 1000 (exclude), there are 99 ($\frac{990-10}{10}$ + 1) integers which are multiples of 10
    499 + 199 – 99 = 599
    The number of integers which are multiples of both 2 and 5 is 599.

13. *Answer: (B)*
    Area of OABC = Base × Height =
    (x+2) × (2x) = 16
    $2x^2 + 4x - 16 = 0$
    $x^2 + 2x - 8 = 0$
    $(x + 4)(x - 2) = 0$
    x = –4 (not applicable, x must be positive)
    or x = 2

14. *Answer: 11*

$$\frac{x^2+17x+66}{x+6} = \frac{(x+6)(x+11)}{x+6} = x+11$$

$$a = 11$$

15. *Answer: (D)*
From the graph, the closest distance between point and line is at 60% of fat.

16. *Answer: (B)*

$$(16x^9 y^3)^{\frac{1}{2}} = (16)^{\frac{1}{2}}(x)^{\frac{9}{2}}(y)^{\frac{3}{2}} = 4(x)^{\frac{9}{2}}(y)^{\frac{3}{2}}$$

17. *Answer: (C)*
It is an exponential growth model according to the graph.
$y = ab^x$, *where a is the initial value.*
$y = 16(b)^x$
Plug in one point (9, 55)
$55 = 16(b)^9$
$b = \left(\frac{55}{16}\right)^{\frac{1}{9}} = 1.14$
$y = 16(1.14)^x$

18. *Answer: (D)*
This research is only for men. Any conclusion for women is not appropriate.
The cause-and-effect of Olive oil use causes a reduction in the risk of heartburn is not clear either. So answer d) is the best answer.

19. *Answer: (D)*
$Slope = \frac{4-1}{2-0} = \frac{3}{2}$
$y = \frac{3}{2}x + b$ *then plug in* $(0,1)$
$b = 1$
The equation of line m:
$y = \frac{3}{2}x + 1$

20. *Answer:* $\frac{3}{2}$
$a_1 x + b_1 y = c_1$
$a_2 x + b_2 y = c_2$
When the system of equations above has no solutions, then $\frac{a_1}{a_2} = \frac{b_1}{b_2} \neq \frac{c_1}{c_2}$
$\frac{3}{4}x - \frac{1}{2}y = 12$
$ax - by = 9$
$\frac{\frac{3}{4}}{a} = -\frac{\frac{1}{2}}{-b} \neq \frac{12}{9} \rightarrow \frac{a}{b} = \frac{3}{2}$

21. *Answer: (A)*
Let the length of the side of the triangle be x and the length of the side of the square be y.
Area of an equilateral triangle $= \frac{\sqrt{3}}{4}x^2$
Area of a square $= y^2$
$\frac{\sqrt{3}}{4}x^2 = \sqrt{3}\,y^2$
$x^2 = 4y^2$
$x : y = 2 : 1$

22. *Answer: (B)*
Total Volume = 100
$x + y = 100$
Total chemical balance:
$x \times 0.1 + y \times 0.5 = 100 \times 0.25$

Math Mock Test 6

22 QUESTIONS

DIRECTIONS

The questions in this section address a number of important math skills.

Use of a calculator is permitted for all questions.

o **Check the answers after the Module 1 test. If there are more than 8 questions answered incorrectly in Module 1, take the Easy part of Module 2. Otherwise, take the Hard part of Module 2.**

NOTES

Unless otherwise indicated:

• All variables and expressions represent real numbers.

• Figures provided are drawn to scale.

• All figures lie in a plane.

• The domain of a given function f i s the set of all real numbers x for which f(x) is a real number.

REFERENCE

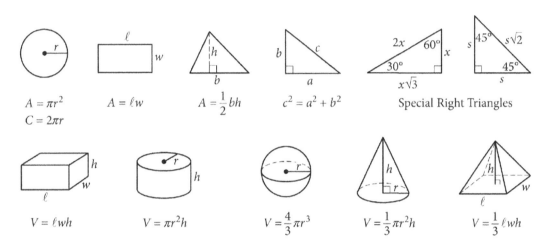

$A = \pi r^2$ $A = \ell w$ $A = \frac{1}{2}bh$ $c^2 = a^2 + b^2$ Special Right Triangles

$C = 2\pi r$

$V = \ell wh$ $V = \pi r^2 h$ $V = \frac{4}{3}\pi r^3$ $V = \frac{1}{3}\pi r^2 h$ $V = \frac{1}{3}\ell wh$

The number of degrees of arc in a circle is **360**.

The number of radians of arc in a circle is 2π.

The sum of the measures in degrees of the angles of a triangle is **180**.

For multiple-choice questions, solve each problem, choose the correct answer from the choices provided, and then circle your answer in this book. Circle only one answer for each question. If you change your mind, completely erase the circle. You will not get credit for questions with more than one answer circled, or for questions with no answers circled.

For student-produced response questions, solve each problem and write your answer next to or under the question in the test book as described below.

• Once you've written your answer, circle it clearly. You will not receive credit for anything written outside the circle, or for any questions with more than one circled answer.

• If you find **more than one correct answer**, write and circle only one answer. Your answer can be up to 5 characters for a **positive** answer and up to 6 characters (including the negative sign) for a **negative** answer, but no more.

• If your answer is a **fraction** that is too long (over 5 characters for positive, 6 characters for negative), write the decimal equivalent.

• If your answer is a **decimal** that is too long (over 5 characters for positive,

• 6 characters for negative), truncate it or round at the fourth digit.

• If your answer is a **mixed number** (such as $3\frac{1}{2}$, write it as an improper fraction (7/2) or its decimal equivalent (3.5).

• Don't include symbols such as a percent sign, comma, or dollar sign in your circled answer.

1. A bike traveled 84 miles in 4 hours. At this rate, how many miles would the bike travel in 5 hours?
   a) 67
   b) 90
   c) 100
   d) 105

$$f(x) = \frac{x+3}{2}$$

2. For the function f above, what is the value of $f(1)$?
   a) $\frac{2}{3}$
   b) $\frac{2}{5}$
   c) 1
   d) 2

3. If 3 times a number is the same as the number itself. What is the number?
   a) $\frac{1}{2}$
   b) 0
   c) 1
   d) 2

$$3(x + b) = ax + c$$

4. In the equation above, a, b, and c are constants. If the equation has infinitely many solutions, which of the following must be equal to a?
   a) 0
   b) 1
   c) 2
   d) 3

All integers in set X are negative.

5. If the statement above is true, which of the following must also be true?
   a) If an integer is negative, it is in set X.
   b) If an integer is positive, it is in set X.
   c) Not all integers in set X are positive.
   d) Some integers in set X are positive.

6. If the side length of a square is an integer and the area of this square is less than 25 but greater than 15, what is the perimeter of the square?

$$4x + 2 = 2$$

7. If x satisfies the equation above, what is the value of $2x + 1$?

8. What is the y-intercept of the linear equation $5y - x = 10$?
   a) –4
   b) –2
   c) 0
   d) 2

9. If $2x + 6y = 12$, then $\frac{1}{3}x + y =$?
   a) 2
   b) 3
   c) 4
   d) 6

10. If $x \neq 0$ and x is inversely proportional to y, which of the following is directly proportional to $\frac{1}{x}$?
    a) $\frac{1}{y}$
    b) $\frac{1}{y^2}$
    c) y
    d) y^2

$$Q = \sqrt{\frac{3dk}{h}}$$

11. The formula above is used to estimate the ideal quantity, Q, of items a store manager needs to order, given the demand quantity, d, the setup cost per order, k, and the storage cost per item, h. Which of the following correctly expresses the storage cost per item in terms of the other variables?

   a) $h = \sqrt{\frac{3dk}{Q}}$

   b) $h = \frac{\sqrt{3dk}}{Q}$

   c) $h = \frac{3dk}{Q^2}$

   d) $h = \frac{Q^2}{3dk}$

12. If $x > x^2$, which of the following must be true?

   I. $x < 1$
   II. $x > 0$
   III. $x^2 > 1$

   a) I only
   b) II only
   c) I and II only
   d) I and III only

13. Let function f be defined by $f(x) = 3x + 1$. If $f(a + 3) = 25$, what is the value of $f(2a)$?

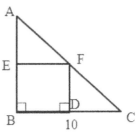

14. In isosceles right triangle $\triangle ABC$ above, EF∥BC and length of $\overline{AF}$ is half of the length of $\overline{AC}$. What is the area of the rectangular region?

15. In the $xy-$plane, line l passes through the points $(1, -1)$ and $(-1, -5)$. Line m is perpendicular to line l and has a y-intercept that is 6 units greater than the y-intercept of line l. What is an equation of line m ?

   a) $y = -\frac{1}{2}x - 6$

   b) $y = -\frac{1}{2}x + 3$

   c) $y = 2x - 3$

   d) $y = 2x + 6$

16. In the figure below, what is the value of x?

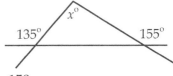

   a) 150
   b) 135
   c) 120
   d) 110

17. Let <I, J> be defined as any integer greater than I but less than J, such as <-3, 3> = {-2, -1, 0, 1, 2}. Which of the following has the same elements as the intersection of <−1, 4> and <1, 6>?

   a) <-2, 2>
   b) <-1, 3>
   c) <-3, 2>
   d) <1, 4>

18. In the xy-plane, the graph of the equation $y = 4x - 3$ intersects the graph of the equation $y = x^2$ at two points. What is the sum of the x-coordinates of the two points?
    a) -4
    b) -3
    c) 3
    d) 4

19. Which of the following is equivalent to $\tan(x^o)$?
    a) $\frac{sin(90^0 - x^o)}{cos(90^0 - x^o)}$
    b) $\frac{cos(90^0 - x^o)}{sin(90^0 - x^o)}$
    c) $-\tan(90^0 - x^o)$
    d) $sin(x^o) - cos(x^o)$

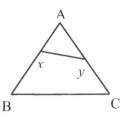

20. The $\triangle ABC$ above is an equilateral triangle. What is the value of $x + y$ in degrees?

21. Bob drove to the school at an average rate of 30 miles per hour. He returned home along the same route at an average rate of 40 miles per hour. If his entire trip took 42 minutes, how many miles did he drive on his way back from school?

22. The number of cats varies inversely with the number of mice. If there are 400 mice when 60 cats are present, how many cats are present when there are 300 mice?
    a) 45
    b) 80
    c) 120
    d) 150

Math Mock Test 6
22 QUESTIONS

DIRECTIONS
The questions in this section address a number of important math skills.
Use of a calculator is permitted for all questions.

NOTES
Unless otherwise indicated:
• All variables and expressions represent real numbers.
• Figures provided are drawn to scale.
• All figures lie in a plane.
• The domain of a given function f i s the set of all real numbers x for which f(x) is a real number.

REFERENCE

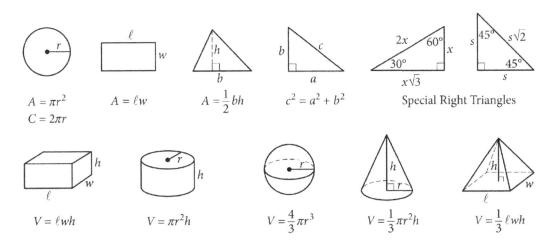

$A = \pi r^2$
$C = 2\pi r$

$A = \ell w$

$A = \frac{1}{2}bh$

$c^2 = a^2 + b^2$

Special Right Triangles

$V = \ell wh$

$V = \pi r^2 h$

$V = \frac{4}{3}\pi r^3$

$V = \frac{1}{3}\pi r^2 h$

$V = \frac{1}{3}\ell wh$

The number of degrees of arc in a circle is **360**.
The number of radians of arc in a circle is 2π.
The sum of the measures in degrees of the angles of a triangle is **180**.

For multiple-choice questions, solve each problem, choose the correct answer from the choices provided, and then circle your answer in this book. Circle only one answer for each question. If you change your mind, completely erase the circle. You will not get credit for questions with more than one answer circled, or for questions with no answers circled.

For student-produced response questions, solve each problem and write your answer next to or under the question in the test book as described below.
• Once you've written your answer, circle it clearly. You will not receive credit for anything written outside the
• circle, or for any questions with more than one circled answer.
• If you find **more than one correct answer**, write and circle only one answer. Your answer can be up to 5 characters for a **positive** answer and up to 6 characters (including the negative sign) for a **negative** answer, but no more.
• If your answer is a **fraction** that is too long (over 5 characters for positive, 6 characters for negative), write the decimal equivalent.

• If your answer is a **decimal** that is too long (over 5 characters for positive,
• 6 characters for negative), truncate it or round at the fourth digit.
• If your answer is a **mixed number** (such as $3\frac{1}{2}$, write it as an improper fraction (7/2) or its decimal equivalent (3.5).
• Don't include symbols such as a percent sign, comma, or dollar sign in your circled answer

1. Ms. Anderson currently has 550 contacts on an online professional networking site. Her goal is to have at least 1,000 contacts. If she wants to meet this goal in 25 weeks, what is the minimum number of contacts per week, on average, she should add?
   a) 18
   b) 19
   c) 21
   d) 22

2. In the figure below, points A and B lie on circle O. If $\angle AOB = 2y°$, what is the value of x in term of y?

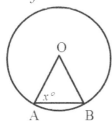

   a) y
   b) $90 - y$
   c) $180 - y$
   d) $90 - \frac{1}{2}y$

3. If $x = \frac{2}{3}yz$, what is the value of y when $z = 6$ and $x = 20$?
   a) 2
   b) 4
   c) 5
   d) 10

4. A political scientist wants to predict how the residents of New Jersey will react to a new bill proposed in the state senate. Which of the following study designs is most likely to provide reliable results for the political scientist?
   a) Mailing a questionnaire to each of 200 randomly selected residents of New Jersey
   b) Surveying a group of 300 randomly selected New Jersey residents

   c) Interviewing a group of students randomly selected from a large public university in New Jersey
   d) Surveying a group of 1,500 randomly selected US residents

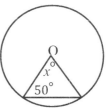

5. In the figure above, point O is the center of the circle. What is the value of x?
   a) 40
   b) 50
   c) 60
   d) 80

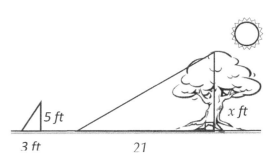

6. At a certain time of day, a tree casts a 21-foot shadow and a 5-foot stick casts a 3-foot shadow. What is the height, in feet, of the tree?

7. A sack contains red, blue, and yellow marbles. The ratio of red marbles to blue marbles to yellow marbles is 3 : 4 : 8. If there are 24 yellow marbles in the sack, how many total marbles are in the sack?

8. A development company is advertising that the mean area of the apartments in a new complex is 1,500 square feet. The complex consists of 10 buildings with a total of 1,000 apartments. A sample of 100 apartments will be selected from the complex to test the company's statement about the mean apartment area. Which of the following is an unbiased sampling method?

    a) Select the first 100 apartments built.

    b) Select the first 100 apartments that are occupied.

    c) Select at random 5 top-floor apartments from each of the buildings.

    d) Select at random 100 apartments from all the apartments in the 10 buildings.

9. A 15-foot wire and a 5-foot wire were each cut completely into 10-inch pieces. How many more 10-inch pieces resulted from the 15-foot wire than from the 5-foot wire? (12 inches = 1 foot)

    a) 6

    b) 9

    c) 12

    d) 188

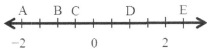

10. On the number line above, A, B, C, D and E are coordinate points. Which of the following is closest in value to $|A - 2 \times C|$?

    a) A

    b) B

    c) C

    d) D

11. The total population in all five cities increased by approximately what percent from 2012 to 2013?

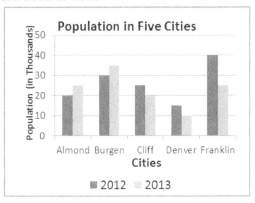

    a) 13.5%

    b) 11.5%

    c) −11.5%

    d) −13.5%

12. On an Algebra final exam, class A has an average score of 90 with 15 students. Class B has an average score of 86.5 with 20 students. When the scores of class A and B are combined, what is the average score of class A and B?

    a) 86

    b) 86.5

    c) 88

    d) 88.5

13. In a triangle, one angle measures $x°$, where $(x°) = \frac{4}{5}$. What is $\cos(90° - x°)$?

14. The figure above shows an arrangement of 14 squares, each with side length of x inches. The perimeter of the figure is P inches and the area of the figure is A square inches. If $21P = A$, what is the value of x?

15. If $f(x) = x^2 + x^{3/2}$, what is the value of $f(3)$ =?

    a) $3 \times (1 + 3\sqrt{3})$

    b) $(1 + 3\sqrt{3})$

    c) $3 \times (1 + 3\sqrt{3})$

    d) $3 \times (3 + \sqrt{3})$

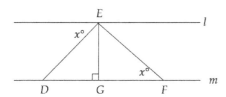

Note: Figure not drawn to scale.

16. In the figure above, line l is parallel to line m. If $x = 40$, what is the measure of $\angle DEF$?

    a) $140°$

    b) $100°$

    c) $80°$

    d) $50°$

Roof Type			
Asphalt Shingle	Slate	Cedar Shake	Total
Single-Story	8	4	3	15
Two-Story	21	10	2	33
Total	29	14	5	48

17. The table above shows the distribution of single-story and two-story houses in a neighborhood classified according to roof type. If one of the houses is selected at random, what is the probability that it will be a single-story house with a slate roof?

    a) $\frac{1}{12}$

    b) $\frac{4}{15}$

    c) $\frac{4}{14}$

    d) $\frac{7}{24}$

18. If John gives Sally $5, Sally will have twice the amount of money that John will have. Originally, there was a total of $45 between the two of them. How much money did John initially have?

    a) 25

    b) 20

    c) 18

    d) 15

19. A bike traveled 80 miles in 5 hours. At this rate, how many miles would the bike travels in 6 hours?

    a) 64

    b) 90

    c) 96

    d) 100

20. In the xy-plane, the circle with radius 5 and center $(6, 4)$ contains the point $(w, 0)$. what is one possible value of w?

21. On a certain test, the highest possible score is 100 and the lowest is 0. If the average score of 5 students is 86, what is the lowest possible score of the fifth student?

    a) 0

    b) 10

    c) 20

    d) 30

22. 36 marbles, all of which are red, blue, or green, are placed in a bag. If a marble is picked from the bag at random, the probability of getting a red marble is $\frac{1}{4}$ and the probability of getting a blue marble is $\frac{1}{2}$. How many green marbles are in the bag?

    a) 9

    b) 10

    c) 12

    d) 15

Math Mock Test 6
22 QUESTIONS

DIRECTIONS
The questions in this section address a number of important math skills.
Use of a calculator is permitted for all questions.

NOTES
Unless otherwise indicated:
• All variables and expressions represent real numbers.
• Figures provided are drawn to scale.
• All figures lie in a plane.
• The domain of a given function f i s the set of all real numbers x for which f(x) is a real number.

REFERENCE

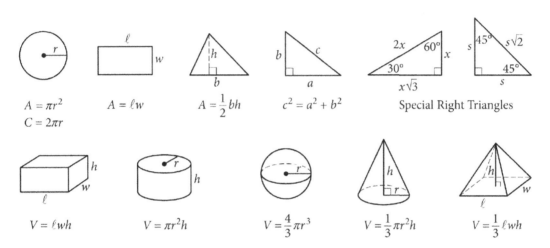

$A = \pi r^2$ $A = \ell w$ $A = \frac{1}{2}bh$ $c^2 = a^2 + b^2$ Special Right Triangles
$C = 2\pi r$

$V = \ell wh$ $V = \pi r^2 h$ $V = \frac{4}{3}\pi r^3$ $V = \frac{1}{3}\pi r^2 h$ $V = \frac{1}{3}\ell wh$

The number of degrees of arc in a circle is **360**.
The number of radians of arc in a circle is 2π.
The sum of the measures in degrees of the angles of a triangle is **180**.

For multiple-choice questions, solve each problem, choose the correct answer from the choices provided, and then circle your answer in this book. Circle only one answer for each question. If you change your mind, completely erase the circle. You will not get credit for questions with more than one answer circled, or for questions with no answers circled.

For student-produced response questions, solve each problem and write your answer next to or under the question in the test book as described below.
• Once you've written your answer, circle it clearly. You will not receive credit for anything written outside the circle, or for any questions with more than one circled answer.
• If you find **more than one correct answer**, write and circle only one answer. Your answer can be up to 5 characters for a **positive** answer and up to 6 characters (including the negative sign) for a **negative** answer, but no more.
• If your answer is a **fraction** that is too long (over 5 characters for positive, 6 characters for negative), write the decimal equivalent.
• If your answer is a **decimal** that is too long (over 5 characters for positive,
• 6 characters for negative), truncate it or round at the fourth digit.
• If your answer is a **mixed number** (such as $3\frac{1}{2}$, write it as an improper fraction (7/2) or its decimal equivalent (3.5).
• Don't include symbols such as a percent sign, comma, or dollar sign in your circled answer.

1. When r is divided by 12, the remainder is 9. What is the remainder when $r + 1$ is divided by 4?

    a) 0
    b) 1
    c) 2
    d) 3

2. A certain colony of bacteria began with one cell, and the population doubled every 30 minutes. What was the population of the colony after 3 hours?

    a) 8
    b) 16
    c) 32
    d) 64

3. A pump can be set to extract water from a pool at one of three different rates: 1 gallon per minute, 4 gallons per minute, or 8 gallons per minute. The graph below shows the amount of water left in the pool from the time the pump was turned on. How many minutes after being turned on was the pump switched to a rate of 8 gallons per minute?

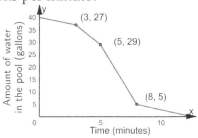

    a) 3
    b) 5
    c) 8
    d) 29

4. If $x^2 - y^2 = 24$, and $x - y = 4$, what is the value of $x + 2y$?

    a) 1
    b) 3
    c) 5
    d) 7

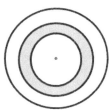

5. The figure above consists of three circles that share the same center. The circles have radii of 2, 3, and 5 respectively. What is the probability that a randomly chosen point will be in the shaded region?

    a) $\dfrac{1}{5}$

    b) $\dfrac{1}{4}$

    c) $\dfrac{5}{16}$

    d) $\dfrac{7}{16}$

6. If $f(x) = 3x^2 - 1$ and $f(x + a) = 3x^2 + 20x + 11$, what could be the value of a?

    a) -11
    b) -3
    c) 2
    d) 4

7. The scatterplot above represents the salary y, in thousands of dollars, and the number of years of experience, x, for each of six employees at a company. A line of best fit for the data is also shown. Which of the following could be an equation of the line of best fit?

     a) $y = \frac{3}{2}x$

     b) $y = \frac{3}{2}x + \frac{95}{2}$

     c) $y = \frac{2}{3}x + \frac{95}{2}$

     d) $y = \frac{2}{3}x + 55$

8. If $a + bi = \frac{1+i}{2-i}$, what is the value of $a + b =$?

     a) 0.4

     b) 0.6

     c) 0.8

     d) 1.0

9. In the xy-plane, the graph of the polynomial function f crosses the x-axis at exactly two points, $(a, 0)$ and $(b, 0)$, where a and b are both positive. Which of the following could define f ?

     a) $f(x) = (x - a)(x - b)$

     b) $f(x) = (x + a)(x + b)$

     c) $f(x) = (x - a)(x + b)$

     d) $f(x) = x(x - a)(x - b)$

10. In $\triangle ABC$ and $\triangle DEF$, $AC = DF$ and $BC = EF$. Which of the following additional information is NOT sufficient to prove that $\triangle ABC$ is congruent to $\triangle DEF$?

     a) $AB = DE$

     b) $m\angle CAB = m\angle FDE$

     c) $m\angle ACB = m\angle DFE$

     d) $AB + BC = DE + EF$

11. The table below shows the number of lakes in the United Kingdom classified by alkalinity and depth.

Depth Class	Alkalinity Class			
	Low	Medium	High	Total
Shallow	87	61	200	357
Moderate	227	86	100	423
Deep	130	35	50	186
Total	444	182	350	966

If a lake has high alkalinity, which of the following is closest to the probability that the lake also has a shallow depth?

     a) 0.22

     b) 0.45

     c) 0.57

     d) 0.61

$$C = \frac{5}{9}(F - 32)$$

12. The equation above gives the relationship between the temperature measured in degrees Fahrenheit, F, and degrees Celsius, C. At what temperature, in degrees Fahrenheit, will the temperature measured in degrees Celsius be triple he value of the temperature measured in degrees Celsius be twice the value of the temperature measured in degrees Fahrenheit?

     a) $\frac{-160}{32}$

     b) $\frac{-160}{22}$

     c) 160

     d) 320

13. In the xy-coordinate plane, point A has coordinates $(x, -5)$ and point B has coordinates $(3, 7)$. If $\overline{AB} = 13$ and x is a positive value, what is the value of x?

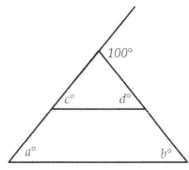

14. In the figure above, what is the value of $2a + 2b - c - d$?

c) 100π
d) 50π

19. Which of the following scatterplots is the best representation of a function, $f(x) = mx + b$, where m is a negative number and b is a positive number?

15. For $b > a$, the product of 4 and $(b - a)$ is equal to the average of a and b. If b is 63, what is a?
     a) 42
     b) 45
     c) 49
     d) 50

a)

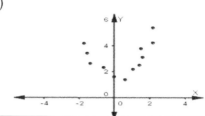

16. Which of the following is a solution to the equation $\sqrt{14 - x} + 2 = x$?
         I. -2
         II. 1
         III. 5
     a) I only
     b) II only
     c) III only
     d) I and III

b)

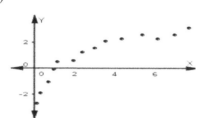

c)

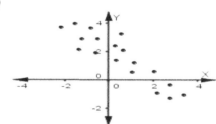

17. If $f(x + 1) = x^2 - 1$, then $f(x) = ?$
     a) $x^2 - 2x + 1$
     b) $x^2 + 2x + 1$
     c) $x^2 - 2x$
     d) $x^2 + 2x$

d)

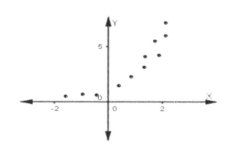

18. Segment $\overline{AB}$ is the diameter of a circle with center O. Another point C lies on circle O. If AC = 5 and BC = 12, what is the area of circle O?
     a) $\dfrac{169}{2}\pi$
     b) $\dfrac{169}{4}\pi$

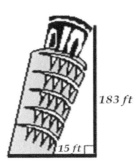

183 ft

15 ft

20. If the Leaning Tower of Pisa is 183 feet tall and the top edge of the tower leans 15 feet out from the bottom edge, what is *tangent* of the angle created between the ground and the tower?

$$f(x) = x\,(x+1)$$

21. The function f is defined above. If the function g is defined by $g(x) = f(x) + 3$, what is the value of $g(3)$?

   a) 9
   b) 15
   c) 22
   d) 27

22. A sample of 500 ninth graders was selected at random and asked how much time they spend on homework each day. Of the ninth graders selected, 200 spend less than 2 hours on homework each day. If the conclusion was drawn that 1.5 million ninth graders spend less than 2 hours on homework each day which of the following is closest to the population, in millions, of ninth graders?

   a) 0.45
   b) 1.35
   c) 3.75
   d) 6.12

Mock Test 6

Module 1 Keys

1. (D)	2. (D)	3. (B)	4. (D)	5. (C)	6. 16	7. 1	8. (D)
9. (A)	10. (C)	11. (C)	12. (C)	13. 31	14. 25	15. (B)	16. (D)
17. (D)	18. (D)	19. (B)	20. 240	21. 12	22. (B)		

Module 2 Easy Keys

1. (A)	2. (B)	3. (C)	4. (B)	5. (D)	6. 35	7. 45	8. (D)
9. (C)	10. (D)	11. (C)	12. (C)	13. $\frac{4}{5}$ or 0.8	14. 27	15. (D)	16. (B)
17. (A)	18. (B)	19. (C)	20. 3 or 9	21. (D)	22. (A)		

Module 2 Hard Keys

1. (C)	2. (D)	3. (B)	4. (D)	5. (A)	6. (C)	7. (B)	8. (C)
9. (A)	10. (B)	11. (C)	12. (B)	13. 8	14. 100	15. (C)	16. (C)
17. (D)	18. (B)	19. (D)	20. 12.2	21. (B)	22. (C)		

Mock Test 6

Module 1 Answers

1. Answer: (D)
    This is a ratio problem.
    $\frac{84}{4} = \frac{x}{5}$ (cross multiply) → $x = 105$

2. Answer: (D)
    $f(1) = \frac{1+3}{2} = 2$

3. Answer: (B)
    Let the number be a.
    $3a = a$
    $3a - a = 0 \rightarrow a = 0$

4. Answer: (D)
    "An equation has infinitely many solutions," means the left expression is exactly same as the right expression.
    $3x + 3b = ax + c$
    $a = 3$

5. Answer: (C)
    If X only contains negative integers, then there are no positive integers in set X.

6. Answer: 16
    Let the side length = d, the area of the square = d^2.
    $15 < d^2 < 25$
    $\sqrt{15} < d < 5 \rightarrow d$ can only be 4.
    $4 \times 4 = 16$

7. Answer: 1
    $4x + 2 = 2$
    $2x + 1 = 1$

8. Answer: (D)
    The y-intercept occurs when x = 0.
    $5y - 0 = 10 \rightarrow y = 2$

9. Answer: (A)
    $2x + 6y = 12$
    $\frac{1}{6}(2x + 6y) = \frac{1}{6} \times 12$
    $\frac{1}{3}x + y = 2$

10. Answer: (C)
    If "x is inversely proportional to y", then xy = k.
    $xy = k \rightarrow y = k\left(\frac{1}{x}\right) \rightarrow \frac{y}{\frac{1}{x}} = k$

    So $\frac{1}{x}$ is directly proportional to y.

11. Answer: (C)
    $Q = \sqrt{\frac{3dk}{h}}$
    $Q^2 = \frac{3dk}{h} \rightarrow h = \frac{3dk}{Q^2}$

12. Answer: (C)
    $x > x^2 > 0$
    $x - x^2 > 0$
    $x(1 - x) > 0$
    Since $x > 0$
    x must be smaller than 1.

13. Answer: 31
    Substitute x with (a + 3).
    $25 = 3 \times (a + 3) + 1$
    $25 = 3a + 10 \rightarrow a = 5$
    $f(2a) = f(10) = 3 \times 10 + 1 = 31$

14. Answer: 25
    $AB = BC$
    $EF = BD = \frac{1}{2}BC = 5$
    $BE = \frac{1}{2}AB = 5$
    Area $= 5 \times 5 = 25$

15. Answer: (B)
    For line l:
    Slope $= \frac{-5-(-1)}{-1-1} = 2$
    $y = 2x + b$
    Plug in $(1, -1)$,
    $-1 = 2(1) + b \rightarrow b = -3$
    For line m:
    Slope $: -\frac{1}{2}$
    y-intercept: $-3 + 6 = 3$
    $y = -\frac{1}{2}x + 3$

16. Answer: (D)
    The three interior angles of the triangle are x°, (180 − 135)°, and (180 − 155)°.
    $x + 45 + 25 = 180$
    $x = 110$

17.   *Answer: (D)*
      Intersection of <-1, 4> and <1, 6> = {0, 1, 2, 3} ∩
      {2, 3, 4, 5} = {2, 3}
      (d) <1, 4> has the same elements of {2, 3}.

18.   *Answer: (D)*
      $4x - 3 = x^2$
      $x^2 - 4x + 3 = 0$
      $(x - 1)(x - 3) = 0$
      $x = 1 \text{ or } 3$
      $1 + 3 = 4$

19.   *Answer: (B)*
      $tan(x^o) = cot(90° - x^o) = \frac{cos(90^o - x^o)}{sin(90^o - x^o)}$

20.   *Answer: 240*
      The sum of the interior angles of a quadrilateral
      triangle is 360°.
      $60^o + 60^o + x + y = 360^o$
      $x + y = 240^o$

21.   *Answer: 12*
      Let one trip have x miles.
      $Time = \frac{Miles}{Rate}$
      Total Time (hours) = $t_{go} + t_{back}$
      $\frac{42}{60} = \frac{x}{30} + \frac{x}{40} = x\left(\frac{1}{30} + \frac{1}{40}\right)$
      x = 12 miles

22.   *Answer: (B)*
      "Varying inversely" is inverse proportion.
      A × B = constant
      A × B (before) = A_1 × B_1 (after)
      $400 × 60 = 300 × B_1 \rightarrow B_1 = 80$

Module 2 Easy Answers

1.   *Answer: (A)*
     The number of contact add each week is C: 25C ≥
     (1000 − 550)
     C ≥ 18

2.   *Answer: (B)*
     ΔOAB is an isosceles Δ.
     2x + 2y = 180
     x + y = 90
     x = 90 – y

3.   *Answer: (C)*
     If x = 20 and z = 6, then $20 = \frac{2}{3}(y)(6)$.
     4y = 20
     y = 5

4.   *Answer: (B)*
     For reliable results:
     1) to pick random sample
     2) Not to use mail (may not mail back)
     Therefore, the answer is b)

5.   *Answer: (D)*
     Two of the legs of the triangle are the radii of the
     circle. This triangle is an isosceles triangle with
     equal base angles.
     180 − 50 − 50 = x → x = 80

6.   *Answer: 35*
     The corresponding sides of two similar triangles are
     proportional.
     $\frac{5}{3} = \frac{x}{21}$
     x = 35 ft

7.   *Answer: 45*
     Total : Yellow = (3 + 4 + 8) : 8 = 15 : 8
     There are 24 yellow marbles.
     15 : 8 = Total Marbles : 24
     8 × Total Marbles = 24 × 15
     Total Marbles = 45

8.   *Answer: (D)*
     It needs to select samples randomly in order to be
     unbiased.

9.   *Answer: (C)*
     From 15-foot: $\frac{(15)(12)}{10} = 18$
     From 5-foot: $\frac{(5)(12)}{10} = 6$
     The difference is 12.

10. *Answer: (D)*
     A = −2 and C = $-\frac{1}{2}$; $|A − 2 × C| = |-2 - 2(-\frac{1}{2})|$
     = |−2 + 1| = |−1| = 1
     D has the coordinate of 1.

11. *Answer: (C)*

Percent Increase = $\frac{2013\ Population - 2012\ Population}{2012\ Population} \times 100\%$

Total Population in 2012 = 20 + 30 + 25 + 15 + 40 = 130 thousand.

Total Population in 2013= 25 + 35 + 20 + 10 + 25 = 115 thousand.

$\frac{115 - 130}{130} \times 100\% = -11.5\%$

12. *Answer: (C)*

This is **not** the average of the averages since the classes have different number of students! The final average is the sum of all students' scores divided by the total number of students.

We know that the sum of all the students' scores in one class is just the average multiplied by the number of students.

Average = $\frac{15 \times 90 + 20 \times 86.5}{15 + 20} = 88$

13. *Answer:* $\frac{4}{5}$ *or 0.8*

$\cos(90^o - x^o) = \sin(x^o) = \frac{4}{5}$

14. *Answer: 27*

The perimeter P is equal to 18x and its area is equal to $14 \times x^2$.

21P = A

$21 \times 18x = 14x^2$

$14x^2 - 378x = 0$

$x^2 - 27x = 0$

$x(x - 27) = 0 \quad \rightarrow \quad x = 27 \ (x > 0)$

15. *Answer: (D)*

The value of f(3) is calculated by replacing x with 3 in the function.

$3^2 + 3^{3/2} = 9 + 3\sqrt{3} = 3(3 + \sqrt{3})$

16. *Answer: (B)*

$m\angle DEF = m\angle DEG + m\angle GEF = (90 - x) + (90 - x) = 50 + 50 = 100°$

17. *Answer: (A)*

$p = \frac{single\ house\ and\ slate\ roof}{total\ house} = \frac{4}{48} = \frac{1}{12}$

18. *Answer: (B)*

Let J be the amount of money John initially had and S be the amount of money Sally initially had. Together, they originally had $45.

J + S =45

J = 45 – S

After John gives Sally $5, John will have J – 5 dollars and Sally will have S + 5 dollars. Therefore,

S + 5 = 2(J – 5).

S + 5 = 2(45 – S – 5) = 80 – 2S

S = 25

Plug J = 45 – S into the equation above to get J = $20.

19. *Answer: (C)*

This is a ratio problem.

$\frac{80}{5} = \frac{x}{6}$ *(cross multiply)*

x = 96

20. *Answer: 3 or 9*

The standard equation of the circle:

$(x - 6)^2 + (y - 4)^2 = 25$

Plug in the point $(w, 0) \rightarrow (w - 6)^2 + 16 = 25$

$w - 6 = \pm 3 \rightarrow w = 9\ or\ 3$

21. *Answer: (D)*

The lowest possible score is equal to the lowest score a student can get if each of other four students got the highest possible score (otherwise we can always increase another student's score and decrease the lowest score). Thus, each of other four students must get 100.

Total Score = 5 × 86 = 430

Lowest Possible Score = 430 – 400 = 30

22. *Answer: (A)*

The probability of getting green marbles: $1 - \frac{1}{4} - \frac{1}{2} = \frac{1}{4}$

$\frac{1}{4} = \frac{x}{36}, \quad x = 9$

Module 2 Hard Answers

1. *Answer: (C)*
   $r = 12 \times q + 9$ (Remainder Theorem)
   $r + 1 = 12 \times q + 10$
   Since $12 \times q$ is divisible by 4, the remainder of $r + 1$ divided by 4 is equal to the remainder of 10 divided by 4, which is 2.
   Or just simply pick an easy number to try out this question, such as 21 (12 + 9) in this case.

2. *Answer: (D)*
   1, 2, 4, 8, 16, 32, 64

3. *Answer: (B)*
   The slope of the line between two points,
   $(5, 29)$ and $(8, 5)$ is $\frac{29-5}{5-8} = -8$.
   The rate of the pump is 8 gallons from the 5th minute. The answer is b).

4. *Answer: (D)*
   $x^2 - y^2 = (x - y)(x + y)$
   $4(x + y) = 24$,
   $x + y = 6$
   $x - y = 4$
   Solve above system equations:
   $x = 5$ and $y = 1$
   $x + 2y = 7$

5. *Answer: (A)*
   The probability that a randomly chosen point will be in the shaded area is equal to $\frac{Area\ of\ Shaded\ Region}{Total\ Area}$
   Area of Shaded Region = Area of Medium Circle – Area of Small Circle
   $\pi \times 3^2 - \pi \times 2^2 = 5\pi$
   Total Area $= \pi \times 5^2 = 25\pi$
   Probability $= \frac{5\pi}{25\pi} = \frac{1}{5}$

6. *Answer: (C)*
   $f(x + a) = 3x^2 + 20x + 11$
   When $x = 0$, $f(a) = 11 = 3a^2 - 1$
   $a^2 = 4 \rightarrow a = \pm 2$

7. *Answer: (B)*
   Slope $= \frac{3}{2}$ and y-intercept $= \frac{95}{2}$
   The answer is b)

8. *Answer: (C)*
   Rationalize the denominator.
   $\frac{2+i}{2+i} \times \frac{1+i}{2-i} = \frac{1+3i}{1+4} = \frac{1}{5} + \frac{3}{5}i$
   $a + bi = \frac{1}{5} + \frac{3}{5}i$
   $a = \frac{1}{5}$ and $b = +\frac{3}{5}$
   $a + b = \frac{4}{5} = 0.8$

9. *Answer: (A)*
   This equation has exactly two roots, a and b.
   $f(x) = (x - a)(x - b)$

10. *Answer: (B)*
    When $m\angle CAB = m\angle FDE$,
    $\triangle ABC$ and $\triangle DEF$ has an SSA relationship that does not guarantee two triangles are congruent. The answer is b).

11. *Answer: (C)*
    $\frac{Shallow\ and\ high\ alkalinity}{high\ alkalinity} = \frac{200}{350} = 0.57$

12. *Answer: (B)*
    $C = 3F = \frac{5}{9}(F - 32)$
    $27F - 5F = -160$
    $F = -\frac{160}{22}$

13. *Answer: 8*
    Use the distance formula.
    $\sqrt{(x - 3)^2 + (-5 - 7)^2} = 13$
    $(x-3)^2 + 12^2 = 13^2$
    $(x-3)^2 = 25$
    $x - 3 = \pm 5 \rightarrow x = -2, 8$

14. *Answer: 100*
    $100 = c + d = a + b$
    $2(a + b) - c - d = 200 - 100 = 100$

15. *Answer: (C)*
    $\frac{63 + a}{2} = 4 \times (63 - a)$.
    $63 + a = 8(63 - a)$
    $63 + a = 8 \times 63 - 8a$
    $9a = 7 \times 63 \rightarrow a = 49$

16. *Answer: (C)*

$$\sqrt{14 - x} = x - 2$$
$$14 - x = (x - 2)^2 = x^2 - 4x + 4$$
$$x^2 - 3x - 10 = 0$$
$$(x - 5)(x + 2) = 0$$
$$x = 5, -2$$
$$\sqrt{14 - (-2)} + 2 \neq -2$$

Therefore, $x = -2$ is not the solution. The answer is c).

17. *Answer: (D)*

$$f(x + 1) = x^2 - 1$$
$$f(x) = f\big((x + 1) - 1\big)$$
$$= (x - 1)^2 - 1$$
$$= x^2 - 2x + 1 - 1 = x^2 - 2x$$

18. *Answer: (B)*

ΔABC is a right triangle.
$$AB^2 = AC^2 + BC^2$$
$$AB = \sqrt{5^2 + 12^2} = 13$$
$$Radius = \frac{1}{2}(13) = 6.5$$
$$Area = \pi \times 6.5^2 = 42.25\,\pi = \frac{169}{4}\,\pi$$

19. *Answer: (D)*

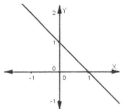

The graph of $f(x) = -x + 1$:
So, answer is (d).

20. *Answer: 12.2*

$$\tan(\theta) = \frac{183}{15} = 12.2$$

21. *Answer: (B)*

$$g(3) = f(3) + 3 = 3(3 + 1) + 3 = 15$$

22. *Answer: (C)*

$$\frac{200}{500} = \frac{1.5}{x}$$
$$x = 3.75$$

Math Mock Test 7

22 QUESTIONS

DIRECTIONS

The questions in this section address a number of important math skills.

Use of a calculator is permitted for all questions.

○ **Check the answers after the Module 1 test. If there are more than 8 questions answered incorrectly in Module 1, take the Easy part of Module 2. Otherwise, take the Hard part of Module 2.**

NOTES

Unless otherwise indicated:

• All variables and expressions represent real numbers.

• Figures provided are drawn to scale.

• All figures lie in a plane.

• The domain of a given function f i s the set of all real numbers x for which f(x) is a real number.

REFERENCE

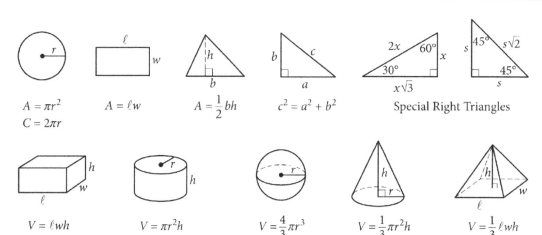

$A = \pi r^2$ $A = \ell w$ $A = \frac{1}{2}bh$ $c^2 = a^2 + b^2$ Special Right Triangles

$C = 2\pi r$

$V = \ell wh$ $V = \pi r^2 h$ $V = \frac{4}{3}\pi r^3$ $V = \frac{1}{3}\pi r^2 h$ $V = \frac{1}{3}\ell wh$

The number of degrees of arc in a circle is **360**.

The number of radians of arc in a circle is 2π.

The sum of the measures in degrees of the angles of a triangle is **180**.

For multiple-choice questions, solve each problem, choose the correct answer from the choices provided, and then circle your answer in this book. Circle only one answer for each question. If you change your mind, completely erase the circle. You will not get credit for questions with more than one answer circled, or for questions with no answers circled.

For student-produced response questions, solve each problem and write your answer next to or under the question in the test book as described below.

• Once you've written your answer, circle it clearly. You will not receive credit for anything written outside the circle, or for any questions with more than one circled answer.

• If you find **more than one correct answer**, write and circle only one answer. Your answer can be up to 5 characters for a **positive** answer and up to 6 characters (including the negative sign) for a **negative** answer, but no more.

• If your answer is a **fraction** that is too long (over 5 characters for positive, 6 characters for negative), write the decimal equivalent.

• If your answer is a **decimal** that is too long (over 5 characters for positive,

• 6 characters for negative), truncate it or round at the fourth digit.

• If your answer is a **mixed number** (such as $3\frac{1}{2}$, write it as an improper fraction (7/2) or its decimal equivalent (3.5).

• Don't include symbols such as a percent sign, comma, or dollar sign in your circled answer.

1. If $x^{\frac{1}{4}} = \sqrt{3}$, then what is the value of x?
   a) 1
   b) 3
   c) 9
   d) 27

2. If $\frac{2}{x} + x = 4 + \frac{1}{2}$, then x can be equal to which of the following?
   a) 1
   b) 2
   c) 3
   d) 4

3. When the number 13 is divided by the positive integer p, the remainder is 1. For how many different values of p is this true?
   a) Six
   b) Five
   c) Four
   d) Three

4. The front of a roller-coaster car is at the bottom of a hill and is 10 feet above the ground. If the front of the roller-coaster car rises at a constant rate of 8 feet per second, which of the following equations gives the height h, in feet, of the front of the roller-coaster car s seconds after it starts up the hill?
   a) $h = 8s + 10$
   b) $h = 10s + \frac{335}{8}$
   c) $h = 8s + \frac{335}{15}$
   d) $h = 10s + 8$

5. In the xy-coordinate plane, line m is the reflection of line l about the y-axis. Which of the following could be the sum of the slopes of lines m and l?
   a) 1
   b) -1
   c) 0
   d) $\frac{1}{2}$

6. In the xy-plane, line k passes through the point (3,1) and is parallel to the line with equation $y = \frac{5}{2}x - \frac{7}{2}$. What is the slope of line k?

7. For every 15 cars sold by a dealer, 3 of them were red. What is the probability that a car sold that is selected at random would be red?

$$3(1 - x) = -3x + b$$

8. In the equation above, b is a constant. If the equation has no solution, which of the following must be true?
   a) $b \neq -3$
   b) $b \neq -1$
   c) $b \neq 1$
   d) $b \neq 3$

9. If $a = \left|\frac{1}{x+4}\right|$ and $b = \frac{1}{y+2}$, what is the value of $a + b$ when $x = -5$ and $y = -3$?
   a) $\frac{1}{2}$
   b) $-\frac{1}{2}$
   c) $\frac{1}{4}$
   d) 0

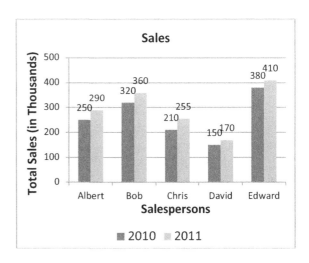

10. Which salesperson had the greatest increase in the number of units sold from 2010 to 2011 according to the graph above?
    a) Albert
    b) Bob
    c) David
    d) Chris

11. The population in 2010 was r. If there is a net population increase of x people each year, which of the following represents the population of y years after 2010?
    a) $x + ry$
    b) $r + xy$
    c) $r + x(2010 - y)$
    d) $r + x(y - 2010)$

$$wxy + xyz = wx + yz$$
12. In the equation above, w, x, and z are each greater than 1. Which of the following is equivalent to y?
    a) $-x$
    b) $-\dfrac{1}{x}$
    c) $\dfrac{1}{xz-z}$
    d) $\dfrac{wx}{wx+xz-z}$

$$1.2(h + 2) = 2h - 1.2$$
13. What value of h is the solution of the equation above?

14. When a number is tripled and then reduced by 15, the result is 300. What is the number?

$$2000 - 61k = 48$$
15. In 1962, the population of a bird species was 2,000. The population k years after 1962 was 48, and k satisfied the equation above. Which of the following is the best interpretation of the number 61 in this context?
    a) The population k years after 1962

b) The value of k when the population was 48
c) The difference between the population in 1962 and the population k years after 1962.
d) The average decrease in the population per year from 1962 to k years after 1962

16. If $x^2 - y^2 = 24$ and $x + y = 6$, find the value of y.
    a) 1
    b) 3
    c) 5
    d) 7

17. If $3 = m^x$, then $9m^2 = ?$
    a) m^{2x}
    b) m^{3x}
    c) m^{2x+2}
    d) m^{2x+3}

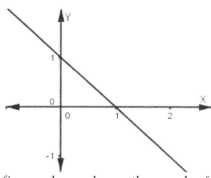

18. The figure above shows the graph of the line $y = mx + b$, where m and b are constants. Which of the following best represents the graph of the line $y = -2mx - b$?
    a)

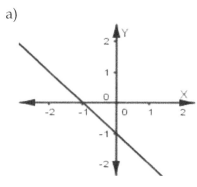

b)

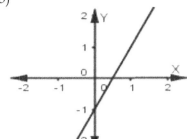

c)

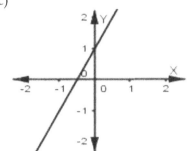

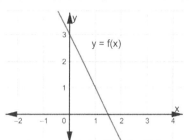

20. The graph of the linear function f is shown in the xy-plane above. The graph of the linear function g (not shown) is perpendicular to the graph of f and passes through the point $(1, 3)$. What is the value of $g(0)$?

21. Find the area of the circle given by the equation $x^2 + y^2 - 4x + 2y = 20$. (Round your answer to the nearest tenth.)

d)

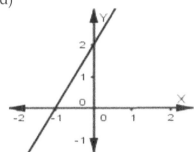

19. Which of the following expressions must be negative if $x < 0$?
    a) $x^2 - 2$
    b) $x^5 - 1$
    c) $x^4 - 3x^2 - 1$
    d) $x^6 + 3x^2 + 1$

22. If Bill can run $\frac{5}{4}$ as fast as Mitt. Sam can run $\frac{6}{5}$ as fast as Bill. Mitt can run how many times as fast as the average speed of Bill and Sam?
    a) $\frac{8}{11}$
    b) $\frac{9}{11}$
    c) 1
    d) $\frac{11}{9}$

Math Mock Test 7
22 QUESTIONS

DIRECTIONS

The questions in this section address a number of important math skills.
Use of a calculator is permitted for all questions.

NOTES

Unless otherwise indicated:
• All variables and expressions represent real numbers.
• Figures provided are drawn to scale.
• All figures lie in a plane.
• The domain of a given function f i s the set of all real numbers x for which f(x) is a real number.

REFERENCE

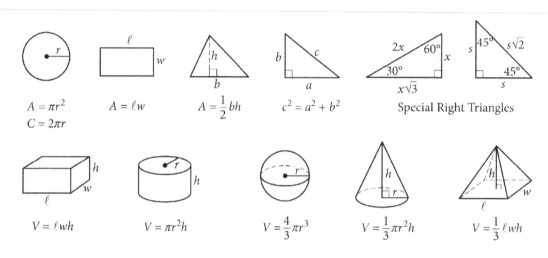

$A = \pi r^2$
$C = 2\pi r$

$A = \ell w$

$A = \frac{1}{2}bh$

$c^2 = a^2 + b^2$

Special Right Triangles

$V = \ell wh$

$V = \pi r^2 h$

$V = \frac{4}{3}\pi r^3$

$V = \frac{1}{3}\pi r^2 h$

$V = \frac{1}{3}\ell wh$

The number of degrees of arc in a circle is **360**.
The number of radians of arc in a circle is 2π.
The sum of the measures in degrees of the angles of a triangle is **180**.

For multiple-choice questions, solve each problem, choose the correct answer from the choices provided, and then circle your answer in this book. Circle only one answer for each question. If you change your mind, completely erase the circle. You will not get credit for questions with more than one answer circled, or for questions with no answers circled.

For student-produced response questions, solve each problem and write your answer next to or under the question in the test book as described below.

• Once you've written your answer, circle it clearly. You will not receive credit for anything written outside the
• circle, or for any questions with more than one circled answer.
• If you find **more than one correct answer**, write and circle only one answer. Your answer can be up to 5 characters for a **positive** answer and up to 6 characters (including the negative sign) for a **negative** answer, but no more.
• If your answer is a **fraction** that is too long (over 5 characters for positive, 6 characters for negative), write the decimal equivalent.

• If your answer is a **decimal** that is too long (over 5 characters for positive,
• 6 characters for negative), truncate it or round at the fourth digit.
• If your answer is a **mixed number** (such as $3\frac{1}{2}$, write it as an improper fraction (7/2) or its decimal equivalent (3.5).
• Don't include symbols such as a percent sign, comma, or dollar sign in your circled answer.

1. Ms. Jang took her 25 students to the library. If 12 students each checked out exactly 2 books, 3 students each checked out exactly 3 books, and the rest of the class each checked out only 1 book, how many total books did the students in Ms. Jang's class check out from the library?
   - a) 27
   - b) 29
   - c) 43
   - d) 47

2. Which of the following sets of numbers has an average (arithmetic mean) that is less than its median?
   - a) {−2, −1, 1}
   - b) {−2, −1, 1, 2, 3}
   - c) {1, 2, 3, 6}
   - d) {1, 2, 3, 4, 5}

3. Number of Flight Arrivals at Kennedy Airport in a Month

	On time	Delayed	Total
Airline A	2,029	861	2,890
Airline B	1,150	700	1,850
Airline C	3,179	1,561	4,740

   Based on the table above, what fraction of the flights for Airline A were delayed?
   - a) $\frac{70}{1850}$
   - b) $\frac{861}{1561}$
   - c) $\frac{861}{2890}$
   - d) $\frac{2079}{2890}$

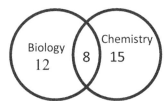

4. The Venn diagram above shows the distribution of 35 students at a school who took biology, chemistry, or both. What percent of the students who take both chemistry and biology?
   - a) 15%

   - b) 20%
   - c) 23%
   - d) 25%

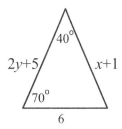

5. In the triangle above, which of the following must be true?
   - a) $x = y$
   - b) $x = 5$
   - c) $x < y$
   - d) $x = 2y + 4$

6. In the figure above, a cube has a volume of 64 cubic units. What is the length of the diameter of a sphere that is inscribed in the cube?

7. The diagram above shows 4 concentric circles, with diameters 2, 4, 6, and 12 respectively. What is the probability that a randomly selected point in the diagram will fall in the shaded region?

8. If $x = \frac{1}{5}yz$, what is the value of y when $z = 15$ and $x = 60$?
    a) 8
    b) 10
    c) 20
    d) 25

9. If $2,500 = 100(2x + 5)$, then $x =$
    a) $\frac{1}{10}$
    b) 1
    c) 10
    d) 100

10. The surface area of a cube is $6\left(\frac{3d}{2}\right)^2$, where d is a positive constant. Which of the following gives the perimeter of one face of the cube?
    a) $\frac{a}{2}$
    b) a
    c) $3a$
    d) $6a$

11. The sum of two different numbers x and y is 70, and the difference when the smaller number is subtracted from the larger number is 30. What is the value of xy?
    a) 100
    b) 210
    c) 1,000
    d) 2,100

x	-2	-1	2	3
y	-7	-4	5	8

12. Which of the following equations satisfies the relationship between x and y in the table above?
    a) $y = x + 6$
    b) $y = -3x + 1$
    c) $y = 3x + 1$
    d) $y = 3x - 1$

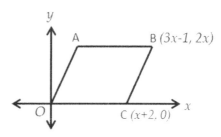

34 In the figure above, if the area of parallelogram OABC is 16, what is the value of x?

14. In a toy factory production line, every 9th toy has their electronic parts checked and every 12th toy will have their safety features checked. In the first 180 toys, what is the probability that a toy will have both its electronic parts and safety features checked?

15. Plant A is currently 20 centimeters tall, and Plant B is currently 15 centimeters tall. The ratio of the heights of Plant A to Plant B is equal to the ratio of the heights of Plant C to Plant D. If Plant C is 60 centimeters tall, what is the height of Plant D, in centimeters?
    a) 32
    b) 45
    c) 60
    d) 75

16. The table below shows the number of students attending Knollwood High School from 2009 through 2013. If the median number of students for the five years was 355, and no two years had the same number of students, what is the most possible value for X?

Old Oak High School Student Population	
Years	Number of Students
2009	X
2010	325
2011	387
2012	376
2013	355

   a) 360
   b) 365
   c) 356
   d) 350

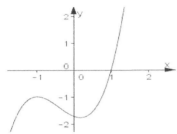

17. The figure above shows the graph of $g(x)$. At what value(s) of x does $g(x)$ equal to 0?

   a) 1
   b) –1
   c) 2
   d) –2

18. To determine if cooking with olive oil reduces the risk of heartburn for men, researchers interviewed a random sample of 5,500 men who had no history of heartburn. Study participants were identified as either regular or occasional olive oil users. Five years later, researchers interviewed the men again. They found that the proportion of men who experienced frequent heartburn was significantly lower for men identified as regular olive oil users Which of the following is the most appropriate conclusion of the study?

   a) Olive oil use causes a reduction in the risk of heartburn for men and women.
   b) Olive oil use causes a reduction in the risk of heartburn for men but not necessarily for women.
   c) There is an association between olive oil use and the risk of heartburn for men and women, but it is not necessarily a cause-and-effect relationship.
   d) There is an association between olive oil use and the risk of heartburn for men, but it is not necessarily a cause-and-effect relationship, and the association may not exist for women.

19. Which of the following could be the coordinates of point R in a coordinate plane, if points P(2, 1), Q(–1, 4), and R(x, y) lie on the same line?

   a) (0, 2)
   b) (3, 2)
   c) (0, –2)
   d) (1, 2)

183 ft

15 ft

20. If the Leaning Tower of Pisa is 183 feet tall and the top edge of the tower leans 15 feet out from the bottom edge, what is *tangent* of the angle created between the ground and the tower?

22. A sample of 500 ninth graders was selected at random and asked how much time they spend on homework each day. Of the ninth graders selected, 200 spend less than 2 hours on homework each day. If the conclusion was drawn that 1.5 million ninth graders spend less than 2 hours on homework each day which of the following is closest to the population, in millions, of ninth graders?
    a) 0.45
    b) 1.35
    c) 3.75
    d) 6.12

Time(days)	Counts
0	5
1	50
2	500
3	5,000
4	50,000
5	500,000

21. The estimated counts of bacteria in a petri dish are over the course of five days, as shown in the table above. Which of the following best describes the relationship between time and the estimated counts of bacteria during the five-day period?
    a) Decreasing linear
    b) Increasing linear
    c) Exponential decay
    d) Exponential growth

Math Mock Test 7
22 QUESTIONS

DIRECTIONS
The questions in this section address a number of important math skills.
Use of a calculator is permitted for all questions.

NOTES
Unless otherwise indicated:
• All variables and expressions represent real numbers.
• Figures provided are drawn to scale.
• All figures lie in a plane.
• The domain of a given function f i s the set of all real numbers x for which f(x) is a real number.

REFERENCE

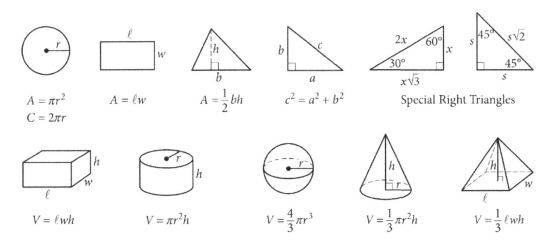

$A = \pi r^2$ $A = \ell w$ $A = \dfrac{1}{2}bh$ $c^2 = a^2 + b^2$ Special Right Triangles
$C = 2\pi r$

$V = \ell wh$ $V = \pi r^2 h$ $V = \dfrac{4}{3}\pi r^3$ $V = \dfrac{1}{3}\pi r^2 h$ $V = \dfrac{1}{3}\ell wh$

The number of degrees of arc in a circle is **360**.
The number of radians of arc in a circle is 2π.
The sum of the measures in degrees of the angles of a triangle is **180**.

For multiple-choice questions, solve each problem, choose the correct answer from the choices provided, and then circle your answer in this book. Circle only one answer for each question. If you change your mind, completely erase the circle. You will not get credit for questions with more than one answer circled, or for questions with no answers circled.

For student-produced response questions, solve each problem and write your answer next to or under the question in the test book as described below.
• Once you've written your answer, circle it clearly. You will not receive credit for anything written outside the circle, or for any questions with more than one circled answer.
• If you find **more than one correct answer**, write and circle only one answer. Your answer can be up to 5 characters for a **positive** answer and up to 6 characters (including the negative sign) for a **negative** answer, but no more.
• If your answer is a **fraction** that is too long (over 5 characters for positive, 6 characters for negative), write the decimal equivalent.
• If your answer is a **decimal** that is too long (over 5 characters for positive,
• 6 characters for negative), truncate it or round at the fourth digit.
• If your answer is a **mixed number** (such as $3\frac{1}{2}$, write it as an improper fraction (7/2) or its decimal equivalent (3.5).
• Don't include symbols such as a percent sign, comma, or dollar sign in your circled answer.

1. In the figure below, the two circles are tangent at point P and OQ = 12. If the area of the circle with center O is nine times the area of the circle with center Q, what is the length of OP?

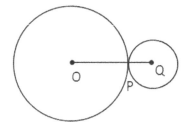

   Note: Figure not drawn to scale.
   a) 3
   b) 4
   c) 6
   d) 9

2. Find the product of 5 and the sum of m and 5. Then, find one-fifth of the difference between that product and 5. In terms of m, what is the final result?
   a) $m - 5$
   b) $m - 4$
   c) $m + 4$
   d) $m + 5$

$$\sqrt[3]{x^b}$$

3. Which of the following is equivalent to the expression above for all $x > 0$, where a and b are positive integers?
   a) x^{3b}
   b) $x^{\frac{3}{b}}$
   c) $x^{\frac{b}{3}}$
   d) x^{3-b}

4. The price of an investment over a period of 5 years is shown in the graph below.

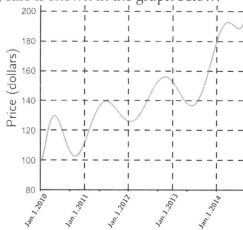

   During which of the following time periods did the price of the investment have the largest increase?
   a) Jan. 1, 2011 to Jan. 1, 2012
   b) Jan. 1, 2011 to Jan. 1, 2013
   c) Jan. 1, 2012 to Jan. 1, 2014
   d) Jan. 1, 2013 to Jan. 1, 2014

5. The ratio of three interior angle measures in a triangle is 2:3:4. What is the measure, in degrees, of the largest angle in this triangle?
   a) 80°
   b) 90°
   c) 100°
   d) 120°

6. According to the consumer price index, the price of a certain product has increased by the same number of percent each month since January 2015. which of the following function types could correctly be used to model this situation, where a and b are positive constants and t is the number of months since January 2015? (Assume the price of the product was not zero in January 2015.)
   a) $f(t) = abt$
   b) $f(t) = ab^t$
   c) $f(t) = a + b^t$
   d) $f(t) = a + bt$

$$y = 2x + 4$$

$$y = (x - 3)(x + 2)$$

7. The system of equations above is graphed in the xy-plane. At which of the following points do the graphs of the equations intersect?
   a) $(-2, 0)$
   b) $(0, -2)$
   c) $(5, -14)$
   d) $(-5, 14)$

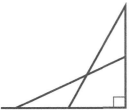

8. In the figure above, a 26-foot-long ladder is placed against a building which is perpendicular to the ground. After the ladder slides down 14 feet vertically, the bottom of the ladder is now 24 feet away from the base of the building, what is the original distance of the bottom of the ladder from the base of the building, in feet?
   a) 10
   b) 13
   c) 20
   d) 24

9. How many different positive three-digit integers begin with an even digit and end with an odd digit?
   a) 100
   b) 120
   c) 200
   d) 120

10. If $y = 3x^2 + 6x + 2$ is graphed in the xy-plane, which of the following characteristics of the graph is displayed as a constant or coefficient in the equation?
   a) y-coordinate of the vertex
   b) x-intercept(s)
   c) y-intercept
   d) x-intercept of the line of symmetry

11. If $a^x \cdot a^4 = a^{10}$ and $(a^4)^y = a^{12}$, what is the value of $x + y$?

a) 7
b) 8
c) 9
d) 10

12. If each edge of a rectangular solid has a length that is an integer greater than one, which of the following could be the volume of the solid, in cubic units?
   a) 9
   b) 15
   c) 18
   d) 21

$$\frac{1}{2}x = a$$
$$x + y = 5a$$

13. In the system of equations above, a is a constant such that $0 < a < \frac{1}{3}$. If (y, x) is a solution to the system of equations, what is one possible value of y?

14. The difference of two consecutive numbers is equal to k. What is the value of k?

15. A rectangular box has dimensions $36 \times 14 \times 18$. Without wasting any space, which of the following could be the dimensions of the smaller boxes which can be packed into the rectangular box?
   a) $2 \times 5 \times 6$
   b) $7 \times 9 \times 12$
   c) $3 \times 5 \times 6$
   d) $4 \times 5 \times 6$

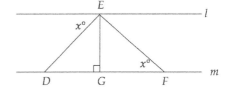

Note: Figure not drawn to scale.

16. In the figure above, line l is parallel to line m. If $x = 40$, what is the measure of $\angle DEF$?
    a) 140°
    b) 100°
    c) 80°
    d) 50°

17. A cargo helicopter delivers only 100-pound packages and 120-pound packages. For each delivery trip, the helicopter must carry at least 10 packages, and the total weight of the packages can be at most 1,100 pounds. What is the maximum number of 120-pound packages that the helicopter can carry per trip?
    a) 2
    b) 4
    c) 5
    d) 6

18. The formula $B = \frac{703w}{h^2}$ is used to determine body mass index, B, based on a person's weight w, in pounds, and height h, in inches. Which of the following can be used to determine a person's height, in inches, based on weight and body mass index?
    a) $h = \sqrt{\frac{703w}{B}}$
    b) $h = \sqrt{\frac{B}{703w}}$
    c) $h = \frac{703w}{B}$
    d) $h = \frac{B}{703w}$

19. The daily cost of phone services in a business building is $.25 per hour from 9 AM through 9 PM, and $.06 per hour at any other hours of the day. Which of the following expressions represents the cost, in dollars, of the phone service starting

from 9 AM and lasting for 20 hours a day over 30 days?
    a) $30 \times 11(.25) + 30(20 - 11)(.6)$
    b) $30 \times 12(.25) + 30(20 - 12)(.6)$
    c) $30 \times 13(.25) + 30(20 - 13)$
    d) $30 \times 12(.25) + 30(.6)$

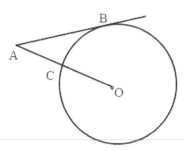

20. In the diagram above, AB is tangent to circle O at point B. AB = 2AC and the radius has length 3. What is the length of $\overline{AO}$?

21. If set A = {1, 3, 8, 10, 15} and set B consists of all the even positive integers less than or equal to 10, how many elements are in the union of the two sets?
    a) 0
    b) 3
    c) 8
    d) 9

22. If x and y are positive and $3x^2y^{-1} = 27x$, what is y^{-1} in term of x?
    a) $\frac{x}{9}$
    b) $\frac{9}{x}$
    c) $\frac{x^2}{9}$
    d) $\frac{x}{3}$

Mock Test 7

Module 1 Keys

1. (C)	2. (D)	3. (B)	4. (A)	5. (C)	6. $\frac{5}{2}$, or 2.5	7. $\frac{1}{5}$ or .2	8. (D)
9. (D)	10. (D)	11. (B)	12. (D)	13. 4.5	14. 105	15. (D)	16. (A)
17. (C)	18. (B)	19. (B)	20. $\frac{5}{2}$	21. 78.5	22. (A)		

Module 2 Easy Keys

1. (C)	2. (B)	3. (C)	4. (C)	5. (D)	6. 4	7. $\frac{5}{6}$ or .833	8. (C)
9. (C)	10. (D)	11. (C)	12. (D)	13. (B)	14. $\frac{1}{36}$	15. (B)	16. (D)
17. (A)	18. (D)	19. (D)	20. 12.2	21. (D)	22. (C)		

Module 2 Hard Keys

1. (D)	2. (C)	3. (C)	4. (C)	5. (A)	6. (B)	7. (A)	8. (A)
9. (C)	10. (C)	11. (C)	12. (C)	13. $0 < y < 1$	14. 1	15. (B)	16. (B)
17. (C)	18. (A)	19. (B)	20. 5	21. (C)	22. (B)		

Mock Test 7

Module 1 Answers

1. *Answer: (C)*
    $(x^{\frac{1}{4}})^4 = x$
    $(\sqrt{3})^4 = 9$

2. *Answer: (D)*
    Compare both sides of the equation and find the corresponding terms.
    $x = 4$

3. *Answer: (B)*
    Find all the factors of (13 − 1) that are greater than 1.
    The factors of 12 that are greater than 1 are 2, 3, 4, 6 and 12. 5 different values of p.

4. *Answer: (A)*
    A linear model: $h = 8s + 10$

5. *Answer: (C)*
    The reflection about y-axis will change all negative slopes to their positives and vice versa. Therefore, the sum of any such pairs of slopes must be zero.

6. *Answer:* $\frac{5}{2}$*, or 2.5*
    Two parallel lines have the same slope.

7. *Answer:* $\frac{1}{5}$ *or .2*
    $\frac{3}{15} = \frac{1}{5}$

8. *Answer: (D)*
    $3(1 - x) = -3x + b$
    $3 - 3x = -3x + b$
    If b ≠ 3, then there is no solution.

9. *Answer: (D)*
    $a + b = |\frac{1}{-5+4}| + \frac{1}{-3+2}$
    $1 - 1 = 0$

10. *Answer: (D)*
    Chris had an increase of 255 − 210 = 45 units, the greatest increase shown.

11. *Answer: (B)*
    A linear model:
    Initial value: r
    Slope: x
    $f(y) = yx + r$

12. *Answer: (D)*
    Grouping all terms with y and factoring out y:
    $y(wx + xz − z) = wx$
    $y = \frac{wx}{wx+xz-z}$

13. *Answer: 4.5*
    $1.2(h + 2) = 2h − 1.2$
    $1.2h − 2h = −1.2 − 2.4$
    $−0.8h = −3.6 \rightarrow h = 4.5$

14. *Answer: 105*
    $3a − 15 = 300 \quad \rightarrow \quad a = 105$

15. *Answer: (D)*
    This is a linear model:
    Slope is −61 and initial value(in 1962) is 2000. The average decrease in the population per year from 1962 to k years after 1962 is 61.

16. *Answer: (A)*
    $x^2 − y^2 = (x − y)(x + y)$
    $24 = (x − y) \times 6$
    $x − y = 4$
    $x + y = 6$
    $x = 5$ *and* $y = 1$

17. *Answer: (C)*
    $9m^2 = 3^2 \times m^2 = m^{2x} \times m^2 = m^{2x+2}$

18. *Answer: (B)*
    From the graph, slope equals −1 and y-intercept is 1.
    $m = −1, \ b = 1$
    $y = −2mx − b = 2x − 1$ *(with positive slope and negative y-intercept)*

19. *Answer: (B)*
    If x < 0, then the result of an odd power of x is negative and the result of an even power of x is positive.

20. *Answer:* $\frac{5}{2}$

    The slope of f is $-\frac{3}{1.5} = -2$

    f and g are perpendicular, so slope of g is $\frac{1}{2}$.

    $g(x): y = \frac{1}{2}x + b$

    Plug in the point (1, 3)

    $3 = \frac{1}{2} + b \to b = \frac{5}{2}$

    $g(x) = y - \frac{1}{2x} + \frac{5}{2}$

    $g(0) = \frac{5}{2}$

21. *Answer: 78.5*

    Rewrite to the equation in standard form.

    $x^2 - 4x + 4 + y^2 + 2y + 1 = 20 + 5$

    $(x - 2)^2 + (y + 1)^2 = 5^2$

    The center of the circle is (2, −1) and the radius is 5.

    The area of the circle is $\pi r^2 = 25\pi = 78.5$.

22. *Answer: (A)*

    Let Mitt can run at speed of x

    Bill has speed of $\frac{5}{4}x$

    Sam has speed of $\frac{6}{5} \times \frac{5}{4}x = \frac{3}{2}x$

    The average speed of Sam and Bill:

    $\frac{1}{2} \times (\frac{5}{4} + \frac{3}{2})x = \frac{11x}{8}$

    Mitt has $\frac{x}{\frac{11}{8}x} = \frac{8}{11}$ *times as fast as their average speed.*

Module 2 Easy Answers

1. *Answer: (C)*

    $12 \times 2 + 3 \times 3 + (25 - 12 - 3) \times 1 = 43$

2. *Answer: (B)*

    To find the median, sort all the numbers in the set from least to greatest. If there are odd amount of numbers in a set, then median is the middle number. If there are even amount of numbers in the set, median is the average of the two middle numbers.

    Average $= -\frac{2}{3}$ *Median* $= -1$

    Average $= 0.6$ *Median* $= 1$

    Average $= 3$ *Median* $= 2.5$

    Average $= 3$ *Median* $= 3$

    Average $= 3.2$ *Median* $= 3$

3. *Answer: (C)*

    $\frac{Delay\ of\ Airline\ A}{Total\ of\ Airline\ A} = \frac{861}{2890}$

4. *Answer: (C)*

    $\frac{8}{35} = 0.23 = 23\%$

5. *Answer: (D)*

    The degree of the 3rd interior angle is $180° - 40° - 70° = 70°$.

    Since this triangle has two angles that are 70°, it is an isosceles triangle.

    $2y + 5 = x + 1$

    $x = 2y + 4$

6. *Answer: 4*

    Diameter of Sphere = Length of Side of Cube

    Length of Side of Cube $= \sqrt[3]{64} = 4$

7. *Answer:* $\frac{5}{6}$ *or .833*

    Total Area – White Area = Shaded Area

    $\pi (6)^2 - \pi (3)^2 + \pi (2)^2 - \pi (1)^2 = 30\pi$

    Probability $= \frac{Shaded\ Area}{Total\ Area} = \frac{30\pi}{36\pi} = \frac{30}{36} = \frac{5}{6}$

8. *Answer: (C)*

    If x = 60 and z = 15, then $60 = \frac{1}{5}(y)(15)$.

    $60 = 3y$

    $y = 20$

9. *Answer: (C)*

    Divide both sides by 100.

    $2,500 = 100(2x + 5)$

    $25 = 2x + 5$

    $2x = 20$

    $x = 10$

10. *Answer: (D)*

    Area of One Face $= Side^2 = \left(\frac{3a}{2}\right)^2 \to Side = \frac{3a}{2}$

    Peimeter $= 4 \times Side = 4 \times \frac{3a}{2} = 6a$

11. *Answer: (C)*

    $x + y = 70$

    $x - y = 30$

    $x = 50; y = 20 \to xy = 1,000$

12. *Answer: (D)*
$Slope = \frac{Rise}{Run} = \frac{-4-(-7)}{-1-(-2)} = 3$
$y - (-7) = 3(x - (-2))$ *(Point-slope-form)*
$y = 3x - 1$

13. *Answer: (B)*
Area of OABC = Base × Height =
$(x+2) \times (2x) = 16$
$2x^2 + 4x - 16 = 0$
$x^2 + 2x - 8 = 0$
$(x + 4)(x - 2) = 0$
$x = -4$ *(not applicable, x must be positive)*
or $x = 2$

14. *Answer:* $\frac{1}{36}$
The LCM of 9 and 12 is 36.
The every 36th toy will have both of their electronic parts and safety features checked.
There are 5 such toys (180 divided by 36).
$\frac{5}{180} = \frac{1}{36}$

15. *Answer: (B)*
$\frac{20}{15} = \frac{60}{D}$
$D = 45$

16. *Answer: (D)*
If the median number of students for the five years was 355, there should be 2 years with number of students more than 355 and 2 years with number of students less than 355.
X should be less than 355.

17. *Answer: (A)*
When g(x) is equal to 0, the graph of the function intersects the x-axis.
The value of x is 1 when the graph intercepts x-axis.

18. *Answer: (D)*
This research is only for men. Any conclusion for women is not appropriate.
The cause-and-effect of Olive oil use causes a reduction in the risk of heartburn is not clear either.
So answer d) is the best answer.

19. *Answer: (D)*
$Slope = \frac{Rise}{Run} = \frac{4-1}{-1-2} = -1$
Point-slope-form: $y - 1 = -(x - 2)$
The point (1, 2) satisfies the above equation.

20. *Answer: 12.2*
$\tan(\theta) = \frac{183}{15} = 12.2$

21. *Answer: (D)*
The number of bacteria counts is ten times more than the day before:
$f(t) = 5 \times 10^t$; t is the number of days.
It is an exponential growth model.

22. *Answer: (C)*
$\frac{200}{500} = \frac{1.5}{x}$
$x = 3.75$

Module 2 Hard Answers

1. *Answer: (D)*
Since the area of circle O is nine times the area of circle Q, the radius of circle O is $\sqrt{9}$ times of the radius of circle Q.
If PQ = r, OP = 3r, then r + 3r = 12.
$r = 3 = PQ$
$OP = 12 - 3 = 9$

2. *Answer: (C)*
$\frac{5(m + 5) - 5}{5} = \frac{5(m + 5 - 1)}{5} = m + 4$

3. *Answer: (C)*
$\sqrt[3]{x^b} = x^{\frac{b}{3}}$

4. *Answer: (C)*
The largest increase will be from Jan. 1, 2012 to Jan. 1, 2014 according to the graph.

5. *Answer: (A)*
We can define the measures of the three angles to be x, 2x and 3x.
$2x + 3x + 4x = 180°$
$x = 20°$
The largest angle is $4x = 80°$

6. *Answer: (B)*
"If it is increased by the same number of percent each month" means this is an exponential growth model.
$f(t) = ab^t$

7. Answer: (A)
    $2x + 4 = (x - 3)(x + 2)$
    $x^2 - 3x - 10 = 0$; $(x + 2)(x - 5) = 0$
    $x = -2$ and $y = 0$ or $x = 5$ and $y = 14$
    Therefore, $(-2, 0)$ or $(5, 14)$

8. Answer: (A)
    After slipping, the height becomes $\sqrt{26^2 - 24^2} = 10$.
    Before slipping, the height was : $10 + 14 = 24$.
    The bottom of the ladder was originally $\sqrt{26^2 - 24^2} = 10$ feet away from the base.

9. Answer: (C)
    Units digit has 5 choices (1, 3, 5, 7, 9).
    Tens digit has 10 choices (0 ~ 9).
    Hundreds digit has 4 choices (2, 4, 6, 8).
    $5 \times 10 \times 4 = 200$

10. Answer: (C)
    The constant of this equation is 2 which means when $x = 0$, then $y = 2$. Therefore, the y-intercept is 2.

11. Answer: (C)
    $a^x \cdot a^4 = a^{(x + 4)} = a^{10}$; $(a^4)^y = a^{4y} = a^{12}$
    $x = 6$ and $y = 3$; therefore, $x + y = 9$

12. Answer: (C)
    The volume should be the product of at least 3 integers greater than one.
    Among the answer choices only 18 can be the product of 3 integers greater than 1.
    $18 = 2 \times 3 \times 3$

13. Answer: $0 < y < 1$
    Solve the system of the equations:
    $x = 2a$
    $y = 3a$
    $0 < a < \frac{1}{3} \rightarrow 0 < 3a < 1$
    $0 < y < 1$

14. Answer: 1
    Let the two consecutive numbers be x and $(x + 1)$.
    $(x + 1) - x = k$; $k = 1$

15. Answer: (B)
    The number 5 is not a factor of 14, 36 or 18; therefore, answers (a), (c), (d) are not possible. Only (b)'s dimensions could be packed into the rectangular box without wasting space.

$\frac{14}{7} \times \frac{36}{12} \times \frac{18}{9} = 12$

16. Answer: (B)
    $m\angle DEF = m\angle DEG + m\angle GEF = (90 - x) + (90 - x) = 50 + 50 = 100°$

17. Answer: (C)
    Let x be the number of 120-pound package and y be the number of 100-pound package.
    $x + y \geq 10$
    $120x + 100y \leq 1100$
    By checking the number of x and y,
    when $x=6$ and $y=4$, then
    $120(6) + 100(4) = 1120$, which is greater than 1,100 pounds;
    when $x=5$ and $y=5$, then
    $120(5) + 100(5) = 1100$, which is equal to 1,100 pounds. Therefore, the answer is c).

18. Answer: (A)
    $B = \frac{703w}{h^2}$
    $h^2 = \frac{703w}{B} \rightarrow h = \sqrt{\frac{703w}{B}}$

19. Answer: (B)
    In order to find the daily price, add the cost from the rush hours, which is 12 (hours) $\times$ (.25), and the cost from the additional hours, which is $(20 - 12)$(hours) $\times$ (.6).
    Multiply the daily cost by 30 to find the total cost for 30 days.

20. Answer: 5
    ΔOAB is a right triangle with hypotenuse $\overline{OA}$, so use the Pythagorean Theorem.
    $OB = OC = 3$
    $AC = x$ $AB = 2x$ $AO = 3 + x$
    $(2x)^2 + 3^2 = (3 + x)^2$
    $4x^2 + 9 = x^2 + 6x + 9$ $3x^2 = 6x \rightarrow x = 2$ so $AO = 5$

21. Answer: (C)
    $A \cup B = A + B - (A \cap B)$
    $A = \{1, 3, 8, 10, 15\}$; $B = \{2, 4, 6, 8, 10\}$
    $A \cap B = \{8, 10\}$
    Number of Elements in $(A \cup B) = 5 + 5 - 2 = 8$

22. Answer: (B)
    Divide by $3x^2$ on both sides of the equation $3x^2y^{-1} = 27x$.
    $y^{-1} = \frac{27x}{3x^2} = \frac{9}{x}$

Math Mock Test 8

22 QUESTIONS

DIRECTIONS

The questions in this section address a number of important math skills.

Use of a calculator is permitted for all questions.

○ **Check the answers after the Module 1 test. If there are more than 8 questions answered incorrectly in Module 1, take the Easy part of Module 2. Otherwise, take the Hard part of Module 2.**

NOTES

Unless otherwise indicated:
- All variables and expressions represent real numbers.
- Figures provided are drawn to scale.
- All figures lie in a plane.
- The domain of a given function f i s the set of all real numbers x for which f(x) is a real number.

REFERENCE

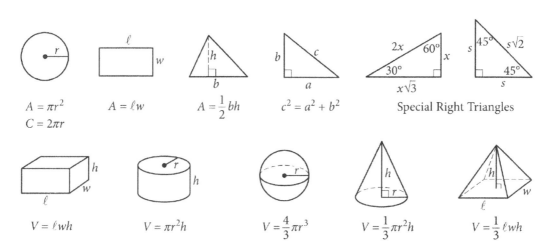

$A = \pi r^2$

$C = 2\pi r$

$A = \ell w$

$A = \frac{1}{2} bh$

$c^2 = a^2 + b^2$

Special Right Triangles

$V = \ell wh$

$V = \pi r^2 h$

$V = \frac{4}{3}\pi r^3$

$V = \frac{1}{3}\pi r^2 h$

$V = \frac{1}{3} \ell wh$

The number of degrees of arc in a circle is **360**.

The number of radians of arc in a circle is 2π.

The sum of the measures in degrees of the angles of a triangle is **180**.

For multiple-choice questions, solve each problem, choose the correct answer from the choices provided, and then circle your answer in this book. Circle only one answer for each question. If you change your mind, completely erase the circle. You will not get credit for questions with more than one answer circled, or for questions with no answers circled.

For student-produced response questions, solve each problem and write your answer next to or under the question in the test book as described below.
- Once you've written your answer, circle it clearly. You will not receive credit for anything written outside the circle, or for any questions with more than one circled answer.
- If you find **more than one correct answer**, write and circle only one answer. Your answer can be up to 5 characters for a **positive** answer and up to 6 characters (including the negative sign) for a **negative** answer, but no more.
- If your answer is a **fraction** that is too long (over 5 characters for positive, 6 characters for negative), write the decimal equivalent.
- If your answer is a **decimal** that is too long (over 5 characters for positive,
- 6 characters for negative), truncate it or round at the fourth digit.
- If your answer is a **mixed number** (such as $3\frac{1}{2}$, write it as an improper fraction (7/2) or its decimal equivalent (3.5).
- Don't include symbols such as a percent sign, comma, or dollar sign in your circled answer.

1. What is the solution of $9n + 20 = -16$?
   a) -4
   b) $-\frac{20}{9}$
   c) $\frac{4}{9}$
   d) 4

2. Which of the following is equivalent to $2(x^2 - x) + 3(x^2 - x)$?
   a) $5x^2 - 5x$
   b) $5x^2 + 5x$
   c) $5x$
   d) $5x^2$

3. If x and y are positive integers and $8 \times 2^x = 4^y$, what is x in terms of y?
   a) y
   b) y^2
   c) $2y$
   d) $2y - 3$

4. To rent a single movie from a DVD lending machine, Mrs. Kinney was charged $1 for the first day. For every day afterwards, she must pay a rental fee of $1 plus a late fee of $.50. If she paid a total of $10, how many days did she keep the DVD?
   a) 7
   b) 6
   c) 5
   d) 4

5. As a part of a store's shoe sale, the first pair of shoes costs x dollars, and each additional pair on sale costs m dollars less than the first pair. Which of the following represents the total cost if a customer buys n pairs of shoes?
   a) $nx + m(n - 1)$
   b) $nx - m(n - 1)$
   c) $x + (n - 1)(x - m)$
   d) $x + n(x - m)$

6. What is the volume, in cubic centimeters, of a right rectangular prism that has a length of 4 centimeters, a width of 9 centimeters, and a height of 5 centimeters?

7. Intersecting three lines are shown below. What is the value of a?

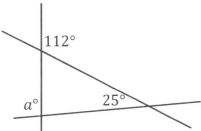

8. The circle above has center O, the length of arc $\overset{\frown}{ADC}$ is 4π, and $x = 100$. What is the length of arc $\overset{\frown}{ABC}$?

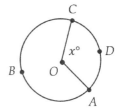

   a) 10.4π
   b) 12.5π
   c) 16.3π
   d) $\frac{75}{2}\pi$

x	$f(x)$
1	a
2	b
3	c

9. For the function f, the table above shows some values of x and their corresponding values of $f(x)$ in terms of the constants a, b, and c. If $a < b < c$, which of the following could NOT be the graph of $y = f(x)$ in the xy-plane?

a)

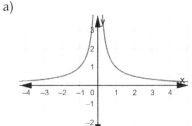

b)

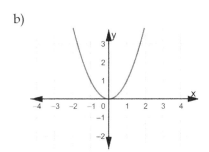

c)

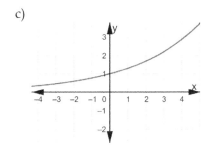

d)

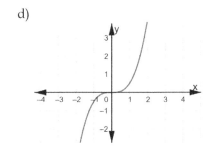

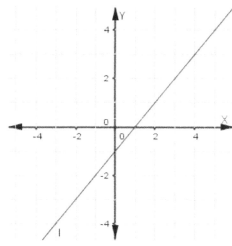

10. Which of the following is an equation of line l in the xy-coordinate plane above?
   a) $x = 1$
   b) $y = 1$
   c) $x = y$
   d) $y = x - 1$

$$x^{16} - x^{14} = k(x^{15} - x^{14}) \qquad x > 1$$

11. Based on the two conditions listed above, what is k in terms of x?
   a) $x + 1$
   b) $x - 1$
   c) $\dfrac{1}{x-1}$
   d) $\dfrac{1}{x+1}$

12. Which of the following expressions is equivalent to $(3x^2 - 2) - (-5x^2 - 3x + 4)$?
   a) $-2x^2 + 3x - 6$
   b) $-2x^2 - 3x - 2$
   c) $8x^2 - 3x + 2$
   d) $8x^2 + 3x - 6$

13. A company sells boxes of marbles in red and green. Helen purchased a box of marbles in which there were half as many green marbles in the box as red ones and 20 marbles were green. How many marbles were in Helen's box?

14. Triangle PQR has right angle Q. If $sin(R) = \frac{4}{5}$, what is the value of $tan(P)$?

15. At West Hill High School, some members of the Key Club are on the math team and no members of the math team are freshmen. Which of the following must also be true?
    a) No members of the Key Club are freshmen.
    b) Some members of the Key Club are freshmen.
    c) Some members of the Key Club are not freshmen.
    d) More tenth graders are on the math team than are on the Key Club.

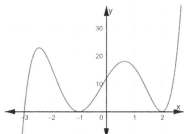

16. The graph of the function f is shown in the xy-plane above, where $y = f(x)$. Which of the following functions could define f ?
    a) $f(x) = (x + 3)(x + 1)^2(x - 2)^2$
    b) $f(x) = (x - 3)^2(x - 1)(x + 2)$
    c) $f(x) = (x - 3)(x - 1)^2(x + 2)^2$
    d) $f(x) = (x + 3)^2(x + 1)(x - 2)$

17. The equation $p = 15 + 0.5d$ approximates the pressure p, in pounds per square inch, exerted on a diver at a depth of d feet (ft) below the surface of the water. What is the increase in depth that is necessary to increase the pressure by 1 pound per square inch?
    a) $\frac{1}{0.5}$ ft
    b) $\frac{1}{15}$ ft
    c) 0.5 ft
    d) 15 ft

18. If $0 > xy$ and $y > 0$, which of the following statements must be true?
    $x < 0$
    $x < y$
    $x > 0$
    a) I only
    b) III only
    c) I and II
    d) II and III

19. If the average (arithmetic mean) of a, b and c is m, which of the following is the average of a, b, c and d?
    a) $\frac{2m+d}{3}$
    b) $\frac{m+d}{2}$
    c) $\frac{3m+d}{4}$
    d) $\frac{m+2d}{2}$

20. Ms. DePietro provides some markers to her Arts class. If each student takes 3 markers, there will be 1 marker left. If 5 students take 4 markers each and the rest of students take 2 markers each, there will be no markers left. How many students are in Ms. DePietro's Arts class?

21. What is the remainder when $2x^4 - 3x^3 + 4x^2 - 5x + 6$ is divided by $x - 3$?

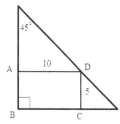

22. In the figure above, if ABCD is a rectangle, what is the area of the triangle?
    a) 150
    b) 122.5
    c) 112.5
    d) 100

Math Mock Test 8
22 QUESTIONS

DIRECTIONS
The questions in this section address a number of important math skills.
Use of a calculator is permitted for all questions.

NOTES
Unless otherwise indicated:
• All variables and expressions represent real numbers.
• Figures provided are drawn to scale.
• All figures lie in a plane.
• The domain of a given function f i s the set of all real numbers x for which f(x) is a real number.

REFERENCE

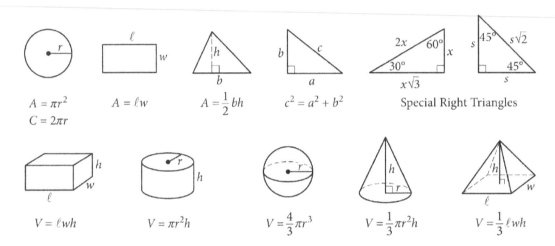

$$A = \pi r^2$$
$$C = 2\pi r$$

$$A = \ell w$$

$$A = \frac{1}{2} bh$$

$$c^2 = a^2 + b^2$$

Special Right Triangles

$$V = \ell wh$$

$$V = \pi r^2 h$$

$$V = \frac{4}{3}\pi r^3$$

$$V = \frac{1}{3}\pi r^2 h$$

$$V = \frac{1}{3}\ell wh$$

The number of degrees of arc in a circle is **360**.
The number of radians of arc in a circle is 2π.
The sum of the measures in degrees of the angles of a triangle is **180**.

For multiple-choice questions, solve each problem, choose the correct answer from the choices provided, and then circle your answer in this book. Circle only one answer for each question. If you change your mind, completely erase the circle. You will not get credit for questions with more than one answer circled, or for questions with no answers circled.

For student-produced response questions, solve each problem and write your answer next to or under the question in the test book as described below.
• Once you've written your answer, circle it clearly. You will not receive credit for anything written outside the
• circle, or for any questions with more than one circled answer.
• If you find **more than one correct answer**, write and circle only one answer. Your answer can be up to 5 characters for a **positive** answer and up to 6 characters (including the negative sign) for a **negative** answer, but no more.
• If your answer is a **fraction** that is too long (over 5 characters for positive, 6 characters for negative), write the decimal equivalent.

• If your answer is a **decimal** that is too long (over 5 characters for positive,
• 6 characters for negative), truncate it or round at the fourth digit.
• If your answer is a **mixed number** (such as $3\frac{1}{2}$, write it as an improper fraction (7/2) or its decimal equivalent (3.5).
• Don't include symbols such as a percent sign, comma, or dollar sign in your circled answer.

1. A parking lot charges $6.00 maintenance fee per day to use its parking space. In addition, there is a charge of $2.5 per hour. Which of the following represents the total charge, in dollars, to park a car in the parking lot for m hours in one day?

   a) $6m + 2.5$
   b) $(6 + 2.5)m$
   c) $6 + 2.5 + m$
   d) $6 + 2.5m$

2. Two units of length used in ancient Egypt were cubits and palms, where 1 cubit is equivalent to 6 palms. The Great Sphinx statue in Giza is approximately 150 cubits long. Which of the following best approximates the length, in palms, of the Great Sphinx statue?

   a) 6
   b) 25
   c) 300
   d) 900

3. A physician prescribes a treatment in which a patient takes 2 teaspoons of a medication every 8 hours for 6 days. According to the prescription, how many teaspoons of the medication should the patient take in a 24-hour period?

   a) 4
   b) 6
   c) 8
   d) 10

4. If $\frac{a}{7} = 4$, what I the value of $2a$?

   a) 14
   b) 16
   c) 56
   d) 112

5. A certain cake recipe calls for 4 cups of flour to make 15 servings. If 60 servings of the cake are being made, how many cups of flour will be needed for this recipe?

   a) 3
   b) 4
   c) 10
   d) 16

6. In a junior high school with seventh and eighth graders, there is the same number of girls as boys. The eighth grade has 220 students, and there are 5 boys for every 6 girls. In the seventh grade there are 5 boys for every 4 girls. How many girls are in the seventh grade?

x	$f(x)$	$g(x)$
1	4	0
3	5	12
5	6	8
7	1	10
9	9	8

7. The table above shows several values of function f and function g. According to the table, if $f(3) = a$, what is the value of $g(a)$?

8. The function f is defined by $f(x) = 3x^2 - 8x + 17$. What is the value of $f(-2)$?

   a) -11
   b) 13
   c) 21
   d) 45

9. According to the graph shown above, how many distinct positive values of x are there on the graph when $y = -0.5$?
    a) 4
    b) 5
    c) 6
    d) 7

10. The table below shows the number of cars sold by a certain brand of car dealerships for the first quarter of 2016 in five different locations. Based on the information in the table, what is the approximately probability of a car sold that is from the region I in March?

    Number of Cars Sold in 1st Quarter of 2016 at Five Locations

Location	Months		
	Jan.	Feb.	Mar.
I	80	75	65
II	76	48	52
III	90	82	68
IV	52	68	72
V	64	62	60

    a) 6.4%
    b) 10.8%
    c) 17.4%
    d) 21.2 %

11. How many positive three-digit integers have the hundreds digit equal to the multiple of 3 and the units digit (ones digit) is an even digit?
    a) 150
    b) 160
    c) 162
    d) 180

12. Class A has X students and class B has Y students. The average of the test scores of class A is 85, and the average of the test scores of class B is 90. When the scores of class A and B are combined, the average score is 88. What is the ratio of X to Y?
    a) $\frac{1}{2}$
    b) $\frac{1}{3}$
    c) $\frac{1}{4}$
    d) $\frac{2}{3}$

13. How many cups, each with a capacity of 8 fluid ounces, can be filled with water from a cooler that contains 10 gallons of water? (1 gallon = 128 fluid ounces)

14. Gina drove at an average of 40 miles per hour from her house to a bookstore. Along the same route, she returned at an average of 60 miles per hour. If the entire trip took her 1 hour, how many miles did Gina drive in total?

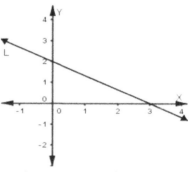

15. What is the equation of line L in the figure above?
    a) $y = 3x + 2$
    b) $y = -3x + 2$
    c) $y = -2x - 3$
    d) $y = -\frac{2}{3}x + 2$

16. Which of the following is a solution to the equation $\sqrt{14 - x} + 2 = x$?

    I. -2

    II. 1

    III. 5

    a) I only

    b) II only

    c) III only

    d) I and III

17. Megan began a one-way 10-mile bicycle trip by riding very slowly for 5 miles. She rested for 30 minutes and then rode quickly for the rest of the trip. Which of the following graphs could correctly represents the trip?

  a)

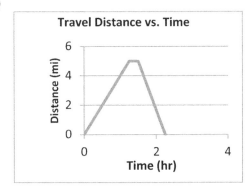

  b)

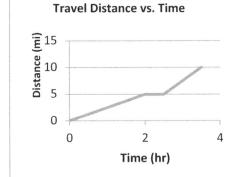

c)

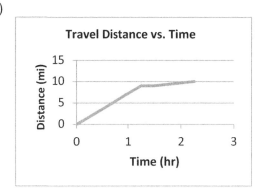

d)

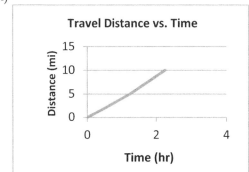

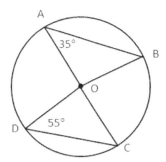

Note: Figure not drawn to scale.

18. In the graph shown above, what is the value of m∠AOD + m∠BOC?

    a) 180

    b) 150

    c) 110

    d) 100

19. The table below shows the number of cars sold in a certain brand of car dealerships for the first quarter of 2016 in five different locations. Based on the information in the table, what is the probability if a car sold in January and February in 2016 is sold from the region II?

Number of Cars Sold in Five Locations

Locations	Months		
	Jan.	Feb.	March
I	80	75	65
II	76	48	52
III	90	82	68
IV	52	68	72
V	64	62	60

a) 6.5%
b) 10.8%
c) 25.3%
d) 31.2 %

20. If $a - bi = i(3 - 7i)$, what is the value of $a + b$?

21. In the xy-plane, line l passes through the origin and is perpendicular to the line $3x + 2y = 2b$, where b is a constant. If the two lines intersect at the point $(2a, a - 1)$, what is the value of b?
    a) –13
    b) –12
    c) –6
    d) 12

22. Let the function f be defined by $f(x) = x^2 + 27$. If $f(3y) = 3f(y)$, what is the one possible value of y?
    a) –1
    b) 1
    c) 2
    d) –3

Math Mock Test 8

22 QUESTIONS

DIRECTIONS

The questions in this section address a number of important math skills.
Use of a calculator is permitted for all questions.

NOTES

Unless otherwise indicated:
- All variables and expressions represent real numbers.
- Figures provided are drawn to scale.
- All figures lie in a plane.
- The domain of a given function f is the set of all real numbers x for which f(x) is a real number.

REFERENCE

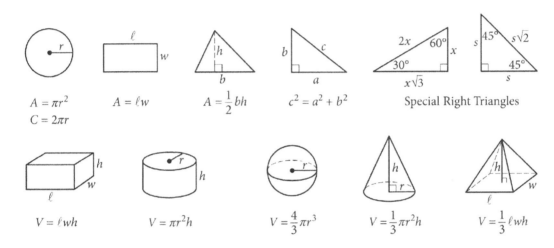

$A = \pi r^2$
$C = 2\pi r$

$A = \ell w$

$A = \frac{1}{2}bh$

$c^2 = a^2 + b^2$

Special Right Triangles

$V = \ell wh$

$V = \pi r^2 h$

$V = \frac{4}{3}\pi r^3$

$V = \frac{1}{3}\pi r^2 h$

$V = \frac{1}{3}\ell wh$

The number of degrees of arc in a circle is **360**.
The number of radians of arc in a circle is 2π.
The sum of the measures in degrees of the angles of a triangle is **180**.

For multiple-choice questions, solve each problem, choose the correct answer from the choices provided, and then circle your answer in this book. Circle only one answer for each question. If you change your mind, completely erase the circle. You will not get credit for questions with more than one answer circled, or for questions with no answers circled.

For student-produced response questions, solve each problem and write your answer next to or under the question in the test book as described below.
- Once you've written your answer, circle it clearly. You will not receive credit for anything written outside the circle, or for any questions with more than one circled answer.
- If you find **more than one correct answer**, write and circle only one answer. Your answer can be up to 5 characters for a **positive** answer and up to 6 characters (including the negative sign) for a **negative** answer, but no more.
- If your answer is a **fraction** that is too long (over 5 characters for positive, 6 characters for negative), write the decimal equivalent.
- If your answer is a **decimal** that is too long (over 5 characters for positive,
- 6 characters for negative), truncate it or round at the fourth digit.
- If your answer is a **mixed number** (such as $3\frac{1}{2}$, write it as an improper fraction (7/2) or its decimal equivalent (3.5).
- Don't include symbols such as a percent sign, comma, or dollar sign in your circled answer.

1. Of 100 people who played a certain video game, 85 scored more than 0 but less than 20,000, 14 scored between 20,000 and 200,000 points, and the remaining player scored 6,000,000 points Which of the following statements about the mean and median of the 100 scores is true?
   a) The mean is greater than the median.
   b) The median is greater than the mean.
   c) The mean and the median are equal.
   d) There is not enough information to determine whether the mean or the median is greater.

2. The scatterplot in the xy-plane above shows the balance y, in dollars, of a savings account after x years. Which of the following functions best models the data in the scatterplot?
   a) $y = (500)^{x+1}$
   b) $y = 500(0.12)^x$
   c) $= 500(0.12)^{x+1}$
   d) $y = 500(1.12)^x$

3. If $f(x) = \frac{x^2 - 15}{x^2 - 20}$, what is the value of $f(5)$?
   a) 0
   b) 2
   c) 4
   d) 6

4. A bag contains red, green, and blue marbles. The probability of randomly pulling out a red marble from the bag is $\frac{1}{4}$ and the probability of randomly pulling out a blue marble is $\frac{3}{7}$. Which of the following could be the total number of marbles in the bag?
   a) 11
   b) 22
   c) 28
   d) 35

5. In 1789, Benjamin Franklin gave an amount of money to Boston, Massachusetts. The money was to be invested for 100 years in a trust fund. If the value of the trust fund doubled every n years, which of the following graphs best models the value of the trust fund over time for the 100 years?

   a)
   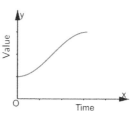

   b)
   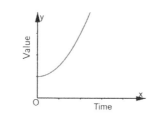

   c)
   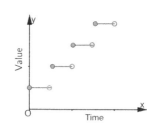

   d)
   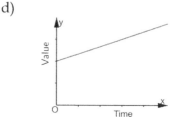

6. We start out with a set of 8 numbers. We subtract 4 from 4 of these numbers. If the average (arithmetic mean) of these eight numbers was 10 originally, what is the new average?
   a) 7
   b) 8
   c) 9
   d) 9.5

7. Vehicle A ran 15 miles an hour for 4 hours. The total distance A traveled was twice the distance of Vehicle B after Vehicle B traveled 10 miles an hour for X hours. What is X?
   a) 3
   b) 4
   c) 4.5
   d) 5

8. In the xy-coordinate system, $(k, 9)$ is one of the points of intersection of the graphs $y = 2x^2 + 1$ and $y = -x^2 + m$, where m and k are constants. What is the value of m?
   a) 13
   b) 12
   c) 10
   d) 8

9. There are 100 students in the school pep rally. What is the largest number of n students such that the statement "At least n student birthdays in this pep rally falling in the same month" is always true?
   a) 8
   b) 9
   c) 10
   d) 12

10. In a sequence of numbers, the leading term is 2. Each successive term is formed by adding 1 to its preceding term and then multiplying the result by 2. What is the fourth term in the sequence?
    a) 30
    b) 32
    c) 42
    d) 46

11. The fruits provided in the student lounge contain pears, apples, and oranges. The ratio of the numbers of pears to apples is 3 : 5 and the ratio of the numbers of apples to oranges is 3 : 5. Find the ratio of the numbers of pears to oranges?
    a) 9 : 25
    b) 25 : 9
    c) 3 : 5
    d) 5 : 3

12. The quadratic function f is given by $f(x) = ax^2 + bx + c$, where a is a negative real number and c is a positive real number. Which of the following is the possible graph of $f(x)$?

a)

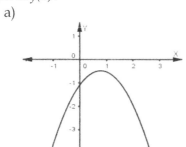

b)

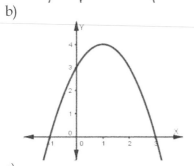

c)

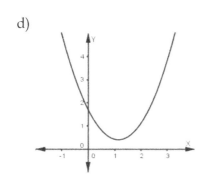

d)

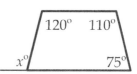

13. If the sum of all consecutive integers from -41 to x, inclusive, is 42, what is the value of x?

| | English Courses | |
Gender	Honor	AP
Male		
Female		
Total	60	20

14. The incomplete table above summarizes the number of students who take English Honor and English AP classes by gender for the Springfield High School. There are 4 times as many English Honor female students as there are AP English female students, and there are 2 times as many as Honor English male students as there are AP English male students. If there is a total of 20 AP English students and 60 Honor English students in the school, which of the following is closest to the probability that an English AP student selected at random is female?

$$3x + 2y = 13$$
$$2x + y = 9$$

15. In the system of equations above, what is the value of $x + y$?

a) 5
b) 4
c) 3
d) 2

Note: Figure not drawn to scale.

16. What is the value of x in the figure above?

a) 90
b) 100
c) 125
d) 120

17. At the beginning of a laboratory experiment, Miguel had 10 milliliters of a solution in a flask. The first step of the experiment consisted of Miguel pouring x milliliters of the solution into a beaker and y milliliters of the solution into a different beaker. There remained at least 4 milliliters of the solution in the flask after the first step. which of the following inequalities can be used to correctly represent this situation?

    a) $10 - x - y \geq 4$
    b) $10 - x + y \geq 4$
    c) $4 - x - y \geq 5$
    d) $4 - x + y \geq 5$

18. The center of a circle is the origin of a rectangular coordinate plane. If $(-5, 0)$, $(0, 5)$, and $(5, 0)$ are three points on the circumference of the circle, what is the probability that a randomly picked point inside the circle would fall inside the triangle formed by those three points?

    a) $\frac{1}{2}$
    b) $\frac{1}{3}$
    c) $\frac{1}{\pi}$
    d) $\frac{2}{\pi}$

19. Machine A makes 250 toys per hour. Machine B makes 350 toys per hour. If both machines begin running at the same time, how many minutes will it take the two machines to make a total of 1800 toys?

    a) 180
    b) 150
    c) 130
    d) 120

20. The graph of lines t and v in the xy-plane are perpendicular. The equation of line t is $\frac{2}{3}x + \frac{5}{6}y = -10$. What is the slope of line v?

21. On a certain test, the highest possible score is 100 and the lowest is 0. If the average score of 5 students is 86, what is the lowest possible score of the fifth student?

    a) 0
    b) 10
    c) 20
    d) 30

$$kx + y = 1$$
$$y = -x^2 + k$$

22. In the system of equations above, k is a constant. When the equations are graphed in the xy-plane, the graphs intersect at exactly two points. Which of the following CANNOT be the value of k?

    a) 3
    b) 2
    c) 1
    d) 0

Mock Test 8

Module 1 Keys

1. (A)	2. (A)	3. (D)	4. (A)	5. (C)	6. 180	7. 93	8. (A)
9. (A)	10. (D)	11. (A)	12. (D)	13. 60	14. $\frac{3}{4}$	15. (C)	16. (A)
17. (A)	18. (C)	19. (C)	20. 9	21. 108	22. (C)		

Module 2 Easy Keys

1. (D)	2. (D)	3. (B)	4. (C)	5. (D)	6. 80	7. 8	8. (D)
9. (B)	10. (A)	11. (A)	12. (D)	13. 160	14. 48	15. (D)	16. (C)
17. (B)	18. (A)	19. (C)	20. 4	21. (A)	22. (D)		

Module 2 Hard Keys

1. A)	2. (D)	3. (B)	4. (C)	5. (B)	6. (B)	7. (A)	8. (A)
9. (B)	10. (A)	11. (A)	12. (B)	13. 42	14. $\frac{1}{2}$	15. (B)	16. (C)
17. (A)	18. (C)	19. (A)	20. $\frac{5}{4}$	21. (D)	22. (D)		

Mock Test 8

Module 1 Answers

1. *Answer: (A)*
   $9n + 20 = -16$
   $9n = -36$
   $n = -4$

2. *Answer: (A)*
   Combine the like terms.
   $2(x^2 - x) + 3(x^2 - x)$
   $= 2x^2 - 2x + 3x^2 - 3x$
   $= 5x^2 - 5x$

3. *Answer: (D)*
   Given that $8(2^x) = 4^y$, *then*
   $2^3 \times 2^x = 2^{2y}$.
   $2^{3+x} = 2^{2y}$
   $3 + x = 2y$
   $x = 2y - 3$

4. *Answer: (A)*
   Let n be the number of days that Mrs. Kinney kept the DVD.
   $1 + 1 \times (n - 1) + 0.5(n - 1) = 10 \rightarrow n = 7$

5. *Answer: (C)*
   The first pair costs x dollars. Each additional pair costs $(x - m)$ dollars. Therefore, the cost of n pairs of shoes would be the price of the first pair plus the cost of the additional $(n - 1)$ pairs.
   $x + (n - 1)(x - m)$

6. *Answer: 180*
   $4 \times 5 \times 9 = 180$

7. *Answer: 93*
   $a = 68 + 25 = 93$

8. *Answer: (A)*
   Find the radius r.
   $\frac{100}{360} = \frac{4\pi}{2\pi r}$
   $720 = 100r$
   $r = \frac{36}{5}$
   $\widehat{ABC} = 2\pi r - \widehat{ADC} = 2\pi r - 4\pi = 2\pi\left(\frac{36}{5}\right) - 4\pi = \frac{52}{5}\pi = 10.4\pi$

9. *Answer: (A)*
   $c > b > a$
   $(3) > f(2) > f(1)$
   The only answer is a), which graph does not fit in that relationship.

10. *Answer: (D)*
    Line l passes through two points $(0, 1)$ and $(-1, 0)$. Only answer d) satisfies these condition.

11. *Answer: (A)*
    $k = \frac{x^{16}-x^{14}}{x^{15}-x^{14}} = \frac{x^{14}(x^2-1)}{x^{14}(x-1)} = \frac{(x+1)(x-1)}{x-1} = x + 1$

12. *Answer: (D)*
    $(3x^2 - 2) - (-5x^2 - 3x + 4)$
    $= 3x^2 - 2 + 5x^2 + 3x - 4$
    $= 8x^2 + 3x - 6$

13. *Answer: 60*
    Let g be the number of green marbles and r be the number of red marbles.
    Translate "half as many green marbles as red ones" into an algebraic statement: $g = \frac{1}{2}r$
    Plug $g = 20$ into the equation to get $r = 40$.
    $20 + 40 = 60$

14. *Answer:* $\frac{3}{4}$

    $QR = \sqrt{5^2 - 4^2} = 3$
    $tan(P) = \frac{QR}{QP} = \frac{3}{4}$

15. *Answer: (C)*
    Some students on Key Club also on math team in which there are no freshmen.

16. *Answer: (A)*
    Information from the graph, the function $y = f(x)$ has one root of -3, double roots of -1, and double roots of 2.

17. *Answer: (A)*
A linear model
Slop = 0.5
For every foot, the pressure increases 0.5 pound per square inch. For every pound per square inch, it needs $\frac{1}{0.5}$ feet.
The answer is a).

18. *Answer: (C)*
If xy < 0 and y > 0 then x < 0 and x < y.

19. *Answer: (C)*
The Average of a, b, and c is equal to the sum of a, b, and c divided by 3.
$a + b + c = 3m$
$a + b + c + d = 3m + d$
Average: $\frac{3m+d}{4}$

20. *Answer: 9*
Let x be the number of students in Ms. DePietro's Arts class.
$3x + 1 = 5 \times 4 + (x - 5) \times 2$
$x = 9$

21. *Answer: 108*
Remainder Theorem: If polynomial $P(x)$ is divided by $x - r$, its remainder is $P(r)$.
$P(3) = 2 \times 3^4 - 3 \times 3^3 + 4 \times 3^2 - 5(3) + 6 = 108$

22. *Answer: (C)*
Both legs of the triangle have length of 10 + 5 = 15.
So the area of the triangle: $\frac{1}{2} \times 15 \times 15 = 112.5$

Module 2 Easy Answers

1. *Answer: (D)*
Parking m hours costs $2.5 × m plus $6 maintenance fee per day, so the total charge would be 6 + 2.5m.

2. *Answer: (D)*
$\frac{1\ cubit}{6\ palms} = \frac{150\ cubits}{x\ palms}$
$x = 900$

3. *Answer: (B)*
$\frac{2}{8} = \frac{x}{24} \rightarrow x = 6$

4. *Answer: (C)*
$\frac{a}{7} = 4 \rightarrow a = 28$
$2a = 56$

5. *Answer: (D)*
A proportion problem
$\frac{4\ Cups}{15\ Serving} = \frac{x}{60\ Serving}$
$x = 16$

6. *Answer: 80*
In the eighth grade, there are $220 \times \frac{5}{6+5} = 100$ boys and $220 - 100 = 120$ girls.
Let x be the number of girls in seventh grade.
Boys of 7th Grade : Girls of 7th Grade = 5 : 4
So the number of boys in 7th grade is $\frac{5}{4}x$.

The total number of boys in two grades is the same as girls:
$100 + \frac{5}{4}x = 120 + x$
$\frac{1}{4}x = 20 \rightarrow x = 80$

7. *Answer: 8*
$f(3) = 5 = a$
$g(5) = 8$

8. *Answer: (D)*
$f(-2) = 3(-2)^2 - 8(-2) + 17 = 45$

9. *Answer: (B)*
Draw a horizontal line y = −0.5 to find how many interceptions with the graph.
From the graph above, there are 5 interceptions with line y = −0.5.

10. *Answer: (A)*
The total number of cars sold: 1,014
The probability that the car sold from the region I in March = $\frac{65}{10.14} = 0.064 = 6.4\%$

11. *Answer: (A)*
The hundreds has 3 choices (3, 6, 9) and the units digit has 5 choices (2, 4, 6, 8, 0). There are 10 possible values of tens digit (0 – 9).
Total = 3 × 5 × 10 = 150

12. *Answer: (D)*

We want to find $\frac{X}{Y}$.

Average: $\frac{Sum\ of\ Terms}{Number\ of\ Terms}$

$\frac{85X + 90Y}{X+Y} = 88$ *(cross multiply)*

$85X + 90Y = 88 \times (X + Y)$

$85X + 90Y = 88X + 88Y$

$2Y = 3X$

$\frac{X}{Y} = \frac{2}{3}$

13. *Answer: 160*

$10(128)\left(\frac{1}{8}\right) = 160$

14. *Answer: 48*

Let one trip have x miles

Total Time = $t_{go} + t_{back}$

$1 = \frac{x}{40} + \frac{x}{60} = x(\frac{1}{40} + \frac{1}{60}) \rightarrow x = 24$

Total miles: $2 \times 24 = 48$ *miles*

15. *Answer: (D)*

$Slope = \frac{Rise}{Run} = \frac{0-2}{3-0} = -\frac{2}{3}$

y-intercept $= 2$

$y = -\frac{2}{3}x + 2$

16. *Answer: (C)*

$\sqrt{14 - x} = x - 2$

$14 - x = (x - 2)^2 = x^2 - 4x + 4$

$x^2 - 3x - 10 = 0$

$(x - 5)(x + 2) = 0$

$x = 5, -2$

$\sqrt{14 - (-2)} + 2 \neq -2$

Therefore, $x = -2$ is not the solution. The answer is c).

17. *Answer: (B)*

Slower speeds have smaller (flatter) slopes. Resting speeds have horizontal slope. Higher speeds have bigger (steeper) slopes.

18. *Answer: (A)*

$m\angle AOD + m\angle BOC = 360 - m\angle DOC - m\angle AOB$

$m\angle AOB = 180 - 2 \times 35 = 110$

$m\angle DOC = 180 - 2 \times 55 = 70$

$m\angle AOD + m\angle BOC = 360 - 110 - 70 = 180$

19. *Answer: (C)*

The total number of cars sold in January and February: 697

The total number of cars sold from region II in Jan. and Feb.: 176.

The probability that the car sold was from the region II $= \frac{176}{697} = 0.2525 = 25.3\%$

20. *Answer: 4*

$a - bi = i(3 - 7i) = 3i - 7i^2$

$= 7 + 3i$

$a = 7$ *and* $b = -3$

$a + b = 4$

21. *Answer: (A)*

The line of $3x + 2y = 2b$ has a slope of $\frac{-3}{2}$.

Line l is perpendicular, so it should have a slope of $\frac{2}{3}$. We also know that it passes through the origin.

$y = \frac{2}{3}x$

$a - 1 = \frac{2}{3}(2a)$

$3a - 3 = 4a \rightarrow a = -3$

point $(-6, -4)$ passing through $3x + 2y = 2b \rightarrow$

$-6 \times 3 - 4 \times 2 = -26 = 2b$

$b = -13$

22. *Answer: (D)*

$f(3y) = (3y)^2 + 27 = 3f(y) = 3(y^2 + 27)$

$9y^2 + 27 = 3y^2 + 3 \times 27$

$6y^2 = 54, \quad y^2 = 9, \quad y = \pm 3$

Module 2 Hard Answers

1. *Answer: A)*

Since most of the people scored are in the lower point group, the mean is greater than the median.
        The answer is a).

2. *Answer: (D)*

This is an exponential growth model.

The initial value is 500.

$y = 500(b)^x$

Use a data point $(8, 1300)$

$1300 = 500(b)^8$

$b = \left(\frac{1300}{500}\right)^{\frac{1}{8}} = 1.12.$

        The answer is d).

3. *Answer: (B)*
Plug the number 5 into the function.
$$f(5) = \frac{5^2 - 15}{5^2 - 20}$$
$$\frac{10}{5} = 2$$

4. *Answer: (C)*
Total number of marbles must be a common multiple of 7 and 4.
LCM of 7 and 4 is 28.
So 28 is one possible number of marbles in the bag.

5. *Answer: (B)*
Let v be the value after t years and let v_0 be the initial value, then
$$v = v_0(2)^{\frac{t}{n}}$$
This is an exponential growth model.
Therefore the graph should be b).

6. *Answer: (B)*
$$Average = \frac{Sum\ of\ Terms}{Number\ of\ Terms}$$
$$New\ Average = \frac{8 \times 10 - 4 \times 4}{8} = 8$$

7. *Answer: (A)*
Total Distance A Traveled = Rate × Time
= 15 miles/hour × 4 hours = 60 miles
Total Distance B Traveled
= 10 miles/hour × x hours = $\frac{1}{2}$ × 60 miles = 30 miles
$$x = \frac{30\ miles}{10\ miles/hour} = 3\ hours$$

8. *Answer: (A)*
Plug in the values for x and y into both equations.
$2(k)^2 + 1 = 9$ → $k^2 = 4$
$9 = -k^2 + m$
$9 = -4 + m$ → $m = 13$

9. *Answer: (B)*
It is a probability question.
The least students can have birthdays in the same month is when every month has the same number of students' birthdays for the first 96 students.
96 ÷ 12 = 8.
The rest of four students' birthdays spread into 4 different months.
So at least 8 + 1 = 9 students' birthdays will be in the same month.

10. *Answer: (A)*
$(((((2+1) \times 2)+1) \times 2)+1) \times 2) = 30$

11. *Answer: (A)*
Use the same ratio number to compare
Pear : Apple = 3 : 5   = 9 : 15
Pear: Orange = 3 : 5   = 15 : 25
Apple : Orange   = 9 : 25

12. *Answer: (B)*
A negative value of a will make the quadratic function's graph open downward and a positive value of c will show that the function has a positive y-intercept.

13. *Answer: 42*
The sum of all integers from –41 to +41 is 0. The next term is 42.
Therefore, x = 42

14. *Answer: $\frac{1}{2}$*

Gender	English Courses	
	Honor	AP
Male	$2y$	y
Female	$4x$	x
Total	60	20

$$\begin{cases} x + y = 20 \\ 2y + 4x = 60 \end{cases}$$
By solving the system of equations, we find x = 10 and y = 10.
Probability = $\frac{10}{20} = \frac{1}{2}$

15. *Answer: (B)*
$(3x + 2y) - (2x + y) = 13 - 9$
$x + y = 4$

16. *Answer: (C)*
The sum of a quadrilateral's interior angles is equal to 360°.
$120 + 110 + 75 + (180 - x) = 360$
$x = 125$

17. *Answer: (A)*
"at least 4" means ≥ 4
$10 - x - y \geq 4$

18. *Answer: (C)*
Radius of the Circle = 5
Area of the Circle = $\pi(5)^2 = 25\pi$
Area of the Triangle = $\frac{1}{2} \times 5 \times 10 = 25$
Probability = $\frac{25}{25\pi} = \frac{1}{\pi}$

19. *Answer: (A)*
Total Time = $\frac{Total\ Toys}{Total\ Rate}$
Total Rate = 250 toys/hour + 350 toys/hour = 600 toys/hour
Total Time = $\frac{1800\ toys}{600\ toys/hour}$ = 3 hours = 180 minutes

20. *Answer: $\frac{5}{4}$*
$\frac{2}{3}x + \frac{5}{6}y = -10$
Line t: $y = -\frac{4}{5}x - 12$
The slope of line $v = \frac{5}{4}$

21. *Answer: (D)*
The lowest possible score is equal to the lowest score a student can get if each of other four students got the highest possible score (otherwise we can always increase another student's score and decrease the lowest score). Thus, each of other four students must get 100.
Total Score = $5 \times 86 = 430$
Lowest Possible Score = 430 – 400 = 30

22. *Answer: (D)*
$y = 1 - kx = -x^2 + kx$
$x^2 - kx - (k-1) = 0$
Since the graphs intersect at exactly two points, its discriminant > 0.
$(-k)^2 - 4(1)\big(-(k-1)\big) > 0$
$k^2 + 4k - 4 > 0$
When $k = 0$, it does not satisfy this inequality. Therefore, the answer is d).

Math Mock Test 9

22 QUESTIONS

DIRECTIONS

The questions in this section address a number of important math skills.

Use of a calculator is permitted for all questions.

○ **Check the answers after the Module 1 test. If there are more than 8 questions answered incorrectly in Module 1, take the Easy part of Module 2. Otherwise, take the Hard part of Module 2.**

NOTES

Unless otherwise indicated:

• All variables and expressions represent real numbers.

• Figures provided are drawn to scale.

• All figures lie in a plane.

• The domain of a given function f is the set of all real numbers x for which f(x) is a real number.

REFERENCE

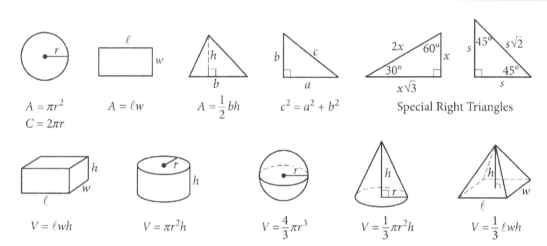

$A = \pi r^2$ $A = \ell w$ $A = \frac{1}{2}bh$ $c^2 = a^2 + b^2$ Special Right Triangles

$C = 2\pi r$

$V = \ell wh$ $V = \pi r^2 h$ $V = \frac{4}{3}\pi r^3$ $V = \frac{1}{3}\pi r^2 h$ $V = \frac{1}{3}\ell wh$

The number of degrees of arc in a circle is **360**.

The number of radians of arc in a circle is 2π.

The sum of the measures in degrees of the angles of a triangle is **180**.

For multiple-choice questions, solve each problem, choose the correct answer from the choices provided, and then circle your answer in this book. Circle only one answer for each question. If you change your mind, completely erase the circle. You will not get credit for questions with more than one answer circled, or for questions with no answers circled.

For student-produced response questions, solve each problem and write your answer next to or under the question in the test book as described below.

•   Once you've written your answer, circle it clearly. You will not receive credit for anything written outside the circle, or for any questions with more than one circled answer.

•   If you find **more than one correct answer**, write and circle only one answer. Your answer can be up to 5 characters for a **positive** answer and up to 6 characters (including the negative sign) for a **negative** answer, but no more.

•   If your answer is a **fraction** that is too long (over 5 characters for positive, 6 characters for negative), write the decimal equivalent.

•   If your answer is a **decimal** that is too long (over 5 characters for positive,

•   6 characters for negative), truncate it or round at the fourth digit.

•   If your answer is a **mixed number** (such as $3\frac{1}{2}$, write it as an improper fraction (7/2) or its decimal equivalent (3.5).

•   Don't include symbols such as a percent sign, comma, or dollar sign in your circled answer.

$$2x + y = 8$$
$$x + 2y = 4$$

1. For the system of equations above, what is the value of $x + y$?

    a)-1
    b) 4
    c) 5
    d) 20

2. If $x > 1$ and $a(x + 3)(x - 1) = 0$, what is the value of a?

    a) 3
    b) 2
    c) 1
    d) 0

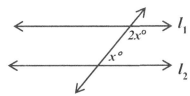

Note: Figure not drawn to scale.

3. In the figure above, $l_1 \parallel l_2$, what is the value of x?

    a) 45
    b) 50
    c) 60
    d) 70

4. If $\frac{3\sqrt{x} + y}{\sqrt{x} + 1} = 3$ then $y =$?

    a) 1
    b) 3
    c) 5
    d) 8

5. Which of the following represents the graph of the equation $x + y = 2$ in the xy-plane?

    a)

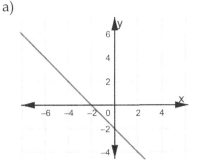

b)

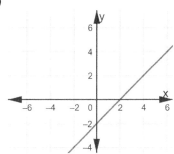

c)

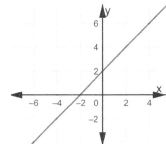

d)

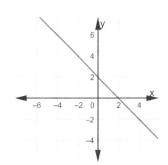

6. If $\frac{5}{q} = \frac{3}{9}$, what is the value of q?

7. Bella sells only rings and necklaces on her website. Rings sell for $50 each, and necklaces sell for $30 each. If Bella sold 25 pieces of jewelry and her sales totaled $1,050, how many necklaces did Bella sell?

$$\sqrt{x+18} - 2\sqrt{x-9} = 0$$

8. What value of x satisfies the equation above?
   - a) 8
   - b) 9
   - c) 12
   - d) 18

9. Which of the following could be the sum of 9 numbers if the average of these 9 numbers is greater than 9 and less than 10?
   - a) 91
   - b) 90
   - c) 85
   - d) 81

10. If $\frac{2x}{3} = \frac{3}{2}$, then $x=$?
   - a) $\frac{2}{3}$
   - b) $\frac{3}{2}$
   - c) 2
   - d) $\frac{9}{4}$

$$x^2 - 4x + 1 = 0$$

11. Which of the following is a solution to the equation above?
   - a) $x = -2 + \sqrt{2}$
   - b) $x = -2 + \sqrt{3}$
   - c) $x = 2 + \sqrt{2}$
   - d) $x = 2 + \sqrt{3}$

$$8x - 2x(c+1) = x$$

12. In the equation above, c is a constant. If the equation has infinitely many solutions, what is the value of c?
   - a) $\frac{11}{2}$
   - b) $\frac{9}{2}$
   - c) $\frac{7}{2}$
   - d) $\frac{5}{2}$

13. If $g(x) = 4x - 12$, then at what value of x does the graph of $g(x)$ cross the x-axis?

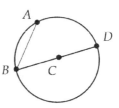

Note: Figure not drawn to scale.

14. In the circle above, C is the center. If the measure of $\angle ABC$ is 60^0 and radius $BC = 8$, what is the length of $\overline{AB}$?

15. If $x^2 - 2x = 8$, which of the following is a possible value of $x^2 - x =$?
   - a) 12
   - b) 9
   - c) −6
   - d) −9

$$y = x^2 + x - 2$$
$$x + y = 1$$

16. If (x, y) is a solution of the system of equations above, which of the following is a possible value of xy?
   - a) 7
   - b) 1
   - c) −1
   - d) −12

17. $a, b, x,$ and y are positive numbers. If $x^{-\frac{2}{3}} = a^{-6}$ and $y^{\frac{2}{3}} = b^6$, what is $(xy)^{-\frac{1}{3}}$ in terms of a and b?
   - a) ab
   - b) $a^{-3}b^{-3}$
   - c) $a^2 b^2$
   - d) $a^{-2}b^{-2}$

$$y \geq x + 2$$
$$2x + 3y \leq 6$$

18. In which of the following does the shaded region represent the solution set in the *xy*-plane to the system of inequalities above?

a)

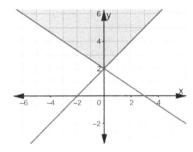

b)

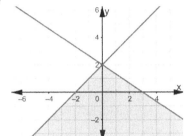

c)

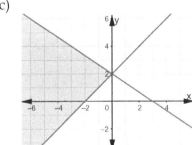

d)

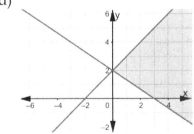

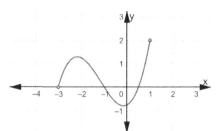

19. The entire graph of $y = f(x)$ is shown in the *xy*-plane above. Which of the following could be the product of all the values of x for which $f(x) = 0$?

     a) -2
     b) 0
     c) $\dfrac{3}{2}$
     d) $\dfrac{2}{3}$

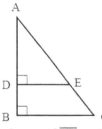

20. In the figure above, if $\overline{AC} = 15$, $\overline{DE} = 3$, and $\overline{AD} = 4$, then what is the length of $\overline{AC}$?

21. A circle with center at coordinates $(4, 5)$ touches the *x*-axis at only one point. What is the radius of the circle?

$$(4x + 4)(ax - 1) - x^2 + 4$$

22. In the expression above, a is a constant. If the expression is equivalent to bx, where b is a constant, what is the value of b ?

     a) -5
     b) -3
     c) 0
     d) 12

Math Mock Test 9

22 QUESTIONS

DIRECTIONS

The questions in this section address a number of important math skills.
Use of a calculator is permitted for all questions.

NOTES

Unless otherwise indicated:
• All variables and expressions represent real numbers.
• Figures provided are drawn to scale.
• All figures lie in a plane.
• The domain of a given function f i s the set of all real numbers x for which f(x) is a real number.

REFERENCE

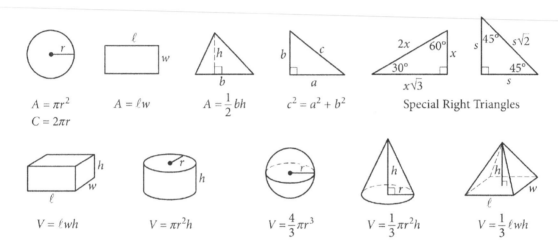

$A = \pi r^2$ $A = \ell w$ $A = \frac{1}{2} bh$ $c^2 = a^2 + b^2$ Special Right Triangles
$C = 2\pi r$

$V = \ell wh$ $V = \pi r^2 h$ $V = \frac{4}{3}\pi r^3$ $V = \frac{1}{3}\pi r^2 h$ $V = \frac{1}{3}\ell wh$

The number of degrees of arc in a circle is **360**.
The number of radians of arc in a circle is 2π.
The sum of the measures in degrees of the angles of a triangle is **180**.

For multiple-choice questions, solve each problem, choose the correct answer from the choices provided, and then circle your answer in this book. Circle only one answer for each question. If you change your mind, completely erase the circle. You will not get credit for questions with more than one answer circled, or for questions with no answers circled.

For student-produced response questions, solve each problem and write your answer next to or under the question in the test book as described below.
• Once you've written your answer, circle it clearly. You will not receive credit for anything written outside the
• circle, or for any questions with more than one circled
  answer.
• If you find **more than one correct answer**, write and
  circle only one answer. Your answer can be up to 5
  characters for a **positive** answer and up to 6 characters
  (including the negative sign) for a **negative** answer,
  but no more.
• If your answer is a **fraction** that is too long (over 5
  characters for positive, 6 characters for negative), write
  the decimal equivalent.

• If your answer is a **decimal** that is too long (over 5
  characters for positive,
• 6 characters for negative), truncate it or round at the
  fourth digit.
• If your answer is a **mixed number** (such as $3\frac{1}{2}$, write it
  as an improper fraction (7/2) or its decimal equivalent
  (3.5).
• Don't include symbols such as a percent sign, comma,
  or dollar sign in your circled answer.

$$(3x + 2)(2x + 1)$$

1. Which of the following is equivalent to the expression above?

    a) $5x^2 + 8x + 5$
    b) $5x^2 + x + 2$
    c) $6x^2 + 7x + 2$
    d) $6x^2 + 7x + 9$

2. The number of people who rode a certain bus each day of a week is shown in the table below.

Day	Number of Riders
Monday	612
Tuesday	798
Wednesday	655
Thursday	773
Friday	808
Saturday	480
Sunday	229

Which of the following is true based on these data?

    a) The bus had the most riders on Tuesday.
    b) Each day from Tuesday through Sunday, the number of riders on the bus was greater than the previous day.
    c) Each day from Tuesday through Sunday, the number of riders on the bus was less than the previous day.
    d) The two days with the fewest number of riders were Saturday and Sunday.

3. Ivan opened a checking account with an initial deposit of x dollars, and then he deposited \$60 into the account each week for 15 weeks. At the end of the 14 weeks, he had deposited \$900 into the account. If no other deposits or withdrawals were made, what is the value of x ?

    a) 60
    b) 80
    c) 120
    d) 200

$$1, 5, 21, 85, t, 1365, \ldots$$

4. In the sequence above, what is the value of t?

    a) 34
    b) 51
    c) 53
    d) 341

5. A cube has 2 faces painted green and the remaining faces painted red. The total area of the green faces is 32 square inches. What is the volume of this cube, in cubic inches?

    a) 9
    b) 27
    c) 36
    d) 64

6. A scale drawing of a room uses the scale 2 centimeters = 1 foot. In the drawing, one wall has a length of 22 centimeters. What is the actual length, in feet, of this wall?

7. Each term in a sequence of numbers is greater than the term before it and the difference between any two consecutive terms is constant. If the 15th and 20th terms in the sequence are 6 and 16, respectively, what is the 300th term?

8. The average score of John's 5 math tests is 80. If the teacher decides not to count his lowest score, which is 60, what will be John's new average score?

    a) 80
    b) 82
    c) 85
    d) 86

$$°F = \frac{9}{5}°C + 32°$$

9. The equation above represents the relationship of temperature scales between Fahrenheit (°F) and Celsius (°C). How many degrees of Celsius changed for each additional degree of Fahrenheit increased?

     a) 1.8
     b) 1
     c) 0.8
     d) 0.55

10. In △ABC below, ∠ACB is 90°. Which of the following segments has the longest length?

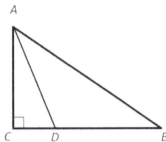

     a) Segment AD
     b) Segment AC
     c) Segment CB
     d) Segment AB

11. The Rockville Reservoir had an original storage capacity of 500,000 acre-feet at the end of 1950, the year in which it was built. Starting in 1951, sediment carried downstream by the Rockville River collected in the reservoir and began reducing the reservoir s storage capacity at the approximate rate of 1,000 acre-feet per year. What was the approximate storage capacity, in acre-feet, of the reservoir at the end of 2020?

     a) 300,000
     b) 400,000
     c) 430,000
     d) 450,000

12. The quadratic function f is defined by $f(x) = 2(x + 2)^2 - 1$. In the xy-plane, which of the following could be the graph of $y = f(x)$ shifted 3 units to the right?

     a)

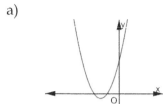

     b)

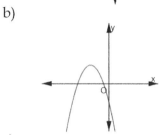

     c)

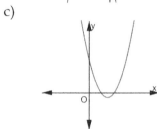

     d)

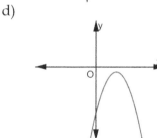

13. If the sum of all consecutive integers from −41 to x, inclusive, is 42, what is the value of x?

$$\frac{(x^2 + 17x + 66)}{x + 6}$$

14. If the expression above is equivalent to an expression of the form $x + a$, where $x \neq -6$, what will be the value of a ?

15. $\frac{1}{5}$ of 80 is equal to what percent of 200?

    a) 5 %

    b) 8 %

    c) 10 %

    d) 16 %

	Courses			
Gender	French	Spanish	Chinese	Total
Male	8	10	11	29
Female	12	14	15	41
Total	20	24	26	70

16. The table above represents the number of freshmen in Stoneville High School who currently enroll in three foreign language classes. Which of the following categories accounts for approximately 20 percent of all the students in those three foreign language classes?

    a) Males taking Chinese

    b) Females taking Spanish

    c) Males taking French

    d) Females taking Chinese

17. At the beginning of a laboratory experiment, Miguel had 10 milliliters of a solution in a flask. The first step of the experiment consisted of Miguel pouring x milliliters of the solution into a beaker and y milliliters of the solution into a different beaker. There remained at least 4 milliliters of the solution in the flask after the first step. which of the following inequalities can be used to correctly represent this situation?

    a) $10 - x - y \geq 4$

    b) $10 - x + y \geq 4$

    c) $4 - x - y \geq 5$

    d) $4 - x + y \geq 5$

$$2x - y = -2$$
$$2x + y = 2$$

18. For the solution of the system of equations above, what is the value of y?

    a) -1

    b) -2

    c) 0

    d) 2

19. A car rental company calculates the price of renting a car by adding the fixed rental fee with an additional charge for every 10 miles traveled. If the charge to rent a car and drive 50 miles is $120 and the charge to rent a car and drive 200 miles is $165, what would be the price, in dollars, to rent a car and travel 300 miles?

    a) 178

    b) 186

    c) 195

    d) 225

20. An isosceles triangle has one side of length 20 and one side of length 30. What is the largest possible value that the perimeter of the triangle could be?

21. If there are 8 points in a plane, no three of which are collinear, how many distinct lines can be formed by connecting two of these points?

    a) 15

    b) 21

    c) 28

    d) 49

22. $18,000 in winnings for a tennis tournament was distributed in the ratio of 6:2:1 to the first-, second-, and third-place finishers, respectively. How much money did the first place finisher receive?

    a) $12,000

    b) $15,000

    c) $10,000

    d) $8,000

Math Mock Test 9

22 QUESTIONS

DIRECTIONS

The questions in this section address a number of important math skills.

Use of a calculator is permitted for all questions.

NOTES

Unless otherwise indicated:

• All variables and expressions represent real numbers.

• Figures provided are drawn to scale.

• All figures lie in a plane.

• The domain of a given function f i s the set of all real numbers x for which f(x) is a real number.

REFERENCE

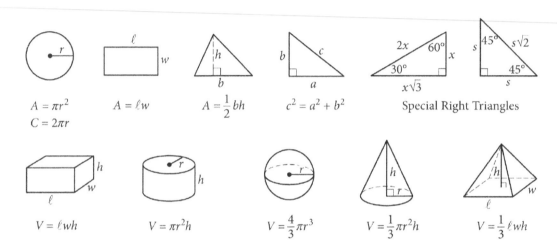

$A = \pi r^2$ $A = \ell w$ $A = \dfrac{1}{2} bh$ $c^2 = a^2 + b^2$ Special Right Triangles

$C = 2\pi r$

$V = \ell wh$ $V = \pi r^2 h$ $V = \dfrac{4}{3}\pi r^3$ $V = \dfrac{1}{3}\pi r^2 h$ $V = \dfrac{1}{3}\ell wh$

The number of degrees of arc in a circle is **360**.

The number of radians of arc in a circle is 2π.

The sum of the measures in degrees of the angles of a triangle is **180**.

For multiple-choice questions, solve each problem, choose the correct answer from the choices provided, and then circle your answer in this book. Circle only one answer for each question. If you change your mind, completely erase the circle. You will not get credit for questions with more than one answer circled, or for questions with no answers circled.

For student-produced response questions, solve each problem and write your answer next to or under the question in the test book as described below.

• Once you've written your answer, circle it clearly. You will not receive credit for anything written outside the circle, or for any questions with more than one circled answer.

• If you find **more than one correct answer**, write and circle only one answer. Your answer can be up to 5 characters for a **positive** answer and up to 6 characters (including the negative sign) for a **negative** answer, but no more.

• If your answer is a **fraction** that is too long (over 5 characters for positive, 6 characters for negative), write the decimal equivalent.

• If your answer is a **decimal** that is too long (over 5 characters for positive,

• 6 characters for negative), truncate it or round at the fourth digit.

• If your answer is a **mixed number** (such as $3\frac{1}{2}$, write it as an improper fraction (7/2) or its decimal equivalent (3.5).

• Don't include symbols such as a percent sign, comma, or dollar sign in your circled answer.

$$y = 3$$
$$y + 1 = x^2$$

1. If (x_1, y_1) and (x_2, y_2) are the solution to the system of equations above, what are the values of x_1 and x_2 ?
   a) $-\sqrt{3}$ and $\sqrt{3}$
   b) $-\sqrt{2}$ and $\sqrt{2}$
   c) -2 and 2
   d) -3 and 3

2. In the xy-plane, the graph of which of the following equations is perpendicular to the graph of the equation below?
$$-3x + 2y = 4$$
   a) $3x - 2y = 4$
   b) $3x + 2y = 3$
   c) $2x + 3y = 4$
   d) $2x - 3y = 3$

3. The graph of the exponential function h in the xy-plane, where $y = h(x)$, has a y-intercept of d, where d is a positive constant. Which of the following could define the function h ?
   a) $h(x) = -3(d)^x$
   b) $h(x) = 3(x)d$
   c) $h(x) = d(-x)^3$
   d) $h(x) = d(3)^x$

4. To make fruit punch, grapefruit juice, orange juice, and lemonade are mixed in with a ratio of $4:3:1$ by volume, respectively. In order to make 4 liters of this drink, how much orange juice, in liters, is needed?
   a) 1
   b) 1.5
   c) 2
   d) 2.5

5. Starting in 1950, the population of a city doubled every 15 years until 2010. The population of the city was 45,000 in 1950. Which of the following expressions gives the population of the city in 2010?
   a) $45000(2)^4$
   b) $45000(2)^{15}$
   c) $45000(2)^{60}$
   d) $45000(2)(60)$

6. Positive integers x, y, and z satisfy the equations $x^{-\frac{1}{2}} = \frac{1}{3}$ and $y^z = 8$, $z > y$, what is the value of $x + y + z$?
   a) 5
   b) 7
   c) 14
   d) 15

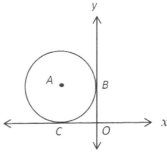

7. In the figure above, a circle with center A is tangent to the x-axis and the y-axis on the xy-coordinate plane. If the coordinates of the center A are $(-3, 3)$, what are the coordinates of point C?
   a) $(-2, 0)$
   b) $(-3, 0)$
   c) $(2, 0)$
   d) $(0, -3)$

8. If w is a positive number and $w > w^2$, which of the following statements is true?
$$w^2 > w^3$$
$$w > \frac{w}{3}$$
$$w > w^3$$
   a) I, II
   b) II, III
   c) I, II, and III
   d) I only

9. The cost of a long-distance call using phone company A is $1.00 for the first three minutes and $.10 for each additional minute. The same call using the phone company B is charged flat rate at $0.15 per minute for any amount of time. For a call that lasts t minutes, the cost using company A is the same as the cost using the company B, what is the value of t?
    a) 15
    b) 14
    c) 12
    d) 10

10. How many points do the graph of function, $f(x) = (x - 1)^2$, cross the x-axis?
    a) 0
    b) 1
    c) 2
    d) 3

11. An ecologist selected a random sample of 30 prairie dogs from a colony and found that the mean mass of the prairie dogs in the sample was 0.94 kilograms (kg) with an associated margin of error of 0.12 kg. Which of the following is the best interpretation of the ecologist's findings?
    a) All prairie dogs in the sample have a mass between 0.82 kg and 1.06 kg.
    b) Most prairie dogs in the colony have a mass between 0.82 kg and 1.06 kg.
    c) Any mass between 0.82 kg and 1.06 kg is a plausible value for the mean mass of the prairie dogs in the colony.
    d) Any mass between 0.82 kg and 1.06 kg is a plausible value for the mean mass of the prairie dogs in the sample.

12. A poster has an area of 436 square inches. The length x, in inches, of the poster is 6 inches longer than the width of the poster. Which of the following equations can be solved to determine the length, in inches, of the poster?
    a) $x^2 - 436 = 6$
    b) $x^2 + 6x = 436$
    c) $x^2 + 6 = 436$
    d) $x^2 - 6x = 436$

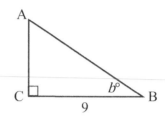

Note: Figure not drawn to scale

13. In the triangle above, if $\sin(b°) = 0.6$ and the BC = 9, what is the perimeter of the triangle?

14. Lines t and w are parallel in the xy-plane. The equation of line t is $4x + 7y = 11$, and line w passes through the point $(2, -1)$. What is the value of the y-intercept of line w?

15. When the number 99 is divided by the positive integer N, the remainder is 4. For how many different values of N is this true?
    a) One
    b) Two
    c) Three
    d) Four

16. If the center of the circle defined by $x^2 + y^2 - 4x + 2y = 20$ is (a, b), then $a + b = ?$
    a) 0
    b) 1
    c) 3
    d) 4

17. Megan began a one-way 10-mile bicycle trip by riding very slowly for 5 miles. She rested for 30 minutes and then rode quickly for the rest of the trip. Which of the following graphs could correctly represents the trip?

a)

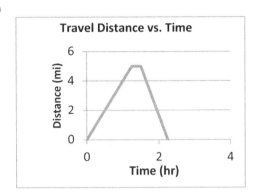

b)

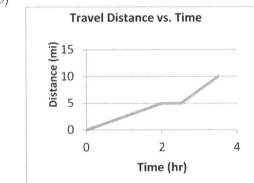

c)

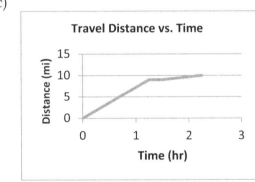

d)

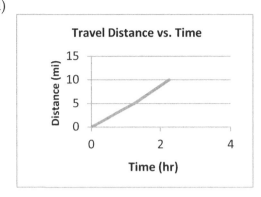

18. According to the graph below, how many employees have salary less than or equal to $60,000?

    a) 300
    b) 550
    c) 250
    d) 100

19. The load capacity of a certain washing machine is 14 pounds. What is the approximate load capacity of the same washing machine, in kilograms? (1 kilogram = 2.2046 pounds)
    a) 2.6
    b) 5.8
    c) 6.4
    d) 12.5

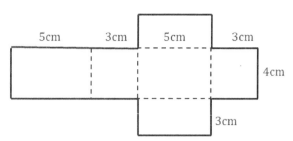

20. If the figure above is folded along the dashed lines, a rectangular box will be formed. What is the surface area of the box in square centimeters?

x	1	2	3	4
y	$\dfrac{17}{4}$	$\dfrac{35}{4}$	$\dfrac{41}{4}$	$\dfrac{71}{4}$

21. Which of the following equations relates y to x for the values in the table above?

   a) $y = \frac{1}{2} \times \left(\frac{17}{2}\right)^x$

   b) $y = 2 \times \left(\frac{17}{8}\right)^x$

   c) $y = \frac{9}{2}x - \frac{1}{4}$

   d) $y = \frac{1}{4}x + 4$

22. $18,000 in winnings for a tennis tournament was distributed in the ratio of 6:2:1 to the first-, second-, and third-place finishers, respectively. How much money did the first place finisher receive?

   a) $12,000

   b) $15,000

   c) $10,000

   d) $8,000

Mock Test 9

Module 1 Keys

1. (B)	2. (D)	3. (C)	4. (B)	5. (D)	6. 15	7. 10	8. (D)
9. (C)	10. (D)	11. (D)	12. (D)	13. 3	14. 8	15. (A)	16. (D)
17. (B)	18. (C)	19. (C)	20. 25	21. 5	22. (B)		

Module 2 Easy Keys

1. (C)	2. (D)	3. (A)	4. (D)	5. (D)	6. 11	7. 576	8. (C)
9. (D)	10. (D)	11. (C)	12. (C)	13. 42	14. 11	15. (B)	16. (B)
17. (A)	18. (D)	19. (C)	20. 80	21. (C)	22. (A)		

Module 2 Hard Keys

1. (C)	2. (C)	3. (D)	4. (B)	5. (A)	6. (C)	7. (B)	8. (C)
9. (B)	10. (B)	11. (C)	12. (D)	13. 27	14. $\frac{1}{7}$	15. (C)	16. (B)
17. (B)	18. (B)	19. (C)	20. 94	21. (C)	22. (A)		

Mock Test 9

Module 1 Answers

1. *Answer: (B)*
   $(2x + y) + (x + 2y) = 8 + 4$
   $3x + 3y = 12$
   $x + y = 4$

2. *Answer: (D)*
   Solve by zero-product rule.
   $a(x - 1)(x + 3) = 0$
   One of the terms a, (x − 1), and (x + 3) must be equal to zero.
   Given that x > 1, only a can be equal to zero.

3. *Answer: (C)*
   Consecutive interior angles are supplementary.
   $2x + x = 180$
   $x = 60$

4. *Answer: (B)*
   $3\sqrt{x} + y = 3\sqrt{x} + 3$
   $y = 3$

5. *Answer: (D)*
   $x + y = 2$
   $y = -x + 2$
   Slope = −1 and y-intercept = 2
   The answer is d).

6. *Answer: 15*
   Cross multiply.
   $5 \times 9 = 3 \times q$
   $q = 15$

7. *Answer: 10*
   Number of necklaces sold=x
   Number of ring sold=y
   $x + y = 25$
   $30x + 50y = 1050$
   Solve the system of the equations above: x = 10; y = 15

8. *Answer: (D)*
   When x = 18,
   $\sqrt{x + 18} - 2\sqrt{x - 9} = \sqrt{18 + 18} - 2\sqrt{18 - 9} = \sqrt{36} - 2\sqrt{9} = 6 - 6 = 0$

9. *Answer: (C)*
   Sum = Number of Elements × Average

$9 \times 9 < Sum < 10 \times 9$
$81 < Sum < 90$

10. *Answer: (D)*
    Use cross multiplication to solve fraction equations.
    $\frac{2x}{3} = \frac{3}{2}$
    $2 \times 2x = 3 \times 3$
    $4x = 9$ *(divide both sides by 4)*
    $x = \frac{9}{4}$

11. *Answer: (D)*
    Quadratic formula
    $x = \frac{4 \pm \sqrt{16 - 4}}{2} = 2 \pm \sqrt{3}$

12. *Answer: (D)*
    "An equation has infinitely many solutions" means left side expression is the same as the right side expression.
    $8x - 2x(c + 1) = x$
    $(8 - 2c - 2)x = x$
    $8 - 2c - 2 = 1$
    $2c = 5 \rightarrow c = \frac{5}{2}$

13. *Answer: 3*
    The value of x where g(x) crosses the x-axis is the value of x where g(x) is equal to 0.
    $0 = 4x - 12$
    $x = 3$

14. *Answer: 8*

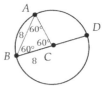

An isosceles triangle with an angle measurement of 60° is also an equilateral triangle.

15. *Answer: (A)*
    Factor $x^2 - 2x - 8$.
    $(x - 4)(x + 2) = 0$
    $x = 4$ *or* -2
    Plug x = 4 and −2 into the expression.
    $x^2 - x = (4)^2 - 4 = 12$ *or*
    $x^2 - x = (-2)^2 - (-2) = 6$

16. *Answer: (D)*
Solve the system of equations.
$$y = 1 - x = x^2 + x - 2$$
$$x^2 + 2x - 3 = 0$$
$$(x - 1)(x + 3) = 0$$
$$x = 1 \text{ or } -3 \rightarrow y = 0 \text{ or } 4$$
$$xy = 0 \text{ or } 4 \text{ or } -12$$

17. *Answer: (B)*
$$x^{-\frac{2}{3}} = a^{-6} \rightarrow x = (a^{-6})^{-\frac{3}{2}} = a^9$$
$$y^{\frac{2}{3}} = b^6 \rightarrow y = (b^6)^{\frac{3}{2}} = b^9$$
$$(xy)^{-\frac{1}{3}} = (a^9 b^9)^{-\frac{1}{3}} = a^{-3} b^{-3}$$

18. *Answer: (C)*

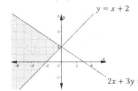

$y \geq x + 2$ means the solution set locates at the upper side of y-axis and $2x + 3y \leq 6$ means the solution set locates at the lower side of y-axis. Therefore, the answer is c).

19. *Answer: (C)*
The x-intercepts are the roots of $y = f(x)$.
$$(-3)(-1)(0.5) = \frac{3}{2}$$

20. *Answer: 25*

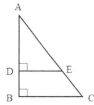

Since $\overline{DE} \parallel \overline{BC}$, $BC = 15$, $DE = 3$, and $AD = 4$
$$AE = \sqrt{3^2 + 4^2} = 5$$
$$\frac{AE}{AC} = \frac{DE}{C}$$
$$\frac{5}{AC} = \frac{3}{15} \rightarrow AC = 25$$

21. *Answer: 5*
The circle is tangent to the x−axis, since otherwise it would touch the axis at zero or two points (try drawing it out to see). Its radius is the distance from the center to the x-axis which is 5.

22. *Answer: (B)*
$$(4x + 4)(ax - 1) - x^2 + 4 = 4ax^2 - 4x + 4ax - 4 - x^2 + 4 = x^2(4a - 1) + x(4a - 4)$$
$$a = \frac{1}{4}$$
$$x(4a - 4) = -3x = bx$$
$$b = -3$$

Module 2 Easy Answers

1. *Answer: (C)*
$$(3x + 2)(2x + 1) = 6x^2 + 7x + 2$$

2. *Answer: (D)*

3. *Answer: (A)*
A linear model:
Let y is the total money after w weeks:
$$y = x + 60(w)$$
$$900 = x + 60(14)$$
$$x = 60$$

4. *Answer: (D)*
Examine the first few terms to figure out the pattern.
$$1 + 4^1 = 5$$
$$5 + 4^2 = 21$$
$$21 + 4^3 = 85$$

$$85 + 4^4 = 341 = t$$
$341 + 4^5 = 1365$ (Doing this is to verify that the answer is correct.)
This is also a sequence constructed by multiplying the previous term by 4 and then adding 1 to the product each time to get the next term.
$$1 \times 4 + 1 = 5$$
$$5 \times 4 + 1 = 21$$
$$21 \times 4 + 1 = 85$$
$$85 \times 4 + 1 = 341$$
$$t = 341$$
$341 \times 4 + 1 = 1365$ (Doing this is to verify that the answer is correct.)

5. *Answer: (D)*
   Let x be the length of the side. The area of one face is
   x^2. *The total area of the two green faces is then $2x^2$,*
   which is equal to 32.
   $2x^2 = 32 \quad \rightarrow \quad x^2 = 16 \quad \rightarrow \quad x = 4 \ (x > 0)$
   The volume of cube:
   $x \times x \times x = 4 \times 4 \times 4 = 64$ *cubic inches*

6. *Answer: 11*
   $\frac{2 \ cm}{1 \ ft} = \frac{22}{x}$
   $x = 11 \ feet$

7. *Answer: 576*
   Because the difference between any two consecutive
   terms is constant $= \frac{16-6}{20-15} = 2$
   15th term: 6
   300th term: 15th term + (300 – 15) × 2
   $= 6 + 285 \times 2 = 576$

8. *Answer: (C)*
   John's original average is 80 for 5 tests.
   5 × 80 = 400 (sum for 5 tests)
   400 – 60 = 340 (sum for 4 tests)
   $\frac{340}{4} = 85$ *(average of 4 tests)*

9. *Answer: (D)*
   $\frac{9}{5}°C = °F - 32$
   $°C = \frac{5}{9}(°F - 32)$
   For each degree of Fahrenheit increased will increase
   $\frac{5}{9}$ *(or 0.555) degrees of Celsius.*

10. *Answer: (D)*
    In a triangle, bigger angles will always face longer
    sides. No angle in ΔABC will have degree greater
    than 90, so the side facing ∠ACB will be longest.
    AB > AD > AC and CD.

11. *Answer: (C)*
    $y = -1000x + 500000$
    $x = 2020 - 1950 = 70$
    $y = (-1000)(70) + 500000 = 430,000$

12. *Answer: (C)*
    $f(x) = 2(x + 2)^2 - 1$
    Vertex is at $(-2, -1)$.
    After shift 3 units to the right, the vertex is at
    $(1, -1)$, in the fourth quadrant.
         The answer is c)

13. *Answer: 42*
    The sum of all integers from –41 to +41 is 0. The
    next term is 42.
    Therefore, x = 42

14. *Answer: 11*
    $\frac{x^2+17x+66}{x+6} = \frac{(x+6)(x+11)}{x+6} = x + 11$
    $a = 11$

15. *Answer: (B)*
    $\frac{1}{5}$ *of 80* $\rightarrow \frac{1}{5} \times 80 = 16$
    $16 = \frac{x}{100} \times 200$
    $16 = 2x$
    $x = 8$
    Therefore, $\frac{1}{5} \times 80 = 16$, which is equal to 200 ×
    8% = 16

16. *Answer: (B)*
    $70 \times 0.2 = 14$
    There are 14 female students taking Spanish.

17. *Answer: (A)*
    "at least 4" means ≥ 4
    $10 - x - y \geq 4$

18. *Answer: (D)*
    $2x - y = -2$ ---(1)
    $2x + y = 2$ ---(2)
    $(1) + (2) \rightarrow 4x = 0$
    $x = 0$, *so y = 2*

19. *Answer: (C)*
    Let initial charge be \$x, and the fee for every 10
    miles be \$y.
    $x + 5 y = 120$
    $x + 20y = 165$
    $15y = 45, \quad y = 3, \quad x = 105$
    For traveling 300 miles, the total charge is
    $105 + 30 \times 3 = 195.$

20. *Answer: 80*
    An isosceles triangle must have two sides with the
    same length. The third side has a length of either 20
    or 30.
    The largest perimeter can be 20 + 30 + 30 = 80.

21. *Answer: (C)*
This is combination. The number of ways to select m objects from n objects ($n \geq m$), where order does not matter:

$$C_m^n = \frac{n!}{m!(n-m)!}$$

To choose any two points among the 8 points: $C_2^8 =$ 28

22. *Answer: (A)*
1st place will have $\frac{6}{6+2+1} \times 18000 = \$12,000$

Module 2 Hard Answers

1. *Answer: (C)*
$3 + 1 = x^2$
$x = \pm 2$

2. *Answer: (C)*
Rewrite $-3x + 2y = 4$ to slope-intercept form:
$2y = 3x + 4$
$y = \frac{3}{2}x + 2 \rightarrow Slope = \frac{3}{2}$
Its perpendicular line should has a slope $-\frac{2}{3}$.
The answer (c) $2x + 3y = 4$ has a slope $-\frac{2}{3}$.

3. *Answer: (D)*
The y-intercept, d, is the initial value of this exponential function.
$h(x) = d(3)^x$

4. *Answer: (B)*
Every 8 liters, (4+3+1), of drink, 3 liters of orange juice will be needed. So 4 liters of this drink, we need $\frac{3}{8} \times 4$ of orange juice.
Orange Juice = 1.5 liters

5. *Answer: (A)*
This is an exponential growth model.
$P = P_0 (2)^{\# \, of \, double}$
$P = 45000(2)^{\frac{60}{15}} = 45000(2)^4$

6. *Answer: (C)*
$x^{-\frac{1}{2}} = \frac{1}{3}, \quad x = (\frac{1}{3})^{-2} = 3^2 = 9$
$8 = 2^3 = y^z$
$y = 2 \, and \, z = 3$
$x + y + z = 2 + 3 + 9 = 14$

7. *Answer: (B)*
$AC = AB$
The coordinates of B: (0, 3)
The coordinates of C: (–3, 0)

8. *Answer: (C)*
w is a positive number and $w < w^2$.
$w^2 - w > 0$
$w (1 - w) > 0$
$w > 0 \, and \, 1 - w > 0$
$-w > -1, \quad w < 1$
So $0 < w < 1$.
If $0 < w < 1$, then any number multiplied by w produces a number smaller than the original number. Therefore, $w^2 > w^3$, $w^3 > w^4$, and so on.
I, II, III are all correct.

9. *Answer: (B)*
$1 + (t - 3) \times 0.1 = 0.15t \rightarrow t = 14$

10. *Answer: (B)*
The graph of f(x) intersects the x-axis when f(x) = 0.
$0 = (x - 1)^2 \rightarrow x = 1$

11. *Answer: (C)*
x = Mass of prairie dogs
$0.94 - 0.12 \leq x \leq 0.94 + 0.12$
$0.82 \leq x \leq 1.06$
x is a plausible value for the mean mass in the colony.

12. *Answer: (D)*
Width = $x - 6$
$(x)(x - 6) = 436$
$x^2 - 6x = 436$

13. *Answer: 27*
Use the Pythagorean Theorem to find the lengths of sides of the right triangle.
$cos (b^o) = \sqrt{1 - 0.6^2} = 0.8$
$cos(b^o) = 0.8 = \frac{9}{AB} \rightarrow AB = 11.25$
$AC = A \times sin(b^o) = 11.25 \times 0.6 = 6.75$
$11.25 + 6.75 + 9 = 27$

14. *Answer:* $\frac{1}{7}$

Since line l and line w are parallel, the equation of line w is $4x + 7y = k$.
Plug in $(2, -1)$,
$4(2) + 7(-1) = k$
$k = 1$
Therefore, the equation of line w is $4x + 7y = 1$.
When $x = 0$, *y-intercept is* $\frac{1}{7}$.

15. *Answer:* (C)

Find all the factors of $(99 - 4)$ *that are greater than 4.*
$95 = 5 \times 19$
The total number of factors of 95: $(1+1)(1+1) = 4$
N must be greater than 4, so we need to deduct factors that are smaller than or equal to 4 which are 1.
The total number of different values of N: $4 - 1 = 3$

16. *Answer:* (B)

Rewrite to the equation in standard form.
$x^2 - 4x + 4 + y^2 + 2y + 1 = 20 + 5$
$(x - 2)^2 + (y + 1)^2 = 5^2$
The center of the circle is $(2, -1)$ *and the radius is 5.*
$a = 2, b = -1$
$a + b = 1$

17. *Answer:* (B)

Slower speeds have smaller (flatter) slopes. Resting speeds have horizontal slope. Higher speeds have bigger (steeper) slopes.

18. *Answer:* (B)

According to the bar graph, there are 100 + 150 + 300 = 550 employees with a salary of $60,000 or less.

19. *Answer:* (C)
$x = \frac{14}{2.2064} = 6.345$

20. *Answer:* 94

After folding, the height of the box will be 3 cm, the length will be 5 cm, and the width will be 4cm.
Surface Area $= (3 \times 4 + 4 \times 5 + 5 \times 3) \times 2 = 94$ *cm*^{2}

21. *Answer:* (C)

Plot in some of the x and y values to each equation and find the equation c) $y = \frac{9}{2}x - \frac{1}{4}$ *satisfies the values in the talbe.*

22. *Answer:* (A)

1st *place will have* $\frac{6}{6+2+1} \times 18000 = \$12,000$

Math Mock Test 10
22 QUESTIONS

DIRECTIONS

The questions in this section address a number of important math skills.

Use of a calculator is permitted for all questions.

- **Check the answers after the Module 1 test. If there are more than 8 questions answered incorrectly in Module 1, take the Easy part of Module 2. Otherwise, take the Hard part of Module 2.**

NOTES

Unless otherwise indicated:

- All variables and expressions represent real numbers.
- Figures provided are drawn to scale.
- All figures lie in a plane.
- The domain of a given function f is the set of all real numbers x for which f(x) is a real number.

REFERENCE

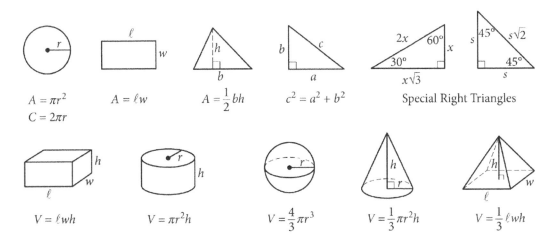

$A = \pi r^2$ $A = \ell w$ $A = \dfrac{1}{2}bh$ $c^2 = a^2 + b^2$ Special Right Triangles

$C = 2\pi r$

$V = \ell wh$ $V = \pi r^2 h$ $V = \dfrac{4}{3}\pi r^3$ $V = \dfrac{1}{3}\pi r^2 h$ $V = \dfrac{1}{3}\ell wh$

The number of degrees of arc in a circle is **360**.

The number of radians of arc in a circle is 2π.

The sum of the measures in degrees of the angles of a triangle is **180**.

For multiple-choice questions, solve each problem, choose the correct answer from the choices provided, and then circle your answer in this book. Circle only one answer for each question. If you change your mind, completely erase the circle. You will not get credit for questions with more than one answer circled, or for questions with no answers circled.

For student-produced response questions, solve each problem and write your answer next to or under the question in the test book as described below.

- Once you've written your answer, circle it clearly. You will not receive credit for anything written outside the circle, or for any questions with more than one circled answer.
- If you find **more than one correct answer**, write and circle only one answer. Your answer can be up to 5 characters for a **positive** answer and up to 6 characters (including the negative sign) for a **negative** answer, but no more.
- If your answer is a **fraction** that is too long (over 5 characters for positive, 6 characters for negative), write the decimal equivalent.
- If your answer is a **decimal** that is too long (over 5 characters for positive,
- 6 characters for negative), truncate it or round at the fourth digit.
- If your answer is a **mixed number** (such as $3\frac{1}{2}$, write it as an improper fraction (7/2) or its decimal equivalent (3.5).
- Don't include symbols such as a percent sign, comma, or dollar sign in your circled answer.

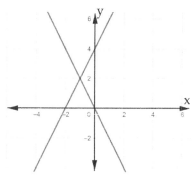

1. The lines in the xy-plane above are the graphs of two linear equations. What is the solution (x,y) to the system formed by the equations?
    a) $(-2, 4)$
    b) $(-1, 2)$
    c) $(0, 0)$
    d) $(0, 4)$

2. If $2x + 1 = 9$, what is the value of $\sqrt{5x - 4}$?
    a) 4
    b) –4
    c) 3
    d) –3

3. What are the solutions of the quadratic equation $2x^2 - 4x - 6 = 0$?
    a) $x = -1$ or $x = -3$
    b) $x = -1$ or $x = 3$
    c) $x = 1$ or $x = -3$
    d) $x = 1$ or $x = 3$

$$D = 60 - \frac{2}{3}P$$
$$S = \frac{1}{3}P$$

4. In economics, the equilibrium price is defined as the price at which quantity demanded and quantity supplied are equal. If the quantity demanded, D, and quantity supplied, S, in terms of the price in dollars, P, are given by the equations above, what is the equilibrium price?
    a) $0
    b) $60
    c) $80
    d) $120

5. Which of the following is equivalent to $x^{\frac{5}{2}}$, where $x > 0$?
    a) $\frac{x^5}{x^2}$
    b) $x^5 - x^2$
    c) $\sqrt{x^5}$
    d) $\left(\sqrt[5]{x} \right)^2$

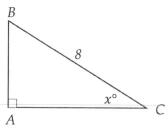

6. Note: Figure not drawn to scale.
In right triangle ABC above, $\overline{BC} = 8$. If the sine of $x^o = \frac{\sqrt{3}}{2}$, what is the length of $\overline{AC}$?

7. If $x = 7 + (6 \times 5^3 + 1)$, Find the value of x.

$$\begin{cases} 8x - 5y = 17 \\ 7x + 5y = 15 \end{cases}$$

8. For the solution (x, y) to the system of equations above, what is the value of ?
    a) 1
    b) $\frac{2}{5}$
    c) $-\frac{3}{5}$
    d) -1

9. A school choir consists of one row of singers, half of which are boys and the other half girls. Which of the following must be true?
    a) The first person and the last person have different genders.
    b) There are two girls next to each other.
    c) If the last two are girls, there are at least two adjacent boys.
    d) If there are two adjacent boys, there are also two adjacent girls.

$$2ax - 15 = 3(x + 5) + 5(x - 1)$$

10. In the equation above, a is a constant. If no value of x satisfies the equation, what is the value of a ?
    a) 1
    b) 2
    c) 3
    d) 4

11. Which of the following is an equation of the line that is perpendicular to the y-axis and passes through the point (2, 1)?
    a) $y = 1$
    b) $y = -1$
    c) $y = x$
    d) $y = -x$

$$(ax + 3)(5x^2 - bx + 4)$$
$$= 20x^3 - 9x^2 - 2x + 12$$

12. The equation above is true for all x, where a and b are constants. What is the value of ab ?
    a) 18
    b) 20
    c) 24
    d) 40

$$\frac{1}{x - 4} = \frac{-1}{x - 5}$$

13. What value of x satisfies the equation above?

14. The two acute angles of a right triangle have degree measures of x and y. If $sin(x) = \frac{3}{5}$, what is the value of $cos(y)$?

$$y = x^2$$
$$y = 3x + 4$$

15. The system of equations above is graphed in the xy-plane. The graphs of the equations intersect at a point (x, y) where $x > 0$ and $y > 0$. What is the y-coordinate of this point of intersection?
    a) 4
    b) 9
    c) 16
    d) 25

16. If $\frac{x}{y} = 4$, $x = 4z$, and $z = 6$, what is the value of y?
    a) 6
    b) 7
    c) 8
    d) 10

$$3x - y = -2$$
$$2x^2 - y = 0$$

17. If (x, y) is a solution to the system of equations above, which of the following is a possible value of xy ?
    a) 0
    b) ¼
    c) 4
    d) 16

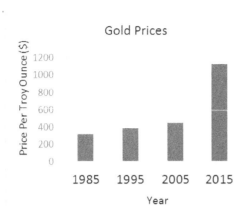

**Annual Average Gold Price from 1985 to 2015
(U.S. dollars per troy ounce)**

18. The figure above shows the change of the annual average gold price between 1985 and 2015, in U.S. dollars per troy ounce. A troy ounce is a traditional unit of gold weight. In 1985, a troy ounce of gold had an annual average price of around $317. Based on the information shown, which of the following conclusions is valid?
    a) A troy ounce of gold cost more in 1995 than in 2005.
    b) The price more than doubled between 2005 and 2015.
    c) The percent increase from 1985 to 2015 is more than 300%.
    d) The overall average gold price between 1985 and 2015 is around US $555.

19. If one triangle has two sides that have lengths of 3 and 7, which of the following CANNOT be the length of the third side of the triangle?
    a) 5
    b) 6
    c) 8
    d) 10

20. If $3(x - 5) = 15$, what does $\frac{x-5}{x+5}$ equal?

21. Last year, Gary's tomato plants produced 20 kilograms of tomatoes. This year, Gary increased the number of tomato plants in his garden by 20%. If his plants produce tomatoes this year at the same rate per plant as last year, how many kilograms of tomatoes can Gary expect the plants to produce this year?

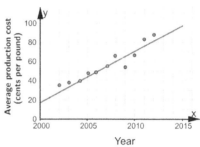

22. The scatterplot above shows the average production cost, in cents per pound, of coffee in Ecuador for the years from 2002 to 2012. A line of best fit is also drawn. Which of the following is closest to the difference, in cents per pound, between the actual average production cost in 2012 and the average production cost in 2012 predicted by the given line of best fit?
    a) 4
    b) 8
    c) 16
    d) 50

Math Mock Test 10

22 QUESTIONS

DIRECTIONS

The questions in this section address a number of important math skills.
Use of a calculator is permitted for all questions.

NOTES

Unless otherwise indicated:
• All variables and expressions represent real numbers.
• Figures provided are drawn to scale.
• All figures lie in a plane.
• The domain of a given function f i s the set of all real numbers x for which f(x) is a real number.

REFERENCE

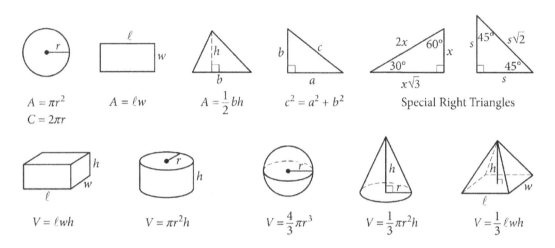

$A = \pi r^2$ $A = \ell w$ $A = \frac{1}{2}bh$ $c^2 = a^2 + b^2$ Special Right Triangles
$C = 2\pi r$

$V = \ell w h$ $V = \pi r^2 h$ $V = \frac{4}{3}\pi r^3$ $V = \frac{1}{3}\pi r^2 h$ $V = \frac{1}{3}\ell w h$

The number of degrees of arc in a circle is **360**.
The number of radians of arc in a circle is 2π.
The sum of the measures in degrees of the angles of a triangle is **180**.

For multiple-choice questions, solve each problem, choose the correct answer from the choices provided, and then circle your answer in this book. Circle only one answer for each question. If you change your mind, completely erase the circle. You will not get credit for questions with more than one answer circled, or for questions with no answers circled.

For student-produced response questions, solve each problem and write your answer next to or under the question in the test book as described below.
• Once you've written your answer, circle it clearly. You will not receive credit for anything written outside the
• circle, or for any questions with more than one circled answer.
• If you find **more than one correct answer**, write and circle only one answer. Your answer can be up to 5 characters for a **positive** answer and up to 6 characters (including the negative sign) for a **negative** answer, but no more.
• If your answer is a **fraction** that is too long (over 5 characters for positive, 6 characters for negative), write the decimal equivalent.

• If your answer is a **decimal** that is too long (over 5 characters for positive,
• 6 characters for negative), truncate it or round at the fourth digit.
• If your answer is a **mixed number** (such as $3\frac{1}{2}$, write it as an improper fraction (7/2) or its decimal equivalent (3.5).
• Don't include symbols such as a percent sign, comma, or dollar sign in your circled answer.

1. An hour hand of a clock rotates through $\frac{9\pi}{7}$ radians clockwise. If the hour hand is 4 inches long, what is the length of the arc that the tip of the hour hand moves through?
   a) 5π inches
   b) 5.14π inches
   c) 6.17π inches
   d) 8.78π inches

2. If a number was rounded to 20.3, which of the following could have been the original number?
   a) 20.24
   b) 20.249
   c) 20.35
   d) 20.25

3. If $(0.10) \times y = 10^2$, then $y =$?
   a) 0.01
   b) 0.001
   c) 100
   d) 1000

$$y - 7x = 13$$
$$8x = 3y$$

4. Which ordered pair (x, y) is the solution to the system of equations above?
   a) $(8, 3)$
   b) $(-3, -8)$
   c) $(1, \frac{3}{8})$
   d) $(\frac{8}{3}, 1)$

5. For each repair job, an elevator technician charges r dollars per hour for each hour worked plus a flat fee of k dollars. If the technician charges \$210 for a 2-hour job, which of the following represents the relationship between r and k?
   a) $210 = k + 2r$
   b) $210 = 2k + r$
   c) $210 = 2r - k$
   d) $210 = r - 2k$

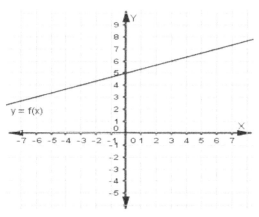

6. The graph of the linear function f is shown in the xy-coordinate plane above. If the slope of the graph g is 6 times the slope of the graph of f, and the graph of g passes through the point $(0, -3)$, what is the value of $g(10)$?

7. A movie company invited a total of 600 people to complete their review survey after watching a new release movie. Of the 420 people who finished that survey so far, 55 percent are male and 45 percent are female. Assuming all 600 people will eventually complete the survey, how many of the rest of the respondents must be female in order for half of the total respondents to be female?

8. Which of the following is equivalent to $\dfrac{1}{\frac{1}{x-1} - \frac{1}{x+1}}$?
   a) 2
   b) $\frac{1}{2x}$
   c) $\frac{1}{(x-1)(x+1)}$
   d) $\frac{x^2-1}{2}$

9. The functions f and g are defined by $f(x) = 4x$ and $g(x) = x^2$. For what value of x does $f(x) - g(x) = 4$?

    a) -2
    b) -1
    c) 1
    d) 2

10. Parabola D in the xy-plane has equation $x - 2y^2 - 8y - 11 = 0$. Which equation shows the x-intercept(s) of the parabola as constants or coefficients?

    a) $x = 2y^2 + 8y + 11$
    b) $x = 2(y + 2)^2 + 3$
    c) $x - 3 = 2(y + 2)^2$
    d) $y = -\sqrt{\frac{x-3}{2}} - 2$

11. The graph below shows a certain brand of TV sales in four different continents. From 2011 to 2012, the total sales in the four continents decreased by what percentage?

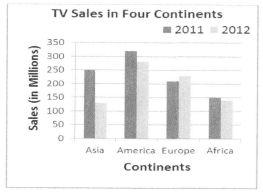

    a) 17
    b) 15
    c) 12
    d) 1

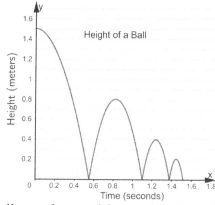

12. A ball was dropped from a height of 1.5 meters and hit the ground several times. The graph above represents the height h, in meters, of the ball t seconds after it was dropped. Of the following, which best approximates the maximum height, in meters, of the ball between the second and third time it hit the ground?

    a) 0.2
    b) 0.4
    c) 0.8
    d) 1.5

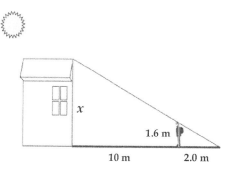

13. Jon walks 10 meters away from a wall outside his school building as shown in the figure above. At the point he stands, he notices that his shadow reaches to the same spot as the shadow of the school. If Jon is 1.6 meters tall and his shadow is 2 meters long, how high is the school building, in meters?

14. Gisela would owe $23,750 in taxes each year if she were not eligible for any tax deductions. This year, Gisela is eligible for tax deductions that reduce the amount of taxes she owes by $2,850.00. If these tax deductions reduce the taxes Gisela owes this year by d%, what is the value of d ?

15. Which of the following is an equation of the circle in the xy-plane that has center (0,0) and radius 4?
   a) $x^2 + y^2 = 4$
   b) $x^2 + y^2 = 8$
   c) $x^2 + y^2 = 16$
   d) $x^2 + y^2 = 64$

16. What is the remainder of 2013^{2014} divided by 10?
   a) 1
   b) 3
   c) 7
   d) 9

$$h(t) = -16t^2 + 320t + h_o$$

17. At time $t = 0$, a rocket was launched from a height of h_o feet above the ground. Until the rocket hit the ground, its height, in feet, after t seconds was given by the function h above. For which of the following values of t did the rocket have the same height as it did when $t = 5$.
   a) 10
   b) 15
   c) 18
   d) 20

18. If x and y are positive integers and $2^{2x} + 2^{(2x+2)} = y$, what is 2^x in terms of y?
   a) $\frac{y}{5}$
   b) $\frac{\sqrt{y}}{\sqrt{5}}$
   c) $\frac{y}{12}$
   d) $\frac{\sqrt{y}}{5}$

19. Which of the following scatterplots is the best representation of a function, $f(x) = mx + b$, where m is a negative number and b is a positive number?
   a)
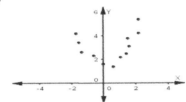
   b)
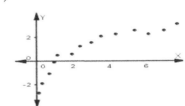
   c)
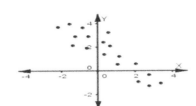
   d)
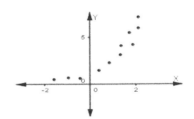

$$\frac{3}{4}x - \frac{1}{2}y = 12$$
$$ax - by = 9$$

20. The system of equations above has no solutions. If a and b are constants, what is the value of $\frac{a}{b}$?

21. If the area of an equilateral triangle equals the area of a square multiplied by $\sqrt{3}$, what is the ratio of the length of a side of the triangle to the length of a side of the square?

    a) $2:1$
    b) $2:3$
    c) $1:2$
    d) $4:3$

22. In the figure below, what is the value of $a + b + 2c + 2d$?

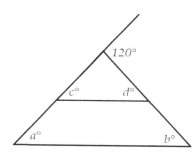

Note: Figure not drawn to scale.

    a) 240
    b) 300
    c) 360
    d) 380

Math Mock Test 10
22 QUESTIONS

DIRECTIONS
The questions in this section address a number of important math skills.
Use of a calculator is permitted for all questions.

NOTES
Unless otherwise indicated:
- All variables and expressions represent real numbers.
- Figures provided are drawn to scale.
- All figures lie in a plane.
- The domain of a given function f i s the set of all real numbers x for which f(x) is a real number.

REFERENCE

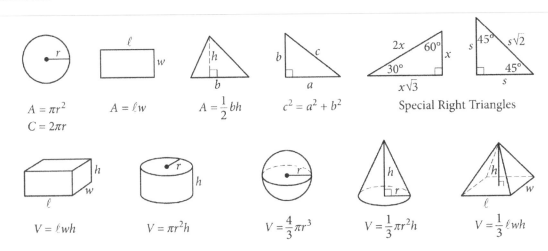

$A = \pi r^2$ $A = \ell w$ $A = \frac{1}{2} bh$ $c^2 = a^2 + b^2$ Special Right Triangles
$C = 2\pi r$

$V = \ell wh$ $V = \pi r^2 h$ $V = \frac{4}{3}\pi r^3$ $V = \frac{1}{3}\pi r^2 h$ $V = \frac{1}{3}\ell wh$

The number of degrees of arc in a circle is **360**.
The number of radians of arc in a circle is 2π.
The sum of the measures in degrees of the angles of a triangle is **180**.

For multiple-choice questions, solve each problem, choose the correct answer from the choices provided, and then circle your answer in this book. Circle only one answer for each question. If you change your mind, completely erase the circle. You will not get credit for questions with more than one answer circled, or for questions with no answers circled.

For student-produced response questions, solve each problem and write your answer next to or under the question in the test book as described below.
- Once you've written your answer, circle it clearly. You will not receive credit for anything written outside the circle, or for any questions with more than one circled answer.
- If you find **more than one correct answer**, write and circle only one answer. Your answer can be up to 5 characters for a **positive** answer and up to 6 characters (including the negative sign) for a **negative** answer, but no more.
- If your answer is a **fraction** that is too long (over 5 characters for positive, 6 characters for negative), write the decimal equivalent.
- If your answer is a **decimal** that is too long (over 5 characters for positive,
- 6 characters for negative), truncate it or round at the fourth digit.
- If your answer is a **mixed number** (such as $3\frac{1}{2}$, write it as an improper fraction (7/2) or its decimal equivalent (3.5).
- Don't include symbols such as a percent sign, comma, or dollar sign in your circled answer.

5, 13, 29, 61, ...

1. The leading term in the sequence above is 5, and each successive term is formed by multiplying the preceding term by x and then adding y. What is the value of y?

    a) 1
    b) 2
    c) 3
    d) 4

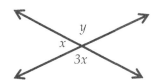

2. In the figure above, what is the value of $3x + 2y$?

    a) 405
    b) 135
    c) 270
    d) 360

3. After 8 new customers entered the grocery store and 2 customers left the store, there were three times as many customers in the store as there were before. How many customers were originally in the grocery store?

    a) 1
    b) 2
    c) 3
    d) 4

4. To get a job done, a machine needs to produce x boxes of toys, in which each box contains y toys. If this machine runs 10 hours per day and produces an average of z toys per minute, how many days will it take to finish the job?

    a) $\frac{xy}{z}$

    b) $\frac{xy}{60 \times 10 \times z}$

    c) $\frac{xy}{60 \times 60 \times 10 \times z}$

    d) $\frac{60 \times 10 \times xy}{z}$

5. If $x > y > 0.1$, which of the following is less than $\frac{x}{y}$?

    a) $\frac{x+0.1}{y+0.1}$

    b) $\frac{2x}{2y}$

    c) $\frac{x-0.1}{y-0.1}$

    d) $(\frac{x}{y})^2$

$$s = 9.8t$$

6. The equation above can be used to approximate the speed s, in meters per second (m/s), of an object t seconds after being dropped into a free fall. Which of the following is the best interpretation of the number 9.8 in this context?

    a) The speed, in m/s, of the object when it hits the ground
    b) The increase in speed, in m/s, of the object for each second after it is dropped
    c) The speed, in m/s, of the object t seconds after it is dropped
    d) The initial speed, in m/s, of the object when it is dropped

7. A magazine article on video game habits in the United States reported that in 2010 gamers spent an average of 5.1 hours per week playing games. The article also reported the average for 2011 to be 6.0 hours per week. Based on the article, how did the average number of hours that gamers spent playing games per week change from 2010 to 2011?

    a) It decreased by 17.6%.
    b) It increased by 15%.
    c) It increased by 15%.
    d) It increased by 17.6%.

$$y = (x - h)^2(x + h)(x + k)$$

8. The equation above is graphed in the xy-plane. If h and k are positive constants and $h \neq k$, how many distinct x-intercepts does the graph have?

    a) 1
    b) 2
    c) 3
    d) 4

d)

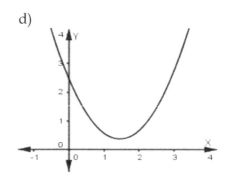

9. If the function f is defined by $f(x) = ax^2 + bx + c$, where a > 0, and c > 0, which of the following could be the graph of $f(x)$?

    a)

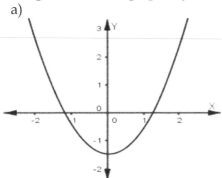

    b)

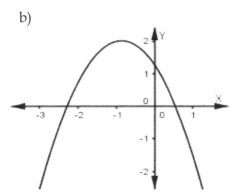

    c)

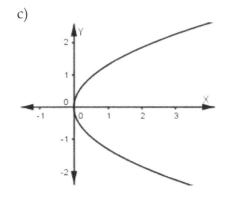

10. In the xy-plane, the graph of $y = 3 - (x - 2)^2$ is the image of the graph of $y = 4 - x^2$ after which of the following transformations?

    a) A translation of 1 unit up and 2 units to the right
    b) A translation of 1 unit down and 2 units to the right
    c) A translation of 1 unit up and 2 units to the left
    d) A translation of 2 units down and 1 unit to the right

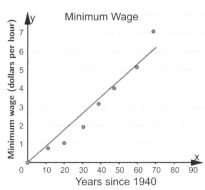

11. The scatterplot above shows the federal-mandated minimum wage every 10 years between 1940 and 2010. A line of best fit is shown, and its equation is $y = 0.096x - 0.488$. What does the line of best fit predict about the increase in the minimum wage over the 70-year period?

    a) Each year between 1940 and 2010, the average increase in minimum wage was 0.096 dollars.

    b) Each year between 1940 and 2010, the average increase in minimum wage was 0.49 dollars.

    c) Every 10 years between 1940 and 2010, the average increase in minimum wage was 0.096 dollars.

    d) Every 10 years between 1940 and 2010, the average increase in minimum wage was 0.488 dollars.

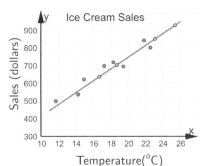

12. The scatterplot above shows a company's ice cream sales d, in dollars, and the high temperature t, in degrees Celsius (°C), on 12 different days. A line of best fit for the data is also shown. Which of the following could be an equation of the line of best fit?

    a) $d = 0.03t + 402$

    b) $d = 10t + 402$

    c) $d = 33t + 300$

    d) $d = 33t + 84$

13. Jacob bought two types of pens: blue pens that cost $0.70 each and red pens that each cost m times as much as a blue pen. If the cost of 5 blue pens and 4 red pens was $13.30, what is the value of m?

14. The first term of the sequence above is 1, and every term after the first term is −2 times the preceding term. How many of the first 100 terms of this sequence are less than 100?

15. $\frac{1}{5}$ of 80 is equal to what percent of 200?

    a) 5 %

    b) 8 %

    c) 10 %

    d) 16 %

16. Which of the following expressions is equivalent to $\sqrt[3]{8x^3y^5}$, where x and y are positive?

    a) $2xy^{\frac{5}{3}}$

    b) $8xy^{\frac{5}{3}}$

    c) $2x^3y^5$

    d) $\frac{8}{3}xy^2$

17. The three interior angle measures of a triangle have the ratio 3 : 4 : 5. What is the measure, in degrees, of the largest angles?
    a) 60°
    b) 70°
    c) 75°
    d) 85°

18. In the figure below, what is the value of $a - b$?

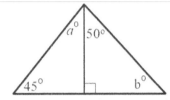

Note: Figure not drawn to scale.

    a) 0
    b) 5
    c) 10
    d) 15

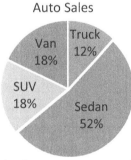

Auto Sales

19. The pie graph above represents the automobiles that were sold by a dealer in 2010, according to their records. If the dealer sold 50 more Sedans than all others combined, how many automobiles did it sell altogether?
    a) 1,000
    b) 1,150
    c) 1,250
    d) 1,500

20. How many combinations of three dishes can be prepared if you have the recipes for 9 dishes?

21. Emma mows grass at a constant rate of 2 acres per hour. She mowed 3 acres before lunch and plans to spend t hours mowing after lunch. If Emma wants to mow at least 10 acres of grass today, which of the following inequalities best represents this situation?
    a) $2t \geq 10$
    b) $2t - 2 \geq 10$
    c) $2t + 2 \geq 10$
    d) $2t + 3 \geq 10$

22. A "square-root-factor" is an integer greater than 1 with exactly three positive integer factors: itself, its square root, and 1. Which of the following is a square-root-factor?
    a) 128
    b) 81
    c) 64
    d) 49

Mock Test 10

Module 1 Keys

1. (B)	2. (A)	3. (B)	4. (B)	5. (C)	6. 4	7. 758	8. (B)
9. (C)	10. (D)	11. (A)	12. (C)	13. $\frac{9}{2}$, or 4.5	14. $\frac{3}{5}$	15. (C)	16. (A)
17. (D)	18. (D)	19. (D)	20. $\frac{1}{3}$ or 0.33	21. 24	22. (B)		

Module 2 Easy Keys

1. (B)	2. (D)	3. (D)	4. (B)	5. (A)	6. 17	7. 111	8. (D)
9. (D)	10. (A)	11. (A)	12. (B)	13. 9.6	14. 12	15. (C)	16. (D)
17. (B)	18. (B)	19. (D)	20. $\frac{3}{2}$	21. (A)	22. (C)		

Module 2 Hard Keys

1. (C)	2. (A)	3. (C)	4. (B)	5. (A)	6. (B)	7. (D)	8. (C)
9. (D)	10. (B)	11. (A)	12. (C)	13. 3.5	14. 54	15. (B)	16. (A)
17. (C)	18. (B)	19. (C)	20. (D)	21. (D)	22. (D)		

Mock Test 10

Module 1 Answers

1. *Answer: (B)*
   The graph shows the point of the interception is
   $(-1, 2)$.

2. *Answer: (A)*
   2x + 1 = 9
   x = 4
   5(4) – 4 = 16
   $\sqrt{16} = 4$

3. *Answer: (B)*
   $2x^2 - 4x - 6 = 0$
   $2(x^2 - 2x - 3) = 0$
   $2(x - 3)(x + 1) = 0$
   $x = -1 \text{ or } x = -3$

4. *Answer: (B)*

   $\frac{1}{3}P = 60 - \frac{2}{3}P$
   $p = 60$

5. *Answer: (C)*
   $x^{\frac{5}{2}} = \left(\sqrt{x}\right)^5 = \sqrt{x^5}$

6. *Answer: 4*
   $sin(x°) = \frac{\overline{AB}}{\overline{BC}} = \frac{\overline{AB}}{8}$
   $\frac{\overline{AB}}{8} = \frac{\sqrt{3}}{2} \rightarrow \overline{AB} = 4\sqrt{3}$
   $(\overline{AC})^2 = (\overline{BC})^2 - (\overline{AB})^2$
   $= 64 - 48 = 16$
   $\overline{AC} = 4$

7. *Answer: 758*
   Apply PEMDAS.
   x = 7 + (6 × 125 + 1) = 7 + (750 + 1) = 7 + 751 = 758

8. *Answer: (B)*
   $\begin{cases} 8x - 5y = 15 \quad ----(1) \\ 7x + 5y = 15 \quad ----(2) \end{cases}$
   $(1) + (2) \rightarrow 15x = 30$
   $x = 2$
   $7(2) + 5y = 15 \rightarrow y = \frac{1}{5}$
   $xy = 2 \times \frac{1}{5} = \frac{2}{5}$

9. *Answer: (C)*
   There are no rules about how to arrange boys and girls, so (a) and (b) are incorrect.
   If there is one girl at each end, then two boys must be adjacent. Therefore, (d) is wrong.
   If the last two seated are girls, then two boys must be adjacent. (c) is correct.

10. *Answer: (D)*
    $2ax - 15 = 3(x + 5) + 5(x - 1)$
    $2ax - 15 = 8x + 10$
    If a = 4, then the equation has no solution because $-15 \neq 10$. The answer is d).

11. *Answer: (A)*
    The line perpendicular to the y-axis is a horizontal line. The value of the y coordinate is constant for a horizontal line.
    y = 1

12. *Answer: (C)*
    "True for all x" means the expressions on both sides need to be identical.
    $(ax + 3)(5x^2 - bx + 4) = 20x^3 - 9x^2 - 2x + 12$
    The coefficients of x^2 on both sides should be the same:
    $-ab + 15 = -9$
    $ab = 24$

13. *Answer: $\frac{9}{2}$, or 4.5*
    Cross multiply
    $x - 5 = -x + 4$
    $x = \frac{9}{2}$

14. *Answer: $\frac{3}{5}$*
    When $x + y = 90°$,
    $cos(y) = sin(y) = \frac{3}{5}$

15. *Answer: (C)*
    Solve the system of equations.
    $x^2 = 3x + 4$
    $x^2 - 3x - 4 = 0$
    $(x - 4)(x + 1) = 0$
    $x = 4, y = 16$

16. *Answer: (A)*
   Plug the value of z into x = 4z.
   $x = 4 \times 6 = 24$
   $\frac{x}{y} = 4$, $\frac{24}{y} = 4$, $4y = 24$, $y = 6$

17. *Answer: (D)*
   Solve the system of equations by subtracting 1st equation from 2nd equation to eliminate y.
   $3x - 2x^2 = -2$
   $2x^2 - 3x - 2 = 0$
   $(x - 2)(2x + 1) = 0$
   $x = 2$ and $y = 8 \to xy = 16$
   Or $x = -\frac{1}{2}$ and $y = \frac{1}{2}$ $xy = -\frac{1}{4}$

18. *Answer: (D)*
   Percent Change: $\frac{1100-310}{310} \times 100\% \approx 255\%$
   Overall Average: $\frac{310+390+420+1100}{4} = \$555$

19. *Answer: (D)*
   The length of the 3rd side should be smaller than the sum of the lengths of the other two sides and greater than their difference.
   $7 - 3 < x < 7 + 3$
   $4 < x < 10$

20. *Answer:* $\frac{1}{3}$ *or 0.33*
   $3(x - 5) = 15$
   $x - 5 = 5 \to x = 10$
   $\frac{x-5}{x+5} = \frac{5}{10+5} = \frac{5}{15} = \frac{1}{3}$

21. *Answer: 24*
   $20 \times (1 + 0.2) = 24$

22. *Answer: (B)*
   Based on the graph, the difference is $89 - 81 = 8$.

Module 2 Easy Answers

1. *Answer: (B)*
   $l = \theta r = \frac{9\pi}{7} \times 4$
   $= \frac{36\pi}{7} = 5.14\pi$ *inches*

2. *Answer: (D)*
   According to the rounding rules, the original number can be in the range: $25.25 \le x \le 25.34$

3. *Answer: (D)*
   Divide both sides by 0.1.
   $(0.10) \times y = 100$
   $y = \frac{100}{0.1} = 1000$

4. *Answer: (B)*
   Solve the system of equations.
   $y - 7x = 13 \to y = 7x + 13$
   $8x = 3y \to 8x = 3(7x + 13)$
   $8x = 21x + 39$
   $13x = -39$
   $x = -3$ and $y = -8$

5. *Answer: (A)*
   A linear model:
   $y = rx + k$
   $210 = 2r + k$

6. *Answer: 17*
   The graph of f passes through the points (0, 5) and (3, 6)
   Slope of f $= \frac{6-5}{3-0} = \frac{1}{3}$
   $y - 5 = \frac{1}{3}x$
   $y = f(x) = \frac{1}{3}x + 5$
   $g(x) = \frac{6}{3}x - 3 = 2x - 3$
   $g(10) = 20 - 3 = 17$

7. *Answer: 111*
   We need 300 females but only 189 (420 × 0.45) females who complete the survey so far.
   $300 - 189 = 111$

8. *Answer: (D)*
   $\frac{1}{\frac{x+1}{(x-1)(x+1)} - \frac{x-1}{(x-1)(x+1)}} = \frac{1}{\frac{2}{(x+1)(x-1)}} = \frac{(x+1)(x-1)}{2} = \frac{x^2-1}{2}$

9. *Answer: (D)*
   $4x - x^2 = 4$
   $x^2 - 4x + 4 = 0$
   $(x - 2)(x - 2) = 0$
   $x = 2$

10. *Answer: (A)*
    The x-intercept(s) is when y = 0.
    The x-intercept(s) is 11.
    Only answer a) has constant or coefficient of 11.

11. *Answer: (A)*
    Total sales in 2011: 250 + 325 + 210 + 150 = 935
    Total sales in 2012: 130 + 280 + 230 + 140 = 780
    Percent Change = $\frac{780-935}{935}$ = -16.57% ~ -17%

12. *Answer: (B)*
    The time between the second and third time it hit the ground is about 1.3 seconds. Its max height is 0.4 meters.

13. *Answer: 9.6*
    Let the height of the school building be x.
    The two triangles are similar; therefore, their corresponding sides are proportional.
    $\frac{2}{10+2} = \frac{1.6}{x}$

    $x = 9.6\ m$

14. *Answer: 12*
    $\frac{2850}{23750} \times (100\%) = 12\%$

15. *Answer: (C)*
    Standard equation of a circle:
    $(x - h)^2 + (y - k)^2 = r^2$
    $(x - 0)^2 + (y - 0)^2 = 4^2$

16. *Answer: (D)*
    2013^1 has units digit of 3
    2013^2 has units digit of 9 (3 × 3 = 9)
    2013^3 has units digit of 7 (3 × 9 = 27)
    2013^4 has units digit of 1 (3 × 7 = 21)
    2013^5 has units digit of 3 (3 × 1 = 3)
    Only the units digit needs to be concerned.
    So every fourth power of 2013 repeats its units digit.
    2014 ÷ 4 has remainder of 2
    2013^{2014} has the same units digit as 2013^2, which is 9.

17. *Answer: (B)*
    $h(5) = -16(5)^2 + 320(5) + h_0 = -16t^2 + 320t + h_0$ divided by 16

18. *Answer: (B)*
    $2^{2x} + 2^{(2x+2)} = 5 \times 2^{2x}$
    $5 \times 2^{2x} = y \quad \rightarrow \quad 2^{2x} = \frac{y}{5}$
    $(2^x)^2 = \frac{y}{5} \quad \rightarrow \quad 2^x = \frac{\sqrt{y}}{\sqrt{5}}$

19. *Answer: (D)*

    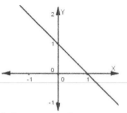

    The graph of f (x) = -x + 1:
    So, answer is (d).

20. *Answer: $\frac{3}{2}$*
    $a_1 x + b_1 y = c_1$
    $a_2 x + b_2 y = c_2$
    When the system of equations above has no solutions, then $\frac{a_1}{a_2} = \frac{b_1}{b_2} \neq \frac{c_1}{c_2}$
    $\frac{3}{4} x - \frac{1}{2} y = 12$
    $ax - by = 9$
    $\frac{\frac{3}{4}}{a} = -\frac{\frac{1}{2}}{-b} \neq \frac{12}{9} \rightarrow \frac{a}{b} = \frac{3}{2}$

21. *Answer: (A)*
    Let the length of the side of the triangle be x and the length of the side of the square be y.
    Area of an equilateral triangle= $\frac{\sqrt{3}}{4} x^2$
    Area of a square = y^2
    $\frac{\sqrt{3}}{4} x^2 = \sqrt{3}\ y^2$
    $x^2 = 4\ y^2$
    $x : y = 2 : 1$

22. *Answer: (C)*
    $120 = c + d = a + b$
    $a + b + 2(c + d) = 120 + 2 \times 120 = 360$

Module 2 Hard Answers

1. *Answer: (C)*
   $13 - 5 = 8$
   $29 - 13 = 16$
   $61 - 29 = 32$
   So each successive term is multiplying the proceeding term by 2 and adding 3.
   $13 = 2 \times 5 + 3$, *so* $y = 3$
   $61 = 29 \times 2 + 3$ *(double check the answer)*

2. *Answer: (A)*
   $3x + x = 180°$ *and* $y = 3x$
   $4x = 180°$
   $x = 45°$
   $3x = 135° = y$
   $2y = 135 \times 2 = 270°$
   $3x + 2y = 135 + 270 = 405°$

3. *Answer: (C)*
   Let x be the number of customers before the changes. After adding 8 new customers and subtracting 2 customers who left, the number of customers equals three times as many as x.
   $x + 8 - 2 = 3x$
   $x = 3$

4. *Answer: (B)*
   $Number\ of\ Days = \frac{Total\ Work}{Work\ per\ Hour}$
   Total Number of Toys to Make= xy
   Machine runs 10 hours (10 × 60 minutes) per day.
   Number of Toys Made per Day = $z \times 60 \times 10$
   $Number\ of\ Days = \frac{xy}{60 \times 10 \times z}$

5. *Answer: (A)*
   $x > y > 0.1$
   Plug in x = 2, and y = 1
   Only answer (a), $\frac{2.1}{1.1}$, *less than 2.*

6. *Answer: (B)*
   "The slope of 9.8" means speed increase 9.8 per second. The answer is b).

7. *Answer: (D)*
   $\frac{6.0 - 5.1}{5.1} \times 100\% = 17.6\%$
   It increased by 17.6%.

8. *Answer: (C)*
   "x-intercepts" $\rightarrow y = 0$
   $(x - h)^2(x + h)(x + k) = 0$
   $x = h, -h, -k$
   There are 3 distinct x-intercepts.

9. *Answer: (D)*
   The positive leading coefficient of a quadratic function means the curve goes upwards; a positive constant c means y-intercept is positive. Only (d) meets all these conditions.

10. *Answer: (B)*
    It is right shift 2 units and down shift 1 unit.

11. *Answer: (A)*
    $y = 0.096x - 0.488$
    The slope, 0.096, means that each year between 1940 and 2010, the average of increasing in minimum wage was 0.096 dollars.

12. *Answer: (C)*
    Based on the graph, the slope of the line is 33 and its y-intercept is about 300.
    The equation of this line: $d = 33t + 300$

13. *Answer: 3.5*
    $5 \times 0.7 + 4 \times m \times 0.7 = 13.3$
    $m = \frac{9.8}{2.8} = 3.5$

14. *Answer: 54*
    Among the first 100 terms, there are 50 negative numbers and 4 positive numbers less than 100: 1, 4, 16, and 64.
    Total numbers less than 100 is 50 + 4 = 54

15. *Answer: (B)*
    $\frac{1}{5}$ *of* $80 \rightarrow \frac{1}{5} \times 80 = 16$
    $16 = \frac{x}{100} \times 200$
    $16 = 2x$
    $x = 8$
    Therefore, $\frac{1}{5} \times 80 = 16$, *which is equal to* $200 \times 8\% = 16$

16. *Answer: (A)*
    $\sqrt[3]{8x^3y^5} = (8x^3t^5)^{\frac{1}{3}} = 2xy^{\frac{5}{3}}$

17. *Answer: (C)*
We can define the measures of the three angles to be 3x, 4x, and 5x.
$3x + 4x + 5x = 180° \rightarrow x = 15°$
$5 \times 15 = 75°$

18. *Answer: (B)*
$a = 45$ *and* $b = 40$
$a - b = 5$

19. *Answer: (C)*
Solve this problem using proportions.
There were 4% (52% − 48%) more Sedans sold than all other cars combined.
$4\% : 50 = 100\% : x$
$x = 1,250$ *cars*

20. *Answer: (D)*
This is combination. The number of ways to select m objects from n objects ($n \geq m$), where order does not matter: ($C_m^n = \frac{n!}{m!(n-m)!}$)
To choose 3 from 9: $C_3^9 = \frac{9!}{3! \times 6!} = 84$

21. *Answer: (D)*
$3 + 2t \geq 10$

22. *Answer: (D)*
The square root of the number must be a prime number.
Only $\sqrt{49}$ *is a prime number.*

Index

More Books by Dr. Jang:

Dr. Jang's SAT 800 Series:

Dr. Jang's SAT 800 Math Workbook
Dr. Jang's SAT 800 Chemistry Subject Test
Dr. Jang's SAT 800 Physics Subject Test
Dr. Jang's SAT 800 Math Subject Test Level 2
Dr. Jang's SAT 800 Math Ten Practice Tests

Dr. Jang's AP 5 Series:

Dr. Jang's AP 5 Physics 1 Workbook
Dr. Jang's AP 5 Chemistry Workbook

Dr. Jang's ACT:
Dr. Jang's ACT 36 Math Workbook

Visit Our Website for More Services and More Practice Questions:
www.DrJang800.com

The Goals of Dr. Jang's Books:

~For students:
To help you study based on your skill level.

~For teachers:
To help you plan lessons based on students' needs.

Made in the USA
Las Vegas, NV
03 November 2024

11042652R00208